THE ONE SHOW ANNUAL

ADVERTISING'S BEST PRINT, DESIGN, RADIO & TV

VOLUME 25

THE ONE CLUB FOR ART & COPY

PRESIDENT
John Butler
Butler, Shine, Stern & Partners, Sausalito

EXECUTIVE DIRECTOR/EXECUTIVE EDITOR
Mary Warlick

EDITOR
Tiffany Meyers

EDITORIAL ASSISTANTS
Maiko Shiratori
Matt Helland

ONE SHOW MANAGER
Steve Marchese

BOOK DESIGNER
Lise Mardon Smith
EMAIL: italics12@earthlink.net

COVER AND DIVIDER PAGE CONCEPT AND DESIGN
Graham Clifford
Graham Clifford Design, New York
212 645 0909
www.grahamclifforddesign.com

COVER AND DIVIDER PAGE PHOTOGRAPHER
Peter Cunningham
New York
212 533 8006
www.wordwiseweb.com

ONE SHOW SPONSORS
Getty Images
Yahoo!
The Newspaper Association of America
The Creative Group

PUBLISHED BY
One Club Publishing
21 East 26th Street, 5th Floor
New York, NY 10010
TEL: 212 979 1900
FAX: 212 979 5006
WEBSITE: www.oneclub.com

FIRST PRINTING
ISBN 0-929837-20-7

PRODUCTION AND SEPARATION
AVA Book Production Pte. Ltd.
EMAIL: production@avabooks.com.sg

DISTRIBUTED IN THE US AND CANADA BY
Sterling Publishing
387 Park Avenue South
New York, NY 10016-8810

DISTRIBUTED EX-NORTH AMERICA BY
AVA Distribution
TEL: +41 78 600 5109
EMAIL: sales@avabooks.ch
WEBSITE: www.avabooks.ch

IMAGE PARTNER: GETTY IMAGES
PHOTO CREDITS
FRONT OF BOOK: 218279 Harald Sund/Getty Images
GOLD, SILVER, BRONZE: EA8479-001 Steven Weinberg/Getty Images
BEST OF SHOW: CA23717 Ron Chapple/Getty Images
JUDGES CHOICE: David S. Waitz
GOLD ON GOLD: 395515-004 Hiroyuki Matsumoto/Getty Images
RADIO MERIT: CA31671 Christoph Wilhelm/Getty Images
TELEVISION MERIT: CA25357 Ken Ross/Getty Images
INNOVATIVE & INTEGRATED MERIT: AB13241 Bald Headed Pictures/Getty Images
COLLEGE MERIT: 10164659 Richard Kolker/Getty Images

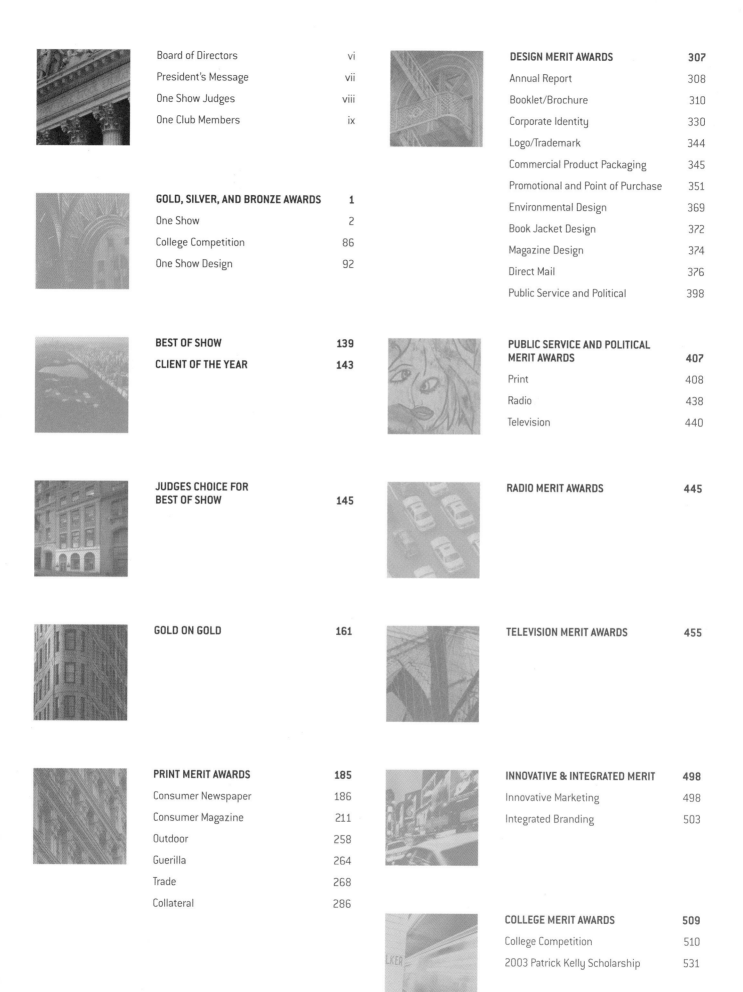

PRESIDENT'S MESSAGE

This is a rotten business.

This is what I keep hearing, anyways.

Everywhere I go this tends to be the commentary I get about this business that I am in. It doesn't seem to matter if I'm talking to people who are in the trenches, actually doing the work, or to those charged with inspiring the latter, it's generally always the same. Our business just doesn't seem to be that much fun anymore is how it usually starts, cascading into a droning whimper that ultimately becomes a self-fulfilling prophecy.

Time to own up. There are times when I find myself agreeing. It's pretty easy to be seduced by the febrile musings of your peers. Especially when the business tends to be in a state of flux. Yep, this is a terrible, terrible business indeed.

But then something happens. One of my teams invariably shows me something wonderful. (A glimmer of hope!) Or, this book you hold in your hands arrives in the mail, and the rest of the day is shot. (How many pencils did ___ get this year?)

I wind up slamming the book shut after a time, and instantly become "motivated." I check all previous apathetic tendencies and get down to the business of making ads again. I see the thinking that CPB has created for MINI, and I am reminded of the seminal car work of yesterday, with a fresh, contemporary spin. Volkswagen continues to inspire with its simplicity and insight, and a little known campaign for MTV by la comunidad in Miami makes me laugh so hard I hurt myself. This year, Miami certainly seems the place to be.

One of the perks of this Presidency gig is that not only do I get comped tickets to the best advertising show in the free world, I also get a front-seat perspective about what is really going on in this business before everyone else. This is what I will miss most about being here when my tenure comes to a halt at the end of the year.

Make no mistake, great work is still being done out there. Don't fall into the trap that I fall into from time to time. It's not all doom and gloom. There is plenty of interesting work being done by people who frankly don't have the time to whine. Become inspired by them.

Could this be the start of something new and exciting in this "dreadful" business? I tend to believe so.

Today.

Tomorrow, I'll probably be whining again.

John Butler
PRESIDENT

2003 ONE SHOW JUDGES

John Butler, PRESIDENT
Butler, Shine, Stern & Partners, Sausalito

David Abbott
London

Alex Bogusky
Crispin Porter + Bogusky, Miami

Ross Chowles
The Jupiter Drawing Room (South Africa), Cape Town

Mimi Cook
Goodby, Silverstein & Partners, San Francisco

Craig Davis
Saatchi & Saatchi, Hong Kong

Jackie End
TBWA/Chiat/Day, New York

Kara Goodrich
Arnold Worldwide, Boston

Mike Hughes
The Martin Agency, Richmond

Akira Kagami
Dentsu, Tokyo

Gary Koepke
Modernista!, Boston

Chris Lange
Fallon, Minneapolis

Jamie Mambro
McCarthy Mambro Bertino, Boston

Kevin McKeon
Bartle Bogle Hegarty, New York

Jim Riswold
Wieden + Kennedy, Portland

Tim Roper
Crispin Porter + Bogusky, Venice

Jader Rossetto
DM9 DDB, São Paulo

Eric Silver
Cliff Freeman & Partners, New York

Kash Sree
Leo Burnett, Chicago

Scott Wild
Cramer-Krasselt, Chicago

Jon Wyville
Young & Rubicam, Chicago

ONE SHOW RADIO JUDGES

Carl Loeb, ONE SHOW RADIO CO-CHAIR
Bartle Bogle Hegarty, New York

Bob Winter, ONE SHOW RADIO CO-CHAIR
DDB, Chicago

Steve Dildarian
Goodby, Silverstein & Partners, San Francisco

Marc Gallucci
Fort Franklin, Boston

Austin Howe
Radioland, Portland

Peter Kain
Bartle Bogle Hegarty, New York

Roy Kamen
Kamen Audio, New York

Dylan Lee
Wieden + Kennedy, Portland

Mark Nardi
Hill Holliday, Boston

Bobby Pearce
Fallon, Minneapolis

Ian Reichenthal
Freelance, New York

Rob Rosenthal
Moffatt Rosenthal, Portland

ONE SHOW DESIGN JUDGES

Dana Arnett, ONE SHOW DESIGN CHAIR
VSA Partners, Chicago

Rick Anwyl
EAI, Atlanta

Peter Bell
Fairly Painless Advertising, Holland, MI

Brian Collins
Ogilvy & Mather/Brand Integration Group, New York

Robynne Raye
Modern Dog, Seattle

Stefan Sagmeister
Sagmeister Inc., New York

MEMBERS

A

Jeffrey Abbott
Tara Adams
Daniel X. Ahearn
Darius Edward Alaie
Joe Alexander
Christine Aliferis
Mark Allen
Gideon Amichay
Cheri Anderson
Claire Anderson
Stephanie Anderson
Gil Arevalo
Elizabeth Asdorian
David Augustyn
Brian Avenius

B

Kristina Backlund
John Bade
Chris Baier
Rob Baiocco
Rob Baird
Larry Baisden
Roger Baldacci
David Baldwin
Lisa Balser
Matthew Barker
Chuck Barkey
Bob Barrie
Daniel Barry
Stephen Bassett
Paul Belford
Gregg Benedikt
Mitch Bennett
Cheryl Berman
Becca Bernstein
David Bernstein
Eric Bertuccio
Scott Bevier
Arthur Bijur
Bruce Bildsten
Hillary Black
Gary Bloomer
Nick Bontaites
Darlene Bosch

Robert Braden
Clarence Bradley
Yvonne Brandt-Cousin
Daniel Bremmer
Bill Brokaw
Brian Brooker
Mark Brown
Rebecca Brown
Chavy Broyde
Mike Burns
Ron Burkhardt
John Butler

C

Larry Cadman
Elizabeth Caguin
Jason Campbell
Susan Carroll
Pablo Castro
David Chang
Soo Mean Chang
Andy Cheng
Hong Choi
Chris Churchill
Bart Cleveland
Christopher Cole
Marco Colín
Chris Collins
Julie Commack
Adam Cook
Doug Cook
Candice Corlett
Nicole Cota
Chris Covington
Jennifer Covington
Josephine Craig-Carey
Rob Cramer
Steve Crane
Darrell Credeur
Angelo Cushman

D

Joanna D'Avanzo
Trish Daley
Aaron Dalton

Kevin Daly
Tonya Daniel
Sankha Das
Douglas Dauzier
Angela Denise
Yvonne DeSanti
Robert Devol
Kristie DiCostanzo
Sara DiOrazio
Ryusuke Dohi
Timothy Donza
Steve Doppelt
Linda Dorup
Tom Doud
Scott Duncan
Nathan Duval
Jason Duvall

E
Jason English

F
Simon Fairweather
Lauren Feiman
Isabella Ferreora
Monique Fikar
Matt Fischvogt
Tim Fisher
Kevin Flatt
Katie Forte
Melanie Foster
Brian Fouhy
Kevin Freidberg
Glen Fruchter

G
Jason Gaboriau
Tom Gabriel
Walita Ganmanee
Mark Ganton
Robin Gara
Denise Garcia
Elena Garrigues
Danny Gellert
Richard Gerdes
Kevin Gladwin
Colin Glaum
Kenneth Gleason
Leisa Glispy
Kevin Goff

Keith Goldberg
Ian Goldy
Mitch Gordon
Doug Green
Adam Greenhood
Norm Grey
Aaron Griffiths
Jed Grossman
Philip Growick
Ted Guidotti
Juan Carlos Gutierrez

H
Lori Habas
Eddie Hahn
Shyamlee Handa
Kristin Hanson
Megan Happ
Emily Harrington
Lawrence Harris
Jackie Hathiramani
Larry Hauser
Tim Heckman
Brendan Hemp
Roy Herbert
Armando Hernandez
Rony Herz
Ralf Heuel
Heather Higgins
William Hillsman
Woody Hinkle
Sally Hogshead
Dave Holloway
Kelly Hood
Hugh Hough
Jonathan Huang
John Huggins
David Hughes
Mike Hughes
John Hynes

I
Brenda Innocenti
Matias Irbarne

J
Rob Jackson
Chris Jacobs
Harry Jacobs
Per Robert Jacobson

Anne Marie Jeffrey
Bob Jeffrey
Edward Johnson
Kevin Johnson
Marcus Johnson
Michael Johnson
Will Johnson
Ed Jones
Stephen Jones
Angelo Juliano
William Jurewicz

K
Kevin Kantrowitz
Adam Kanzer
Simon Kao
Laurel Katz
Leslie Kay
Scott Keglovic
Carol Lee Kelliher
Alan Kelly
Daniel Kenneally
Jeff Kidwell
Monica Kim
Chaz King
Erika Kirkland
Joe Knezic
Mark Knight
Bob Kochuk
Matej Kodric
Tomas Kohoutek
Jane Kornacki

L
Ming Lai
Stephen Land
Robin Landa
Richard Lao
Adam LaRocca
David Laskarzewski
Llysa Lederkramer
Howard Lenn
Mike Lescarbeau
Jamie Levey
Kate Levin
John Liegey
David Liewellyn
Meredith Light
Adrian Lim
Julio Lima

Kenneth Lin
Frank Lopresti
Eileen Lovern

M
Sam Maclay
Vanessa Maganza
Sharoz Makarechi
Karen Mallia
John Mannion
Alex Manosalvas
Sarah Marden
Joel Maron
Rhoda Marshall
Jeff Martin
Michael Mastrullo
Brian J. Mattlin
Marie Matulewicz
Richard May
Scott McAfee
Meredith McBride
Lisa McHugh
Rick McHugh
Samantha McKinlay
Sean McLaughlin
Lewis McVey
Robert Mellett
Mark Mendelis
Andy Mendelsohn
Lucy Meredith
Mark Millar
Christopher Miller
Matt Miller
Sakol Mongkolkasetarin
Ty Montague
Michael Mooney
Beverly Ann Moore
Adam Morgan
Jeanna Morgan
Scott Mortimore
Jim Mountjoy
Matthew Moyer
Zak Mroueh
Meredith Muegge
Mark Musto

N
Bob Needleman
Arun K. Nemali
Alec Nightingale

Cinthia Gabriela Novick

Christina Nyberg

O

David Oakley

Tim O'Donnell

Elanor Oliver

Hollie Ontrop

Christina Orlando

Ricardo Ortega

Reuben Orter

Alejandro Ortiz

Jamie Overkamp

Erol Ozlevi

P

Paula Pagano

Woonhwa Paik

Chantal Panozzo

Dmitry Paperny

Blaine Parker

Babita Patel

Lance Paull

Bill Pauls

Ladd Peterson

Dimitrios Petsas

Adam Piantanida

Robert Pienciak

Bonnie Pihl

Donna Pilch

Jeremy Pipenger

Owen Plotkin

Demir Karpat Polat

Jim Scott Polsinelli

Darya Porat

Glenn Price

Belinda Pruyne

Tony Pucca

Michael Pudim

Dave Pullar

Stephanie A. Putter

Q

Keith Quesenberry

Aldo Quevedo

Dan Quiterio

R

Pamela Raitt

Heather Ratana

Alexander Rehm

Kevin Reilly

Richard Rhodes

Allen Richardson

Hank Richardson

Alexander Ridore

Nigel Roberts

John Robertson

Kerri Rodenbaugh

Adam Rogers

Eric Rojas

Jennifer Rosenthal

Meryl Rothstein

Charles Rouse

Ann Rudig

John Ruebush

Robby Russell

S

Neeraj Sabharwal

Vicki Sander

Alexandra Sann

Emmanuel Santos

Robert Sawyer

Lyle Schemer

Dennis Scheyer

Chris Schlegel

Jonathan Schoenberg

Trevor Schoenfeld

Chad Schomber

Michael Schwabenland

Heinz Schwegler

George Scombulis

Mark Scott

Joan Sechrist

Sheridan Sechter

Tod Seisser

Rob Semos

Alexandra Setnikar

Tonice Sgrignoli

Matthew Sharpe

Rick Sheehan

Bill Shelton

Sasha Andres Shenoy

Christopher Sheppard

Mark Silber

German Silva Vasquez

J.C. Sisson

Lauren Slaff

Marc Sobier

William Spencer

Andy Spreitzer

Emily St. Germaine

Catherine St. Jean

John Staffen

Jason Stefanik

Eric Stephens

Fred Stesney

Larry Stone

Alan Stuart

Wade Sturdivant

Mark Svartz

Steve Swartz

T

Daniel Tanenbaum

Ron Tapia

Nick Terzis

Danielle Teschner

Greg Thomas

Adam Tompkins

John Topacio

Susan Treacy

Jay Tsukamoto

Roman Tsukerman

Lauren Tucker

Tracey Turner

Mark Tutssel

U

Rodney Underwood

Alfredo Ustara

V

Vassil Valkov

Roussina Valkova

Paul Venables

Larry Vine

John Vitro

Ted Voss

W

Elaine Wagner

Mark Waites

David Waitz

Judy Wald

Melinda Ward

Michael Ward

Regan Warner

Bob Warren

Mandy Way

Iwan Weidmann

Patrick Weir

Jean Weisman

Craig Welsh

Sean Welsh

Lawrence Werner

Robert Shaw West

Brian Wheeler

Scott Wild

Michael Wilde

Stephanie Wildman

Donna Williams

Steve Williams

Tim Williams

Ellen Wilson

Michael Winslow

Bob Winter

Stewart Winter

Alan Wolk

David Wong

Rena Wong

Jacqueline Woo

Jon Wyville

Y

Betsy Yamazaki

Ken Young

Z

Rachel Zargo

Qi Zhou

Leslie Ziegler

GOLD
SILVER
and
BRONZE

GOLD
**Newspaper Over 600 Lines
Single**

ART DIRECTOR
Georgia Arnott

WRITER
Craig Crawford

PHOTOGRAPHER
Scott Downing

CREATIVE DIRECTORS
James Dalthorp
Tom Cordner

CLIENT
Lexus

AGENCY
Team One Advertising/El Segundo

03001A

THIS IS AN ADVERTISEMENT FOR THE FINEST LUXURY SEDAN IN AMERICA.
SO WHICH LOGO BELONGS IN THE BOTTOM RIGHT-HAND CORNER?

DO YOU KNOW? Or is it possible you merely *think* you know? Well, there's only one way to be certain and that's to put aside your perceptions and prejudices and focus purely on the facts: the tangible, measurable, provable evidence. (In other words, you have to completely ignore the emblems and instead scrutinize the automobiles beneath them.)

And that's what the researchers at Automotive Marketing Consultants Incorporated (AMCI) did to identify "The Finest Luxury Sedan in America."

So what exactly was required to achieve this?

Hallmarks of integrity.

AMCI is the nation's leading independent vehicle testing company. They design objective, third-party studies to substantiate claims that can truthfully be made about an automobile. They drive and evaluate more cars than the federal government, car-enthusiast magazines or any other organization in the United States. Consequently, they have substantiated most claims made in broadcast automobile advertising.

franchised dealers, and began the arduous process of subjecting all of them to a barrage of one hundred and ninety-three dynamic, static and luxury-feature tests and evaluations in seven exhaustive categories.

Success. Not symbols.

Distinguishing a luxury sedan from an ordinary car is rather simple because a luxury sedan has many measurable, defining characteristics—other than the hood ornament. But even more important, these same attributes can also differentiate one luxury sedan from another, and that's what AMCI was looking for.

Here's some of what their evaluation discovered:

For any tests that required driving, AMCI used two of their most experienced test drivers. Each test was repeated until they had both achieved eighteen "perfect" runs in every car for all the tests.

One of the most significant of these trials was the 50-0 mph braking on wet pavement. In this test the BMW 750iL took 95.3 feet to stop. And while this is rather remarkable, it pales when compared to

Traditionally a concours d'élégance is for cars that have been restored to their former glory. But what if you convened one for brand-new cars? Well, that's exactly what AMCI did. And to judge their concours they enlisted the help of three independent paint experts, three wood experts and three leather experts—all highly respected in their fields.

Yet again "The Finest Luxury Sedan in America" took home the trophies in this category. Although, that doesn't mean it was the Jaguar Vanden Plas Supercharged. In fact, no Jaguar made it far enough into the study to have the honor of participating in AMCI's concours. (And for those still keeping tabs, that's one less logo for you to contemplate.)

Ergonomics is the science of designing things that people use so that the people and things interact in the most efficient, effective and safe manner.

Sounds rather Germanic, doesn't it? But it seems as though that stereotype is only partly true. You see, while the three independent experts who evaluated this category chose the Mercedes-Benz S600 as one

AMCI-substantiated claims are in fact among the most highly respected in the automotive industry. And perhaps that's why they were asked to assist when the federal guidelines were originally established for all forms of comparative automotive advertising.

Trademark thoroughness.

In order to certify this claim, AMCI undertook their most sophisticated study to date, by far.

Their unprejudiced, three-phase evaluation took more than a year and 4,000 man-hours to complete.

Phase one was a comprehensive paper review of the most luxurious sedans available in America. The study imposed a few basic criteria to identify only the finest automobiles and those most germane to the U.S. buyer. Ten vehicles were then promoted to phase two, initial Comparative Vehicle Assessment (CVA®) Testing. (Of course, many more were eliminated.)

All were carefully examined in an effort to define the most competitive set possible. An example of each vehicle was procured and thoroughly evaluated.

From this a very clear picture emerged of which automobiles could be considered true contenders. In all, just five remarkable luxury sedans proceeded to the final phase of evaluation, Certification Testing.

To ensure a nonpartisan evaluation of the facts, AMCI then acquired the most luxurious versions available of each of the finalist vehicles from official

"The Finest Luxury Sedan in America," which stopped over three feet sooner. And it didn't stop there.

In fact, the 750iL failed to win a single test in the performance category and only ranked third overall. (Clearly, this is not an advertisement for a BMW.)

If a reputation for refinement were all it took to be considered "The Finest Luxury Sedan in America," one brand would certainly have to be acknowledged as the most obvious contender: Rolls-Royce.

But upon closer examination you might begin to question that reputation. For example, if you counted the exposed screw heads and fasteners inside "The Finest Luxury Sedan in America," you wouldn't find a single one. Do the same in a Silver Seraph and you'd find a total of sixty. (From which you can probably surmise that it's not the Rolls-Royce logo either.)

Is it possible that "The Finest Luxury Sedan in America" is also the quietest? AMCI thinks so. With a decibel reading of just 31.1 at idle, measured in the front seat, it's certainly the most tranquil vehicle they have ever evaluated. And when you consider that the background sound in a typical library is a deafening 40 decibels, chances are you will promptly conclude they're more than likely right in their assessment.

All told, twelve interior-sound, ride-quality and refinement evaluations were performed. "The Finest Luxury Sedan in America" took the honors in most, and quietly drove off with victory in this category.

of the finest German-made sedans, overall it ranked just second to "The Finest Luxury Sedan in America." (Apparently, it's not the three-pointed star either.)

At this point, you may be wondering if it could possibly have been a Bentley that was acknowledged as "The Finest Luxury Sedan in America."

However, just like its matriarch, the Rolls-Royce, even the Bentley Arnage Red Label did not make the final round. (Needless to say, that leaves just one logo to take its rightful place in the corner of this page.)

If the badge fits, wear it.

Finally, after meticulous analysis of the results, AMCI certified that only one luxury sedan has earned the distinction of positioning its logo at the bottom of this advertisement for "The Finest Luxury Sedan in America." By now you have probably concluded, as AMCI did, that the Lexus LS 430 is that sedan.

And that's not merely something they happen to believe. It's a fact they can prove conclusively.

FOR MORE DETAILS VISIT US AT FINESTSEDAN.COM.

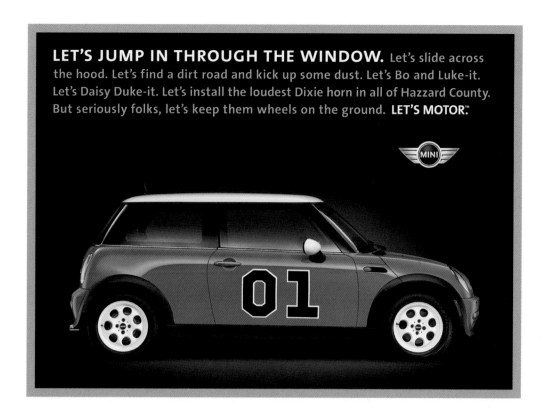

LET'S JUMP IN THROUGH THE WINDOW. Let's slide across the hood. Let's find a dirt road and kick up some dust. Let's Bo and Luke-it. Let's Daisy Duke-it. Let's install the loudest Dixie horn in all of Hazzard County. But seriously folks, let's keep them wheels on the ground. **LET'S MOTOR.**

SILVER
**Newspaper Over 600 Lines
Single**

ART DIRECTORS
Alex Burnard
Mark Taylor

WRITER
Brian Tierney

PHOTOGRAPHER
Daniel Hartz

CREATIVE DIRECTORS
Alex Bogusky
Andrew Keller

CLIENT
MINI

AGENCY
Crispin Porter + Bogusky/Miami

03002A

LET'S SIP, NOT GUZZLE. Let's leave the off-road vehicles off road. Let's stop pretending we live in the jungle. Let's stop intimidating each other. Let's not use the size of our vehicle to compensate for other shortcomings. Let's reclaim our garage space. Let's be nimble. Let's be quick. Let's be honest. **LET'S MOTOR.**

MINI COOPER

SILVER
**Newspaper Over 600 Lines
Single**

ART DIRECTOR
Mark Taylor

WRITERS
Ari Merkin
Steve O'Connell

PHOTOGRAPHER
Daniel Hartz

CREATIVE DIRECTORS
Alex Bogusky
Andrew Keller

CLIENT
MINI

AGENCY
Crispin Porter + Bogusky/Miami

03003A

BRONZE
**Newspaper Over 600 Lines
Single**

ART DIRECTOR
Georgia Arnott

WRITER
Craig Crawford

PHOTOGRAPHER
Scott Downing

CREATIVE DIRECTORS
James Dalthorp
Tom Cordner

CLIENT
Lexus

AGENCY
Team One Advertising/El Segundo

03004A

ANY EVALUATION OF LUXURY SEDANS THAT ELIMINATES A ROLLS-ROYCE AND A BENTLEY IN THE FIRST ROUND MUST HAVE AN IMPRESSIVE WINNER.

IS IT POSSIBLE that popular opinions regarding the icons of motoring luxury are, in fact, *wrong*?

If so, perhaps it is time to replace conventional wisdom with regular wisdom. That's what the experts at Automotive Marketing Consultants Incorporated (AMCI) did when they set out to identify "The Finest Luxury Sedan in America" once and for all.

AMCI is a respected, independent automotive testing company that specializes in the analysis of automobiles. They drive and evaluate more cars than the federal government, car-enthusiast magazines or any organization in the United States. The results of their impartial evaluations are used by car companies when making superiority claims like the ones you're accustomed to seeing in car commercials.

Contrary to what many believe, the restrictions governing advertising are extraordinarily stringent. In fact, the federal guidelines require that advertisers always substantiate claims *before* they make them.

So, how did AMCI conclusively determine the identity of "The Finest Luxury Sedan in America"? Or, more pertinently, how did they negate all others?

Banish bias.

In order to substantiate this claim to a point far beyond mere conjecture, AMCI undertook their most comprehensive and sophisticated study to date.

More significantly, though, this evaluation (like all performed by AMCI) rejected prejudice, partiality and favoritism and, instead, embraced the tangible, measurable and, of course, provable evidence.

By way of example, to evaluate the wood, leather and paint of the five vehicles that made the final round, AMCI did something they have never done before. They recruited three independent experts in each of these fields to do the judging for them. They also did the same for the ergonomics category, thus effectively setting a new standard in impartiality.

In truth, AMCI's reputation for neutrality is so revered that when the federal guidelines that govern comparative automotive advertising were originally established, they were asked to assist in the process.

Expel expediency.

Although the experts at AMCI drive a great deal, they do not believe in shortcuts—of any kind.

Consequently, this comprehensive three-phase evaluation took over a year and 4,000 man-hours to complete. To appreciate just how thorough this study really was, consider the scope of the driving tests: Multiple test drivers repeated every test until each achieved eighteen "perfect" runs in every car.

This would effectively eliminate any differences in driving styles, and therefore could be used to draw factual conclusions about each car's capability, rather than the individual driver's. (And that, after all, is the point of this exceptionally thorough evaluation.)

Phase one was a preliminary paper review of the most luxurious sedans available in the United States. The study imposed some basic criteria to distinguish only the finest automobiles commonly available. Ten were promoted to the second phase of evaluation, Comparative Vehicle Assessment (CVA®) Testing.

An example of each was acquired and scrutinized even further. After careful comparison, five of the ten proved capable of competing for the title of "The Finest Luxury Sedan in America." Consequently, they proceeded to phase three, Certification Testing.

Next, AMCI sourced the most luxurious versions available of each of the five from official franchised dealers. Then they began the task of subjecting them to one hundred and ninety-three dynamic, static and luxury-feature trials in a total of seven categories.

Focus on facts.

A luxury sedan is not simply an ordinary sedan with wood and leather thrown in for good measure. It is a vehicle built to deliver an extraordinary driving experience on every level imaginable. Accordingly, when AMCI performed their in-depth analysis, they reviewed these cars on every level imaginable.

Here are some of their astonishing discoveries:

As the headline at the top of this advertisement attests, certain automobile brands have a considerable reputation for refinement. And, arguably, none quite exemplifies this to the same degree as Rolls-Royce. However, upon closer examination, the validity of this reputation must surely be called into question. (And that is precisely what we're doing here.)

Nothing illustrates this point as well as simply counting all the exposed screw heads and fasteners inside a Rolls-Royce Silver Seraph. At AMCI's count there are sixty. Which is sixty more than you will find in "The Finest Luxury Sedan in America."

Apparently, the Rolls-Royce of luxury sedans is not in fact a Rolls-Royce. (Sorry, old chaps.)

Chances are, if you considered the Rolls-Royce a contender, the possibility that it was a Bentley also

crossed your mind. But much like its matriarch, the Rolls-Royce, the Bentley Arnage Red Label did not have what was required to even make the final phase of AMCI's study. (Surprised? We don't blame you.)

Since these brands obviously require no further deliberation, what others should be considered?

Is it possible that the BMW 750iL actually has the required pedigree? After all, it certainly boasts the heritage. Unfortunately, in the 50–0 mph braking on wet pavement evaluation, the BMW 750iL stopped more than three feet after "The Finest Luxury Sedan in America." More astonishingly, it did not triumph in even a single test in the performance category.

Perhaps you thought the Mercedes-Benz S600 could be considered as a serious contender?

And, truthfully, had this study aimed to identify the finest German-made luxury sedan in America, it would have triumphed. But regrettably (for them), the "German-made" qualifier wasn't one of the criteria.

Appropriately, the luxury sedan that decisively conquered it was also, by far, the quietest in the next evaluation. By achieving a decibel reading of 31.1 at idle, measured in the front seat, it became the most silent vehicle AMCI has ever tested. (And they have been doing this for twenty years.) If you're wondering what 31.1 decibels may sound like, your typical local library comes in at an earsplitting 40 decibels.

AMCI researchers could also give you a decibel reading for a lot of other day-to-day environments. Because of the incredibly low measurement achieved in "The Finest Luxury Sedan in America," they began attempting to record an even lower score. What they discovered was rather astounding. You see, the truth is, they found few places that were as tranquil.

Of the twelve interior-sound, ride-quality and refinement evaluations, "The Finest Luxury Sedan in America" came out ahead in most and quietly drove off with the overall victory in this category.

On the subject of victory, "The Finest Luxury Sedan in America" also won the category judged by the independent wood, leather and paint specialists. In the ergonomics category "The Finest Luxury Sedan in America" once again lived up to its reputation.

All told, "The Finest Luxury Sedan in America" won many individual comparisons, three categories outright and never finished lower than second in any category. In other words, it proved that preconceived notions of luxury should be replaced by the facts.

Dismiss delusions.

Finally, all the results were analyzed and AMCI declared that "The Finest Luxury Sedan in America," to the exclusion of all others, is the Lexus LS 430.

And that's not simply an opinion you can choose to disregard. It's a fact they can support conclusively.

FOR MORE DETAILS VISIT US AT FINESTSEDAN.COM.

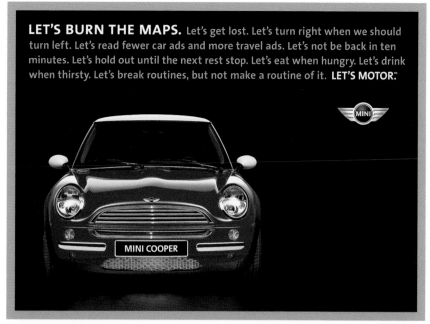

LET'S BURN THE MAPS. Let's get lost. Let's turn right when we should turn left. Let's read fewer car ads and more travel ads. Let's not be back in ten minutes. Let's hold out until the next rest stop. Let's eat when hungry. Let's drink when thirsty. Let's break routines, but not make a routine of it. **LET'S MOTOR."**

MINI COOPER

MERIT

LET'S PUT AWAY THE MIDDLE FINGER. Let's lay off the horn. Let's volunteer jumper cables. Let's pay a stranger's toll. Let's be considerate of cyclists. Let's keep in mind automobiles were created to advance civilization. And for crying out loud, let's remember to turn off those blinkers. **LET'S MOTOR."**

MINI COOPER S

MERIT

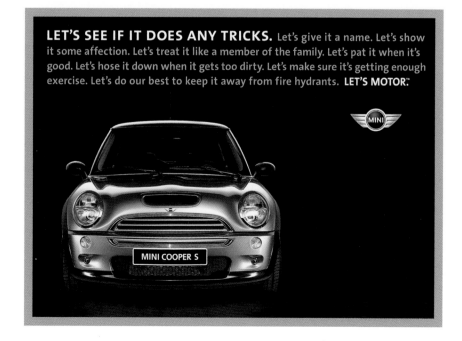

LET'S SEE IF IT DOES ANY TRICKS. Let's give it a name. Let's show it some affection. Let's treat it like a member of the family. Let's pat it when it's good. Let's hose it down when it gets too dirty. Let's make sure it's getting enough exercise. Let's do our best to keep it away from fire hydrants. **LET'S MOTOR."**

MINI COOPER S

GOLD
Newspaper Over 600 Lines Campaign

ART DIRECTOR
Mark Taylor

WRITERS
Ari Merkin
Steve O'Connell

PHOTOGRAPHER
Daniel Hartz

CREATIVE DIRECTORS
Alex Bogusky
Andrew Keller

CLIENT
MINI

AGENCY
Crispin Porter + Bogusky/Miami

03005A

Also won:
MERIT AWARDS
Newspaper Over 600 Lines Single

SILVER

**Newspaper Over 600 Lines
Campaign**

ART DIRECTORS
Philippe Taroux
Stephanie Thomasson
Jessica Gerard-Huet
Emmanuel Bougneres
Thierry Burriez

WRITERS
Benoit Leroux
Bertrand de Demandolx
Jean-François Bouchet
Mattieu Elkaim
Alain Jalabert

PHOTOGRAPHERS
Jean-François Campos
Alain Dercourt
Andre Vayssade

CREATIVE DIRECTOR
Erik Vervroegen

CLIENT
Sony Playstation

AGENCY
TBWA\Paris

03006A

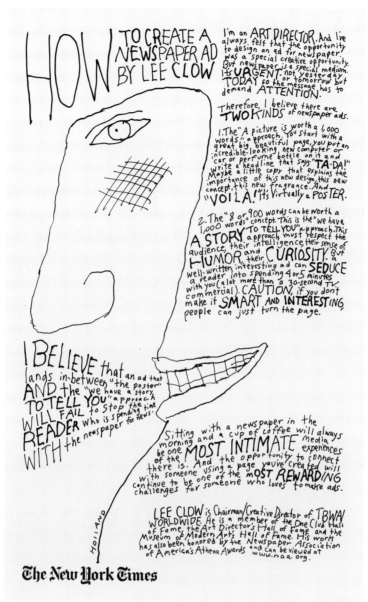

MERIT

BRONZE
Newspaper Over 600 Lines Campaign

ART DIRECTORS
Michael Wright
Mark Braddock

WRITERS
Luke Sullivan
Mike Hughes
Lee Clow
Alon Shoval

ILLUSTRATORS
Brad Holland
Paul Davis
Jack Unruh

AGENCY PRODUCER
Jenny Schoenherr

CREATIVE DIRECTOR
Alon Shoval

CLIENT
Newspaper Association of
America

AGENCY
The Martin Agency/Richmond

03007A

Also won:
MERIT AWARDS
**Newspaper Over 600 Lines
Single**

MERIT

BRONZE
Newspaper 600 Lines or Less Single

ART DIRECTOR
David Damman

WRITER
Dean Buckhorn

CREATIVE DIRECTORS
David Lubars
David Damman

CLIENT
Finnegans

AGENCY
Fallon/Minneapolis

03009A

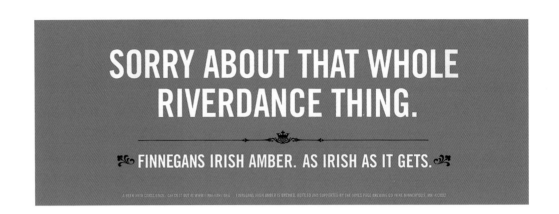

SILVER
Newspaper 600 Lines or Less Campaign

ART DIRECTOR
Ian Grais

WRITER
Ian Grais

PHOTOGRAPHER
Hans Sipma

AGENCY PRODUCER
Chris Raedcher

CREATIVE DIRECTORS
Ian Grais
Chris Staples

CLIENT
Playland

AGENCY
Rethink/Vancouver

03010A

Also won:
SILVER AWARD
Newspaper 600 Lines or Less Single

MERIT AWARDS
Outdoor: Campaign

Newspaper 600 Lines or Less Single

Outdoor: Single

SILVER AWARD **Newspaper Single**

Open daily starting June 15th. Admission includes
unlimited access to over 25 rides. See pne.bc.ca for details.

MERIT AWARDS **Newspaper and Outdoor Single**

Open daily starting June 15th. Admission includes unlimited access to over 25 rides. See pne.bc.ca for details.

9

BRONZE
**Newspaper 600 Lines or Less
Campaign**

ART DIRECTOR
Bob Gates

WRITER
Marty Senn

CREATIVE DIRECTORS
Edward Boches
Jim Hagar

CLIENT
Vespa Naples

AGENCY
Mullen/Wenham

03011A

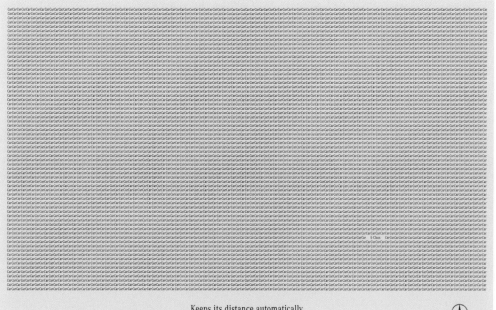

Keeps its distance automatically.
The E-Class with DISTRONIC.

Mercedes-Benz
The Future of the Automobile.

BRONZE
Magazine B/W
Full Page or Spread: Single

ART DIRECTOR
Christian Jakimowitsch

CREATIVE DIRECTORS
Amir Kassaei
Dirk Haeusermann

CLIENT
Mercedes-Benz

AGENCY
Springer & Jacoby/Hamburg

03014A

GOLD
Magazine Color
Full Page or Spread: Single

ART DIRECTOR
Andrew Keller

WRITER
Bill Wright

PHOTOGRAPHER
Sebastian Gray

CREATIVE DIRECTORS
Alex Bogusky
Andrew Keller

CLIENT
MINI

AGENCY
Crispin Porter + Bogusky/Miami

03015A

Reassuringly Expensive.

GOLD
Magazine Color
Full Page or Spread: Single

ART DIRECTOR
Mary-Ann Schmittzehe
Steve Williams

WRITER
Holly Budgen

PHOTOGRAPHER
Coppi Barbieri

AGENCY PRODUCER
Lee Tully

CREATIVE DIRECTOR
Paul Weinberger

CLIENT
Interbrew UK

AGENCY
Lowe/London

03016A

SILVER

Magazine Color
Full Page or Spread: Single

ART DIRECTORS
Don Shelford
Nicole McDonald

WRITER
Joe Fallon

AGENCY PRODUCERS
Aidan Finnan
Andrea Ricker

CREATIVE DIRECTOR
Alan Pafenbach

CLIENT
Volkswagen of America

AGENCY
Arnold Worldwide/Boston

03017A

Beach

The New Beetle Convertible.
Coming soon.

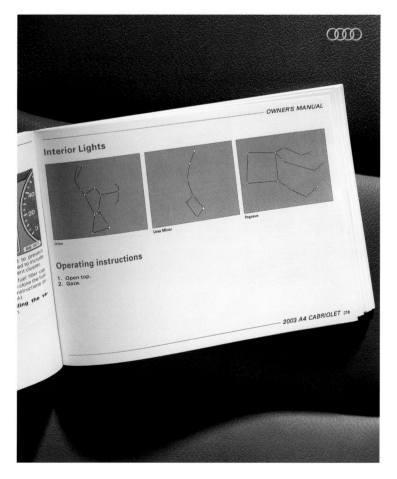

GOLD
Magazine Color
Full Page or Spread: Campaign

ART DIRECTOR
Steve Williams

WRITER
Adrian Lim

PHOTOGRAPHER
Coppi Barbieri

AGENCY PRODUCER
Lee Tully

CREATIVE DIRECTOR
Paul Weinberger

CLIENT
Interbrew UK

AGENCY
Lowe/London

03020A

Also won:
MERIT AWARDS
Magazine Color
Full Page or Spread: Single

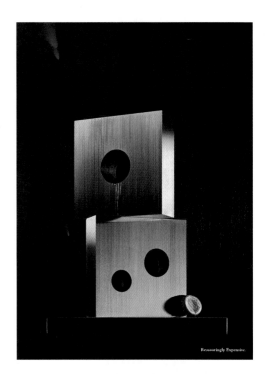

MERIT

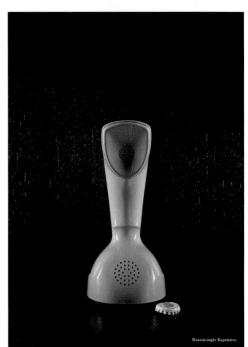

MERIT

MERIT

MERIT

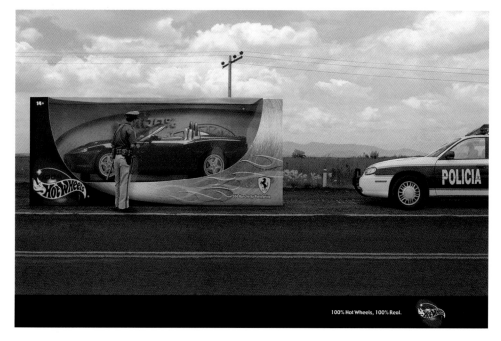

17

SILVER
Magazine Color
Full Page or Spread: Campaign

ART DIRECTOR
Danielle Flagg

WRITER
Mike Byrne

PHOTOGRAPHERS
James Smolka
Michael Jones

CREATIVE DIRECTORS
Susan Hoffman
Carlos Bayala

CLIENT
Nike

AGENCY
Wieden + Kennedy/Portland

03022A

You are completely naked.
Immobile because you're covered
from head to toe in sap.
A pack of hungry wild dogs approaches.
The river is 4.2 miles away.
You're wearing only a pair of the Air Hydrous by Nike ACG.
You also have a box of baking soda,
a tank of propane,
and a pack of Looby's Sweet-N-Tasty Jerky Bites.

GO.

All of a sudden you wake up naked on your back.
Floating down a roaring river towards a 28' drop-off.
Both your arms are totally asleep.
The river is 46 yards wide.
You're wearing only the Air Hydrous by Nike ACG.
You also have a vintage 1972 harmonica,
two competition yo-yos,
and 40 feet of 8-lb. test fishing line.

GO.

Suddenly you are naked.
Hanging upside down in a tree,
feet trapped between two branches.
It's about 125 degrees due to the
disturbingly nearby volcanic activity.
You have cottonmouth.
You're wearing only the Air Hydrous by Nike ACG.
The only other things you have are:
a half a longboard with wax,
one iodine tablet,
and twelve bucks.

GO.

BRONZE
Magazine Color
Full Page or Spread: Campaign

ART DIRECTOR
Sebastien Vacherot

WRITER
Manoelle Van Der Vaeren

PHOTOGRAPHERS
Eastcott Momatiuk
Art Wolfe
Nigel Dennis
Brian Hawkes
Pete Atkinson
Martin Harvey

CREATIVE DIRECTORS
Erik Vervroegen
Chris Garbutt

CLIENT
Nissan

AGENCY
TBWA\Paris

03023A

GOLD
Magazine B/W or Color
Less Than A Page: Single

ART DIRECTOR
Tony Calcao

WRITER
Rob Strasberg

PHOTOGRAPHERS
Daniel Hartz
Sebastian Gray

ILLUSTRATOR
Maggie Baker

CREATIVE DIRECTORS
Alex Bogusky
Andrew Keller

CLIENT
MINI

AGENCY
Crispin Porter + Bogusky/Miami

03024A

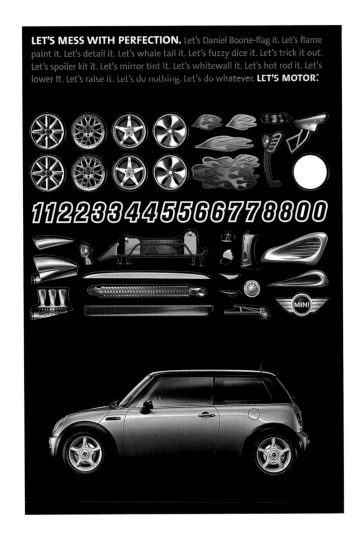

DAYS OF MAGIC. Idaho's Middle Fork of the Salmon. Legendary white water, luxury camping, fabulous fly ... breathtaking scenery, gourmet Dutch oven cuisine, ... hot springs and the best guides on the river. ... Fork Wilderness Outfitters. (800) 726-0575. ...rapids.com

EXCLUSIVE GRAND CANYON BASECAMP Havasupai Waterfalls - Sonoran Desert. Since 1990, exhilarating & educational HIKING and BIKING adventure vacations. 1-6 Day Tours Expert guides-All abilities-Exceptional service 1-866-455-1601 www.azoutbackadventures.com

IDAHO'S MIDDLE FORK OF THE SALMON! Paddle 105 miles through a spectacular wilderness canyon that offers surging rapids, hot springs, wildlife, and some of the best cutthroat trout fishing in the U.S. 5 & 6 day trips with everything provided. Middle Fork River Tours, 800-445-9738 or www.middlefork.com

THE BONDURANT SUPERKART SCHOOL 0-60 ...PH IN 6 SEC., 60-0 IN 4 SEC! Individuals or Corporate ...ract. KGB 125cc Shifter Karts and Briggs & Stratton ...engine ProKarts. Questions? Call 800-652-KART ...visit us at www.bondurantsuperkarts.com

ARTA RIVER TRIPS-Join us for an unforgettable adventure on one of the great rivers of the West. Experience the majesty of a wilderness river canyon, the camaraderie of friendly guides, and the service of a great outfitter. Call for a free catalog (800)323-2782 www.arta.org

GRAB LUNCH! Pull into a fast food drive-thru and wait! Say hello in that crackling speaker language. Order the best looking menu picture. Ask them to colossal-size your straw. Turn up your radio so the fry cook can hear. Hand the money through your sunroof. MINIUSA.COM

SILVER
**Magazine B/W or Color
Less Than A Page: Campaign**

ART DIRECTOR
Matt Peterson

WRITER
Ian Cohen

PHOTOGRAPHERS
Sipa USA
Jean Catuffe

CREATIVE DIRECTORS
Hal Curtis
Dan Wieden

CLIENT
Nike

AGENCY
Wieden + Kennedy/Portland

03027A

Also won:
MERIT AWARD
**Newspaper 600 Lines or Less
Campaign**

Dear Mac,

Hey. I'm thinking of using a headband. I know you used to play with a headband and you looked cool. Do they really work?

— Bandit

Dear Bandit,

I don't have time for this. Yes I did look cool but that was only because I was ranked #1 in the freakin' world. When you're number one you can get away with anything. Also, it was the EIGHTIES. Hey, I've got an idea, why don't you get some leg warmers too? Just let it go.

— Mac

*Got a problem?
askmac@nike.com*

Dear Mac,

My doubles partner and I have been playing together for seven years, but recently I saw him playing with another guy. He seemed to be enjoying playing with that guy more. Now I feel like I'm trying too hard when we play together. Am I crazy?

— Seeing Doubles

Dear Seeing Doubles,

Well, let's see. I played many years with the same guy. He and I were the top doubles team in the world and won everything we played, so no, I never had that problem. But I've seen it happen. Maybe all you need is to add some excitement into your relationship. Mix it up a little. Poach more. Try Australian doubles. Switch sides; you play the forehand for a change. If that doesn't work, give it up and try badminton.

— Mac

*Got a problem?
askmac@nike.com*

Dear Mac,

I play on a Thursday morning women's doubles league. The other day Fran called a ball out that was clearly in. Fran and I got into a heated debate and Fran left crying, leaving us one person short. Should I call and apologize or find a new fourth?

— Suddenly Singles

Dear Suddenly Singles,

Never apologize when you're right. This whole Fran thing reminds me of the time I was playing a certain hot-headed Romanian in the '79 Richmond Open. The umpire called a ball out that was clearly in. I had a little tantrum and he never did reverse the call. But I never apologized. Because I was clearly right. It was in by a mile. So I'd call Fran really late tonight, and just say the word "in" and hang up.

— Mac

*Got a problem?
askmac@nike.com*

WEEK 1

WEEK 2

WEEK 3

GOLD
Outdoor: Single

ART DIRECTOR
Simon Wooller

WRITER
Simon Wooller

ILLUSTRATOR
Morten Meldgaard

AGENCY PRODUCER
Rikke Bondam

CREATIVE DIRECTOR
Simon Wooller

CLIENT
Scandinavian Motor Company

AGENCY
Saatchi & Saatchi/Copenhagen

03028A

SILVER
Outdoor: Single

ART DIRECTOR
Ian Grais

WRITER
Ian Grais

PHOTOGRAPHER
Hans Sipma

AGENCY PRODUCER
Chris Raedcher

CREATIVE DIRECTORS
Ian Grais
Chris Staples

CLIENT
Playland

AGENCY
Rethink/Vancouver

03029A

BRONZE
Outdoor: Single

ART DIRECTORS
Kent Suter
Diane Magid

WRITER
Mike Ward

PHOTOGRAPHER
Michael Jones

CREATIVE DIRECTOR
Terry Schneider

CLIENT
Columbia Sportswear

AGENCY
Borders Perrin Norrander/
Portland

03030A

MERIT

MERIT

GOLD
Outdoor: Campaign

ART DIRECTORS
Tony Calcao
Paul Stechschulte

WRITERS
Rob Strasberg
Ari Merkin

PHOTOGRAPHERS
Tim Damon
Daniel Hartz

CREATIVE DIRECTORS
Alex Bogusky
Andrew Keller

CLIENT
MINI

AGENCY
Crispin Porter + Bogusky/Miami

03032A

Also won:
MERIT AWARDS
Outdoor: Single

25

BRONZE
Outdoor: Campaign

ART DIRECTOR
Noel Haan

WRITER
G. Andrew Meyer

PHOTOGRAPHER
Tony D'Orio

CREATIVE DIRECTORS
Noel Haan
G. Andrew Meyer
Steffan Postaer
Mark Faulkner

CLIENT
Kraft-Altoids Sours

AGENCY
Leo Burnett/Chicago

03033A

Also won:
MERIT AWARDS
**Magazine Color
Full Page or Spread: Campaign**

**Magazine Color
Full Page or Spread: Single**

MERIT

MERIT

MERIT

MERIT

GOLD
Guerilla Advertising: Single

ART DIRECTORS
Slade Gill
Mark Mason

WRITERS
Mark Mason
Slade Gill

PRODUCTION COMPANY
CEA Studios

CREATIVE DIRECTOR
Vanessa Pearson

CLIENT
Guinness UDV

AGENCY
Saatchi & Saatchi/Cape Town

03034A

These magnetic, mock keyholes were placed on cars outside pubs, nightclubs, restaurants, and other drinking establishments. On the reverse of the magnetic keyhole is a decal that provokes people to consider whether indeed they are fit to drive.

BRONZE
Guerilla Advertising: Single

ART DIRECTOR
Christiane Pfennig

WRITER
Philipp Schrenk

CLIENT
Video World

AGENCY
Scholz & Friends/Hamburg

03035A

GOLD
Guerilla Advertising: Campaign

ART DIRECTORS
Erik Heisholt
Marianne Heckmann

WRITER
Erik Heisholt

CREATIVE DIRECTOR
Erik Heisholt

CLIENT
Oslo Piercing Studio

AGENCY
Leo Burnett/Oslo

03036A

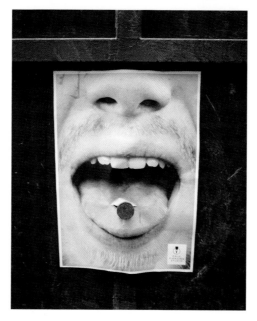

29

SILVER
Guerilla Advertising: Campaign

ART DIRECTORS
Eva Ortner
Kristine Holzhausen

PHOTOGRAPHER
Stephan Foersterling

CREATIVE DIRECTORS
Oliver Kapusta
Thim Wagner

CLIENT
IGFM - International Foundation
of Human Rights

AGENCY
Jung von Matt/Hamburg

03037A

BRONZE
Guerilla Advertising: Campaign

ART DIRECTOR
Hans-Juergen Kaemmerer

WRITER
Robert Junker

PHOTOGRAPHER
Elisabeth Herrmann

CREATIVE DIRECTORS
Uwe Marquardt
Christoph Barth

CLIENT
Amnesty International

AGENCY
Michael Conrad & Leo Burnett/
Frankfurt

03038A

SILVER

Trade B/W
Full Page or Spread: Single

ART DIRECTOR
Mitch Gordon

WRITER
Mark Fenske

PHOTOGRAPHERS
Ibid
Morton Shapiro

CREATIVE DIRECTORS
Mitch Gordon
Joe Sciarrotta
Mark Fenske

CLIENT
Ibid

AGENCY
Ogilvy & Mather/Chicago

03012A

How to know when you've done a good ad.

It's not an easy thing to know.

A good ad isn't like a ball everybody sees sail over the fence for a home run.

Or a kiss, that when it's over your eyes open on someone else's in heat.

A good ad is a tricky, slippery, evasive beast that doesn't like to be caught, won't stand still, won't come out when called.

A good ad is a greased pig when it comes time to put your hands on one.

Masters of disguise, good ads sneak out of you in bars, the shower, dreams, even in advertising meetings, and run away to lost pages in your workbook or torn up sheets in office wastebaskets.

There are even good ads that hide inside other ads and remain unrecognized even when shown on television. (Heck, there's likely a good ad hiding inside this one.)

Some people think you can only tell a good ad when it appears in an advertising award show.

Some people would say the only good ad is one that "sells product."

Whether or not these are helpful identifiers of what makes an ad good is not the point here. (I would say emphatically they are not.)

What we're interested in is how do you know—at the moment you've done it—when you've done a good ad. How do you decide when to stop writing, talking or thinking and grab the little bastard before he makes a getaway, pin him down on the floor and call for the creative director?

One word.

There's one word that, if it fairly describes your ad, tells you you're done.

It's not *honesty* though that's an excellent virtue good ads often contain. It's not *funny* or *provocative* or *wow* or ….

The word is art.

In my gentle opinion, the word is art.

An undefinable monster of a word that means something slightly different to each person is the secret to good advertising.

When you've made art, stop.

Until you have, don't.

I believe it's that simple.

Now, you've looked around this page and noticed it's sponsored by ibid.

Am I suggesting there is something about the conceptual nature of their black and white stock photos that brings an ad closer to art?

That's an easy thing to know.

Thanks for listening.

— *Mark Fenske*

ibidphoto.com

SILVER

Trade B/W
Full Page or Spread: Single

ART DIRECTORS
Mitch Gordon
Neil French

WRITER
Neil French

CREATIVE DIRECTORS
Mitch Gordon
Joe Sciarrotta
Mark Fenske

CLIENT
Ibid

AGENCY
Ogilvy & Mather/Chicago

03013A

Don't bother to read this, the picture's missing.

I mean, seriously, where's the visual joke?

All ads have visual jokes these days. Well, they do if they want to win awards, anyway.

Flick your eyes down to the bottom right-hand corner, and you'll see that the client for this epic is ibid, an excellent source of stock snaps.

My recommendation is that you log on to their site, choose a really clever photo, and build your next ad around that.

With a bit of luck, you won't have to do any writing at all. Which is not only handy, but totally defensible, because nobody reads copy anyway.

Sure, they read newspapers, and magazines, and great dollops of type on Internet sites, but we're talking advertising here. And that's the *real* world, right?

Well, yes. Admittedly, book sales are at an all-time high, but our consumer-insights research tells us that this is because books, artfully displayed, are an ideal décor ploy for the illiterate.

But nobody actually *reads* the damn things! Dearie me, no.

I haven't read them personally, of course, but I'll bet the Bible, and the Koran, for instance, are chock-full of pics.

"A joke a page" was, I believe, the catchphrase of the original authors.

"Have you heard the one about Jonah and the pig? Alright, alright, not the pig then…the camel? You can't draw a camel. What can you draw? A fish. That's it? A fish? OK, this fish walks into a bar…"

The point is, obviously they needed pictures.

How can you expect to get anyone's attention, let alone their interest, with just a load of old words…ridiculous. Prove it for yourself.

Let's say the chap at the next desk has breath that could drop a Doberman at twenty paces.

You don't want to tell him personally. Not face to face, for sure.

So, do you write, "Your breath smells" on a Post-it note and stick it to his desktop?

Of course you don't.

You log on to ibidphoto.com; you download a picture of a dog. You scan a snap of the breather (which you find or take or . look, I can't do all the work for you.) You flip the dog on its back, patch in the breather's face, and do some squiggly lines from his mouth to the dog. (A few hours on Photoshop is all it'll take.)

Then you print the photo and stick *that* to his desktop.

So much more powerful.

And if he's so crass as to say, "What the fuck's that about?", and sling it in the bin, that only proves that he's a boring old reactionary as well as being a both-end farter. His loss.

Now, the only thing that ibid lacks, I notice, is a really good tagline.

How about "A picture is worth a thousand words?" (I just made that up. That's why I get the big bucks.)

Now, if we can just find a picture that expresses those *seven* words, we'll be in business.

— *Neil French*

ibidphoto.com

GOLD
Trade B/W or Color
Any Size: Campaign

ART DIRECTOR
Mark Taylor

WRITER
Ari Merkin

PHOTOGRAPHERS
Stock
Sebastian Gray

CREATIVE DIRECTOR
Alex Bogusky

CLIENT
BELL

AGENCY
Crispin Porter + Bogusky/Miami

03043A

Also won:
SILVER AWARD
Trade Color
Full Page or Spread: Single

SILVER

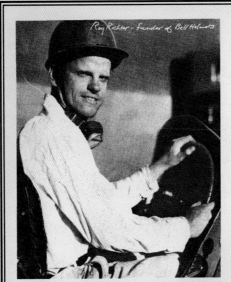

FRUSTRATIONS GROW BEST IN ARTIFICIAL LIGHT.

SEEK OUT

Timberland

MERIT

EXIT

THIS IS NOT A SIGN. IT IS A CALLING.

SEEK OUT

Timberland

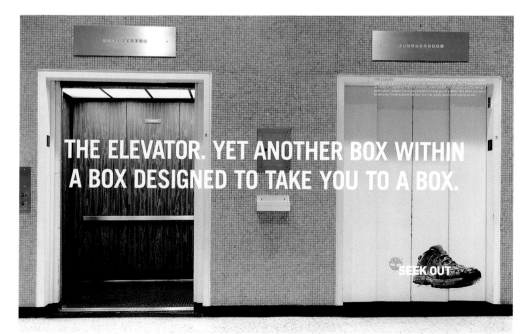

THE ELEVATOR. YET ANOTHER BOX WITHIN A BOX DESIGNED TO TAKE YOU TO A BOX.

SEEK OUT

Timberland

SILVER
Trade B/W or Color
Any Size: Campaign

ART DIRECTORS
David Damman
Dan Bryant

WRITER
Greg Hahn

PHOTOGRAPHER
David Harriman

AGENCY PRODUCER
Louise Raicht

CREATIVE DIRECTORS
David Lubars
Kevin Roddy

CLIENT
Timberland

AGENCY
Fallon/New York

03044A

Also won:
MERIT AWARD
Trade Color
Full Page or Spread: Single

BRONZE
Trade B/W or Color
Any Size: Campaign

ART DIRECTOR
Carlos Rubio

WRITER
Pablo Monzón

CREATIVE DIRECTORS
Pablo Monzón
Jorge López

CLIENT
The Design House

AGENCY
Cathedral The Creative Center/
Madrid

03045A

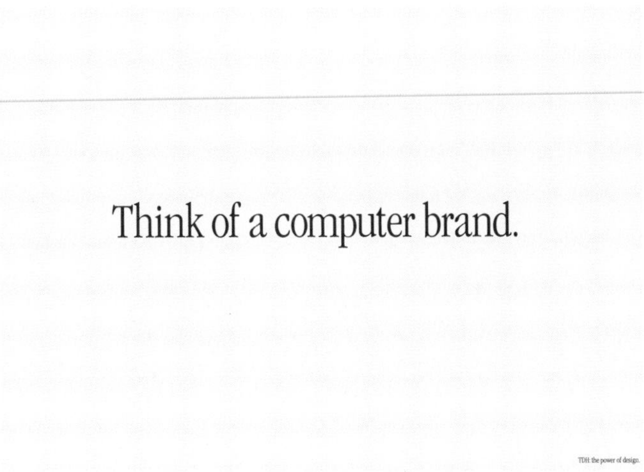

Think of a computer brand.

TDH: the power of design.

THINK OF A
FASHION BRAND.

TDH: THE POWER OF DESIGN.

Think of a beer brand.

TDH ·The power of design.

Think of a
business magazine.

TDH: The power of design.

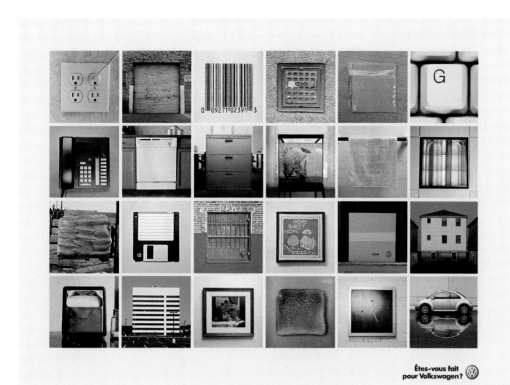

GOLD
**Collateral: Point of Purchase
and In-Store**

ART DIRECTORS
Stephen Cafiero
Jorge Carreño

WRITER
Vincent Lobelle

PHOTOGRAPHER
Oliver Rheindorf

CREATIVE DIRECTOR
Erik Vervroegen

CLIENT
Sony Playstation

AGENCY
TBWA\Paris

03047A

Also won:
SILVER AWARD
**Trade Color
Full Page or Spread: Single**

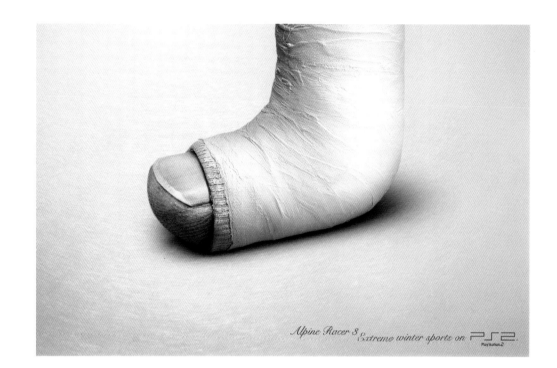

DESK WALLET WALLET

PANORAMIC

We're proud to announce the new limited edition, motorsport-inspired 330i Performance Package. Welcome to the family.

SILVER
Collateral: Point of Purchase and In-Store

ART DIRECTOR
Gerard Caputo

WRITER
Reuben Hower

PHOTOGRAPHER
Simon Stock

CREATIVE DIRECTORS
David Lubars
Bruce Bildsten

CLIENT
BMW of North America

AGENCY
Fallon/Minneapolis

03048A

TAKE YOUR CHILDREN TO WORK DAY
LOWE · THURSDAY, APRIL 25

Mommy

Daddy

Gary Goldsmith

ME

SILVER
Collateral: Self-Promotion

ART DIRECTOR
Mark Andeer

WRITER
Tom Hamling

ILLUSTRATOR
Mark Andeer

CREATIVE DIRECTORS
Gary Goldsmith
Dean Hacohen

CLIENT
Lowe

AGENCY
Lowe/New York

03049A

GOLD, SILVER, BRONZE

SILVER
Collateral: Self-Promotion

ART DIRECTOR
Tracy Wong

WRITER
John Schofield

AGENCY PRODUCER
Angie Anderson

CREATIVE DIRECTOR
Tracy Wong

CLIENT
WONGDOODY

AGENCY
WONGDOODY/Seattle

03050A

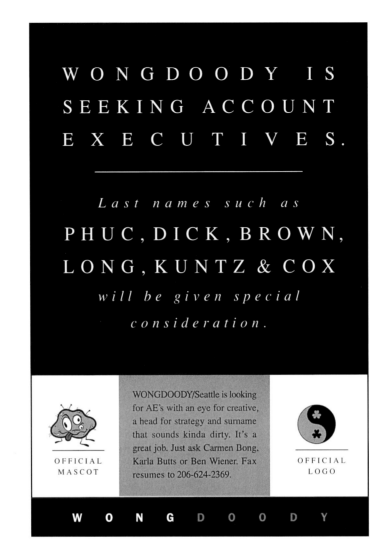

WONGDOODY IS SEEKING ACCOUNT EXECUTIVES.

Last names such as

PHUC, DICK, BROWN, LONG, KUNTZ & COX

will be given special consideration.

OFFICIAL MASCOT

WONGDOODY/Seattle is looking for AE's with an eye for creative, a head for strategy and surname that sounds kinda dirty. It's a great job. Just ask Carmen Bong, Karla Butts or Ben Wiener. Fax resumes to 206-624-2369.

OFFICIAL LOGO

W O N G D O O D Y

BRONZE
Collateral: Self-Promotion

ART DIRECTOR
Dean Lee

WRITER
James Lee

PHOTOGRAPHER
CWS

ILLUSTRATOR
Artefact

CREATIVE DIRECTOR
Alan Russell

CLIENT
Palmer Jarvis DDB

AGENCY
Palmer Jarvis DDB/Vancouver

03051A

Palmer Jarvis DDB ☐
Ideas ☐

GOLD
**Collateral: Posters
Single**

ART DIRECTOR
Amee Shah

WRITERS
Andy Carrigan
Scott Linnen

PHOTOGRAPHER
Mark Laita

CREATIVE DIRECTORS
Alex Bogusky
Andrew Keller

CLIENT
MINI

AGENCY
Crispin Porter + Bogusky/Miami

03052A

SILVER

Collateral: Posters
Single

ART DIRECTOR
William Hammond

WRITER
Steve Straw

PHOTOGRAPHER
Michael Lewis

ILLUSTRATOR
Grant Linton

CREATIVE DIRECTOR
Brett Wild

CLIENT
Guinness

AGENCY
Saatchi & Saatchi/Johannesburg

03053A

BRONZE

Collateral: Posters
Single

ART DIRECTOR
Isabela Ferreira

WRITER
Pete Figel

PHOTOGRAPHER
Isabela Ferreira

CREATIVE DIRECTOR
Dan Fietsam

CLIENT
The Apartment People

AGENCY
Young & Rubicam/Chicago

03054A

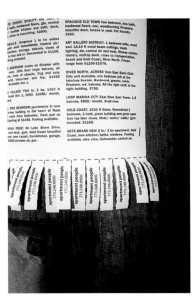

These "For Rent" signs were hung around
Chicago neighborhoods to demonstrate
that Apartment People offers the largest
selection of apartments for rent in the city.

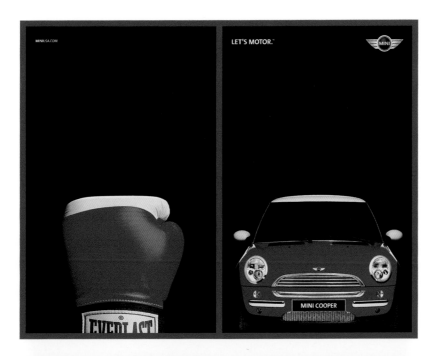

GOLD
**Collateral: Posters
Campaign**

ART DIRECTOR
Amee Shah

WRITERS
Scott Linnen
Andy Carrigan

PHOTOGRAPHER
Mark Laita

CREATIVE DIRECTORS
Alex Bogusky
Andrew Keller

CLIENT
MINI

AGENCY
Crispin Porter + Bogusky/Miami

03055A

Also won:
SILVER AWARD
Outdoor: Campaign

43

SILVER
**Collateral: Posters
Campaign**

ART DIRECTOR
Leong Wai Foong

WRITER
Troy Lim

PHOTOGRAPHER
Geoff Ang

ILLUSTRATOR
Dave Phung

AGENCY PRODUCER
Celeste Pua

CREATIVE DIRECTOR
Francis Wee

CLIENT
Kentucky Fried Chicken
Management

AGENCY
BBDO/Singapore

03056A

Also won:
MERIT AWARDS
**Collateral: Posters
Single**

MERIT

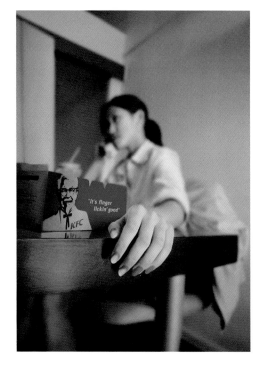

MERIT

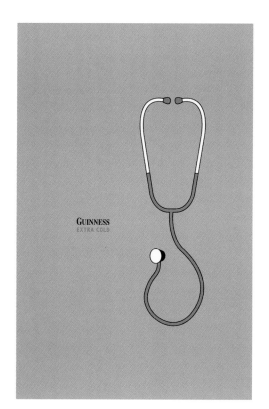

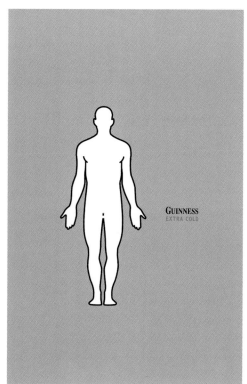

BRONZE
**Collateral: Posters
Campaign**

ART DIRECTORS
Chris Bakay
Jackie Hathiramani

WRITERS
Jackie Hathiramani
Chris Bakay

ILLUSTRATOR
Chris Bakay

CREATIVE DIRECTORS
Jackie Hathiramani
Rich Wakefield

CLIENT
Players Billiards Bar/Guinness

AGENCY
The Third Eye/Atlanta

03057A

GOLD
**Public Service/Political
Newspaper or Magazine
Single**

ART DIRECTOR
Roberto Fernandez

WRITER
Flavio Casarotti

PHOTOGRAPHER
Richard Kohout

CREATIVE DIRECTORS
Jader Rossetto
Pedro Cappeletti
Erh Ray

CLIENT
MASP Museum of Art of
São Paulo

AGENCY
DM9 DDB/São Paulo

03058A

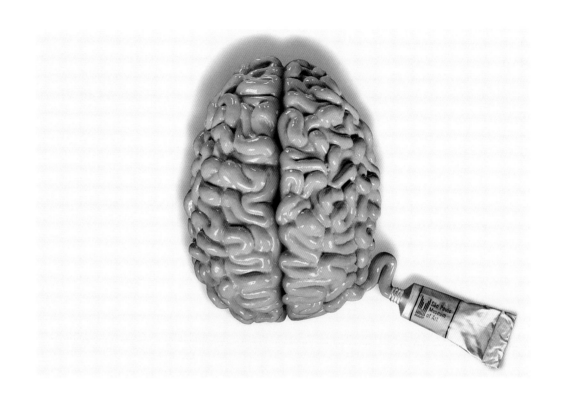

NOT ALL KIDS WANT THE SAME
THING FOR CHRISTMAS.

COVENANT HOUSE. 1-800-HELP-308

SILVER
**Public Service/Political
Newspaper or Magazine
Single**

ART DIRECTOR
Alan Madill

WRITER
Terry Drummond

PHOTOGRAPHER
Frank Hoedl

AGENCY PRODUCERS
Judy Boudreau
Connie Gorsline

CREATIVE DIRECTORS
Zak Mroueh
Paul Lavoie

CLIENT
Covenant House

AGENCY
Taxi/Toronto

03059A

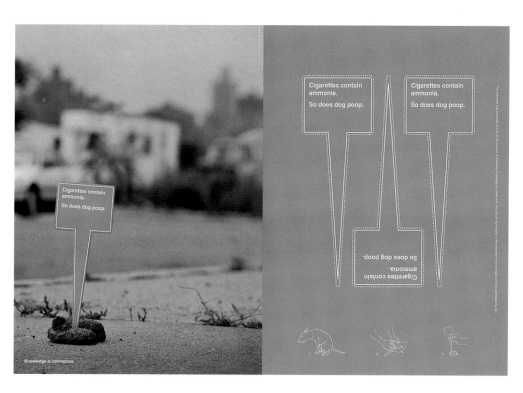

Cigarettes contain ammonia.
So does dog poop.

Knowledge is contagious.

BRONZE
**Public Service/Political
Newspaper or Magazine
Single**

ART DIRECTORS
Rob Baird
Alex Burnard
Mike Del Marmol

WRITER
Rob Strasberg

PHOTOGRAPHERS
Rob Baird
Alex Burnard
Greg Carter
Mike Del Marmol

ILLUSTRATOR
Jasper Goodall

AGENCY PRODUCERS
Aidan Finnan
Sally Hunter
Andrea Ricker

CREATIVE DIRECTORS
Ron Lawner
Alex Bogusky
Pete Favat
Ari Merkin
Roger Baldacci

CLIENT
American Legacy Foundation

AGENCY
Arnold Worldwide/Boston and
Crispin Porter + Bogusky/Miami

03060A

GOLD

**Public Service/Political
Newspaper or Magazine
Campaign**

ART DIRECTORS
Mike Keane
Ed Clark

WRITERS
Tony Veazey
Mike Keane

PHOTOGRAPHER
Ed Clark

TYPOGRAPHER
Simon Warden

CREATIVE DIRECTOR
Tony Veazey

CLIENT
Trees for London

AGENCY
FBA/Manchester

03061A

NOT ALL KIDS WANT THE SAME THING FOR CHRISTMAS.

COVENANT HOUSE ✉ 1-800-HELP-308

MERIT

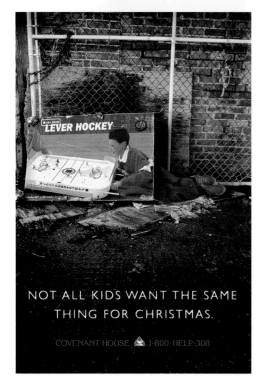

NOT ALL KIDS WANT THE SAME THING FOR CHRISTMAS.

COVENANT HOUSE ✉ 1-800-HELP-308

NOT ALL KIDS WANT THE SAME THING FOR CHRISTMAS.

COVENANT HOUSE ✉ 1-800-HELP-308

SILVER
Public Service/Political Newspaper or Magazine Campaign

ART DIRECTOR
Alan Madill

WRITER
Terry Drummond

PHOTOGRAPHER
Frank Hoedl

AGENCY PRODUCERS
Judy Boudreau
Connie Gorsline

CREATIVE DIRECTORS
Zak Mroueh
Paul Lavoie

CLIENT
Covenant House

AGENCY
Taxi/Toronto

03062A

Also won:
MERIT AWARDS
Public Service/Political Outdoor and Posters Campaign

Public Service/Political Newspaper or Magazine Single

GOLD, SILVER, BRONZE

BRONZE
**Public Service/Political
Newspaper or Magazine
Campaign**

ART DIRECTORS
Martin Pasecky
Michael Martin
Basil Mina

WRITERS
Basil Mina
Jirka Pleskot
Michael Yee

CREATIVE DIRECTOR
Basil Mina

CLIENT
Museum of Communism Prague

AGENCY
Leo Burnett/Prague

03063A

In order to tell people what Terry Fox did after losing a leg to cancer, a 6-foot-long poster that narrated the entire story of Terry Fox was placed in schools, offices, malls, hospitals, and other crowded places.

SILVER
Public Service/Political Outdoor and Posters Single

ART DIRECTOR
Dinesh Tharippa

WRITER
Vinod Lal Heera Eshwer

PHOTOGRAPHER
Bhabananda Mishra

ILLUSTRATOR
Dinesh Tharippa

CREATIVE DIRECTOR
Ramesh Ramanathan

CLIENT
Terry Fox Foundation

AGENCY
Saatchi & Saatchi/Bangalore

03064A

BRONZE
Public Service/Political Outdoor and Posters Single

ART DIRECTORS
Brent Ladd
Tonda Mueller

WRITER
Daniel Russ

PHOTOGRAPHERS
Peter Marlow
Magnum Photos

CREATIVE DIRECTORS
Daniel Russ
Brent Ladd

CLIENT
Peace Council

AGENCY
GSD&M/Austin

03065A

SILVER

Public Service/Political Collateral: Brochures and Direct Mail

ART DIRECTORS
Gavin Bradley
Steve Cooper
Maggie Mouat
Louise Studholme

WRITERS
Ken Double
Kate Benton

PHOTOGRAPHER
Ross Brown

CREATIVE DIRECTOR
Gavin Bradley

CLIENT
Women's Refuge

AGENCY
Saatchi & Saatchi New Zealand/
Wellington

03066A

HOW VISIBLE DOES DOMESTIC VIOLENCE HAVE TO BE BEFORE WE DO SOMETHING ABOUT IT?

Women's Refuge Annual Appeal 22-29 July. Call 0900 REFUGE to make a $20 donation.

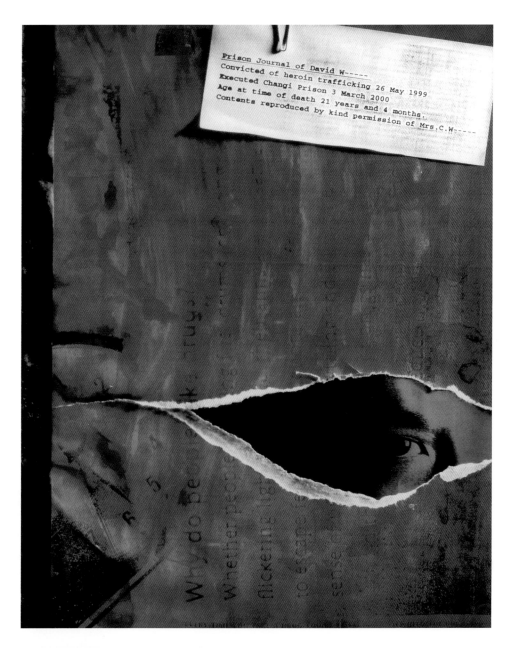

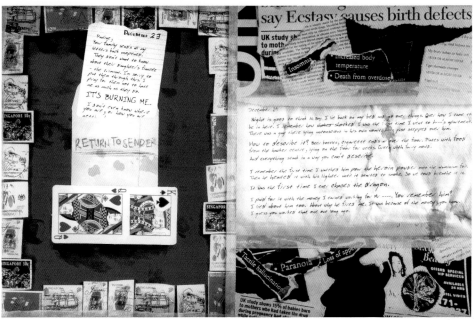

BRONZE
Public Service/Political Collateral: Brochures and Direct Mail

ART DIRECTORS
Anna Peters
Drew Lees

WRITERS
Malcolm Pryce
Drew Lees

PHOTOGRAPHER
Phenomenon

ILLUSTRATOR
Anna Peters

CREATIVE DIRECTOR
Quentin Berryman

CLIENT
Ministry of Home Affairs

AGENCY
Batey/Singapore

03067A

GOLD
**Public Service/Political
Radio: Single**

WRITERS
Paul Brazier
Nick Worthington

AGENCY PRODUCER
Debbie Dillon

PRODUCTION COMPANY
COI Communications

CREATIVE DIRECTORS
Paul Brazier
Nick Worthington

CLIENT
COI/DTLR

AGENCY
Abbott Mead Vickers.BBDO/
London

03001R

ANNOUNCER 1: You're four times more likely to have a road accident when on a mobile phone.

ANNOUNCER 2: It's hard to concentrate on two things at the same time.

ANNOUNCER 1: You're four times more likely to have a road accident when on a mobile phone.

ANNOUNCER 2: It's hard to concentrate on two things at the same time.

ANNOUNCER 1: You're four times more likely to have a road accident when on a mobile phone.

ANNOUNCER 2: It's hard to concentrate on two things at the same time.

ANNOUNCER 1: You're four times more likely to have a road accident when on a mobile phone.

ANNOUNCER 2: It's hard to concentrate on two things at the same time.

TOGETHER: Think. Switch it off when you drive.

SILVER
**Public Service/Political
Radio: Single**

WRITERS
Matt Syberg-Olsen
Chris Hall

AGENCY PRODUCER
Francesca DeRose

PRODUCTION COMPANY
Keen Music

CREATIVE DIRECTORS
Tim Kavander
Bill Newbery

CLIENT
Canadian Psychiatric Research
Foundation

AGENCY
Arnold Worldwide/Toronto

03002R

OPERATOR: Emergency, what are you reporting?

WOMAN: Oh my God! Oh my God! A man just got hit by a car!

OPERATOR: Okay, ma'am. Can you tell me where you are?

WOMAN: I'm at Oak and 16th. Oh God! Send an ambulance!

OPERATOR: Okay, ma'am, I need you to calm down. Can you see the man who got hit?

WOMAN: Yes.

OPERATOR: Is he bleeding?

WOMAN: No. He's not bleeding.

OPERATOR: But he's alive?

WOMAN: I think so. He's breathing.

OPERATOR: He's probably fine, then.

WOMAN: But I saw him get hit.

OPERATOR: Don't worry, ma'am. He's probably looking for attention.

WOMAN: Are you sure?

OPERATOR: Oh, yeah. Either that or he just doesn't want to go to work.

WOMAN: Really?

OPERATOR: Yeah. Just walk away. He'll have to learn to deal with his problems like everyone else. Really, it's for his own good.

ANNOUNCER: Imagine if we treated everyone like we treat the mentally ill. This message from the Canadian Psychiatric Research Foundation. Mental illness is real. Help us find a cure.

INTERVIEWER: Hi. Do you mind answering some questions for us?

TEEN: No.

INTERVIEWER: All right. For 25.4 million dollars, would you live in your parents' basement until you were 40 years old?

TEEN: Yeah!

INTERVIEWER: All right. Would you sleep in a cemetery for one year for 25.4 million dollars?

TEEN: I sure would—and have a good time, too.

INTERVIEWER: Would you cut off your pinky toe?

TEEN: Yeah, sure would! I'd have nine toes.

INTERVIEWER: Would you eat your own vomit for 25.4 million?

TEEN: I'd eat it like it was lasagna.

INTERVIEWER: Here's your final question: For 25.4 million dollars, would you market a product to teenagers that's responsible for killing 3 million people a year?

TEEN: No, that's stupid!

INTERVIEWER: Well, the CEO of the tobacco company that makes Marlboro cigarettes would. Last year, he made 25.4 million dollars in salary with stock options.

TEEN: I think he's a, a jerk.

ANNOUNCER: Corporate Tobacco won't tell you the truth. So we will. Target Market. Go to tmvoice.com.

SILVER
**Public Service/Political
Radio: Campaign**

WRITER
Troy Longie

AGENCY PRODUCERS
Rose Pennington
Jenee Schmidt

PRODUCTION COMPANY
Babble-On

CREATIVE DIRECTOR
Jac Coverdale

CLIENT
Target Market

AGENCY
Clarity Coverdale Fury/
Minneapolis

03003R

WOMAN: Hello.

INTERVIEWER: Hi. I have a quick product survey. Would you mind participating?

WOMAN: Okay.

INTERVIEWER: This widely used product has a few downsides I am going to tell you about. You tell me whether you "don't care," "care," or "care a lot."

WOMAN: Okay.

INTERVIEWER: Okay. This product may wrinkle your skin.

WOMAN: I care about that.

INTERVIEWER: Okay. This product smells bad to some people.

WOMAN: I don't care.

INTERVIEWER: This product exposes people who use it to radiation.

WOMAN: Well, I care about that.

INTERVIEWER: Okay. This product can cause a few things. I'll list them, okay? Erectile Dysfunction.

WOMAN: A who? Ere-ere-erectile Dysfunction?

INTERVIEWER: Yes.

WOMAN: Oh, I care about that.

INTERVIEWER: Okay. Sudden Infant Death Syndrome.

WOMAN: And I care about that. That's dangerous.

INTERVIEWER: And every fifth death in America.

WOMAN: I care about that.

INTERVIEWER: Are you familiar with this product?

WOMAN: No. I don't know what you are talking about.

INTERVIEWER: It's cigarettes.

WOMAN: Oh.

INTERVIEWER: Thanks for your time.

ANNOUNCER: Knowledge is contagious. Infect truth.

BRONZE
**Public Service/Political
Radio: Campaign**

WRITER
Annie Finnegan

AGENCY PRODUCER
Chris Jennings

PRODUCTION COMPANY
Blast Audio

CREATIVE DIRECTORS
Ron Lawner
Alex Bogusky
Pete Favat
Ari Merkin
Roger Baldacci

CLIENT
American Legacy Foundation

AGENCY
Arnold Worldwide/Boston and
Crispin Porter + Bogusky/Miami

03004R

Also won:
MERIT AWARD
**Public Service/Political
Radio: Single**

GOLD
Public Service/Political
Television: Single

ART DIRECTOR
Duncan Marshall

WRITER
Howard Willmott

AGENCY PRODUCER
Sally-Ann Dale

PRODUCTION COMPANY
Gorgeous Enterprises

DIRECTOR
Frank Budgen

ANIMATION PRODUCTION
Passion Pictures

DIRECTOR OF ANIMATION
Russell Brooke

CREATIVE DIRECTOR
David Droga

CLIENT
NSPCC

AGENCY
Saatchi & Saatchi/London

03068A

SILVER
Public Service/Political
Television: Single

ART DIRECTOR
Ryan O'Rourke

WRITER
Steve O'Connell

AGENCY PRODUCER
Michelle Lazzarino

PRODUCTION COMPANY
Hundred Street Films

DIRECTOR
Simon Levene

CREATIVE DIRECTOR
Alex Bogusky

CLIENT
Florida Department of Health

AGENCY
Crispin Porter + Bogusky/Miami

03069A

(Throughout this commercial, a real, live-action man abuses a cartoon boy, who recovers quickly from each assault, just as cartoons do.)

MAN: What's this, then? Had a hard day, have you? Sitting here all day watching telly? Now what the hell are you up to? Look at the state of this place, look at the state of it, look at it. What did I tell you about running indoors? What did I tell you? There you are. What are you up to? I just asked you, what are you up to? *(The father throttles the cartoon boy until his eyes bulge. The cartoon recovers.)* Why do you make me do this to you? You dirty ba—Get out, that's it, go on, you run, get out of here. *(He hurls the cartoon boy down the stairs. The next shot shows the boy; this time, he is not a cartoon but a real child, crumpled and concussed at the landing.)*

SUPER: Real children don't bounce back. If you think a child is being abused, do something. 0808 800 5000. Your call can be anonymous. Together we can stop child abuse.

HERO: Do you really expect me to talk?

VILLAIN: Only to the angels. *(Ceiling vents start billowing in gas.)* So long, fancy man.

(Henchmen, sitting on the other side of the cell wall, inhale deeply on cigarettes and blow smoke through the vents to the other side of the cell.)

SUPER: With over 200 poisons, second-hand smoke kills 53,000 people a year.

VILLAIN: Faster!

SUPER: Truth.

INSTRUCTOR: Ben, we're gonna skip parallel parking and go straight to tailgating. So let's get out there on the interstate, find us a semi, show him who's boss. No, no. Don't use your turn signal. It's nobody's business where you're going. What are you doing? *[Yelling at the car next to them, expecting the boy to repeat after him.]*

STUDENT: What are you doing?

INSTRUCTOR: What are you doing? *[He hands the student a coffee mug and sugar packets.]* Ben, I'm a two cream, one sugar guy. This is a cell phone, son. *[Throws it in the back seat.]* Why don't you get that for me?

ANNOUNCER: You didn't learn to drive this way. So why do you drive this way?

SUPER: If you don't stop driving dangerously, we'll stop you. New Mexico Law Enforcement.

BRONZE
Public Service/Political Television: Single

ART DIRECTOR
Mike Penn

WRITER
Sam Maclay

AGENCY PRODUCER
Sterling Grant, Jr.

PRODUCTION COMPANY
Sterling Productions

DIRECTOR
Jason Reitman

CREATIVE DIRECTORS
Scott Johnson
Sam Maclay

CLIENT
New Mexico State Highway & Transportation Department's Traffic Safety Bureau

AGENCY
Rick Johnson & Company/ Albuquerque

03070A

WOMAN: I have been in prison since 1992. People need to know that I will probably spend the rest of my life here. I do not live in fear of dying. I have not been beaten. No one has been subjected to brutality or violent attacks, and no one has died while in custody. I know that trying to find my husband was wrong, and that I have no right to be calling for human rights. I deserve to be here. They have stopped passing your letters on to me, so you should stop writing. They have no effect.

SUPER: Amnesty International. Become a Freedom Writer. www.amnesty.org.nz.

SILVER
Public Service/Political Television: Campaign

ART DIRECTOR
Billy McQueen

WRITERS
Chris Schofield
Oliver Maisey

AGENCY PRODUCER
Terry Slade-Baker

PRODUCTION COMPANY
Curious Films

DIRECTOR
Darryl Ward

CREATIVE DIRECTOR
Oliver Maisey

CLIENT
Amnesty International

AGENCY
GeneratorBates/Auckland

03071A

BRONZE
Public Service/Political
Television: Campaign

ART DIRECTORS
Ryan O'Rourke
Amee Shah
Jennifer Meinders

WRITERS
Steve O'Connell
Scott Linnen
Jeff Baxter

AGENCY PRODUCER
Spring Clinton-Smith

PRODUCTION COMPANY
Harvest Films

DIRECTOR
Baker Smith

CREATIVE DIRECTORS
Ron Lawner
Alex Bogusky
Pete Favat
Ari Merkin
Roger Baldacci

CLIENT
American Legacy Foundation

AGENCY
Arnold Worldwide/Boston and
Crispin Porter + Bogusky/Miami

03072A

Also won:
MERIT AWARD
Public Service/Political
Television: Single

[A truth teen pulls plastic baby dolls from a duffel
bag. Soon, baby dolls flood the sidewalk. Commuters
and pedestrians stop to pick them up. The message
printed on the baby dolls' shirts read: How do
infants avoid second-hand smoke? "At some point,
they begin to crawl."—Tobacco Executive, 1996.]

SUPER: *Knowledge is contagious. Infect truth.
infect-truth.com.

TOM: Hi, Tom Bodett for Motel 6, with a word for business travelers. Seems business has its own language these days, full of buzzwords. Like "buzzword" or "net-net." And after a day spent white boarding a matrix of action items and deliverables, it's nice to know you can always outsource your accommodation needs to the nearest Motel 6. You'll get a clean, comfortable room for the lowest price, net-net, of any national chain. Plus dataports and free local calls in case you tabled your discussion and need to reconvene offline. So you can think of Motel 6 as your total business travel solution provider, vis-a-vis cost-effective lodging alternatives for Q-1 through Q-4, I think. Just call 1-800-4-MOTEL-6 or visit motel6.com. I'm Tom Bodett for Motel 6, and we'll maintain the lighting device in its current state of illumination for you.

ANNOUNCER: Motel 6. An Accor hotel.

FATHER: George?

GEORGE: Yeah?

FATHER: I have to talk to you about something.

GEORGE: Okay.

FATHER: Come sit here. Listen. Something terrible has happened.

GEORGE: It wasn't me.

FATHER: No, it's okay, George. I'm not cross with you. Do you remember what happened to granny last year?

GEORGE: She went to sleep with angels forever and ever.

FATHER: That's right, George. The same thing's happened again. Only this time it's not granny. It's someone else you love very, very much.

GEORGE: Not mommy!

FATHER: No, no. It's worse. It's much worse, son. It's Santa. Santa Claus is dead.

(George starts crying.)

ANNOUNCER: If you want to save money this Christmas, stay in a City Lodge Hotel room.

GOLD
Consumer Radio: Single

WRITER
Chris Smith

AGENCY PRODUCER
Sheri Cartwright

PRODUCTION COMPANY
Bad Animals

CREATIVE DIRECTOR
Mike Malone

CLIENT
Motel 6

AGENCY
The Richards Group/Dallas

03005R

SILVER
Consumer Radio: Single

WRITERS
Cathy Thomson
Paul Warner

AGENCY PRODUCER
Melanie Gray

PRODUCTION COMPANY
Sterling Sound

DIRECTOR
Cathy Thomson

CREATIVE DIRECTOR
Sandra de Witt

CLIENT
City Lodge

AGENCY
TBWA Hunt Lascaris/
Johannesburg

03006R

GOLD
Consumer Radio: Campaign

WRITERS
Ralf Heuel
Christoph Nann

PRODUCTION COMPANY
Studio Funk

DIRECTOR
Ralf Heuel

CREATIVE DIRECTORS
Ralf Heuel
Ralf Nolting

CLIENT
Volkswagen

AGENCY
Grabarz & Partner Werbeagentur/
Hamburg

03008R

(Dialogue is played in extreme slow-motion.)

MAN: Morning, Miss Stevenson.

WOMAN: Morning, sir.

MAN: Do I have any appointments today?

WOMAN: Actually, today is your wedding anniversary.

MAN: Oh, I'd almost forgotten! You are an angel!

BOTH: Ha ha ha ha ha.

ANNOUNCER: *(At normal speed.)* After a ride in the new Volkswagen Passat W8, everything else will seem slower than usual. The new Passat W8. The 8-cylinder by Volkswagen.

(Dialogue is played in extreme slow-motion.)

MAN 1: Good evening, sir.

MAN 2: Good evening, I've reserved a table under the name, "Horseborough-Porter."

MAN 1: Ah, yes, Mr. Horseborough-Porter. Table for two?

MAN 2: Exactly.

ANNOUNCER: *(At normal speed.)* After a ride in the new Volkswagen Passat W8, everything else will seem slower than usual. The new Passat W8. The 8-cylinder by Volkswagen.

(Dialogue is played in extreme slow-motion.)

MAN 1: Ah, boss! Am I glad to see you!

MAN 2: Why, what is it that's so urgent?

MAN 1: Er, it's about the Hennings builder's merchant veneered masonite exterior hardboard delivery.

ANNOUNCER: *(At normal speed.)* After a ride in the new Volkswagen Passat W8, everything else will seem slower than usual. The new Passat W8. The 8-cylinder by Volkswagen.

ANNOUNCER: Hollywood Video presents "60 Second Theater," where we try (unsuccessfully) to pack a two-hour Hollywood production into 60 seconds. Today's presentation: "A Beautiful Mind."

PROFESSOR: Gentlemen, who among you will be the next tortured genius of your generation?

NASH: I'm a tortured genius.

STUDENT 1: Yeah, me, too.

PROFESSOR: Well, perhaps one of you will distinguish yourself from the others.

NASH: I know, I'll come up with a truly original idea.

STUDENT 1: I just had an original idea yesterday.

STUDENT 2: I'm having one right now.

NASH: Professor?

PROFESSOR: Ah, John Nash. Have you come up with your original idea?

NASH: Yes, sir. I call it, "the shoe."

PROFESSOR: I think someone's thought of that.

NASH: What about lawn furniture?

PROFESSOR: That, too.

NASH: Jalapeño poppers.

PROFESSOR: No.

NASH: A law of governing dynamics which can create an equilibrium in nonsingular events.

PROFESSOR: Wait, that one after jalapeño poppers. That's the discovery of a lifetime. What will you do now?

NASH: Oh, I was thinking I'd go work for the government breaking secret Soviet codes, get a chip implanted in my arm, meet a brilliant, beautiful woman, get chased by Russian spies, go crazy, take pills that rob me of my manhood, start smoking, get old, and yell at people who probably aren't there.

PROFESSOR: Nash, you're nuts!

ANNOUNCER: If this doesn't satisfy your urge to see "A Beautiful Mind" (and we can't say we blame you), then rent it today at Hollywood Video. Where every rental is yours for five days, and where "A Beautiful Mind" is guaranteed to be in stock or next time it's free. Hollywood Video. Celebrity voices impersonated.

MAN: Hey, uh, this is me on the moon. I have just taken a step that's very big, uh, but is more big for you and everyone there at home, uh, that's not...here.

ANNOUNCER: A good education can make all the difference. Start investing in your child's future, today, from as little as 120 rand per month. Metropolitan Life. Make your world a better place.

SILVER
Consumer Radio: Campaign

WRITERS
Richard Ardito
Grant Smith

AGENCY PRODUCER
Katherine Cheng

PRODUCTION COMPANY
Kamen Entertainment

CREATIVE DIRECTOR
Arthur Bijur

CLIENT
Hollywood Video

AGENCY
Cliff Freeman & Partners/
New York

03009R

BRONZE
Consumer Radio: Campaign

WRITERS
Slade Gill
Conn Bertish

AGENCY PRODUCER
Caryn Brits

PRODUCTION COMPANY
B&S Studios

CREATIVE DIRECTOR
Vanessa Pearson

CLIENT
Metropolitan Life

AGENCY
Saatchi & Saatchi/Cape Town

03010R

SILVER
Consumer Television
Over :30 Single

ART DIRECTOR
Vince Squibb

WRITER
Vince Squibb

AGENCY PRODUCER
Sarah Hallatt

PRODUCTION COMPANY
Academy Films

DIRECTOR
Jonathan Glazer

CREATIVE DIRECTOR
Paul Weinberger

CLIENT
Interbrew UK

AGENCY
Lowe/London

03074A

[On a crowded ship filled with Devil's Island-bound prisoners, a convict comes into possession of a bottle of Stella Artois. Any surreptitious attempt to open the bottle is thwarted by the suspicions of his fellow inmates to whom he is chained. Striking a guard with a soup ladle lands the prisoner in the one place on the entire ship where he may enjoy the Stella Artois in solitude: the coffin-like box that serves as solitary confinement.]

SUPER: Stella Artois. Reassuringly expensive.

BRONZE
Consumer Television
Over :30 Single

ART DIRECTOR
Storm Tharp

WRITER
Jonathan Cude

AGENCY PRODUCER
Henry Lu

PRODUCTION COMPANY
Park Pictures

DIRECTOR
Lance Accord

CREATIVE DIRECTORS
Carlos Bayala
Hal Curtis

CLIENT
Nike

AGENCY
Wieden + Kennedy/Portland

03075A

[To the sound of an orchestra tuning its instruments, sportsmen and women are shown in the moment prior to action: Walter Davis spits, Randy Johnson stands on the mound, Nikolai Khabibulin stretches in front of the net, a sumo wrestler throws rice, Vince Carter prays, a female boxer stands in the corner, Lisa Leslie puts in a mouthpiece, Jen Holdren spins a ball, Jason Kidd kisses his hand before a freethrow, Lance Armstrong waits at the starting gate.]

SUPER: Just Do It. Swoosh.

SNOOP DOGG: Welcome back to the P. We're about to get real funky up in here right now with this brand new, stone-cold groove entitled the "Funkship."

SUPER: 1975 Omega Quadrant.

[George Clinton leads a funk band on a 1975 TV show. An afro-wearing dance couple pop-lock on the dance floor. Two streetballers dribble up a storm with red, white, and blue basketballs. Sports figures—including Dirk Nowitzki, Steve Nash, Robert Horry, Derek Fisher, Elton Brand, and Lisa Leslie—groove on the floor. In the control panel, Jason Kidd and K-Mart—wearing Roswell Raygun uniforms—display their skillz.]

SUPER: nikebasketball.com.

SILVER
Consumer Television Over :30 Campaign

ART DIRECTOR
Andy Fackrell

WRITER
Jimmy Smith

AGENCY PRODUCER
Henry Lu

PRODUCTION COMPANY
Oil Factory

DIRECTOR
Hughes Bros.

CREATIVE DIRECTORS
Hal Curtis
Carlos Bayala

CLIENT
Nike

AGENCY
Wieden + Kennedy/Portland

03076A

[A 70's couple walks down the beach in matching knitted sweaters.]

ANNOUNCER: The Bud Light Institute presents the ultimate soft rock compilation for men: Ulterior Emotions. You'll get hits like...

80'S GUY: *[Singing.]* I love you dearly because you let me go out with my friends on a weekly basis.

ANNOUNCER: Play it soft, play it often.

4 MEN: *[Singing.]* Our relationship is getting stronger with every golf game that I play.

70'S GUY: *[Singing.]* Woman, it takes a special kind of woman to make sandwiches for the guys.

ANNOUNCER: Who could forget...

60'S GUY: *[Singing.]* You said it was okay. I should have known it wasn't. Nooo.

SOUL GUY: *[Singing.]* You're beautiful. Baby, can I go up North this weekend?

ANNOUNCER: And the classic...

METAL GUY: *[Singing.]* Girl, you didn't have to get me that beer.

ANNOUNCER: The gift of love. Visit budlightinstitute.ca for details.

ISAAC FROM THE LOVE BOAT: This calls for a Bud Light.

BRONZE
Consumer Television Over :30 Campaign

ART DIRECTOR
Rich Pryce-Jones

WRITER
David Chiavegato

AGENCY PRODUCER
Johnny Chambers

PRODUCTION COMPANY
Avion Films

DIRECTOR
Martin Granger

CREATIVE DIRECTOR
Dan Pawych

CLIENT
Labatt Breweries

AGENCY
Downtown Partners DDB/Toronto

03077A

Also won:
MERIT AWARD
Consumer Television Over :30 Single

GOLD
**Consumer Television
:30/:25 Single**

ART DIRECTORS
Eric King
Ben Nott

WRITER
Susan Treacy

AGENCY PRODUCER
Richard O'Neill

PRODUCTION COMPANY
MJZ

DIRECTOR
Rocky Morton

CREATIVE DIRECTOR
Chuck McBride

CLIENT
Fox Sports Net

AGENCY
TBWA/Chiat/Day/San Francisco

03079A

SUPER: Game 5.

(A guy holds a lobster over a pot of boiling water. He lets the lobster go, but it clamps itself to his arm. He doesn't react.)

SUPER: Game 18.

(A woman slams a door repeatedly on the guy's hand. He calmly removes his hand.)

SUPER: Game 59.

(The same guy stands over the open hood of his car. Sizzling, steaming-hot, lime-green antifreeze sprays all over him. No reaction.)

SUPER: The more hockey you watch, the tougher you get. Red Wings vs. Islanders, Tonight 7 pm. Fox Sports Net.

SILVER
**Consumer Television
:30/:25 Single**

WRITER
John Immesoete

AGENCY PRODUCERS
Greg Popp
Gary Gassel

PRODUCTION COMPANY
MJZ

DIRECTOR
Kuntz & Maguire

CREATIVE DIRECTORS
John Immesoete
John Hayes
Barry Burdiak

CLIENT
Anheuser-Busch

AGENCY
DDB/Chicago

03080A

GREG: This is just a wonderful home you have. I could really see myself living here with Leslie, when the two of you pass on. Not that you're going to pass on any time soon, because you both still look great— for your age. You both still have your motor skills, got your dexterity, you know, you can still function, you can still lift stuff, which is great! So, Leslie tells me you're loaded.

SUPER: Budweiser logo. TRUE. www.budweiser.com.

BOY: *(In the back seat, speaking to his father.)* Stop. *(The boy's father slams the brakes just as a dog runs into the road. Next, the boy and his father are shown walking in the rain.)*

BOY: Wait. *(A tree crashes right in front of them.)*

(We next see the boy at a birthday party.)

BOY: Don't eat the cake. *(The partygoers ignore him and eat the cake.)*

WOMAN: Oh, no! *(She frantically shakes an empty milk carton.)*

ANNOUNCER: Got Milk?

BRONZE
**Consumer Television
:30/:25 Single**

ART DIRECTOR
Sean Farrell

WRITER
Colin Nissan

AGENCY PRODUCER
Cindy Epps

PRODUCTION COMPANY
Biscuit Filmworks

DIRECTOR
Noam Murro

CREATIVE DIRECTORS
Jeffrey Goodby
Rich Silverstein

CLIENT
California Milk Processor Board

AGENCY
Goodby, Silverstein & Partners/
San Francisco

03081A

GOLD
Consumer Television
:30/:25 Campaign

ART DIRECTORS
Eric King
Ben Nott

WRITER
Susan Treacy

AGENCY PRODUCER
Richard O'Neill

PRODUCTION COMPANY
MJZ

DIRECTOR
Rocky Morton

CREATIVE DIRECTOR
Chuck McBride

CLIENT
Fox Sports Net

AGENCY
TBWA/Chiat/Day/San Francisco

03082A

Also won:
MERIT AWARDS
Consumer Television
:30/:25 Single

MERIT

SUPER: Game 4.

(A guy irons his shirt while watching a hockey game. He bumps his arm on the hot iron. Showing no pain, he turns back to the game.)

SUPER: Game 15.

(The same guy, now in his yard, is bitten by a mad dog. He barely notices.)

SUPER: Game 61.

(The guy unloads groceries from his car. A van backs into him, pinning his legs between the two cars. He continues with his groceries.)

SUPER: The more hockey you watch, the tougher you get. Red Wings vs. Hurricanes, Tonight 7 pm. Fox Sports Net.

SUPER: Game 1.

(A guy plucks out a nose hair. He barely reacts.)

SUPER: Game 16.

(The same guy sits in front of a fireplace. Without hesitating, he picks up a smoldering log with his bare hand.)

SUPER: Game 45.

(The guy, on a scooter, slams into the open door of a parked van. He gets up and continues on his way.)

SUPER: The more hockey you watch, the tougher you get. Red Wings vs. Sharks, Tonight 7 pm. Fox Sports Net.

SUPER: Game 1.

(A woman pulls a strip of hot wax off a guy's hairy back. He doesn't wince.)

SUPER: Game 17.

(The guy is playing foosball. A stray dart sticks him in the neck. He looks over his shoulder to see who lost their dart.)

SUPER: Game 56.

(He throws a bag of trash into a dumpster. The dumpster's lid slams on his neck. He pulls his head out and calmly walks away.)

SUPER: The more hockey you watch, the tougher you get. Red Wings vs. Blackhawks, Tonight 7 pm. Fox Sports Net.

SILVER
Consumer Television
:30/:25 Campaign

ART DIRECTOR
Jeff Williams

WRITERS
Brant Mau
Jed Alger

AGENCY PRODUCER
Jeff Selis

PRODUCTION COMPANY
@radical.media

DIRECTOR
Errol Morris

CREATIVE DIRECTORS
Roger Camp
Susan Hoffman

CLIENT
Miller Brewing Company

AGENCY
Wieden + Kennedy/Portland

03083A

Also won:
MERIT AWARD
Consumer Television
:30/:25 Single

ANNOUNCER: I bet you Noah got pretty hungry staring at those two cows while holed up on that boat. Probably thought to himself: There are a lot of other animals. Who's gonna miss 'em? Hats off, Noah...

SUPER: Miller High Life logo.

ANNOUNCER: You're a stronger man than me.

MOM: Oh, Greg. This one you gotta see. That's Leslie's first bath. Look at her little bottom.

GREG: That's her little bottom all right. Who would have thought that that little bottom would have grown up into such a nice, big, full-body bottom, you know? She's grown into quite a woman. *[To father.]* Just like your wife, your wife is very attractive. I look at her and think, I would date you. I wouldn't date her because you're dating her—you're married to her.

SUPER: Budweiser logo. TRUE. www.budweiser.com.

BRONZE
**Consumer Television
:30/:25 Campaign**

WRITER
John Immesoete

AGENCY PRODUCERS
Greg Popp
Gary Gassel

PRODUCTION COMPANY
MJZ

DIRECTOR
Kuntz & Maguire

CREATIVE DIRECTORS
John Immesoete
John Hayes
Barry Burdiak

CLIENT
Anheuser-Busch

AGENCY
DDB/Chicago

03084A

Also won:
MERIT AWARD
**Consumer Television
:30/:25 Single**

VICTOR: Ready?

JOHN: Yes.

VICTOR: This is called action.

VOICE 3: No batta, no batta.

JOHN: That was pretty lame.

VICTOR: No, that was all there—

[Travis, at the copy machine, hurls the ball at them.]

JOHN: Easy does it, man!

TRAVIS: I want a rematch.

JOHN: Whatever, wait your turn!

VICTOR: Yeah, ya know, why don't you stand over there, copy boy?

JOHN: Yes, less coffee.

SUPER: Without sports, a shelf would just be a shelf. ESPN logo.

GOLD
**Consumer Television
:20 and Under: Single**

ART DIRECTOR
Kim Schoen

WRITER
Kevin Proudfoot

AGENCY PRODUCER
Brian Cooper

PRODUCTION COMPANY
RSA USA

DIRECTOR
ACNE

CREATIVE DIRECTORS
Ty Montague
Todd Waterbury

CLIENT
ESPN

AGENCY
Wieden + Kennedy/New York

03085A

SILVER
**Consumer Television
:20 and Under: Single**

ART DIRECTOR
Lou Flores

WRITERS
Bill Johnson
Cameron Day

AGENCY PRODUCER
Khrisana Edwards

PRODUCTION COMPANY
MJZ

DIRECTOR
Craig Gillespie

CREATIVE DIRECTORS
Brent Ladd
Mark Ray

CLIENT
7-Eleven

AGENCY
GSD&M/Austin

03086A

(A guy, finishing a Taquito, is shown licking his fingers. But the camera reveals that he is actually licking his friend's fingers.)

ANNOUNCER: Maybe 7-Eleven's new Go-go Taquitos are a little too tasty. Go-go Taquitos. They're a fresh new take on food to go.

SUPER: 7-Eleven logo. Oh, thank heaven.

SFX: Slurp, "Ah."

BRONZE
**Consumer Television
:20 and Under: Single**

ART DIRECTOR
Alvaro Sotomayor

WRITER
Joe Ventura

AGENCY PRODUCER
Marije de Graaff

PRODUCTION COMPANY
Baby Enterprises

DIRECTOR
Steve Bendelack

CREATIVE DIRECTOR
Paul Shearer

CLIENT
Nike-Footlocker

AGENCY
Wieden + Kennedy/Amsterdam

03087A

(A Footlocker manager and 12 employees are gathered around a single sneaker box.)

MANAGER: *(Speaking dramatically.)* Finally, the Air Max Plus 5. Witness the future of footwear.

(A choir of angelic voices is heard, and a heavenly glow comes from the Air Max box as he raises its lid.)

MANAGER: Behold the—*(He looks down into the box.)* Wait, this is just a box with a light in it.

EMPLOYEE 1: Sorry, my fault. *(He hands the manager the correct box.)*

MANAGER: The future looks good, my friends.

(He solemnly raises the shoe as though it's the Holy Grail. Employee 1 imitates angelic choir and attempts to touch the shoe. The manger snatches it away.)

ANNOUNCER: Only at Footlocker.

SUPER: Footlocker logo.

KIDS: We love corn! We love corn! We love potatoes! We love potatoes! We love tomatoes! We love tomatoes! We love beets! We love beets!

JAY MOHR: *(Pointing off camera to a boy's mother.)* Hey, let's ride the fake horse and go say "hi" to your mom. She's *hot*.

SUPER: Jay Mohr. Wrong for them. Just right for us. Mohr Sports logo.

SILVER
**Consumer Television
:20 and Under: Campaign**

ART DIRECTOR
Jeff Church

WRITER
Steve McElligott

AGENCY PRODUCERS
Michelle Price
Monique Veillette

PRODUCTION COMPANY
Anonymous Content

DIRECTOR
John Dolan

CREATIVE DIRECTOR
Court Crandall

CLIENT
ESPN Mohr Sports

AGENCY
Ground Zero/Los Angeles

03088A

GOLD, SILVER, BRONZE

GOLD
Consumer Television
Varying Lengths Campaign

ART DIRECTORS
Kevin Dailor
Don Shelford

WRITERS
Tim Gillingham
Joe Fallon
Susan Ebling Corbo

AGENCY PRODUCERS
Bill Goodell
Keith Dezen

PRODUCTION COMPANIES
Anonymous Content
The Directors Bureau

DIRECTORS
Malcolm Venville
Mike Mills

CREATIVE DIRECTOR
Alan Pafenbach

CLIENT
Volkswagen of America

AGENCY
Arnold Worldwide/Boston

03089A

Also won:
GOLD AWARD
Consumer Television
Over :30 Single

GOLD AWARD
Consumer Television
:30/:25 Single

MERIT AWARD
Consumer Television
Over :30 Single

GOLD Consumer Television Over :30 Single

MUSIC: ELO's "Mr. Blue Sky."

[Bill Briggs is trapped in the bubble of corporate America. We watch him wake up, go to work, ponder his existence, and return home. Every day is like the last. Until one day, when Bill spies a Volkswagen New Beetle Convertible through a window. He stops and stares as the Beetle retracts its roof. The bubble is burst. A glimmer of hope emerges on "Bubble Boy's" face as the Beetle pulls away, leaving him alone but enlightened.]

SUPER: The New Beetle Convertible. Coming soon. Drivers wanted.

[A woman sees something that makes her smile. She turns and passes the smile to a guy entering a market. The contagious smile moves down the street from person to person. The action then reverses until eventually, we land on the original woman. The catalyst for this chain reaction is revealed: a Volkswagen New Beetle Convertible.]

ANNOUNCER: The New Beetle Convertible. One good thing leads to another.

SUPER: Drivers wanted. VW logo.

MERIT

■

[This commercial opens on a square clock, then cuts to a square electrical outlet. Throughout the spot, various squares are shown, including an apartment building, a box, a slice of processed cheese, a bar code, a fish tank, a ceiling tile, a fluorescent light, a slice of toast. As the music reaches its crescendo, the final cut shows a round Volkswagen New Beetle.]

SUPER: Drivers wanted. VW logo.

GOLD **Consumer Television :30/:25 Single**

SILVER
Consumer Television
Varying Lengths Campaign

ART DIRECTOR
Kim Schoen

WRITER
Kevin Proudfoot

AGENCY PRODUCER
Brian Cooper

PRODUCTION COMPANY
RSA USA

DIRECTOR
ACNE

CREATIVE DIRECTORS
Ty Montague
Todd Waterbury

CLIENT
ESPN

AGENCY
Wieden + Kennedy/New York

03090A

Also won: MERIT **Consumer Television :30/:25 Single**

JOHN: Homer! Yes.

EMMIT: Nice, nice.

JOHN: Yes, yes.

VICTOR: It only bounced twice.

JOHN: No, no. I cleared it.

EMMIT: So what? It's a home run.

VICTOR: No, it's a double.

JOHN: No, it didn't even hit the back of the shelf.

VICTOR: It bounces twice, it's a double.

EMMIT: What are you talking about?

VICTOR: I'm talking about rules...doesn't hit the back.

JOHN: Those aren't the rules. You're talking about making up the rules.

VICTOR: No, I'm talking about...look, I play with shoes, you don't.

JOHN: So what?

VICTOR: That's a rule.

JOHN: I have a medical condition.

SUPER: Without sports, a shelf would just be a shelf. ESPN logo.

EMMIT: This is why no one wants to play with you.

VICTOR: Why? Because I'm right and I'm better at it than you?

JOHN: Take a nap.

BRONZE
Consumer Television
Varying Lengths Campaign

ART DIRECTORS
Ricky Vior
Luis Ghidotti
Mariano Cassisi
Federico Callegari

WRITERS
Jose Molla
Joaquín Molla
Matias Ballada
Leo Prat

AGENCY PRODUCERS
Facundo Perez
Fernando Lazzari

PRODUCTION COMPANIES
Emma sin Emma
La Banda Films
Wasabi Films

DIRECTORS
Jose Antonio Prat
Diego Kaplan

CREATIVE DIRECTORS
Jose Molla
Joaquín Molla
Cristian Jofre

CLIENT
MTV

AGENCY
la comunidad/Miami Beach

03091A

MUSIC: R.E.O. Speedwagon's "I Can't Fight This Feeling."

[A mother breast feeds her baby. Shyly, the baby moves his hand toward her breast. He slips his hand into the bra cup, testing the waters. Then he grabs the other nipple and plays with it. His mother looks down, confused. The baby smiles at her knowingly.]

SUPER: I watched MTV once.

Also won: MERIT **Consumer Television Over :30 Single**

YOUNG MAN: *(Stopping a woman on the street.)* Hey, can you tell me... *(The woman sprays mace into his face.)* Aaagh! Oh my God!

SUPER: There's a better way to get directions.

(The woman, having run out of mace, pulls a taser from her purse. The young man tries to crawl away; she tasers him from behind.)

SUPER: California Map and Travel Center.

GOLD
Consumer Television
Under $50,000 Budget

ART DIRECTORS
Jason Sperling
Craig Lederman

WRITERS
Jason Sperling
Craig Lederman

AGENCY PRODUCER
Yuko Ogata

PRODUCTION COMPANY
Blind Spot Media

DIRECTOR
Alex Von David

CREATIVE DIRECTOR
Rick Colby

CLIENT
California Map & Travel

AGENCY
Colby & Partners/Santa Monica

03092A

SILVER

**Consumer Television
Under $50,000 Budget**

ART DIRECTORS
Marc Sobier
Chris Polak

WRITER
Hart Rusen

AGENCY PRODUCER
Tracie Davis

PRODUCTION COMPANY
Hidden City

DIRECTOR
Derek Barnes

CREATIVE DIRECTOR
Rob Stout

CLIENT
Suburban

AGENCY
R/west/Portland

03093A

ROAD RAGER: Who do you think you're honking at, huh?! You don't like the way I drive?! Why don't you come on out here, I'll give you a driving lesson! You want a piece of me?! Why don't you come on out and get you some?! Where you gonna go now? You can't speed off by anybody now! *(The driver pushes a button marked, "Trunk Monkey.")* You think you're better than me! Well, I don't like the way you drive! *(A monkey hops out of the trunk with a tire iron.)* What, you got a fancy new button? *(The monkey thumps the road rager on the head.)*

ANNOUNCER: The Trunk Monkey: A revolutionary idea you'll only find at Suburban Auto Group, pending approval by Attorney General.

DRIVER: Okay, back in the trunk.

BRONZE

**Consumer Television
Under $50,000 Budget**

ART DIRECTOR
Andy Nordfors

WRITER
Cal McAllister

PRODUCTION COMPANY
Spring Avenue

DIRECTOR
Todd Factor

CREATIVE DIRECTOR
Cal McAllister

CLIENT
Diadora

AGENCY
The Wexley School for Girls/
Seattle

03094A

(In this version of skeet shooting for the soccer-obsessed, a player has armed himself with a supply of soccer balls to shoot at clay goalies.)

SOCCER PLAYER: *(In Italian.)* Pull!

SUPER: Diadora. Power.

Oh, Pill Popping Suburban Housewife.

(At the check-in desk of The Mill Valley Film Festival 25th Reunion.)

HOOKER WITH A HEART OF GOLD: And you are?

MYSTERIOUS STRANGER: Mysterious Stranger.

HOOKER: Would that be Mysterious Stranger Who Lives With His Mother or Mysterious Stranger In Town To Shake Things Up?

STRANGER: In Town To Shake Things Up.

LONELY CHILD PRODIGY: *(At the bar.)* You know, I just got to the point where I was like, "If I see another script about playing chess, I'm gonna throw up."

INSPIRATIONAL TEACHER: But you're Lonely Child Prodigy. You give smart kids hope.

PRODIGY: How about I get to nail a cheerleader? That would give smart kids hope.

RACIST WHO LEARNS A LESSON: But you're in everything. Seems like every film I go see, there's Ghetto Mom Tryin' To Make It. Is there some sort of advice that you could give me?

GHETTO MOM: All I can say is...be the best damn Racist Who Learns A Lesson you can be.

LONELY PILL-POPPING HOUSEWIFE: And these are my two children. That's Amnesia Victim With A Dark Secret and that's School Burning Hillbilly.

WISE-CRACKING CONVENIENCE STORE OWNER: *(In Urdu, with subtitles.)* Oh, Pill-Popping Suburban Housewife, they're adorable!

HOOKER: *(At check-in desk.)* Okay, you're not here. I've got Free-Spirited New Age Grandmother, Genius Reclusive Mathematician, then it goes to Insane Ventriloquist Hitchhiker.

HAPPY ENDING: Are you sure? Could you look again? H-A-P...Could it be under my last name? E-N-D...

HOOKER: Listen, sister, this is a film festival. We don't really need a Happy Ending.

SUPER: See who makes it this year. Mill Valley Film Festival logo.

GOLD
**Non Broadcast
Cinema**

ART DIRECTOR
Lauren Harwell

WRITER
Paul Johnson

AGENCY PRODUCERS
Bryan Sweeney
Karena Dacker

PRODUCTION COMPANY
Anonymous Content

DIRECTOR
Carter & Blitz

CREATIVE DIRECTORS
Rob Bagot
Terry Rietta

CLIENT
Mill Valley Film Festival

AGENCY
Hill Holliday/San Francisco

03095A

[A man with short hair walks into a small-town barber shop. Instead of cutting the man's hair, the barber grabs a patch from the floor and sticks it to the man's head. He continues to add more, finally giving him sideburns and long hair.]

SUPER: I watched MTV once.

SILVER
Non Broadcast
Cinema

ART DIRECTORS
Ricky Vior
Luis Ghidotti
Mariano Cassisi
Federico Callegari

WRITERS
Jose Molla
Joaquín Molla
Matias Ballada
Leo Prat

AGENCY PRODUCERS
Facundo Perez
Fernando Lazzari

PRODUCTION COMPANY
Wasabi Films

DIRECTOR
Diego Kaplan

CREATIVE DIRECTORS
Jose Molla
Joaquín Molla
Cristian Jofre

CLIENT
MTV

AGENCY
la comunidad/Miami Beach

03096A

GOLD
Innovative Marketing
Category Sponsor:
Yahoo!

ART DIRECTOR
Paul Stechschulte

WRITER
Ari Merkin

CREATIVE DIRECTORS
Alex Bogusky
Andrew Keller

CLIENT
MINI

AGENCY
Crispin Porter + Bogusky/Miami

03001G

SILVER
Innovative Marketing

ART DIRECTORS
David Carter
Tom Riddle

WRITERS
Greg Hahn
David Carter
Joe Sweet
Vincent Ngo

PHOTOGRAPHER
Michael Crouser

AGENCY PRODUCERS
Brian DiLorenzo
Kate Talbott
Ted Knutson

PRODUCTION COMPANY
RSA USA

DIRECTORS
John Woo
Joe Carnahan
Tony Scott

CREATIVE DIRECTORS
David Lubars
Bruce Bildsten
Kevin Flatt

CLIENT
BMW of North America

AGENCY
Fallon/Minneapolis

03002G

Also won:
MERIT AWARD
Integrated Branding

(Decades ago, James Brown sold his soul to the devil for fame and fortune. Now he wishes to re-negotiate. Hired to take Mr. Brown to a rendezvous with the devil, the Driver finds himself entangled in fiendish plans, culminating in a race through Vegas for Mr. Brown's soul.)

(When a hostage negotiation takes a turn for the worse, the Driver races to locate a kidnapped victim locked in the trunk of a sinking car. Linked to her only by cell phone, the Driver narrows in on her location in a desperate race against time and tide.)

(The Driver rescues a mysterious messenger carrying an even more mysterious briefcase. As a helicopter gunman relentlessly pursues them, a game of political intrigue plays out. Not until the climactic end does the Driver gets the answers he's been after.)

BRONZE
Innovative Marketing

ART DIRECTOR
Mark Taylor

WRITER
Ari Merkin

PHOTOGRAPHER
Daniel Hartz

CREATIVE DIRECTORS
Alex Bogusky
Andrew Keller

CLIENT
MINI

AGENCY
Crispin Porter + Bogusky/Miami

03003G

Also won:
MERIT AWARD
Outdoor: Single

MERIT AWARD
Outdoor: Campaign

MERIT Outdoor Single

BRONZE
Innovative Marketing

ART DIRECTOR
Mark Taylor

WRITER
Ari Merkin

PHOTOGRAPHER
Daniel Hartz

CREATIVE DIRECTORS
Alex Bogusky
Andrew Keller

CLIENT
MINI

AGENCY
Crispin Porter + Bogusky/Miami

03004G

BRONZE
Innovative Marketing

ART DIRECTOR
Mark Taylor

WRITER
Ari Merkin

PHOTOGRAPHER
Daniel Hartz

CREATIVE DIRECTORS
Alex Bogusky
Andrew Keller

CLIENT
MINI

AGENCY
Crispin Porter + Bogusky/Miami

03005G

83

SILVER
Integrated Branding

ART DIRECTOR
Kim Schoen

WRITER
Kevin Proudfoot

ILLUSTRATOR
Deanna Cheuk

AGENCY PRODUCERS
Brian Cooper
Chris Noble

PRODUCTION COMPANIES
Epoch Films
Partizan
RSA USA
@radical.media

DIRECTORS
Stacy Wall
David Palmer
ACNE
Errol Morris

CREATIVE DIRECTORS
Ty Montague
Todd Waterbury

CLIENT
ESPN

AGENCY
Wieden + Kennedy/New York

03007G

VICTOR: All right, watch the English on this one, Chief.

JOHN: Foul ball, and...

VICTOR: Ahhh.

JOHN: Third out.

VICTOR: Let's see what ya got.

JOHN: I step up to the plate.

VICTOR: Watch the line, watch the line.

JOHN: Watch the pro in action.

VICTOR: Pro, yeah, that's a good one.

JOHN: I doubled that one.

VICTOR: What are you talkin' about, double?

JOHN: Am I on a roll or what?

EMMIT: It's a double.

JOHN: It's a double, you had to get it!

EMMIT: It's a double...

JOHN: It's a double. Kiss it.

VICTOR: I don't know what game you guys are playing.

JOHN: Kiss the double.

VICTOR: Kiss the double?

JOHN: Yeah.

VICTOR: You're a moron.

SUPER: Without sports, a shelf would just be a shelf.
ESPN logo.

JOHN: It's my turn.

VICTOR: It doesn't count, it doesn't count—

JOHN: What are you talking about?

DON'T BE AFRAID TO EXPLORE YOUR ALTOIDS.
www.gonesour.com

BRONZE
Integrated Branding

ART DIRECTOR
Noel Haan

WRITER
G. Andrew Meyer

PHOTOGRAPHER
Tony D'Orio

AGENCY PRODUCER
Vince Geraghty

PRODUCTION COMPANIES
Backyard Productions
WDDG New York

DIRECTOR
Bob Pritts

CREATIVE DIRECTORS
G. Andrew Meyer
Noel Haan

CLIENT
Kraft-Altoids Sours

AGENCY
Leo Burnett/Chicago

03008G

SUPER/ANNOUNCER: Your curious body.

ANNOUNCER: Meet Jimmy. Jimmy's turning the corner from boyhood to Manville. *(Looking in the bathroom mirror, Jimmy sees a shadow on his upper lip.)* Let it grow, Jimmy. Nothing says gentleman more than a thick, luxuriant moustache.

MOTHER: *(At Jimmy's door, hearing grunts from within.)* Everything all right in there, honey?

JIMMY: *(Doing curls in a muscle T-shirt.)* Just working on that term paper, mom.

ANNOUNCER: Jimmy knows he can go to dad with "man" questions.

DAD: Don't be ashamed if your body starts sprouting hair, or if you have an urge to try on your mother's high heels. Even your Altoids will be changing.

ANNOUNCER: Remember, as you grow older, your Altoids may change. Don't be afraid to enjoy the Curiously Strong fruit flavor of Altoids Tangerine Sours.

85

GOLD
College Advertising
Competition Sponsor:
The Newspaper Association
of America

ART DIRECTOR
Alan Buchanan

WRITER
Nick Prout

SCHOOL
VCU Adcenter/Richmond

CC048

Assignment:
**Promote newspaper readership
among young adults.**

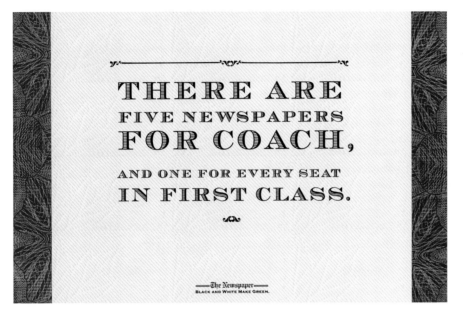

SILVER
College Advertising

ART DIRECTOR
Rosie Guirgis

WRITERS
Graham McCann
Steven H. Miller

DESIGNER
Rosie Guirgis

SCHOOL
The Book Shop/Culver City

CC220

BRONZE
College Advertising

ART DIRECTORS
Katie Rompel
Kevin Poor

WRITER
Robby Russell

SCHOOL
Portfolio Center/Atlanta

CC028

READ

GOLD
College Design

ART DIRECTOR
Aziz Rawat

WRITER
Julie Dulude

SCHOOL
VCU Adcenter/Richmond

CCD059

READ

READ

SILVER
College Design

DESIGNER
Eric Yeager

WRITER
Eric Yeager

SCHOOL
Tyler School of Art -
Temple University/Elkins Park

CCD051

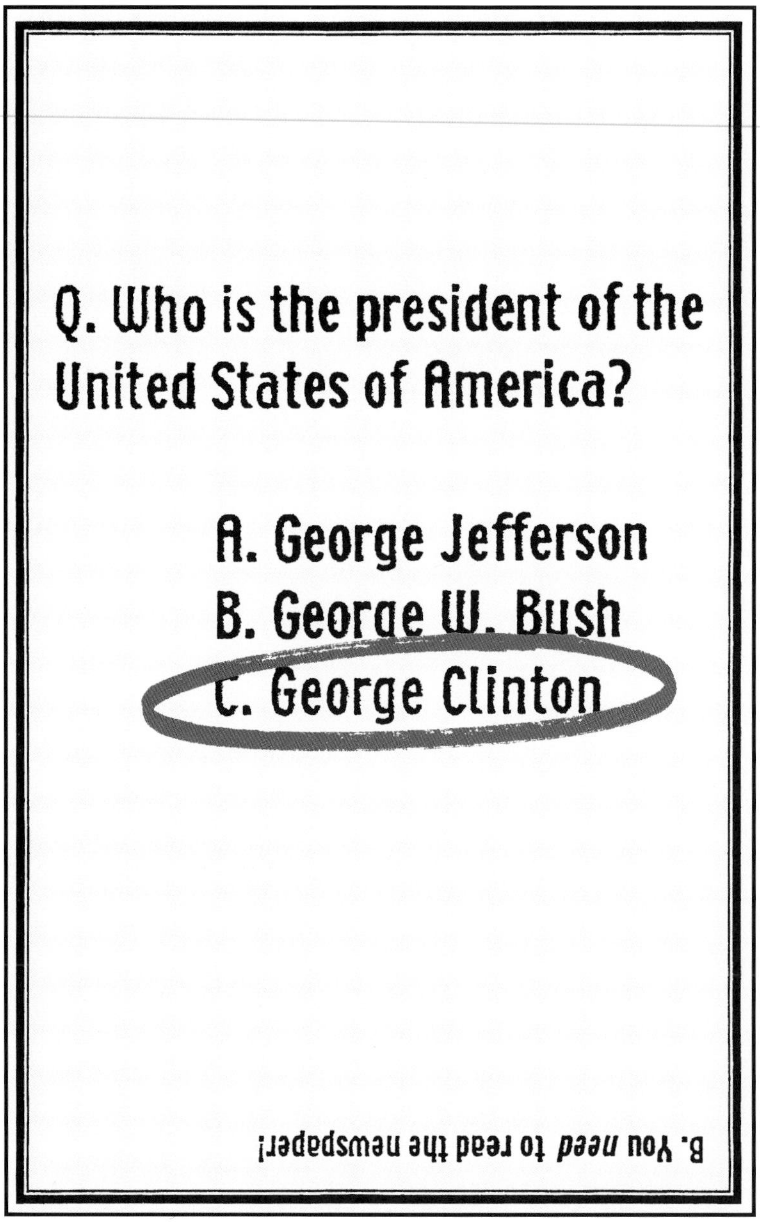

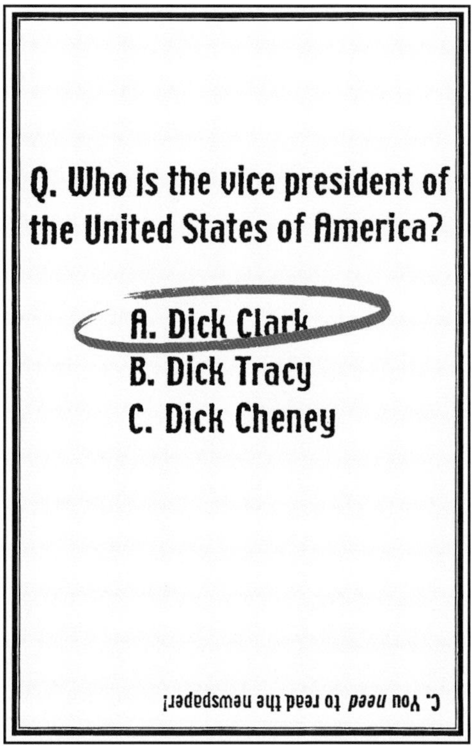

Q. Who is the president of the United States of America?

A. George Jefferson
B. George W. Bush
C. George Clinton

B. **You** *need* **to read the newspaper!**

Q. Who is the vice president of the United States of America?

A. Dick Clark
B. Dick Tracy
C. Dick Cheney

C. **You** *need* **to read the newspaper!**

Q. Who is the secretary of defense of the United States of America?

A. Donald Rumsfeld
B. Donald Trump
C. Donald Osmond

A. **You** *need* **to read the newspaper!**

BRONZE
College Design

DESIGNER
Alberto Landron

SCHOOL
Tyler School of Art -
Temple University/Elkins Park

CCD060

GOLD
One Show Design
Annual Report

DESIGNER
Matthias Ernstberger

ART DIRECTOR
Stefan Sagmeister

WRITER
Otto Riewoldt

PHOTOGRAPHER
Bela Borsodi

CREATIVE DIRECTOR
Stefan Sagmeister

CLIENT
Zumtobel

AGENCY
Sagmeister Inc./New York

03001D

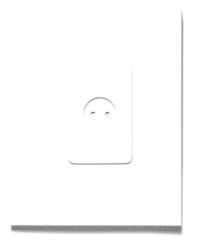

SILVER
One Show Design
Annual Report

DESIGNERS
Denis Kakazu Kushiyama
Alexandre Sartori

ART DIRECTOR
Denis Kakazu Kushiyama

PHOTOGRAPHER
Arnaldo Pappalardo

CREATIVE DIRECTORS
Rita Corradi
José Roberto D'Elboux

CLIENT
Aneel

AGENCY
Young & Rubicam Brazil/
São Paulo

03002D

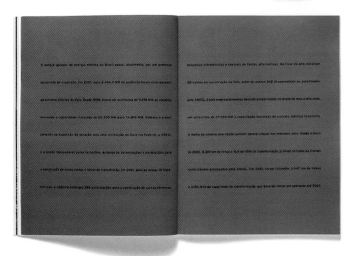

BRONZE
One Show Design
Annual Report

DESIGNER
Leng Soh

ART DIRECTORS
Leng Soh
Pann Lim
Roy Poh

WRITERS
Alex Goh
Carolyn Teo

PHOTOGRAPHERS
Jimmy Fok
Peter Merlin

ILLUSTRATOR
Leng Soh

CREATIVE DIRECTOR
Kinetic

CLIENT
Amara Holdings Limited

AGENCY
Kinetic/Singapore

03003D

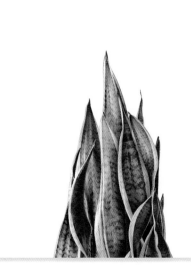

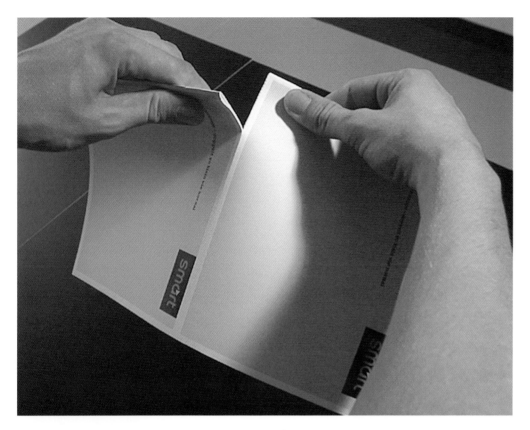

GOLD
One Show Design
Booklet/Brochure

DESIGNER
Niko Willborn

ART DIRECTOR
Niko Willborn

WRITER
Gerald Meilicke

PHOTOGRAPHER
Gaukler Studios

CREATIVE DIRECTORS
Martin Pross
Matthias Schmidt

CLIENT
DaimlerChrysler AG, DCVD

AGENCY
Scholz & Friends/Berlin

03004D

Also won:
SILVER AWARD
Direct Mail
Single

SILVER
One Show Design
Booklet/Brochure

DESIGNERS
Urs Frick
Alfredo Ustara
Kiko Argomaniz

ART DIRECTOR
Urs Frick

WRITER
Pablo de Castro

ILLUSTRATOR
Ixone Sadaba

CREATIVE DIRECTORS
Urs Frick
Uschi Henkes

CLIENT
Buenavista Disney

AGENCY
Zapping/Madrid

03005D

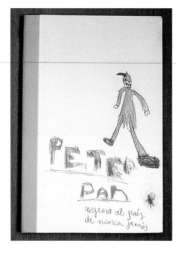
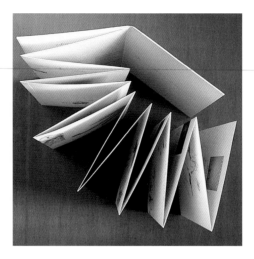
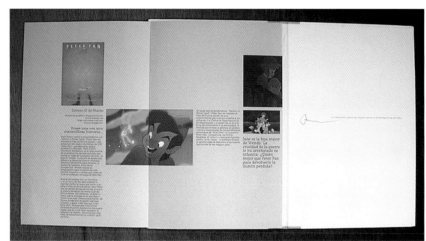

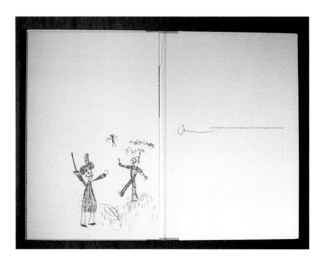

BRONZE
One Show Design
Booklet/Brochure

ART DIRECTORS
Sebastian Hahn
Jerôme Kasunke

WRITER
Jung von Matt

ILLUSTRATORS
Sebastian Hahn
André Price
André Flentje

CLIENT
Jung von Matt

AGENCY
Jung von Matt/Hamburg

03006D

BRONZE
One Show Design
Booklet/Brochure

DESIGNER
Megan Futter

WRITER
Felix Kessel

PHOTOGRAPHERS
Various

CREATIVE DIRECTOR
Nathan Reddy

CLIENT
Apartheid Museum

AGENCY
TBWA/Gavin/Reddy/Johannesburg

03007D

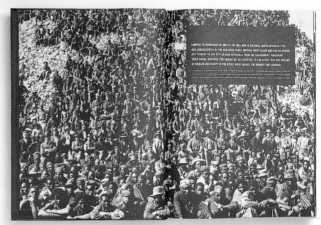

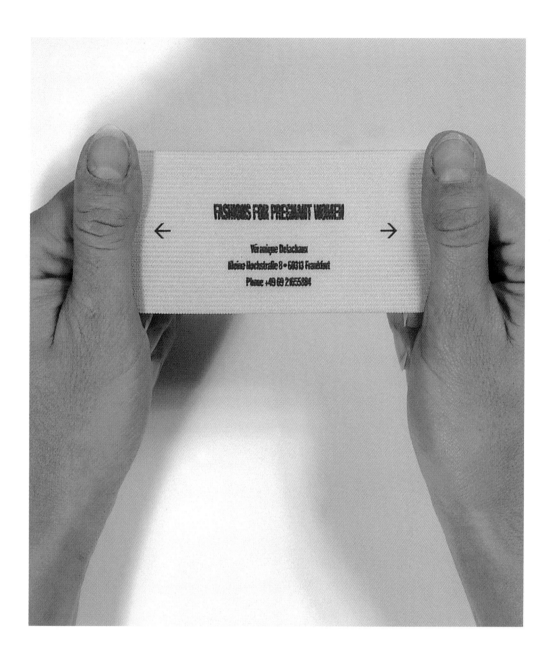

GOLD
One Show Design
Corporate Identity

ART DIRECTOR
Nina Murray

WRITER
Henning Mueller-Dannhausen

CREATIVE DIRECTOR
Andreas Pauli

CLIENT
Veronique Delachaux

AGENCY
Michael Conrad & Leo Burnett/
Frankfurt

03008D

GOLD
One Show Design
Corporate Identity

DESIGNER
Megan Futter

ART DIRECTOR
Marike Stapleton

WRITER
Felix Kessel

PHOTOGRAPHERS
Various

CREATIVE DIRECTORS
Louis Gavin
Nathan Reddy

CLIENT
Apartheid Museum

AGENCY
TBWA/Gavin/Reddy/Johannesburg

03009D

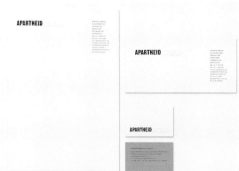

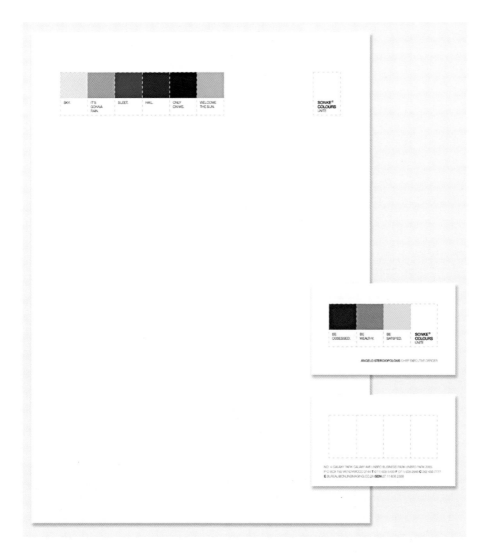

GOLD
One Show Design
Corporate Identity

DESIGNER
Terri Santos

WRITER
Felix Kessel

CREATIVE DIRECTOR
Nathan Reddy

CLIENT
Sonke Printing House

AGENCY
TBWA/Gavin/Reddy/Johannesburg

03010D

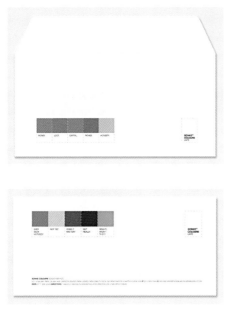

SILVER
One Show Design
Corporate Identity

DESIGNERS
Peh Chee Way Larry
Shaun Sho

ART DIRECTORS
Peh Chee Way Larry
Shaun Sho

WRITERS
Peh Chee Way Larry
Shaun Sho

ILLUSTRATOR
Peh Chee Way Larry

CREATIVE DIRECTORS
Peh Chee Way Larry
Shaun Sho

CLIENT
neighbor

AGENCY
neighbor/Singapore

03011D

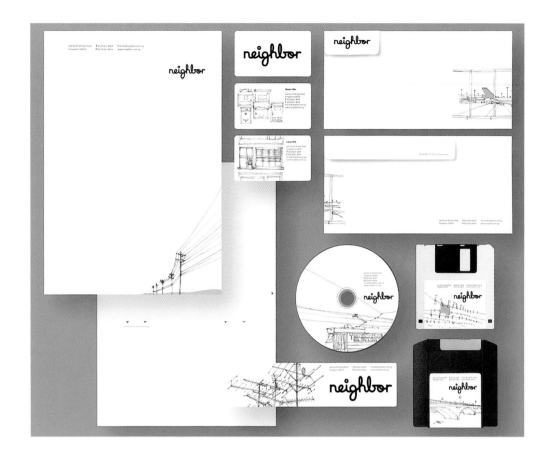

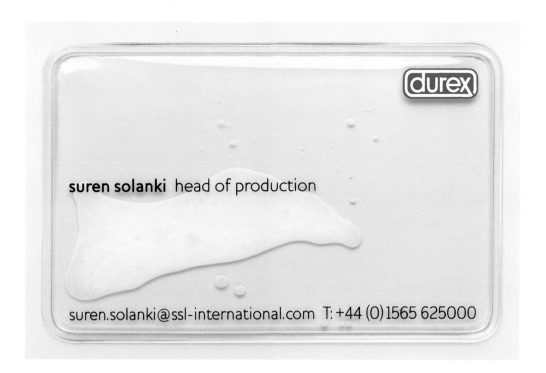

BRONZE
One Show Design
Corporate Identity

DESIGNERS
Dave Price
Neil Lancaster

CREATIVE DIRECTORS
Neil Lancaster
Dave Price

CLIENT
Durex Condoms-SSL
International

AGENCY
McCann-Erickson/Manchester

03012D

BRONZE
One Show Design
Corporate Identity

ART DIRECTORS
Luke Williamson
Thomas Hilland

CREATIVE DIRECTORS
Robert Saville
Mark Waites

CLIENT
Mother

AGENCY
Mother/London

03013D

GOLD
One Show Design
Logo/Trademark

ART DIRECTORS
Julio Lima
Luba Lukova

ILLUSTRATOR
Luba Lukova

CREATIVE DIRECTOR
Julio Lima

CLIENT
Say it Loud!

AGENCY
Say it Loud!/Orlando

03014D

SILVER
One Show Design
Logo/Trademark

DESIGNERS
Gerardo Vichich
Robert Schroeder
Graham Clifford

ART DIRECTOR
Michael Doyle

CREATIVE DIRECTOR
Peter Arnell

CLIENT
Gateway

AGENCY
Arnell Group/New York

03015D

SILVER
One Show Design
Logo/Trademark

DESIGNER
Sarah Moffat

ILLUSTRATOR
John Geary

CREATIVE DIRECTORS
Bruce Duckworth
David Turner

CLIENT
Boa Housewares

AGENCY
Turner Duckworth/London

03016D

GOLD
One Show Design
Commercial Product Packaging

DESIGNER
Tim Stuebane

ART DIRECTOR
Tim Stuebane

WRITER
Birgit van den Valentyn

CREATIVE DIRECTORS
Martin Pross
Matthias Schmidt
Robert Krause

CLIENT
Kurt Hoppenstedt

AGENCY
Scholz & Friends/Berlin

03017D

Also won:
SILVER AWARD
**Environmental Design
Retail, Office, Restaurant,
Outdoor**

SILVER
One Show Design
Commercial Product Packaging

DESIGNER
Pontus Höfvner

ART DIRECTORS
Pontus Höfvner
Anders Kornestedt

ILLUSTRATOR
Anton Nordenstierna

CREATIVE DIRECTOR
Anders Kornestedt

CLIENT
Polar Music Prize

AGENCY
Happy Forsman & Bodenfors/
Göteborg

03018D

Also won:
MERIT AWARD
Booklet/Brochure

BRONZE
One Show Design
Commercial Product Packaging

DESIGNER
Reina Endo

ART DIRECTOR
Tatsuya Miyake

WRITER
Makoto Takahashi

TYPOGRAPHER
Yasuhiro Tominaga

CREATIVE DIRECTOR
Junkichi Uemura

CLIENT
Asabiraki

AGENCY
Hakuhodo/Tokyo

03019D

GOLD
One Show Design
**Promotional and Point of
Purchase Posters: Single**

ART DIRECTOR
Marc Leitmeyer

WRITERS
Manuel Kruck
Jonas Bernschneider

PHOTOGRAPHER
Hans Starck

CREATIVE DIRECTORS
Michael Reissinger
Kay Eichner

CLIENT
Endless Pain Studio

AGENCY
Weigertpirouzwolf/Hamburg

03020D

SILVER
One Show Design
**Promotional and Point of
Purchase Posters: Single**

DESIGNER
Eric Yeo

ART DIRECTOR
Eric Yeo

WRITER
Robert Gaxiola

PHOTOGRAPHER
Teo Studio

CREATIVE DIRECTORS
Rob Sherlock
Robert Gaxiola

CLIENT
KHL Marketing

AGENCY
FCB/Singapore

03021D

BRONZE
One Show Design
Promotional and Point of
Purchase Posters: Single

DESIGNERS
Radhika Vissanji
Andrew Lok

ART DIRECTORS
Radhika Vissanji
Andrew Lok

WRITERS
Andrew Lok
Radhika Vissanji

PHOTOGRAPHER
Jimmy Fok

ILLUSTRATOR
Sally Liu

CREATIVE DIRECTOR
Andrew Lok

CLIENT
UNZA

AGENCY
onemanbrand.com/Singapore

03022D

GOLD
One Show Design
**Promotional and Point of
Purchase Posters: Campaign**

DESIGNERS
Kou Kagiya
Koji Fujioka

ART DIRECTOR
Kou Kagiya

WRITER
Ryuichiro Akamatsu

PHOTOGRAPHER
Hiroshi Azechi

CREATIVE DIRECTOR
Ryuichiro Akamatsu

CLIENT
FM Interwave

AGENCY
Dentsu West/Matsuyama

03023D

SILVER
One Show Design
**Promotional and Point of
Purchase Posters: Campaign**

ART DIRECTOR
Dave Dye

WRITER
Sean Doyle

ILLUSTRATORS
Gary Baseman
Martin Haake
Olaf Hajek
Clayton Bros.
Michael Johnson
Brian Cronin
Sara Fanelli
Jeff Fisher
Andrew Kulman
Giles Revell
Mick Marston
Helen Wakefield

CREATIVE DIRECTORS
Walter Campbell
Sean Doyle
Dave Dye

CLIENT
Merrydown

AGENCY
Campbell Doyle Dye/London

03024D

Also won:
MERIT AWARD
**Direct Mail
Campaign**

Genuine functional style!

Light and space characterise this typical house from 1937. Former business premises with open-plan design and fantastic potential! One of more than a hundred items on display at *A thousand years of architecture in Sweden.*

AVAILABLE TO VIEW TUES–SUN

MUSEUM OF ARCHITECTURE (Skeppsholmskyrkan)

Öppet tisdag–söndag kl 13–17. Sommarlovsprogram för barn och ungdom tisdag–söndag kl 13–15. Fri entré.
Arkitekturmuseet finns även på Fredsgatan 12 i Stockholm. Tel 08-587 270 00. Fax 08-587 270 70. www.arkitekturmuseet.se

The island of sun and wind!

Picturesque ancient castle on Öland. Charming atmosphere, exposed beams, original materials throughout incl. limestone and earth floor! Spacious hall with room for family, animals, tools and storage. One of more than a hundred items on display at *A thousand years of architecture in Sweden.*

AVAILABLE TO VIEW TUES–SUN

MUSEUM OF ARCHITECTURE (Skeppsholmskyrkan)

Öppet tisdag–söndag kl 13–17. Sommarlovsprogram för barn och ungdom tisdag–söndag kl 13–15. Fri entré.
Arkitekturmuseet finns även på Fredsgatan 12 i Stockholm. Tel 08-587 270 00. Fax 08-587 270 70. www.arkitekturmuseet.se

Romantic 18th century property!

Delightful wooden mansion dating back to 1784. Lovingly restored with beautiful contents and a lovely atmosphere. Just like walking into a doll's house! One of more than a hundred items on display at *A thousand years of architecture in Sweden.*

AVAILABLE TO VIEW TUES–SUN

MUSEUM OF ARCHITECTURE (Skeppsholmskyrkan)

Öppet tisdag–söndag kl 13–17. Sommarlovsprogram för barn och ungdom tisdag–söndag kl 13–15. Fri entré.
Arkitekturmuseet finns även på Fredsgatan 12 i Stockholm. Tel 08-587 270 00. Fax 08-587 270 70. www.arkitekturmuseet.se

Designed by an architect!

Modern timber house in simple, modern style. Flexible, open-plan design for the small family. Can be dismantled and moved. One of more than a hundred items on display at *A thousand years of architecture in Sweden.*

AVAILABLE TO VIEW TUES–SUN

MUSEUM OF ARCHITECTURE (Skeppsholmskyrkan)

Öppet tisdag–söndag kl 13–17. Sommarlovsprogram för barn och ungdom tisdag–söndag kl 13–15. Fri entré.
Arkitekturmuseet finns även på Fredsgatan 12 i Stockholm. Tel 08-587 270 00. Fax 08-587 270 70. www.arkitekturmuseet.se

Genuine gingerbread work!

Characteristic of the period, national romanticism at its best with a beautifully decorated wooden façade. Chip-clad roof and large church hall in Viking style. A house with soul! One of more than a hundred items on display at *A thousand years of architecture in Sweden.*

AVAILABLE TO VIEW TUES–SUN

MUSEUM OF ARCHITECTURE (Skeppsholmskyrkan)

Öppet tisdag–söndag kl 13–17. Sommarlovsprogram för barn och ungdom tisdag–söndag kl 13–15. Fri entré.
Arkitekturmuseet finns även på Fredsgatan 12 i Stockholm. Tel 08-587 270 00. Fax 08-587 270 70. www.arkitekturmuseet.se

SILVER
One Show Design
Promotional and Point of
Purchase Posters: Campaign

DESIGNER
Lisa Careborg

ART DIRECTOR
Lisa Careborg

WRITER
Björn Engström

CREATIVE DIRECTOR
Anders Kornestedt

CLIENT
Swedish Museum of Architecture

AGENCY
Happy Forsman & Bodenfors/
Göteborg

03025D

Also won:
MERIT AWARD
Public Service/Political
Posters: Campaign

SILVER
One Show Design
Environmental Design
Signage

DESIGNER
Sharoz Makarechi

ART DIRECTOR
Sharoz Makarechi

WRITER
Harris Silver

ILLUSTRATOR
Matthew Dugas

CREATIVE DIRECTOR
Sharoz Makarechi

CLIENT
Barra + Trumbore

AGENCY
Think Tank 3/New York

03026D

GOLD
One Show Design
**Environmental Design
Retail, Office, Restaurant,
Outdoor**

DESIGNERS
Naoki Kenma
Kazuyuki Kato

ART DIRECTOR
Chie Morimoto

WRITER
Keiichi Sasaki

ILLUSTRATOR
Chie Morimoto

CREATIVE DIRECTOR
Miki Matsui

CLIENT
Oorong-Sha

AGENCY
Hakuhodo/Tokyo

03027D

GOLD
One Show Design
**Environmental Design
Retail, Office, Restaurant,
Outdoor**

DESIGNER
Clay Art

ART DIRECTOR
Hans-Juergen Kaemmerer

WRITER
Robert Junker

PHOTOGRAPHER
Elisabeth Herrmann

CREATIVE DIRECTORS
Uwe Marquardt
Christoph Barth

CLIENT
Amnesty International

AGENCY
Michael Conrad & Leo Burnett/
Frankfurt

03028D

SILVER
One Show Design
**Environmental Design
Retail, Office, Restaurant,
Outdoor**

DESIGNER
Sandra Schilling

ART DIRECTOR
Sandra Schilling

WRITER
Peter Quester

CREATIVE DIRECTORS
Robert Krause
Matthias Schmidt

CLIENT
Tenderloin

AGENCY
Scholz & Friends/Berlin

03030D

BRONZE
One Show Design
**Environmental Design
Retail, Office, Restaurant,
Outdoor**

DESIGNERS
Roman Luba
Michael Ian Kaye

WRITER
Christina Eliopoulos

TYPOGRAPHER
Nigel Kent

PRODUCERS
Madhu Malhan
Cindy Rivet
Gloria Hall

CREATIVE DIRECTORS
Rick Boyko
Brian Collins

CLIENT
FDNY

AGENCY
Ogilvy & Mather/Brand
Integration Group/New York

03031D

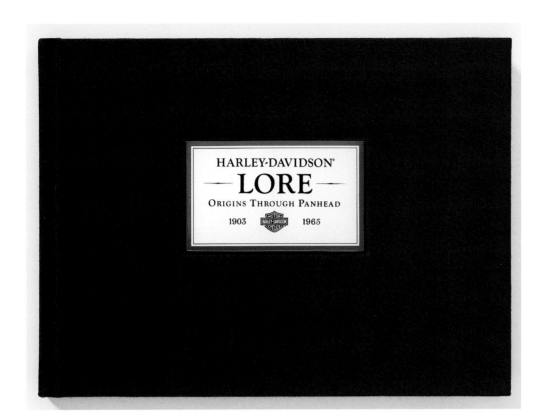

GOLD
One Show Design
Book Jacket Design

DESIGNER
Rob Hicks

ART DIRECTORS
Ken Fox
Mike Petersen

WRITER
Herbert Wagner

PHOTOGRAPHERS
Harley-Davidson Archives
Various

CREATIVE DIRECTOR
Dana Arnett

CLIENT
Harley-Davidson

AGENCY
VSA Partners/Chicago

03032D

SILVER
One Show Design
Book Jacket Design

ART DIRECTORS
Luke Williamson
Thomas Hilland

WRITERS
Thomas Hilland
Luke Williamson

CREATIVE DIRECTORS
Robert Saville
Mark Waites

CLIENT
D&AD

AGENCY
Mother/London

03033D

BRONZE
One Show Design
Book Jacket Design

DESIGNERS
Rob Kester
Carl Glover
Chris Kelly
Nic Hughes

ART DIRECTORS
Chris Ashworth
Cameron Leadbetter

WRITER
Lewis Blackwell

CREATIVE DIRECTOR
Lewis Blackwell

CLIENT
Laurence King Publishing

AGENCY
Getty Images/London

03034D

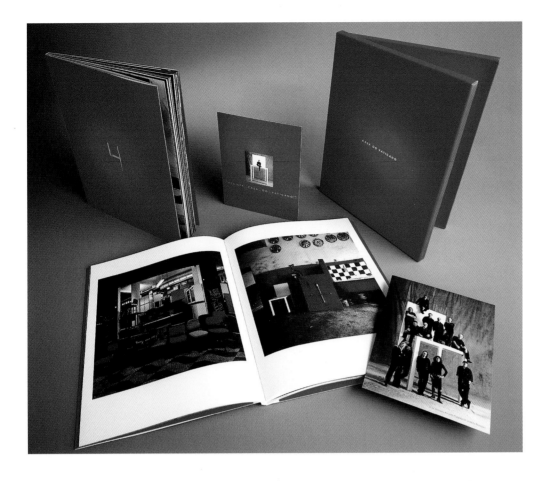

GOLD
One Show Design
Consumer Magazine Full Issue

DESIGNER
Carlos Silvério

ART DIRECTOR
Carlos Silvério

WRITER
Carlos Silvério

PHOTOGRAPHERS
Cristiano Mascaro
Paulo Vainer
Romulo Fialdini
Arnaldo Pappalardo
Willy Biondani
Eustáquio Neves
Klaus Mitteldorf
Reinaldo Cóser
Manolo Moran
Guto Lacaz
Andreas Heiniger
Maurício Nahas
Marcia Xavier
Richard Kohout
Pedro Martinelli
Roberto Donaire

CREATIVE DIRECTOR
Carlos Silvério

CLIENT
Graficos Burti

AGENCY
DPZ/São Paulo

03035D

GOLD
One Show Design
Trade Magazine Full Issue

DESIGNERS
David Mashburn
Alan Leusink

ART DIRECTOR
David Mashburn

PHOTOGRAPHER
Patrick Ibanez

CREATIVE DIRECTORS
Alan Colvin
Joe Duffy

CLIENT
Fractal, LLC

AGENCY
Duffy/New York

03036D

SILVER
One Show Design
Trade Magazine Full Issue

ART DIRECTOR
Douglas Lloyd

CREATIVE DIRECTOR
Douglas Lloyd

CLIENT
Emap Elan East

AGENCY
Lloyd (+ co)/New York

03037D

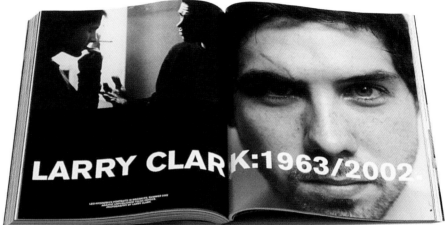

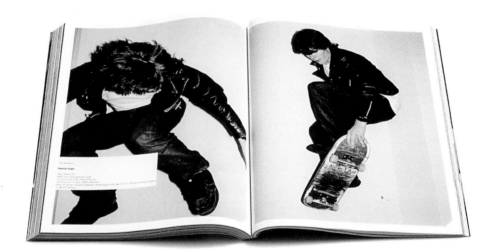

BRONZE
One Show Design
Trade Magazine Full Issue

DESIGNERS
Paul Pensom
Paul Reed

ART DIRECTOR
Dan Moscrop

WRITER
John O'Reilly

CREATIVE DIRECTOR
Lewis Blackwell

CLIENT
Getty Images

AGENCY
Getty Images/London

03038D

GOLD
One Show Design
Direct Mail
Single

DESIGNER
Andreas Kittel

ART DIRECTORS
Andreas Kittel
Anders Kornestedt

WRITER
Björn Engström

ILLUSTRATOR
Io

CREATIVE DIRECTOR
Anders Kornestedt

CLIENT
Munkedals

AGENCY
Happy Forsman & Bodenfors/
Göteborg

03039D

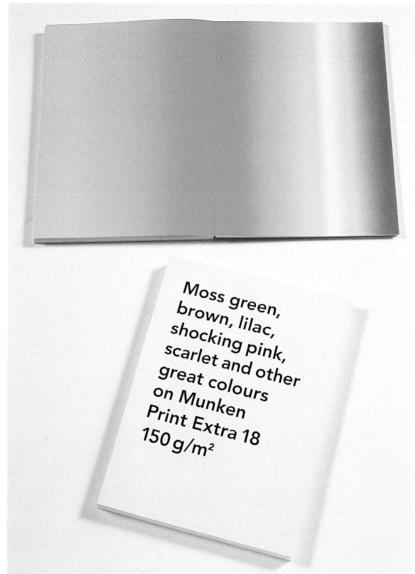

Moss green, brown, lilac, shocking pink, scarlet and other great colours on Munken Print Extra 18 150 g/m²

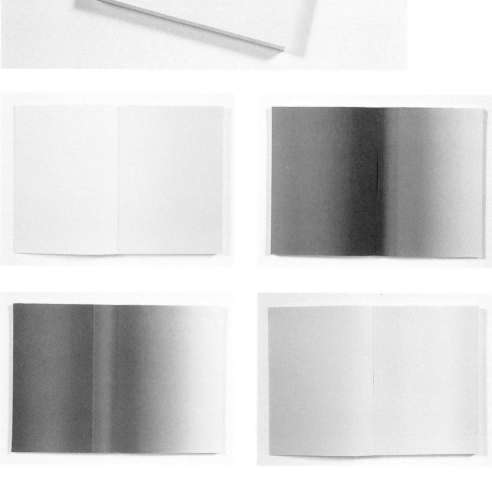

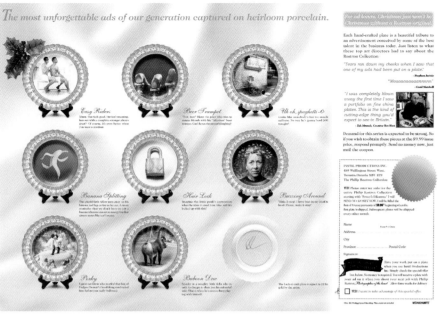

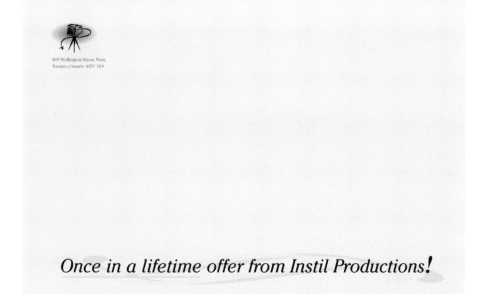

BRONZE
One Show Design
Direct Mail
Single

DESIGNER
Alan Madill

ART DIRECTOR
Alan Madill

WRITER
Terry Drummond

PHOTOGRAPHER
Philip Rostron

CREATIVE DIRECTOR
Zak Mroueh

CLIENT
Instil Productions-Philip Rostron

AGENCY
Taxi/Toronto

03041D

SILVER
One Show Design
Direct Mail
Campaign

ART DIRECTOR
Bernie Hogya

WRITER
Brian Ahern

PHOTOGRAPHER
Clive Stewart

CREATIVE DIRECTORS
Tony Granger
Kerry Keenan

CLIENT
Art Directors Club

AGENCY
Bozell/New York

03042D

Also won:
MERIT AWARD
Direct Mail
Single

MERIT

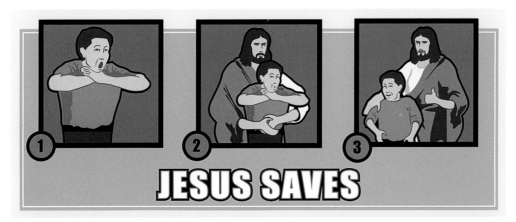

BRONZE
One Show Design
Direct Mail
Campaign

ART DIRECTOR
Paul Liberatore

WRITER
Susan Donovan

CREATIVE DIRECTOR
Jim Mayfield

CLIENT
Bonhomme Church

AGENCY
Schupp Company/St. Louis

03043D

SILVER
One Show Design
Broadcast Design
Typography, Credits, Etc.

DESIGNER
LOBO

CREATIVE DIRECTOR
Mateus de Paula Santos

CLIENT
Diesel

AGENCY
LOBO/São Paulo

03044D

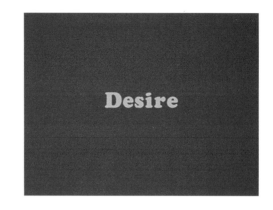

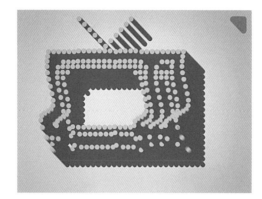

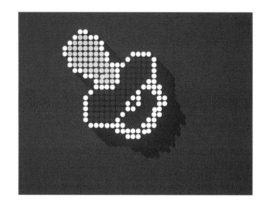

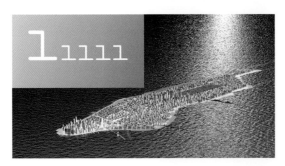

BRONZE
One Show Design
**Broadcast Design
Typography, Credits, Etc.**

DESIGNER
Stephan Valter

ART DIRECTOR
Stephan Valter

WRITER
Kai Zimmermann

ILLUSTRATOR
Stephan Valter

CREATIVE DIRECTOR
Stephan Valter

CLIENT
Grand Marnier

AGENCY
mass/New York

03045D

GOLD
One Show Design
Broadcast Design
Network Identity

DESIGNERS
Roger Guillen
Paul Owen
Lambie-Naim

ART DIRECTORS
Paul Owen
Roger Guillen
Lambie-Naim

WRITERS
Paul Owen
Roger Guillen

PHOTOGRAPHER
Erick Ifergan

CREATIVE DIRECTORS
Michael Eilperin
Dave Howe
Lambie-Naim

CLIENT
SCI FI Channel

AGENCY
SCI FI Channel/New York

03046D

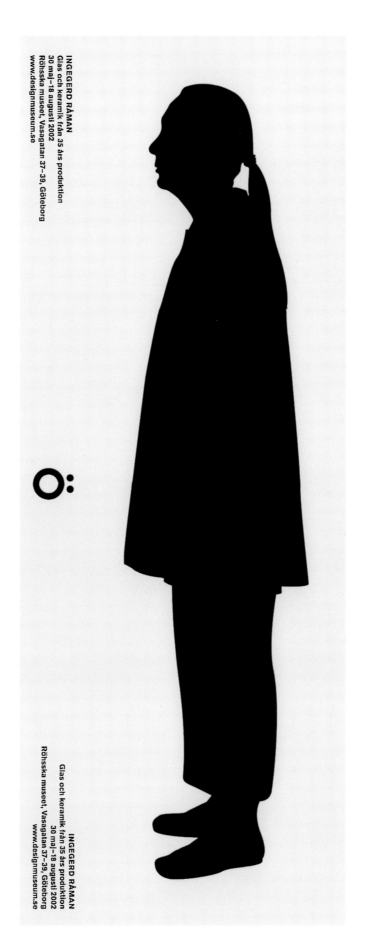

INGEGERD RÅMAN
Glas och keramik från 35 års produktion
30 maj–18 augusti 2002
Röhsska museet, Vasagatan 37–39, Göteborg
www.designmuseum.se

INGEGERD RÅMAN
Glas och keramik från 35 års produktion
30 maj–18 augusti 2002
Röhsska museet, Vasagatan 37–39, Göteborg
www.designmuseum.se

SILVER
One Show Design
**Public Service/Political
Posters: Single**

DESIGNER
Andreas Kittel

ART DIRECTOR
Andreas Kittel

ILLUSTRATOR
Andreas Kittel

CREATIVE DIRECTOR
Anders Kornestedt

CLIENT
Röhsska Design Museum

AGENCY
Happy Forsman & Bodenfors/
Göteborg

03047D

Also won:
MERIT AWARD
**Promotional and Point of
Purchase Posters: Single**

BRONZE
One Show Design
Public Service/Political
Posters: Single

DESIGNER
Norio Takashima

ART DIRECTOR
Ryo Teshima

CREATIVE DIRECTOR
Tetsuya Takizawa

CLIENT
Five Foxes

AGENCY
Hakuhodo/Tokyo

03048D

BLENDS WITH 25% OF THE WORLD'S SKIN. *beyondracism.com*

BRONZE
One Show Design
**Public Service/Political
Posters: Single**

ART DIRECTORS
Laura Hauseman
Bart Cleveland

WRITERS
Sanders Hearne
Brett Compton

PHOTOGRAPHER
Parish Kohanim

CREATIVE DIRECTOR
Bart Cleveland

CLIENT
Beyond Racism

AGENCY
Sawyer Riley Compton/Atlanta

03049D

GOLD
One Show Design
Public Service/Political
Direct Mail

DESIGNERS
Lisa Careborg
Andreas Kittel

ART DIRECTORS
Lisa Careborg
Anders Kornestedt

CREATIVE DIRECTOR
Anders Kornestedt

CLIENT
Swedish Museum of Architecture

AGENCY
Happy Forsman & Bodenfors/
Göteborg

03050D

Also won:
MERIT AWARD
Booklet/Brochure

At the Sydney Dogs Home we have a number of dogs that would love to play fetch. Dogs like Heidi, a female Kelpie cross Whippet we found abandoned, wandering the streets. Like all of our dogs, we nursed her back to full health. Now all we need to do is find her a home. So if you're looking for a loving companion, please call. If you're not, throw this to someone who is! The Sydney Dogs Home is a registered charity desperately in need of help. By offering a home, or making a donation, you can make a real difference to a dog's life. Please help by calling 9587 9611 between 9am and 3pm Mon-Sun or visit www.sydneydogshome.org

The Sydney Dogs Home – finding a home for every dog.

All you need now is a dog.

SILVER
One Show Design
Public Service/Political
Direct Mail

ART DIRECTOR
Gavin McLeod

WRITER
Dave King

CREATIVE DIRECTORS
Tom McFarlane
Dylan Taylor

CLIENT
Sydney Dog's Home

AGENCY
M&C Saatchi/Sydney

03051D

Also won:
MERIT AWARD
Public Service/Political
Collateral: Brochures and
Direct Mail

GOLD, SILVER, BRONZE

GOLD
One Show Design
Public Service/Political
Booklet/Brochure & Other
Collateral

DESIGNERS
Oliver Seltmann
Joakim Revemann
Jens Stein

ART DIRECTORS
Oliver Seltmann
Joakim Revemann
Jens Stein

WRITERS
Ingo Hoentschke
Philipp Woehler

CREATIVE DIRECTORS
Martin Pross
Matthias Schmidt

CLIENT
Aerzte ohne Grenzen e.V.

AGENCY
Scholz & Friends/Berlin

03052D

SILVER
One Show Design
**Public Service/Political
Booklet/Brochure & Other
Collateral**

ART DIRECTORS
Robert Davies
David Day

WRITER
Rafiq Lehmann

PHOTOGRAPHER
Jonathan Tay

CREATIVE DIRECTORS
Sion Scott-Wilson
Trefor Thomas

CLIENT
Republic of Singapore Navy

AGENCY
Saatchi & Saatchi/Singapore

03053D

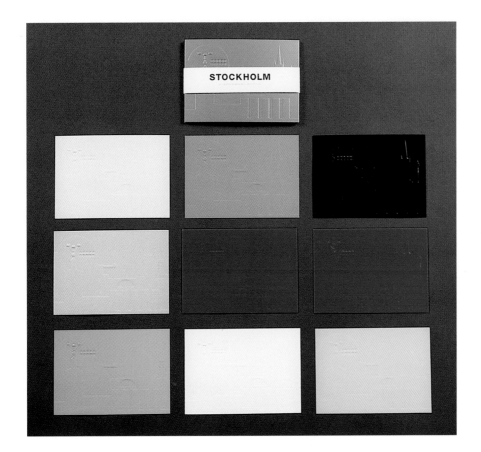

BRONZE
One Show Design
**Public Service/Political
Booklet/Brochure & Other
Collateral**

DESIGNER
Lisa Careborg

ART DIRECTOR
Lisa Careborg

ILLUSTRATOR
Anton Nordenstierna

CREATIVE DIRECTOR
Anders Kornestedt

CLIENT
Swedish Museum of Architecture

AGENCY
Happy Forsman & Bodenfors/
Göteborg

03054D

Also won:
MERIT AWARD
**Environmental Design
Retail, Office, Restaurant,
Outdoor**

BEST

L

SHOW

BEST OF SHOW
GOLD AWARD
Integrated Branding

ART DIRECTORS
Tony Calcao
Andrew Keller
Mark Taylor
Paul Stechschulte
Amee Shah
Alex Burnard
Mike Del Marmol
Paul Keister

WRITERS
Rob Strasberg
Scott Linnen
Steve O'Connell
Bill Wright
Ari Merkin
Andy Carrigan
Brian Tierney
Bob Cianfrone
Tom Adams

CREATIVE DIRECTORS
Alex Bogusky
Andrew Keller

CLIENT
MINI

AGENCY
Crispin Porter + Bogusky/Miami

03006G

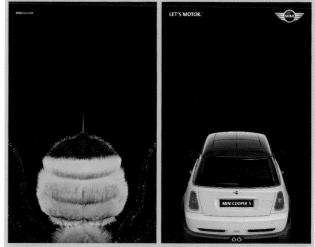

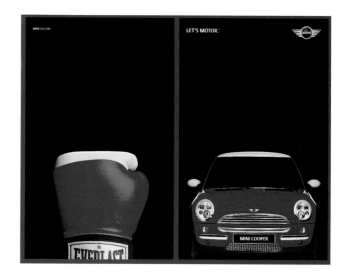

THE BOOK OF MOTORING
(ABRIDGED)

THE BOOK OF MOTORING

MAKES EVERYTHING ELSE
SEEM A LITTLE TOO BIG.

MINI COOPER

[The driver of a MINI Cooper is stopped by a police siren. He pulls over and the policeman approaches. But this is not your typical highway patrolman; it's a British bobby.]

BOBBY: *[With a thick, British accent.]* You do realize you were driving on the wrong side of the road.

MOTORER: This is America, man.

BOBBY: Right then. Good show. Carry on.

SUPER: MINI. Now in America. MINI logo.

THE SUV BACKLASH OFFICIALLY STARTS NOW.

LET'S JUMP IN THROUGH THE WINDOW. Let's slide across the hood. Let's find a dirt road and kick up some dust. Let's Bo and Luke-it. Let's Daisy Duke-it. Let's install the loudest Dixie horn in all of Hazzard County. But seriously folks, let's keep them wheels on the ground. **LET'S MOTOR:**

LET'S SIP, NOT GUZZLE. Let's leave the off-road vehicles off road. Let's stop pretending we live in the jungle. Let's stop intimidating each other. Let's not use the size of our vehicle to compensate for other shortcomings. Let's reclaim our garage space. Let's be nimble. Let's be quick. Let's be honest. **LET'S MOTOR:**

LET'S MESS WITH PERFECTION. Let's window-sticker. Let's bumper sticker. Let's rally-stripe. Let's chrome. Let's fuzzy-dice. Let's graduation-tassel. Let's dashboard-hula-girl. Let's hydraulicize. Let's flame-paint. Let's whitewall. Let's shiny-mamma-mud-flap. Let's do nothing. Let's do whatever. **LET'S MOTOR:**

CLIENT OF THE YEAR

The irony of being named "Client of the Year" is that CP+B rarely refers to MINI USA as "the Client"...we like being called just "MINI." Similarly, the MINI USA team doesn't refer to Crispin as their "Ad Agency," but instead we call CP+B our BAP (Brand Advocacy Partner). It truly is a partnership in every sense of the word. We do our best not to get mired in politics, games, long-just-give-us-what-we-think-we-want creative briefs, and unfounded creative vetoes. A common respect for each other's competencies, a passion for the brand, and chemistry are at the heart of our success as business partners. It's comforting to know that we have a built-in consumer focus group on staff at CP+B with 10 enthusiastic MINI owners active on the account. Though this doesn't come as a surprise to us, since on our first agency search visit to CP+B, they had transformed their parking lot into a used car lot with all staffer cars for sale while they waited for their MINIs. When it comes to the creative content (note: NOT Advertising) development process, all ideas are fair game as long as they fit within our mutually agreed upon goals, strategies, and the Ten Commandments of MINI Marketing. We like to keep each other honest and motivated to motor like no other car company has ever motored before. Ohh, that right...MINI is the only car company that motors...everyone else drives. LET'S MOTOR.

THE MINI USA MARKETING TEAM

LET'S PUT AWAY THE MIDDLE FINGER. Let's lay off the horn. Let's volunteer jumper cables. Let's pay a stranger's toll. Let's be considerate of cyclists. Let's keep in mind automobiles were created to advance civilization. And for crying out loud, let's remember to turn off those blinkers. **LET'S MOTOR:**

LET'S MASTER THE ASPHALT ARTS. Let's perfect our parallel parking. Let's hug the corner. Let's kiss the corner. Heck, let's marry the corner. Let's refine our heel and toe shifting. Let's clip an apex. Let's make graceful lane changes. Let's create our own techniques. Let's teach them unto others. **LET'S MOTOR:**

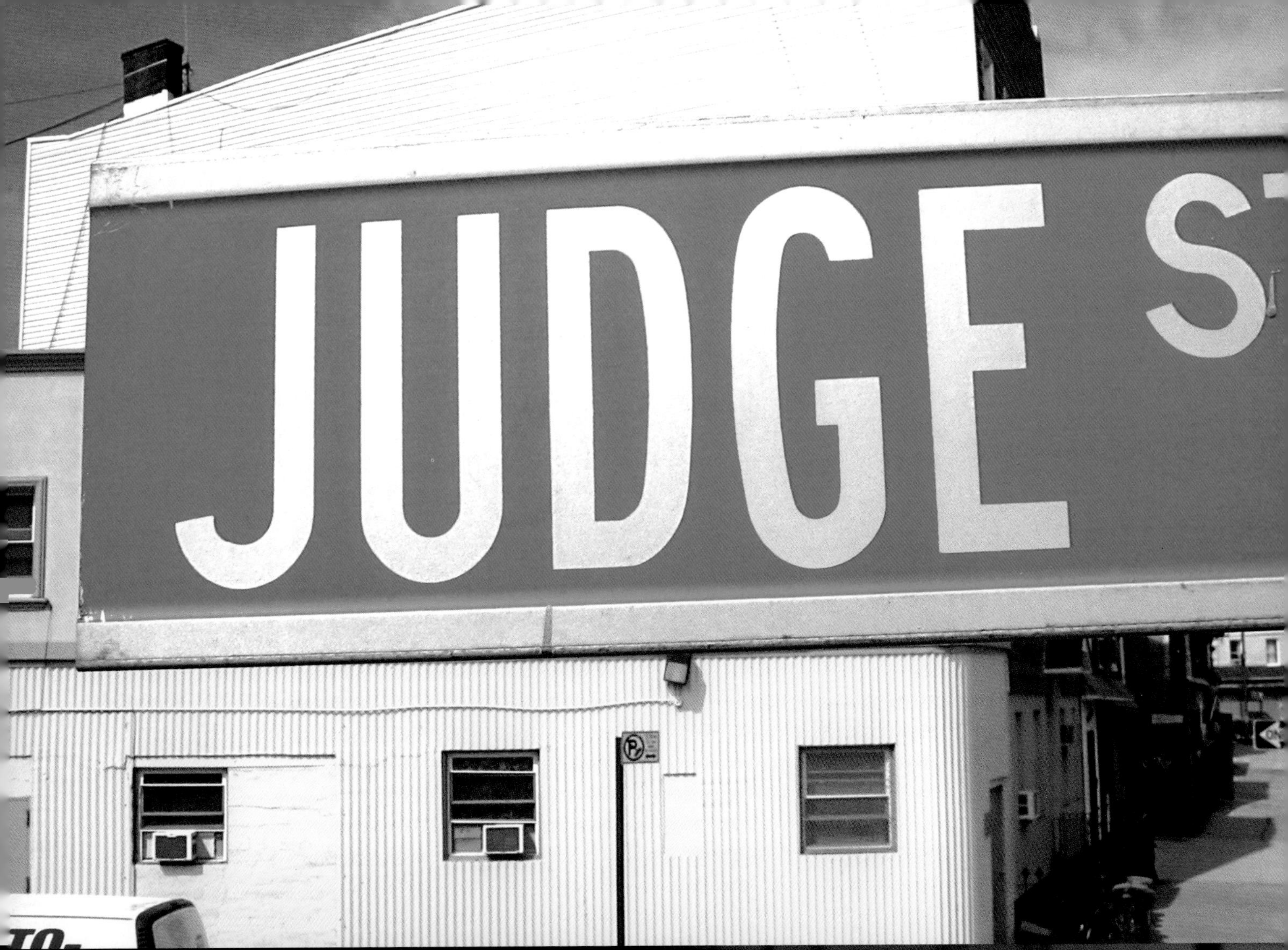
JUDGE

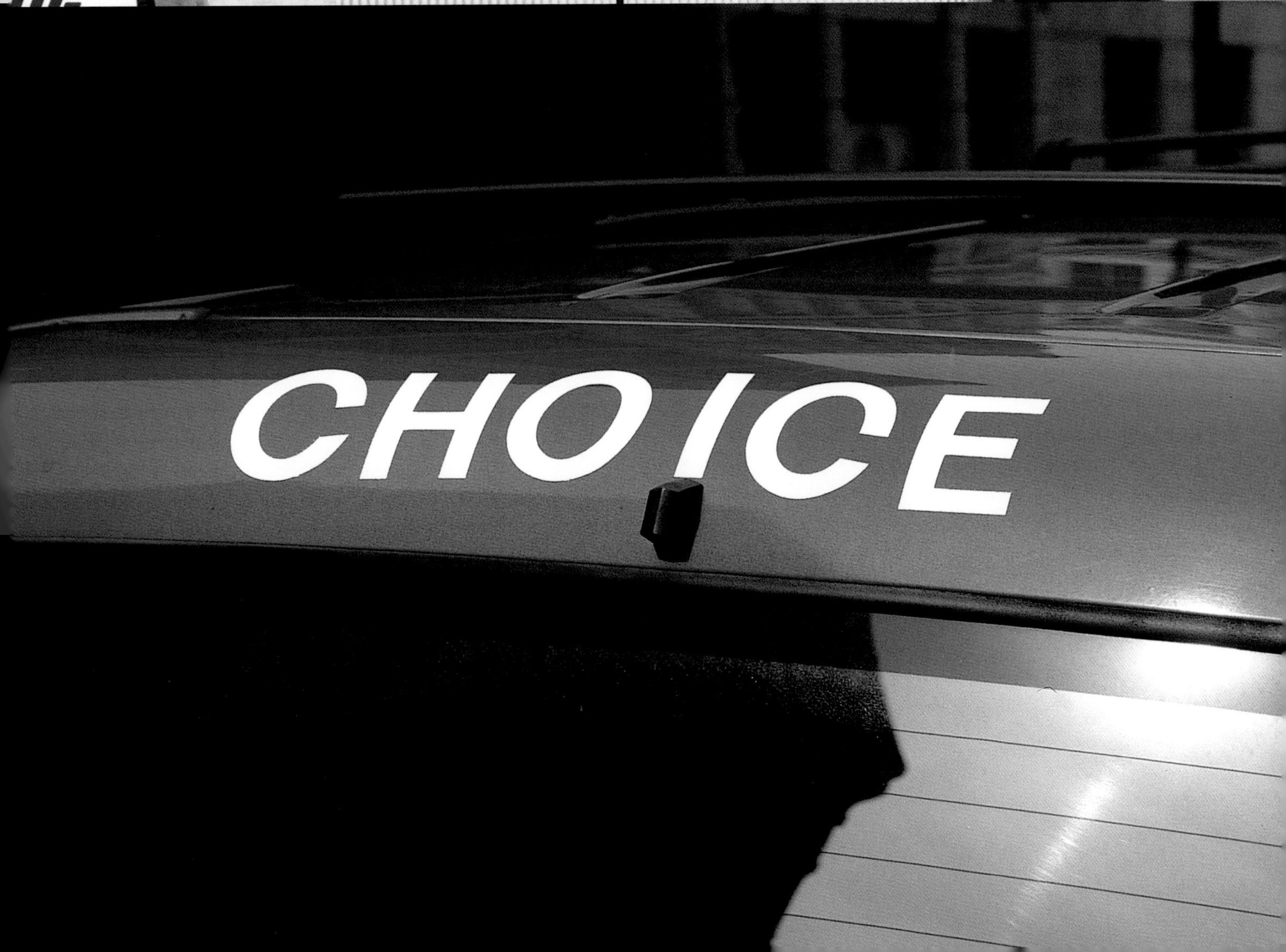
CHOICE

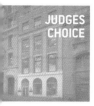

CLIENT
tibornemeth.com

AGENCY
Bubba's Deli/Atlanta

When I was working, photographers would sometimes ask me to produce an ad for them. I never did
anything half as good as the ad for Tibor Nemeth
in this year's show. It's such a perfect idea—the
photograph draws you in, you scan the headline
and realize it's nonsense and move on to the copy
to find out why. It reads: "Great photography can
make you read anything." It's true and you just
proved it. It's not only a great ad for a photographer,
it's a great ad for photography.

CLIENT
Nike

AGENCY
Wieden + Kennedy/Portland

DAVID ABBOTT
London

My personal pick is a TV spot for Nike called "Before."
I guess the reason is simply the classic, "I wish I
did it." But the comment "I wish I did it" seems to
presuppose that one really could have done it given
the chance. This is a bit more humbling than that. I
look at this spot and I honestly have no idea how I
could have ever come up with any of this. The idea
is admittedly very, very simple. Footage of athletes
caught in the moments immediately before the
game begins cut to a soundtrack of an orchestra
warming up. And here is what kills me. There is no
spot without this track. There is hardly a concept
without the track. But the track isn't even a track.
How in the world did these two things get put
together? I have no idea. But it makes me proud to
be part of an industry that includes artists that can
do this kind of work.

ALEX BOGUSKY
Crispin Porter + Bogusky/Miami

CLIENT
Hot Wheels

AGENCY
Ogilvy & Mather/Mexico City

It's always hard to pick one thing, as there are different ads for different situations and lots of great stuff to choose from. That said, there was one campaign that connected with me. Hot Wheels. The creative team took a stock shot of cars in action, a Formula 1 car, a stunt car jumping over other cars. Then over the feature car, the team placed a Hot Wheels box as if it were in the store on the shelf. Simple, yet the right proposition for the product. I wish I had done that campaign.

There was also an ad that challenged my responsibility by charming me. It is a TV ad for MTV. It shows a baby sucking on a woman's breast and really enjoying it. After a while, the baby starts to play with the other nipple with his hand. Stunning performance and totally illogical. I admit it. I have no rational reason to approve this ad, but I do.

ROSS CHOWLES
The Jupiter Drawing Room
(South Africa)/Cape Town

CLIENT
Thomason Autogroup

AGENCY
Nerve/Portland

You know when you are watching the diving at the Olympics and some guy from Uzbekistan comes out to perform a Triple Inverted Upward Dog with a counter-clockwise twist and a degree of difficulty three times that of the other divers and you're thinking, "I hope this doesn't end in tears" and then he rips it into the water without a wiffle to win Gold? Well, that's what I just saw at the One Show.

"The Greatest Auto Dealer Commercial of All Time" was the freshest, funniest thing I saw at the show.

Hats off to the agency who produced an addictive, year-long campaign for a bunch of used car salesmen in downtown Portland. That's no easy assignment.

Part pastiche, large part piss take, this campaign proves that a great idea can subvert an entire category, have you falling about laughing and falling in love with the advertiser all at the same time.

I'm sure that if I lived in Portland I'd feel pretty good about going down to kick a few tires at Thomason Autogroup on the weekend. It might actually be fun.

I've never felt that way about a used car dealer before.

CRAIG DAVIS
Saatchi & Saatchi/Hong Kong

CLIENT
Cartoon Network

AGENCY
Cartoon Network On-Air/Atlanta

CLIENT
IKEA

AGENCY
Crispin Porter + Bogusky/Miami

Although I absolutely loved the HP Mobile TV spot with the cursor nabbing the crook, I just can't get this one Cartoon Network spot out of my head.

It took place in a typical NYPD witness viewing room. Two detectives and Wile E. Coyote were looking through the two-way mirror. The line-up was Foghorn Leghorn, Tweety Bird and the Road Runner. First Foghorn tries to read the card but can't quite get the words out. One of the detectives slams the intercom button and instructs him to just read the words on the card. Finally, Foghorn says: "I say, I say, Meep-Meep." Next Tweety Bird reads the card. But when the Road Runner does a perfect 'Meep-Meep,' you can tell from the look on the Coyote's face that he's the one.

But instead of I.D.ing him, the Coyote just hangs his head and looks at the floor. The detectives are totally frustrated as they escort the Coyote out. One of them says: "C'mon. You know he's just gonna go out there and do it to you again." But the Coyote just shakes his head sadly and leaves. One of the detectives says: "It was number three, right?" The other detective crushes his Styrofoam coffee cup in disgust: "Yeah. It's always three."

I just love that the creative team took all these cartoon characters out of context and put them in another television genre. But what I really love is that they saw the Road Runner as a repeat offender. And the line about doing it again cracks me up every time I think about it.

I guess you could say they had a great subject to deal with but it would've been so easy to just run clips of cartoons. Instead, they did something really smart and made the Cartoon Network seem even more entertaining. So for me, this was really the Best of Show.

JACKIE END
TBWA/Chiat/Day/New York

I was punch drunk by the second day of judging. Battered by illogical, gratuitously violent, stupid stuff that turned out to be for cake mix or something and inane "product origami" where the product was contrived into some ridiculous shape to convey a (more often than not) lame visual concept.

But, then, as always, faith was restored by things like IKEA. The "Lamp" spot is sublime. Beautifully executed, great storytelling and funny. But, all the IKEA work I saw was really admirable. The campaign with the families testing the room settings is great. The print with the people literally uprooting their old furniture is fresh and witty. Even the small insert brochures touting IKEA's unböring strategy are thoughtfully done. Even if IKEA had faced stiffer competition in this show, it still would have been some of the best work.

In a sea of mundane print work, the "Trust Your Guinness" campaign where the pint of Guinness is used as a level was also superb. I just hope the judges weren't so numb by the time they reached it that it went unnoticed. It deserves metal.

KARA GOODRICH
Arnold Worldwide/Boston

Stella Artois. Reassuringly expensive.

CLIENT
Interbrew UK

AGENCY
Lowe/London

Let's face it: We're deep in a creative recession. There aren't a whole lot of home runs being hit right now. You know that's true, because the industry is talking about everything but the work. We're talking about guerilla marketing and about TiVO and about stock prices. Stock prices! One of the things we talk about is how to get our products placed in the entertainment part of television programming. Well, here's an idea: Why don't we make our television commercials entertaining? That way people will actually watch and appreciate our spots. That's exactly what Stella Artois does every year or so with its epic commercials. The one a couple of years ago about the plague was a classic. This one's even better.

I have no idea why they make this look like a 50-year-old movie and I would never claim the idea behind the spot is the biggest idea in the world. All I can say is that everything works beautifully.

When the judges got down to the business of sorting through the finalists, this was the very first thing we saw. I suspect that didn't help it any when the final count was taken. As I write this, I have no idea what won Best of Show. I just know that I never saw anything else at the show that was better than this one.

MIKE HUGHES
The Martin Agency/Richmond

CLIENT
PBS

AGENCY
Fallon/Minneapolis

I've heard people say that to expect morality from creatives is like expecting chastity from prostitutes.

I've heard people say that an ad made up of just positive things is like flat beer.

I've heard people say that emotional ads are not new.

I've also heard that creatives should not listen to others when they do their job.

I agree with just the last one.

So, my Best of Show is the PBS campaign.

AKIRA KAGAMI
Dentsu/Tokyo

149

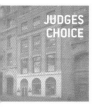

CLIENT
St Mungo's

AGENCY
Saatchi & Saatchi/London

Throughout London, in various snack vending machines, a card was placed. Designed to be roughly the size of a bag of chips, it simply said, "Hungry?" along with some copy about donating to a homeless charity. The machine accepts your donation and the card drops down for more info.

We've all seen great spots or posters for many worthy causes, but in our busy lives we don't always end up making the call or mailing in the check. This was a sure-fire way to collect at the moment of inspiration.

St Mungo's was trying to raise money to feed the homeless. Not a new problem by any means, but the solution I applaud.

CHRIS LANGE
Fallon/Minneapolis

CLIENT
MINI

AGENCY
Crispin Porter + Bogusky/Miami

What did I like best? My first instinct told me it was a tie between Mimi Cook's dashing pants and Alex Bogusky's smart socks, but then I remembered that this whole thing, unfortunately, was supposed to be about advertising and not the exquisite sartorial tastes of Mimi Cook and Alex Bogusky.

So I decided I liked the MINI stuff with the giant newspaper boxes and garbage cans next to pictures of the ungiant car.

Fabulous. Direct. Unique.

Just like Mimi Cook's dashing pants and Alex Bogusky's smart socks.

JIM RISWOLD
Wieden + Kennedy/Portland

CLIENT
MINI

AGENCY
Crispin Porter + Bogusky/Miami

It's been a month since One Show judging. Most of the work I reviewed, some of it very, very good, has long since faded from memory. One piece that still comes to mind immediately is the MINI Kiddie Ride. It's everything I love to see in a piece of communication. It's simple. It's surprising. It's unconventional. It's involving. And it absolutely captures the spirit of that brand. Great idea. I'm jealous.

My personal favorite? Easy. The MINI Kiddie Ride with the coin slot for $16,850. A perfectly contained little truism for a relentlessly likeable brand. I'm emptying my change jar and buying one.

MIMI COOK
Goodby, Silverstein & Partners/San Francisco

KEVIN McKEON
Bartle Bogle Hegarty/New York

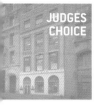

JUDGES
CHOICE

CLIENT
MTV

AGENCY
la comunidad/Miami Beach

Trends of 2002.

1. Risk aversion.
2. Spots with old ladies doing stuff (yuk, yuk) you'd never expect an old lady to do.
3. Europeans really, really jazzed about football (a.k.a. soccer).
4. Japanese iconic characters floating into frame in slow motion from an off-screen trampoline.
5. Spots with little or no dialogue.

I love floating Asians and well-crafted dialogue (see ESPN's "Shelfball" and Mill Valley Film Festival's "Happy Ending") as much as the next guy. But an absence of the spoken word ended up being the common denominator in all my favorite TV work: Umbro's "Goalposts," Volkswagen's "Squares," and Nike's "Before." These probably got a lot of votes. But being a jaded ad person regularly overexposed to ads, I was longing to be surprised. Startled. Knocked out of my uncomfortable plastic chair. And after five long days, I finally was: in the form of a spot for MTV Latin America in which a beautiful baby boy is being breast fed by his beautiful, well-endowed mother. As the soundtrack wails REO Speedwagon's "I Can't Fight This Feeling," the lil' tyke slowly reaches over and cops a feel off mom's other boob. The look they captured on that kid's face was one of the most hilarious and universal moments of 2002. Sure, it's kind of sexist, a little base and it's screwing with something sacred. But that's precisely what MTV is. The "Smells like Britney" spot from the same campaign runs a close second for me. Payoff line: "I watched MTV once." Perfect. Just twisted enough. It's the kind of work our country used to do for the channel. So, for simplicity, originality and fearlessness in an otherwise conservative year, "Baby" gets my personal Best of Show.

The Baby commercial for MTV is a lot of fun and very well-produced. It's the kind of spot you want to see over and over again, even when you've been watching commercials for hours.

JADER ROSSETTO
DM9 DDB/São Paulo

TIM ROPER
Crispin Porter + Bogusky/Venice

The economy sucks. Business sucks. Clients are worried. No one is spending money. So the work has got to suck, right? Well, at the beginning of the week, there seemed to be a fear that the realities of the world would find their way into the show. But, as is the case with talented people, they find a way to overcome even the most difficult situations and come up with great work. By the end of the week, while we were judging the finalists, as usual, there seemed to be plenty of inspired work to choose from. Somehow, no matter what state the business is in, creative people find a way to come up with compelling ideas. Of the entire show, my favorite piece was a commercial for MTV Latin America, where a mother nurses her baby son, in what could be a scene out of some healthcare spot. As the spot progresses, mother and son can't take their eyes off each other. The spot cuts to a close-up of the baby's hand, as it drifts between the mother's breasts, then back to the baby's face as he smiles. The spot cuts to the baby's hand again, as it drifts under the mother's nightgown and begins to fondle her other breast. The spot cuts to the mother's face, showing a bewildered look, as if to say, "what the…?" The last shot shows the baby with a huge smile and the line "I watched MTV once."

I also loved a lot of the work for MINI. The dimensional piece that turned a life-sized MINI into a kid's ride that you might find in an arcade was absolutely brilliant.

My favorite ad of the show was the MTV breast feeding baby spot. The idea was great. The timing was great. The music was great. That and the Volkswagen Beetle convertible commercial with the Mr. Blue Sky track were the only ones that made me jealous. Damn, just thinking about them has set off pangs of insecurity again.

KASH SREE
Leo Burnett/Chicago

JAMIE MAMBRO
McCarthy Mambro Bertino/Boston

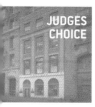

CLIENT
Volkswagen of America

AGENCY
Arnold Worldwide/Boston

CLIENT
Musica

AGENCY
The Jupiter Drawing Room
(South Africa)/Cape Town

Overall, I'd have to say the work done in 2002 was less than stellar and, most likely, suffering from a 9/11 hangover. There were some decent spots in the Budweiser True campaign. Our friends at Fox Sports provided the obligatory violence. I'm pretty sure I saw a commercial where an old man passes gas and, when he does, a snippet of a Britney Spears song comes out of his ass. I think it was for MTV abroad. I have no idea what was trying to be conveyed but I felt compelled to mention it here. Wieden found a way to freshen up the decade-old SportsCenter campaign with a few really funny commercials, in particular the Lance Armstrong gag. Oh yeah, and I love the "Shelfball" spots in the "Without Sports" campaign. The agency that produced the best work was easily Crispin Porter + Bogusky. Alex and crew did fantastic print, posters, and everything else for MINI. The TV campaigns for IKEA were equally inspired. But if I had to pick one spot—the one that stayed with me was the Volkswagen commercial called "Squares." Go to Adcritic and watch it. As Jim Riswold pointed out, "It's like art." And, in the end, isn't that what we aspire to? Shouldn't we?

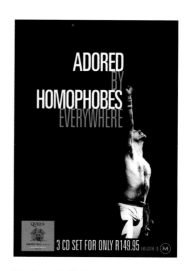

My Judge's Choice for this year's show is the Queen Compilation Poster. One might find it curious as to why this choice, and at times I do as well. However, when I review the show, in my mind this is the only image and copy line that continues to reverberate. It is clear and to the point. It is truthful, honest and above all it is socially relevant and culturally significant, a test of great advertising.

ERIC SILVER
Cliff Freeman & Partners/New York

GARY KOEPKE
Modernista!/Boston

CLIENT
Save the Children

AGENCY
BBDO/Atlanta

Each year it seems like sports ads dominate the best work of the One Show, with maybe some beer ads thrown in for fun.

But this year, it was the Year of Cars.

There was all the innovative MINI launch work, like the "Makes Everything Else Feel Bigger" stuff. The Squares and Mr. Blue Sky ads for Volkswagen... perfectly told and edited commercials. Even "The Greatest Auto Dealer Commercial of All Time" campaign for that small, regional Thomason Autogroup in Portland. And some weird "Trunk Monkey" spot, too.

I was going to pick one of those excellent car ads as my personal Best of Show, but my thoughts kept returning to a small public service ad that had permanently burned itself into my brain, even though I saw it only for a few seconds on the judging table. It was a public service poster for Save the Children. I know, I know...public service is an "easy" category. But I still feel this one is different.

It showed a young teenage girl. By her head was the headline, "My mom is going to kill me." By her belly was the line, "My mom is going to kill me." The instant I saw it, it literally took my breath away. As a parent, all my protective parenting impulses kicked in. I'm a pro-choice guy, but this little poster messed with all that conviction I'd had.

When an ad does that to me, I have to respect its power. And make it my Judge's Choice.

SCOTT WILD
Cramer-Krasselt/Chicago

CLIENT
Guinness

AGENCY
Saatchi & Saatchi/Johannesburg

There are a number of entries this year that have left that pool of great, unused ideas a little bit smaller. The Vauxhall Motors TV spot with the cars playing hide-n-go-seek is a fun demonstration that gives these little cars a lot of personality. As always the Economist work is great. The skin illustration ad is a fun, intelligent way to demonstrate the depth of the magazine. I love the latest additions to the Stella Artois print campaign, particularly "Piano." And the VW television is fantastic, especially the "Squares" spot. But one idea that really stuck out to me is the Guinness "Trust Your Guinness" campaign. Using the head of the beer as a level is a great use of the brown beer/white head icon. And the line that relates it back to the consistent quality of the beer brings it home effortlessly.

They're simple, brilliant and executed beautifully.

JON WYVILLE
Young & Rubicam/Chicago

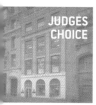

One Show Design

CLIENT
Zumtobel

AGENCY
Sagmeister Inc./New York

The lure of this annual report starts with the assumption of its cover. Product positioned as art can motivate the reader. That big, all-encompassing, plastic molded and de-bossed vase stands alone as solitary reference to what the company ultimately stands for—the simple notion that art and commerce can be powerful partners. The report's design also begs the question, "Who doesn't want to be a skilled artist?"

The Zumtobel annual report, by all admissions, contradicts the entire notion that investor communications have to be stale and uninteresting. Nicely disguised as an annual report, this particular execution gives the reader an immediate emotional and visceral experience which eclipses the typical corporate read. One can see past the obvious documentation of what this company does, ultimately finding the fertile essence of what this enterprise stands for—design, engineering, craftsmanship and integrity. We must give credit to both the client and designer in their collective ability to see beyond the predictable and tap into the emotional power of what great words and pictures can do for corporate storytelling.

Having designed a number of annual reports over the course of my own career, I'll be the first to admit to the challenges of initiating a new approach to current conditions. Based on the "uncommon assumptions" that shine through with this execution, the designer just may have tapped into the secret to cutting through the clutter. Sagmeister opens up a new realm of possibility through his clever design approach, and recognizes that the annual that comes across as the most engaging may just win over the confidence of today's investor. Clearly, it's a win for both sides...Sagmeister and Zumtobel each share a partnership and philosophy that focuses on ideas and possibilities.

DANA ARNETT
VSA Partners/Chicago

I have never viewed the automotive parts and accessories category as being a real hotbed for thoughtful packaging design. However, The Jupiter Drawing Room (South Africa)/Cape Town really got this one right. Their client, Gabriel—manufacturers of [KUBU.], an all-terrain shock absorber—should be ecstatic. This is an excellent example of packaging design that works effectively on a host of levels.

Before I get to the packaging itself, let's start with the brand's promise. "[KUBU.]—Go There. Come Back." What more does a consumer need to know about a shock absorber? This simple idea, a designer's dream, is used to permeate every square inch of space on their package. Further, they tied the packaging into the actual brand experience, communicating a host of sage survival guide tips, pre-trip checklists and memorable pictograms on how to survive for more than 10 minutes in the South African bush country. The packaging, which also functions as a survival tool, includes topics like, "How to use the [KUBU.] shock absorber box to trap food," or "How to use the [KUBU.] shock absorber box to get water."

I'm predisposed to simple, smart design—design that is committed, functional, informative, entertaining and easy. Particularly impressive is design that takes a product and makes a conscious aesthetic leap, allowing a brand and its attributes to emerge and stick in an audience's mind. And, I'm especially drawn to design that is a real category buster—that takes a specific brand in a specific category and breaks out to turn the category stereotype on end. This one effortlessly accomplished all this. The box telescopes open (no industrial tools required to get into the damn thing). It uses a distinctive earth tone palette, straightforward layout and typography, and excellent production values. The end result is a product and brand presentation that both differentiates and is highly memorable.

RICK ANWYL
EAI/Atlanta

It all started off nicely enough. Then the mood shifted. Conspirators whispered. Ballots were covered. "Influence" went from being a noun to being a verb. Brian saw me in front of a piece he didn't like and started in with the Animal House throat clearing. "Ahem—hick." "Ahem—rube." And (I think) "Ahem—blind Nancy." Robynne saw me change a number on my sheet and kicked me—hard. Then, during the slides, Stefan announced that one entry was so awful, anyone voting to let it in the show would "burn in hell." As jury chair, Dana feigned neutrality, parading work he liked above his head like a round-change showgirl at a Vegas prizefight. Rick did the only smart thing, instructing people at his office to call him every 15 minutes, offering him an out.

Like you care.

You want to hear about you. There were nice surprises and wit in self-promotion (a photographer's direct mail, a DJ's business cards) and imaginative use of materials (lace), but annual reports, posters and broadcast design were too darn light.

My Judge's Choice is a piece titled "A Stone in Your Shoe," for MND by Grey in Melbourne. I picked it up thinking it was about golf shoes, and found myself engaged in the horrifying progression of ALS. The stone in the shoe was one man's assumption about a symptom that turned out to be his first encounter with the disease. There was a grace about boiling down a brutal disease to its first innocuous appearance. It overcame a design that was, unfortunately, not as simple. Nevertheless, having gotten in my own way more times than I care to recall, this execution struck the right chord. It makes a disease that will affect a fraction of us real and tangible for the majority.

PETER BELL
Fairly Painless Advertising/Holland, MI

One Show Design

CLIENT
Gabriel Shock Absorbers

AGENCY
The Jupiter Drawing Room (South Africa)/Cape Town

CLIENT
MND

AGENCY
Grey Worldwide/Melbourne

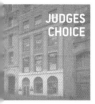

One Show Design

CLIENT
Rheingold Beer

AGENCY
Powell/New York

CLIENT
Oorong-Sha

AGENCY
Hakuhodo/Tokyo

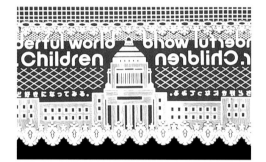

The design profession remains on rewind and fast forward. These two projects highlight that division.

REWIND: The first was Powell's nostalgic but savvy work for Rheingold Beer. Rather than create an of-the-moment, contemporary, pandering design solution as most packaging firms would have done, this idea returns to the core of what the Rheingold brand originally stands for—and sets the stage for a buzz-building brand relaunch. It's a design solution so smart and appropriate that it appears to have been pulled right out of a hole in the space/time continuum. Most branding firms blow this kind of thinking because it requires a level of talent, passion for design/advertising history and craft that most firms do not possess. This solution uses expert mannerism not only to echo a lost golden age of Rheingold Beer in New York City but by remaining true to its brand heritage. Rheingold appears confident and deserving of a second golden age in the 21st century.

FAST FORWARD: Hakuhodo's design system for the Mr. Children tapestry posters was so out of the range of what we normally do in transit advertising in America and Europe that it was almost breathtaking. To hang these complex tapestries as wild-postings in Japanese subway cars was inspired. The choice of the materials unexpected. And the quality of the visuals as beautiful as any poster I have ever judged. The moment I saw these, they were so weird yet so appropriate that I felt like I was looking into a future world I had not anticipated—but one I looked forward to going to.

BRIAN COLLINS
Ogilvy & Mather/Brand Integration Group/
New York

For some time now, I've been feeling that much of what's produced by graphic designers—myself included—is such complete garbage. Literally. Sometimes I just want to scream, "Hey, it's only a cereal box, next stop is the trash." Or, if we're lucky, the recycling bin. That may sound a little harsh but, deep down, don't we all know it's true?

So it was a real pleasure to find a piece in One Show Design that actually mocks our industry, in the form of a photographer's holiday promotion. "The Philip Rostron Collection. Just in time for Christmas" features "the most unforgettable ads of our generation captured on heirloom porcelain." The idea that a photographer would put his best work on porcelain plates cracks me up.

I want to meet Mr. Rostron, "Photographer of the Heart™," and congratulate him for not taking himself too seriously. He allowed the designer and copywriter to go at it, pushing their talents in two very different directions. The designer shows a lot of restraint, never pushing over the edge of believability. I love the cover, with Mr. Rostron's photo in an oval fade (you know what I'm talking about). And I imagine this would be a copywriter's dream job, with lines like, "I was completely blown away the first time I saw a portfolio on fine china plates. This is the kind of cutting-edge thing you'd expect to see in Britain."

I love to laugh and this piece did me in. Who would've expected such a great sense of humor in, of all things, a photographer's promo? In our office, those things usually head right to the trash. I mean recycling bin. So congratulations to Mr. Rostron, and the team that put this together.

ROBYNNE RAYE
Modern Dog/Seattle

One Show Design

CLIENT
Instil Productions-Philip Rostron

AGENCY
Taxi/Toronto

CLIENT
Hong Kong Heritage Museum

AGENCY
Anothermountainman/
Hong Kong

My favorite piece of the show was the poster series for the Hong Kong Heritage Museum, called "Red/Blue/White." It's an ingenious use of an indigenous material; this kind of plastic weave is utilized all over Hong Kong as scaffolding cover on construction sites and other temporary structures. The material always comes in red and blue and white. The decision to sew the images onto the posters (rather than just silk screen them) is the second piece of ingenuity.

A great idea well executed, always a recipe for excellent work.

STEFAN SAGMEISTER
Sagmeister Inc./New York

159

GOLD

On

GOLD

**Newspaper Over 600 Lines
Single**

CLIENT
Lexus

AGENCY
Team One Advertising/El Segundo

03001A

AMCI, an independent automotive research company, conducted a test to determine the finest luxury sedan in America, and named the Lexus LS 430 the winner.

The account people told us the client wanted to make a bunch of noise with this victory. The problem was, considering the prestigious list of luxury cars we defeated included not just Mercedes, Jaguar, and BMW, but Rolls-Royce and Bentley, we were pretty sure consumers might find the results hard to believe.

The automobile business is plagued with credibility issues. Other testing firms, particularly J.D. Power, seem to have an award for everything. Therefore, to validate AMCI's findings, we had to find a way to make them a credible source of information.

We decided to go at it directly. We wanted the ads to look intelligent, authoritative, believable, and most of all, not get in the way of the truth. We wanted people to discover it for themselves.

Needless to say, people were surprised when they saw the work. They told us what was wrong with it: "Nobody will ever read it," "I hate the art direction," "Make the car bigger," "They'll never buy it," and, of course, "Where's the Lexus logo?"

Luckily, many other people believed in our work, and helped defend it. We demonstrated how the idea could extend into every discipline: from radio to outdoor, the Internet, even direct mail. Defending the campaign was daily warfare. People that we had never seen or met before came down to tell us what was wrong with the work. They wanted to see "what else" we had.

That's when it occurred to us that the only way to sell this idea was to not give the client any other option. And that's what we did.

**CRAIG CRAWFORD
GEORGIA ARNOTT
JAMES DALTHORP**

**Newspaper Over 600 Lines
Campaign**

CLIENT
MINI

AGENCY
Crispin Porter + Bogusky/Miami

03005A

Let's concept until our brains go numb. Let's stay later than usual. Let's work on the weekends. Let's toss it out and start over. Let's agree we really nailed it this time. Let's toss it out and start over. Let's enter it into the One Show. Let's win some Pencils. Let's resist the urge to do the "Let's" thing for Gold on Gold. Then again, let's not.

**ARI MERKIN
MARK TAYLOR
STEVE O'CONNELL**

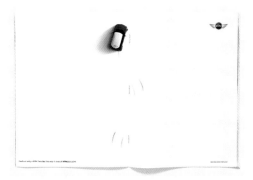

We were sure we'd never be able to get a magazine to bind with orange staples. So we debated whether the idea still worked with plain old silver staples. We convinced ourselves it would be just as good. Finally, our head of media, Jim Poh, asked "Autoweek" and "Rolling Stone" if it would ever be possible to bind with a colored staple. They said, "Sure, pick from one of these 50 colors." Which proves you never know 'til you ask.

ANDREW KELLER
BILL WRIGHT

Magazine Color
Full Page or Spread: Single

CLIENT
MINI

AGENCY
Crispin Porter + Bogusky/Miami

03015A

Never used to like beer. Funny how things change.

HOLLY BUDGEN
MAZ SCHMITTZEHE

Magazine Color
Full Page or Spread: Single

CLIENT
Interbrew UK

AGENCY
Lowe/London

03016A

The art director wanted to shoot simple graphic shapes that would make great still life photographs. The copywriter wanted to feature expensive stuff that would look cool in his living room afterwards. Who says great ads are never a compromise?

ADRIAN LIM
STEVE WILLIAMS

Magazine Color
Full Page or Spread: Campaign

CLIENT
Interbrew UK

AGENCY
Lowe/London

03020A

**Magazine B/W or Color
Less Than A Page: Single**

CLIENT
MINI

AGENCY
Crispin Porter + Bogusky/Miami

03024A

As the writer of this ad I can honestly say, "Tony is in the details."

TONY CALCAO
ROB STRASBERG

Outdoor: Single

CLIENT
Scandinavian Motor Company

AGENCY
Saatchi & Saatchi/Copenhagen

03028A

I got into advertising because it was a glamorous profession. You know, "open on a wide shot of..." Instead, I became an expert on sheet steel.

The Ideas are supposed to be the hardest part. Well, in this case it just flashed into my head while I was out running. It was the production that gave us the headache. The first two posters started rusting under the bits that were supposed to look like aluminum! Not good. But, after some experimentation we figured out how to make it work. And I'm glad it did.

SIMON WOOLLER

Outdoor: Campaign

CLIENT
MINI

AGENCY
Crispin Porter + Bogusky/Miami

03032A

We had another outdoor idea. We wanted to create a MINI roller coaster on a building in Times Square. MINI was all for it. The price came to over $700 thousand, plus media costs. MINI was still all for it. We said it was too much money and recommended that we not move forward with production. MINI stood their ground, pressuring us to build it. It was a tough battle but in the end we won.

Every creative should have a client like MINI at least once in their careers.

ROB STRASBERG
TONY CALCAO
ARI MERKIN
PAUL STECHSCHULTE

■

When we heard the news that we'd won One Show Gold, we both got incredibly drunk. Then called our wives.

SLADE GILL
MARK MASON

Guerilla Advertising: Single

CLIENT
Guinness UDV

AGENCY
Saatchi & Saatchi/Cape Town

03034A

One morning on my way to work, I passed a hook sticking out of a wall.

ERIK HEISHOLT

■

Guerilla Advertising: Campaign

CLIENT
Oslo Piercing Studio

AGENCY
Leo Burnett/Oslo

03036A

■

In a category driven almost entirely by design trends, BELL had something truly unique. A story to tell.

ARI MERKIN
MARK TAYLOR

Trade Color
Full Page or Spread: Single

CLIENT
BELL

AGENCY
Crispin Porter + Bogusky/Miami

03039A

**Trade B/W or Color
Any Size: Campaign**

CLIENT
BELL

AGENCY
Crispin Porter + Bogusky/Miami

03043A

For each of these ads, we were given about a week and a half from concept to finish. It was enough to make a copywriter and an art director stab each other to death with X-acto knives.

We didn't. And we're kinda proud of that.

**MARK TAYLOR
ARI MERKIN**

**Collateral: Point of Purchase
and In-Store**

CLIENT
Volkswagen of America

AGENCY
Arnold Worldwide/Boston

03046A

Knowing that Malcolm Venville is an accomplished photographer as well as a superb director, Tim and I asked him to shoot stills as well as film for each square so we could make posters and print ads out of them. He did and we did. We shot close to 70 different things, then narrowed it down to the ones that read the quickest. Most people think that these images are just screen grabs, but they're actually separate shots. Thanks, Malcolm.

**KEVIN DAILOR
TIM GILLINGHAM**

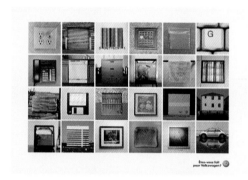

**Collateral: Point of Purchase
and In-Store**

CLIENT
Sony Playstation

AGENCY
TBWA\Paris

03047A

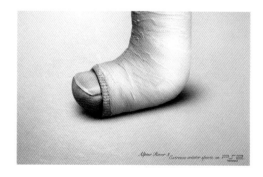

No one would agree on the Alpine Racer briefing. So I made the typical irresponsible creative director's suggestion: "How about giving the game to the creatives so they can try it out?"

The planner wasn't very happy but finally consented. He said, "Go on, guys. Play. The magic is in the product." And for once, the creatives did as they were told.

After a week, I went to their office. They were still playing. They had nothing to present. After the second week, the traffic intervened: "You've got 24 hours. Not one second more."

So the creatives stepped up a gear.

Stephen (writer) is the one who sprained his thumb while playing.

Vincent (art director) is the one who did the layout.

It was the best creative accident of the year.

**STEPHEN CAFIERO
VINCENT LOBELLE
ERIK VERVROEGEN**

This was the first piece of MINI advertising produced. Apparently, it was all downhill after that.

SCOTT LINNEN
AMEE SHAH
ANDY CARRIGAN

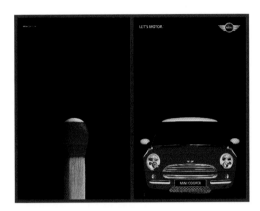

Collateral: Posters
Single

CLIENT
MINI

AGENCY
Crispin Porter + Bogusky/Miami

03052A

As the copywriters on this starkly visual campaign, we didn't get to write a word of copy. So this "Gold on Gold" thing is an absolute godsend. "Nobody reads copy," Amee said to us when we started working on this project. "Let's do something visual. Something bold and graphic that comes right out of the iconic two-tone look of the MINI brand." And so it was. Oh, sure, there was a little tagline. That we got to type. But no headline. And no copy. Not a single word. But now, as fate would have it, we get to write 300 of them. Three hundred sweet, descriptive, little bon mots. For people who actually do read copy, Amee. People who are genuinely interested in knowing a little brand advertising back-story. A little history for God's sake! Like, for instance, the fascinating fact that, back in the 1960's, British race engineering legend John Cooper painted the roofs of his red Mini Cooper S rally racecars white so they'd stand out in the pack. You don't tell a whole story like that with gorgeous Mark Laita photography, no matter how sweet the lighting. We don't care what you say. Did any of you get all that from just looking at these ads? Be honest. Of course not, our esteemed, well-read, fellow copywriters. We say fellow copy-writers because, by now, no word-loathing, monosyllabic-grunting, knuckle-dragging art director would ever have bothered to read this far.

Sadly, they will never know that these posters went up as teasers in US cities with only the non-MINI image filling an entire city wall. Neither will they know that, after one week, the matching MINI side of the equation was added to the walls in a checkerboard pattern. But we copywriters will all know. And why? One word: words.

SCOTT LINNEN
ANDY CARRIGAN

Collateral: Posters
Campaign

CLIENT
MINI

AGENCY
Crispin Porter + Bogusky/Miami

03055A

**Public Service/Political
Newspaper or Magazine
Single**

CLIENT
MASP Museum of Art of
São Paulo

AGENCY
DM9 DDB/São Paulo

03058A

...While trying to come up with a great idea, we said to
each other: "C'mon, think! Use your brain." And that's
exactly what we did.

**FLAVIO CASAROTTI
ROBERTO FERNANDEZ**

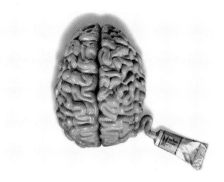

**Public Service/Political
Newspaper or Magazine
Campaign**

CLIENT
Trees for London

AGENCY
FBA/Manchester

03061A

"Trees for London" client Graham Simmonds showed
us some photographs Edmund Clark had taken for
a project called "Treet Street." Great understated
portraits of people holding up handwritten signs of
the streets where they work or live in London. The
streets were named after different kinds of trees.
We thought there was the potential for a great ad
campaign in there. We found some London streets
named after trees that no longer had a blade of
grass, let alone trees. This time we left the people
out and added the line, "Give London Back Its Trees."

MIKE KEANE

ANNOUNCER 1: You're four times more likely to have a road accident when on a mobile phone.

ANNOUNCER 2: It's hard to concentrate on two things at the same time.

ANNOUNCER 1: You're four times more likely to have a road accident when on a mobile phone.

ANNOUNCER 2: It's hard to concentrate on two things at the same time.

ANNOUNCER 1: You're four times more likely to have a road accident when on a mobile phone.

ANNOUNCER 2: It's hard to concentrate on two things at the same time.

ANNOUNCER 1: You're four times more likely to have a road accident when on a mobile phone.

ANNOUNCER 2: It's hard to concentrate on two things at the same time.

TOGETHER: Think. Switch it off when you drive.

It's a great honour for me
I can remember vividly
to win a One Show Gold Award.
the moment that I had
I will pass on the good news
the idea and how I couldn't
to Nick Worthington but frankly
wait to tell my art director,
I don't see why I should as
Paul Brazier.
he had nothing to do with it.

**NICK WORTHINGTON
PAUL BRAZIER**

**Public Service/Political
Radio: Single**

CLIENT
COI/DTLR

AGENCY
Abbott Mead Vickers.BBDO/
London

03001R

The challenge of trying to stir the hearts of a compassion fatigued audience, while at the same time not shocking them so much that they turn away is always there with any charity project. Approaching that head-on gave us the idea. We couldn't show abuse happening to a real child but we could with a cartoon. The result was eerily watchable.

**HOWARD WILLMOTT
DUNCAN MARSHALL
DAVID DROGA**

**Public Service/Political
Television: Single**

CLIENT
NSPCC

AGENCY
Saatchi & Saatchi/London

03068A

Consumer Radio: Single

CLIENT
Motel 6

AGENCY
The Richards Group/Dallas

03005R

When this campaign began, the only writing I'd done was "CRÜE RÜLZ!!" on my Trapper Keeper. Seventeen years later, it's an honor to be one of the folks that gets to work on this campaign. Talk about the shoulders of giants and all that. Thanks to all.

Cocktail party anecdote: This spot was inspired by a completely different client, unaffiliated with Motel 6, who actually talks like this. Really. So I have to thank two clients for this one. Got to be a first.

And a huge tip of the cap to Tom Bodett, easily the friendliest, most helpful, most down-to-earth household name on the planet. Thanks for your help, suggestions, patience and voice, Tom. You made it what it is.

I'm keeping the Pencil, though.

CHRISTOPHER SMITH

TOM: Hi, Tom Bodett for Motel 6, with a word for business travelers. Seems business has its own language these days, full of buzzwords. Like "buzzword" or "net-net." And after a day spent white boarding a matrix of action items and deliverables, it's nice to know you can always outsource your accommodation needs to the nearest Motel 6. You'll get a clean, comfortable room for the lowest price, net-net, of any national chain. Plus dataports and free local calls in case you tabled your discussion and need to reconvene offline. So you can think of Motel 6 as your total business travel solution provider, vis-a-vis cost-effective lodging alternatives for Q-1 through Q-4, I think. Just call 1-800-4-MOTEL-6 or visit motel6.com. I'm Tom Bodett for Motel 6, and we'll maintain the lighting device in its current state of illumination for you.

ANNOUNCER: Motel 6. An Accor hotel.

Consumer Radio: Campaign

CLIENT
Volkswagen

AGENCY
Grabarz & Partner Werbeagentur/
Hamburg

03008R

[Dialogue is played in extreme slow-motion.]

MAN 1: Good evening, sir.

MAN 2: Good evening, I've reserved a table under the name, "Horseborough-Porter."

MAN 1: Ah, yes, Mr. Horseborough-Porter. Table for two?

MAN 2: Exactly.

ANNOUNCER: *[At normal speed.]* After a ride in the new Volkswagen Passat W8, everything else will seem slower than usual. The new Passat W8. The 8-cylinder by Volkswagen.

We'd like to express our thanks for this award.

We are glad, proud, and happy to have succeeded with this many first-rate radio commercials. We congratulate all the other winners. We thank the jury. We are looking forward to next year. (Hey, what's wrong? If you read this at half-speed, it sounds like pretty cool copy.)

**RALF HEUEL
RALF NOLTING
CHRISTOPH NANN**

The concept for "Bubble Boy" was essentially hatched out of our own existence. Working in a skyscraper that's connected to a mall that's connected to a train station made it easy for us to hold a mirror up to ourselves and create this story of a guy trapped in a completely interior world. We all desire for some form of escapism and alas, the Beetle is the perfect vehicle in which to do that, especially in convertible form. Of course, listening to ELO helps, too.

JOE FALLON

Consumer Television
Over :30 Single

CLIENT
Volkswagen of America

AGENCY
Arnold Worldwide/Boston

03073A

We'd like to thank all the people who helped make this spot possible.

But most of all we'd like to thank Mr. James L. Kraft, creator of processed cheese slices.

TIM GILLINGHAM
KEVIN DAILOR

Consumer Television
:30/:25 Single

CLIENT
Volkswagen of America

AGENCY
Arnold Worldwide/Boston

03078A

Day 1. Ben shoves Eric. Eric sucker punches Susan. Susan jabs Ben in the Adam's apple with a fine-point sharpie. Ben staples Eric's ear to the notice board. Eric kicks Ben in the gonads. Susan swings the fire extinguisher into the tailbone of Eric. Ben rips large clump of hair from Susan's head with teeth. Chuck and Markgraf enter with hog ties and pepper spray. Day 2...

BEN NOTT
SUSAN TREACY
ERIC KING

Consumer Television
:30/:25 Single

CLIENT
Fox Sports Net

AGENCY
TBWA/Chiat/Day/San Francisco

03079A

171

**Consumer Television
:30/:25 Campaign**

CLIENT
Fox Sports Net

AGENCY
TBWA/Chiat/Day/San Francisco

03082A

Day 48. Rocky Morton puts Richard O'Neill in a half Nelson grip. Richard eye-gouges the DP. The crew retaliates by sending electric current through agency head sets. Agency restores calm on the set by directing all violence toward talent only. *

* Only seven actors were harmed in the making of these commercials.

**BEN NOTT
SUSAN TREACY
ERIC KING**

**Consumer Television
:20 and Under: Single**

CLIENT
ESPN

AGENCY
Wieden + Kennedy/New York

03085A

Travis, the guy who fires the ball at the two Shelfball players, isn't acting.

At callbacks, we gave him the impression he was going to be one of the lead Shelfball players.

He must have studied the Unofficial Shelfball Rulebook we'd put together for casting—maybe even taken it home and practiced.

On the day of the shoot, we stuck him in the corner next to the copier and told him to keep busy. He was mouthing lines to himself all morning.

At lunch, he cornered us to express his frustration with being relegated to clerical help.

We blamed ACNE.

A few hours later, when we asked him to pick up a stray ball and toss it back to the guys playing Shelfball—he exploded.

Literally.

What you see in this spot is only the first 10 seconds of a four-minute tirade which resulted in RSA's Philip Fox Mills escorting Travis from the set.

It's definitely a lot funnier as a spot than it was in person.

We ended up calling the shoot about an hour after the outburst—everybody was distracted, the guys were having a hard time hitting their shots, and, as long as we're being honest, the boom operator we tried to use as a Travis body double didn't look anything like Travis.

Check out the "Kiss the Double" spot—that's the boom operator in Travis' wardrobe standing at the copy machine—doesn't look anything like him.

**KEVIN PROUDFOOT
KIM SCHOEN**

The Beetle is unique in its relevancy to American culture, and because each spot plays up a different aspect of that relevancy, it just made sense to collect them together as a campaign. In "Squares," the car is about non-conformity. In "Bubble Boy," the car symbolizes freedom. The third spot, "Chain Reaction," relates to how the car makes us feel—happy. Collectively, this campaign is the Beetle.

JOE FALLON

**Consumer Television
Varying Lengths Campaign**

CLIENT
Volkswagen of America

AGENCY
Arnold Worldwide/Boston

03089A

You know your actors are great when during the height of the macing scene, real policemen, unaware of the cameras across the street, drive into frame, hit the brakes and jump out with their guns drawn. Had they not been rear-ended by a lookie-loo shortly after, we would have been smiling instead of cringing.

This spot proves one thing. Good spots can turn great when done right. This does not mean you argue that your bad idea will kick ass with the right 'treatment.' But had it not been for great direction, editing, sound design and of course, painfully brilliant acting, this would have won squat.

**JASON SPERLING
CRAIG LEDERMAN
RICK COLBY**

**Consumer Television
Under $50,000 Budget**

CLIENT
California Map & Travel

AGENCY
Colby & Partners/Santa Monica

03092A

GOLD ON GOLD

Non Broadcast Cinema

CLIENT
Mill Valley Film Festival

AGENCY
Hill Holliday/San Francisco

03095A

A few things entered into our minds when we started working on this project: We wanted to do something special for the festival's 25th anniversary; we thought it should have a cinematic feel; and we knew it was our big chance to get prostitution, racism, drug use and underage sex into a spot.

A world of thanks to our creative directors, Rob Bagot and Terry Rietta; our fabulous directing team, Carter & Blitz; everyone at Anonymous Content; and all those who donated their time, talent and foot rubs to make this spot possible.

We'd like to extend our deepest apologies to Brilliant Yet Schizophrenic Piano Player, Alcoholic Trailer Trash and Sweaty Dwarf Voyeur for ending up on the cutting room floor.

Lastly, if anyone knows who keyed Walter's car during the shoot, please contact the Mill Valley Film Festival office.

**PAUL JOHNSON
LAUREN HARWELL**

Innovative Marketing

CLIENT
MINI

AGENCY
Crispin Porter + Bogusky/Miami

03001G

Recently, a friend of ours told us about a cool thing he saw in a mall. He described it as a kiddie ride with a MINI on top and went on about how people were gathering around, taking pictures and toying with the coin slot. We smiled and said, "Y'know, we work on MINI." He responded, "Yeah, but you just do the advertising."

**ARI MERKIN
PAUL STECHSCHULTE**

Integrated Branding

CLIENT
MINI

AGENCY
Crispin Porter + Bogusky/Miami

03006G

Surprisingly enough, most of the MINI launch work was presented at the pitch. It needs to be said that the real work was done by Account Services, Media, Print/Broadcast Production, and Art Buying.

ANDREW KELLER

We've heard of people who win a One Show Gold Award as students and never win anything else, ever.

**ALAN BUCHANAN
NICK PROUT**

College Competition
Advertising

SCHOOL
VCU Adcenter/Richmond

CC048

Our first mutated frog looked nothing like a frog. Origami doesn't lend itself well to mutation! So we made 20 more until one looked right. The paper doll clones were a cakewalk in comparison. Then we tried making a gas mask out of paper maché, but ended up with a paper maché pig. Or a paper maché Mickey Mouse, depending on whom you asked. God bless Adobe Photoshop.

**AZIZ RAWAT
JULIE DULUDE**

College Competition
Design

SCHOOL
VCU Adcenter/Richmond

CCD059

GOLD ON GOLD

One Show Design

Annual Report

CLIENT
Zumtobel

AGENCY
Sagmeister Inc./New York

03001D

Zumtobel is a leading European manufacturer of lighting systems. The cover of this annual report features a heat molded relief sculpture of five flowers in a vase, symbolizing the five sub-brands under the Zumtobel name.

All images on the inside of the annual report are photographs of this exact cover, shot under different light conditions, illustrating the incredible power of changing light.

It is great to work for a client who trusts his design company in such a way that he proclaims a month before the presentation: "Chances we'll print it exactly as you'll suggest are 99 percent."

STEFAN SAGMEISTER

Booklet/Brochure

CLIENT
DaimlerChrysler AG, DCVD

AGENCY
Scholz & Friends/Berlin

03004D

Why did we show everything twice in the Smart brochure? Because we see the value in being economically minded. For instance, anywhere we might see some attractive free media space, we seize the moment:

For sale!!! Original bicycle from the former GDR, blue, in good shape 200$, for foto and further information mail to gerald.meilicke@s-f.com.

Special offer: Complete collection of old stamps and rare postcards from the 70s. Contact matthias.schmidt@s-f.com

Bargain! Soccer Ball, slightly used, with original signature of Horst Hrubesch, only 19,99$. E-mail for shipping costs to nwillborn@gmx.de

GERALD MEILICKE

Corporate Identity

CLIENT
Veronique Delachaux

AGENCY
Michael Conrad & Leo Burnett/
Frankfurt

03008D

The client, a shop selling fashions especially for pregnant women, asked us to come up with an idea for a giveaway that could be used for different purposes either in the shop, at trade fairs, or as a direct mailing supplement.

The idea was to create a business card that also communicated the benefit of the product. We used a special stretch fabric for the card, so that the card only becomes legible when you stretch it.

Women in particular saw these cards as the perfect example of what they want most in pregnancy fashions—stretchability.

Maybe it helped in the idea that the female part of the creative team was pregnant, too.

ANDREAS PAULI

It's a truly heady feeling realizing that something you have done is actually great. It's equally sobering when you realize the implications. The Apartheid Museum is a beautifully tragic edifice. It stands as a beacon of hope to all nations of the world, proving to them that oppression can be overcome. It stands because millions of people suffered and died. It tells the true history of South Africa's darkest days. It opens wounds to clear them of the festering pus that is racism and inequality, and the pain is often more than people think they can endure. But they do. Endurance is the watchword of the keepers of the flame that is the human spirit. Never give up hope, never give in to despair. Know that one day the will to find peace will find a way. Every piece of work we've done for The Apartheid Museum has had to answer this call. The work is great, the message is far greater. If you ever have a chance, experience our history for yourself and you too will walk away free.

FELIX KESSEL

One Show Design

Corporate Identity

CLIENT
Apartheid Museum

AGENCY
TBWA/Gavin/Reddy/Johannesburg

03009D

Colors are the adjectives of reality. Treat them well, they have feelings, too.

FELIX KESSEL

Corporate Identity

CLIENT
Sonke Printing House

AGENCY
TBWA/Gavin/Reddy/Johannesburg

03010D

One Show Design

Logo/Trademark

CLIENT
Say it Loud!

AGENCY
Say it Loud!/Orlando

03014D

Luba nailed it. She really dove into the Say it Loud! Creative Activist philosophy of my new venture. I'm a huge fan of Luba's work. Her illustration style was perfect for the "Don't try to shut me up, fight for better creative" concept.

Be fearless. Strap on your COJONES. Trust your instincts. Listen to your heart.

JULIO LIMA

It was easy for me to work on this logo with Julio because I liked the name of his new company and the story behind it: After working with a bigger advertising agency for years he decided to venture on his own to create more provocative work on an international level. With my image I wanted to express the process of this transition from limitations to freedom. It was great that Julio gave me total freedom and liked the drawing as his new logo.

LUBA LUKOVA

Commercial Product Packaging

CLIENT
Kurt Hoppenstedt

AGENCY
Scholz & Friends/Berlin

03017D

"Honey?"

"What?"

"Are you sleeping?"

"Sort of..."

"What do you think of people carrying pink plastic udders around?"

(Pause.)

"You're a pervert."

**BIRGIT VAN DEN VALENTYN
TIM STUEBANE**

**Promotional and Point of
Purchase Posters: Single**

CLIENT
Endless Pain Studio

AGENCY
Weigertpirouzwolf/Hamburg

03020D

The 25th door of the Advent Calendar: The image was shot in the lobby of the Radisson Hotel Hamburg. Located beside the lobby, there was the bar, separated from the set by a huge drop curtain. So far so good. But then, Murphy's law took effect: Everything that can go wrong, will go wrong at some point. And what could that be, concerning a drop curtain? That's right: The drop curtain dropped. That happened while all the models were posing in front of the camera half-naked. That way, a quite large, extra door was opened for the guests in advance.

**MANUEL KRUCK
KAY EICHNER
MICHAEL REISSINGER
MARC LEITMEYER
JONAS BERNSCHNEIDER**

Founded in 1996, FM Interwave is a radio station dedicated to music manufactured and played worldwide; its goal is to better serve the international community in the Tokyo metropolitan area and its vicinity. FM Interwave's distinguishing feature is that its listeners are foreigners living in Japan.

These posters were displayed at outdoor entertainment events throughout the summer and fall. The images appear on a simple white background, displaying "BUTT-EaR FLIES" on an antenna. This imagery is intended to inspire listeners to tune in to their favorite radio programs without thinking, and to choose programs by following their instincts. The posters demonstrate the diversity of FM Interwave's listeners by using ears from people of a variety of races. In order to reflect the nature of imagination, the "BUTT-EaR FLY" effect is somewhat grotesque.

KOU KAGIYA

One Show Design

Promotional and Point of Purchase Posters: Campaign

CLIENT
FM Interwave

AGENCY
Dentsu West/Matsuyama

03023D

STRATEGY: Mr. Children is a major band that represents the whole rock scene in Japan. This series of posters is part of a campaign to launch their album, "It's a Wonderful World," which is intended to convey a message of peace, emphasizing the importance of love under the present circumstances of terrorism, war, and crime. These posters were hung in trains jam-packed with people fed up with unpleasant headlines in the news media. Instead of being disgusted with yet another report of disasters, commuters can appreciate and enjoy this small comfort, which is also thought-provoking and refreshing—a quite new experience for the daily commute.

MIKI MATSUI, Creative Director

THE COPY: After discussing our campaign with Mr. Kobayashi, the key person on the client side, the copy line, "Fall in love with the world once more," came naturally to my mind. It was subsequently approved. Indeed, there are just too many miserable things happening in this world, but there still are wonderful things to cherish, as there always have been. Why can't we focus more on this? And that was the message we wanted to relate.

KEIICHI SASAKI, Writer

VISUAL DESIGN: We chose this particular material—lace—because it immediately creates the illusion of happiness and beauty, even with a dark, sorrowful backdrop. Upon closer look, the pattern of the lace reveals the repugnant aspects of the 'real world'—war, money, politics, crime, etc. The white lace, hung from the ceiling, swings in a light breeze and creates a small space of peacefulness.

CHIE MORIMOTO, Art Director

Environmental Design
Retail, Office, Restaurant, Outdoor

CLIENT
Oorong-Sha

AGENCY
Hakuhodo/Tokyo

03027D

GOLD ON
GOLD

One Show Design

Environmental Design
Retail, Office, Restaurant,
Outdoor

CLIENT
Amnesty International

AGENCY
Michael Conrad & Leo Burnett/
Frankfurt

03028D

We would like to invite you to take part in a little experiment. Don't worry, it won't hurt. Well, at least not yet. Want to try?

Okay, so, book a ticket (one-way will do) and fly, today, to any one of the many dictatorial, military or fundamentalist led countries of the world. When you're there, just dress according to your country of origin, or your preferred faith, go out onto the street, show your colors and say out loud exactly what you think.

What, you're scared? What of? Of being beaten, of being arrested, of being thrown in a 16-man cell, of perverted torture methods, of the hopelessness of ever getting out alive, of being forgotten?

Well, don't worry; there's always Amnesty International. They'll work untiringly to help secure your release. They collect donations and signatures globally, send thousands of petitions to the responsible governments, take care of you—psychologically and physically—while you're there and, with every visit they make, give you back what was robbed of you long ago during your torture: hope.

To support AI's tremendous work, we brought the human rights issue right onto the streets of Germany—to show how human rights are treated far too often: trampled under foot.

In the middle of a busy shopping area, desperate hands reach up and cling to a drain, grasping the cover like the bars in a prison cell. The words, "wrong faith," "wrong color," or "wrong opinion," are tattooed on the fingers, reminding casual shoppers of those who are being held unjustly.

A big thank you to all who have given: money, attention and praise.

**HANS-JUERGEN KAEMMERER
ROBERT JUNKER**

Book Jacket Design

CLIENT
Harley-Davidson

AGENCY
VSA Partners/Chicago

03032D

Over the course of Harley-Davidson's 100 year heritage, the stories of experiencing motorcycling have helped shape and define the mystique of this great American brand. Our goal, in creating the Lore series of books, was to bring a visual and verbal presentation of historic milestones to life in the form of words and pictures. Each book in this three edition series chronicles the rise of a modern legend, from its humble beginnings in a 10-foot by 15-foot shed to its present position, a century later, as one of the world's most successful motorcycle manufacturers. The stories highlight the many influences that have shaped the company—wars, the economy, and intense competition from domestic and foreign rivals.

The design of the book takes on a restrained com-position, purposely framing each page with a singular photographic plate. Like an exhibition catalog, an index located at the end of each book details the specific origin and story of each image. The cover title also includes an etched plate, which echoes the mechanical feel of motorcycle hardware.

DANA ARNETT

In my country, no one's bigger in the graphics industry than Luiz Carlos Burti (the client). Not only in reputation but physically as well: He's 6'5" and weighs something in the neighborhood of 290 pounds. In Brazil, he's a true giant in graphics excellence.

This restless man bankrolls the production of the prestigious, biannual "Casa do Vaticano Magazine." It's really a challenge in the form of a magazine. In each edition, a different art director determines its concept and execution from beginning to end. The creative conceives of the subject and invites mostly photographers to illustrate it. The magazine's goal is to serve as a laboratory of creativity.

I wanted the subject, no matter what it was, to force all 16 photographers to produce exclusive images for the magazine. No looking for leftovers in their portfolios. It had to be totally new. So how could I entice them in an equally new way? Why not send the same object to all of them as a subject, with a letter of invitation? An object as the protagonist.

So, what object? A hat? A ladder? A shoe? A roll of toilet paper? A chair? Maybe...Why not? But which one? New or old? Humble or fancy? Ugly or beautiful? Why not design one that was also unique, exclusive, original? I designed it to be as simple as possible. Straight, unadorned, with neither color nor texture. Just structure. A skeleton. With no skin. No past. That's what I made. Or rather, we made. Sixteen identical chairs for 16 very different madmen.

The 17th is Burti himself. A bear that pokes the wasp's nest, but has fun doing so, happily enjoying the stings.

CARLOS SILVÉRIO

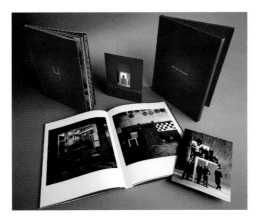

One Show Design

Consumer Magazine Full Issue

CLIENT
Graficos Burti

AGENCY
DPZ/São Paulo

03035D

Beautiful girls, a revolutionary product, crazy scientists from Cleveland, tight low-cut jeans, high-profile parties with too-cool-for-school guest lists, fashion this, fashion that, and, of course, LASERS! Fractal was one of those rare clients who had a revolutionary product with a creative vision. Fractal invented a revolutionary laser that can essentially "unprint" denim fabric—a technology with the potential to change the way people think about the apparel industry as a whole. Finally, a payoff to the designers' workweek. To a designer, this technology screamed: "What? Wait a minute! Do it again! Do it again!"

The graphics of the actual jeans are composed thematically. Each line of jeans is created from a different, inspired topic—Militant, Bohemiana, Blast, and Naked—and "unprinted" with the laser. We used those topics as inspiration for the graphics that were woven through each spread of the book, shooting the models on white so we could have full control of how the graphics interacted with each group. The inside flap of the book was die cut to allow communication pieces like press kits and letterhead to be visible and slide into the book.

**DAVID MASHBURN
ALAN LEUSINK**

Trade Magazine Full Issue

CLIENT
Fractal, LLC

AGENCY
Duffy/New York

03036D

One Show Design

**Direct Mail
Single**

CLIENT
Munkedals

AGENCY
Happy Forsman & Bodenfors/
Göteborg

03039D

One of Happy's assignments in 2002 was to show Munkedals' traditional book paper in a less common context: Not only is it a great paper for novels, but also for more colorful designs, as the Colour Book illustrates, or, as it is actually named, "Moss green, brown, lilac, shocking pink, scarlet and other great colours on Munken Print Extra 18 150 g/m²."

The idea of a book dripping with colors (40 some different Pantone colors mixed in countless combinations) came to us quite easily. The design process went just as smoothly. The absence of selling texts, time-consuming research, and other fuss made the whole project even less complicated. However, the project turned out to be a printer's nightmare in every possible way.

Today the Colour Book has inspired a great number of creative people. However, the fact that it is now totally out of stock could mean that the printer's nightmare has merely just begun...

**BJÖRN ENGSTRÖM
ANDREAS KITTEL
ANDERS KORNESTEDT**

Moss green, brown, lilac, shocking pink, scarlet and other great colours on Munken Print Extra 18 150 g/m²

**Broadcast Design
Network Identity**

CLIENT
SCI FI Channel

AGENCY
SCI FI Channel/New York

03046D

As these things tend to go, the answer to the creative brief came to us in a dream.

We were standing in front of the DQ when a bearded old man, looking for all the world like Steven Spielberg, floated down from the heavens, and spake: "Thou must get the hell away from the UFOs-and-aliens image, and push the magical fantasy thing! Thou must rebrand!"

It was all very David Lynchian. Except for the marketing jargon.

So we followed the instructions we were given and made these spots.

Much later we dreamt ourselves back to the DQ for a couple of hot fudge sundaes, and found the old man working the register.

"Hey, Wise Old Spielbergian Man," we said. "We thought you were God."

"Ah," he replied. "Now you are beginning to grasp the true nature of SCI FI."

**MICHAEL EILPERIN
DAVE HOWE
ROGER GUILLEN
PAUL OWEN**

ARKITEKTUR ÄR YTLIGT!

The Swedish Museum of Architecture wishes to communicate with everyone, not just the "architecture elite." As part of the overall communication, we created this magazine, whose main purpose is to make people look at architecture from different perspectives.

The theme of the first issue was: Do not just look at architecture—feel it, too. We collected a series of rubbings (a technique everyone is familiar with) done on a great number of buildings. Big and small, private and public, old and new— everything from a bridge in Venice, to a colleague's summerhouse, to the famous Arne Jacobsen City Hotel in Copenhagen.

Together, they point out something we are not always thinking about: that architecture is about texture as well.

**LISA CAREBORG
ANDREAS KITTEL
ANDERS KORNESTEDT**

One Show Design

**Public Service/Political
Direct Mail**

CLIENT
Swedish Museum of Architecture

AGENCY
Happy Forsman & Bodenfors/
Göteborg

03050D

Postcards. Simple idea, no comments needed. So let's use this space for some advertising: There are millions of people around the world who need the help of MEDECINS SANS FRONTIERES. And the MEDECINS SANS FRONTIERES needs our help to help others. Simple, isn't it? Please visit www.msf.org and donate.

That's simple, too.

INGO HOENTSCHKE

**Public Service/Political
Booklet/Brochure & Other
Collateral**

CLIENT
Aerzte ohne Grenzen e.V.

AGENCY
Scholz & Friends/Berlin

03052D

183

MERIT AWARD
**Newspaper Over 600 Lines
Single**

ART DIRECTOR
Manish Bhatt

WRITER
Raghu Bhat

PHOTOGRAPHERS
Raj Mistry
Rubin D'Silva

ILLUSTRATORS
Milind Aglave
Ashok Chilla

CREATIVE DIRECTOR
Elsie Nanji

CLIENT
Sil Red Chilli Sauce

AGENCY
Ambience D'Arcy/Mumbai

03098A

MERIT AWARD
**Newspaper Over 600 Lines
Single**

ART DIRECTOR
Dave Galligos

WRITER
John Spalding

PHOTOGRAPHER
Dave Kiesgen

CREATIVE DIRECTORS
Al Jackson
Jim Spruell

CLIENT
Atlanta Pro Percussion

AGENCY
Austin Kelley/Atlanta

03099A

Also won:
MERIT AWARD
**Magazine Color
Full Page or Spread: Single**

MERIT AWARD
Newspaper Over 600 Lines
Single

ART DIRECTOR
Scott Hidinger

WRITER
Al Jackson

CREATIVE DIRECTOR
Al Jackson

CLIENT
Retromodern

AGENCY
Austin Kelley/Atlanta

03100A

Also won:
MERIT AWARDS
Magazine Color
Full Page or Spread: Single

Collateral: Posters
Single

Electronic Stabilisation Programme as standard.

MERIT AWARD
Newspaper Over 600 Lines
Single

ART DIRECTOR
Grant Parker

WRITER
Patrick McClelland

PHOTOGRAPHER
Gary Simpson

CREATIVE DIRECTORS
Jeremy Craigen
Ewan Paterson

CLIENT
Volkswagen

AGENCY
BMP DDB/London

03101A

Also won:
MERIT AWARD
Magazine Color
Full Page or Spread: Single

PRINT
MERIT

MERIT AWARD
**Newspaper Over 600 Lines
Single**

ART DIRECTORS
Molly Sheahan
Jan Jacobs

WRITER
Amber Logan

PHOTOGRAPHER
Simon Harsent

AGENCY PRODUCER
Maggie Meade

CREATIVE DIRECTORS
Tony Granger
Jan Jacobs

CLIENT
The New York Times

AGENCY
Bozell/New York

03102A

MERIT AWARD
**Newspaper Over 600 Lines
Single**

ART DIRECTORS
Takeru Kawai
Masahito Yoshizaki

WRITERS
Konosuke Kamitani
Yutaka Tsujino

ILLUSTRATOR
Masahito Yoshizaki

AGENCY PRODUCER
Koji Wada

PRODUCTION COMPANIES
Dentsu Inc.
Common Design

CREATIVE DIRECTOR
Konosuke Kamitani

CLIENT
Japan Football Association

AGENCY
Dentsu/Tokyo

03105A

WINDOWS ARE PUT INTO BUILDINGS TO MAKE YOU THINK YOU ARE OUTSIDE. DO NOT BE FOOLED, YOU ARE NOT OUTSIDE. ALAS, THIS IS NOTHING MORE THAN ANOTHER THINLY VEILED ATTEMPT TO KEEP YOU SECURELY LOCKED WITHIN THE WARM BERBER-CARPETED GRASP OF THIS PLACE KNOWN AS "IN." THIS IS THE SAME KIND OF THINKING THAT HAS LED TO PLASTIC POTTED PLANTS, NATURE CD'S AND HORROR AMONG HORRORS, THE TREADMILL. BUT FEAR NOT, THESE PLOYS HAVE NOT GONE UNNOTICED. THERE ARE STILL THOSE WHO REALIZE THAT THE OUTDOORS IS NOT TO BE SIMULATED, VIRTUALIZED, OR OTHERWISE "BROUGHT INDOORS" (A FAVORITE EXPRESSION AMONG THE PURVEYORS OF "IN"). THE OUTDOORS IS TO BE EXPERIENCED IN ALL ITS GLORIOUS, HUMBLING, AND REFRESHINGLY UN-SANITIZED OUT-NESS. AS SUCH, WE ARE LAUNCHING A HIGHLY POTENT ARSENAL OF FINELY CRAFTED OUTDOOR WEAR GEARED TO HELP YOU VENTURE BEYOND THE CONFINES OF "IN." FOOTWEAR AND APPAREL DESIGNED TO LET YOU SUCK UP EVERY LAST MOMENT OF "OUT" UNTIL YOUR SPIRIT HAS BEEN FULLY PURGED OF EACH AND EVERY ION OF FLUORESCENCE AND FREON, AND THE CHATTERING WHITE NOISE IN YOUR HEAD HAS BEEN REPLACED BY A VOICE YOU SWEAR BELONGS TO THAT 10-YEAR-OLD KID IN YOUR MOM'S PICTURES. AND THAT, FRIENDS, IS WHEN YOU WILL KNOW THAT YOU ARE OUTSIDE. TIMBERLAND. SEEK OUT

MERIT AWARD
Newspaper Over 600 Lines
Single

ART DIRECTOR
David Damman

WRITER
Greg Hahn

PHOTOGRAPHER
David Harriman

AGENCY PRODUCER
Louise Raicht

CREATIVE DIRECTORS
David Lubars
Kevin Roddy

CLIENT
Timberland

AGENCY
Fallon/New York

03106A

MERIT AWARD
**Newspaper Over 600 Lines
Single**

ART DIRECTOR
Derik Meinköhn

WRITERS
Martien Delfgaauw
Thies Schuster

PHOTOGRAPHER
Nico Weymann

CREATIVE DIRECTORS
Ralf Nolting
Patricia Pätzold

CLIENT
Volkswagen

AGENCY
Grabarz & Partner Werbeagentur/
Hamburg

03107A

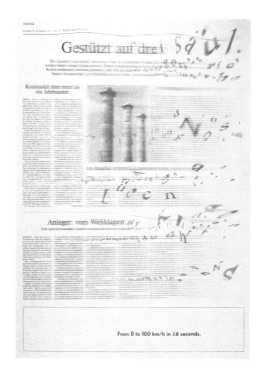

From 0 to 100 km/h in 7.8 seconds.

45° hill-climbing ability.

580 mm wading depth.

The Touareg

MERIT AWARD
Newspaper Over 600 Lines
Single

ART DIRECTOR
Ivan Pols

WRITER
Justin Wanliss

PHOTOGRAPHER
David Prior

ILLUSTRATOR
Ivan Pols

CREATIVE DIRECTOR
Gerry Human

CLIENT
Harley-Davidson

AGENCY
HarrisonHuman Bates/Sandton

03108A

Also won:
MERIT AWARD
Magazine B/W or Color
Less Than A Page: Single

MERIT AWARD
Newspaper Over 600 Lines
Single

ART DIRECTORS
Michael Wright
Mark Braddock

WRITER
Neil French

AGENCY PRODUCER
Jenny Schoenherr

CREATIVE DIRECTOR
Alon Shoval

CLIENT
Newspaper Association
of America

AGENCY
The Martin Agency/Richmond

03112A

Nobody reads long copy any more. Here's why.

Americans either don't read, won't read, or can't read. Somebody famous said that, so it must be true.

More importantly, absolutely no-one reads newspapers any more. That is a well-known fact.

And yet, blissfully ignorant of this, thousands of journalists and reporters spend their lives, pointlessly gathering information, news, and opinions, and writing about it. Day in, day out. Day after wasted day.

Sadder still, many more thousands of lost souls are glumly occupied in setting the result in type, designing the pages, and printing the damned things.

And strangely enough, millions of otherwise seemingly-sane people go out and buy...yes, buy...newspapers every day. This is presumably, one imagines, because they need a cheap substitute for an umbrella, drawer-liners, or an inexhaustible supply of kitty-litter, for a herd of terminally incontinent cats.

But nobody actually reads the newspaper. Dearie me, no.

By the way, Elvis was abducted by aliens, but has returned and is now working as a singing coconut for a time-share in Boca Raton.

So there is a God.

Oh, and I'm a little teapot.

Go away!

You're not still reading this drivel are you? Why, for heaven's sake? Believe me, it's not going to get any better. Go and do something useful. Count your socks.

Run along now. Shoo!

(Have they gone?)

Right then. Sorry about that, but you've got to get rid of the riff-raff. That's the only problem with writing for newspapers. All sorts of people pick them up. Beastly people, a lot of them, probably. Probably clip their toe-nails in bed. That sort of thing.

Where were we?

Erm...nobody reads newspapers, that was it. Well, I suppose we might admit that the people who write the newspapers read their own stuff. So do their Mums, unless there's wrestling on the tele.

For example, this particular exercise in futility was intended to be one in a series of ads headlined 'How I write a newspaper ad,' by (in this case) Neil French'. Surely a headline so mind-numbingly dull as to rival the marvellous all-time great, 'Small earthquake in Peru. Nobody hurt,' as the most boring ever.

It was. God 'elp us, going to feature an illustration of me. My mother would have liked that, except she's dead, and one assumes, no longer collects my bits.

The fact is that the vast majority of the folks that bought this rag are never, ever, going to write an ad, and still less give a rat's bottom who Neil French is. And there are no words to describe how very little they care what a bloke they've never heard of looks like.

So, we changed the look of the ad, to somewhat disguise the fact that it is, on the one hand, insanely incestuous, and on the other, seems to contradict the very point it hopes to make.

Now, anyone still with us will be the anally-retentive sort of loser who has to deconstruct everything, and will have recognised the first bit of this epic as a rather plodding attempt at heavy irony. A useful tool for debunking, is the old irony-ploy.

But did you know that there's a myth that Americans don't understand irony? Since they apparently don't read either, all-friends here, so for what it's worth, and to give us all a break, here's my favourite irony-story.

An American chap goes on holiday to England. On his return, he's telling his pal all about it:

"I was coming out of a shop, one day, and it was raining outside, so I took shelter in the doorway.

Another feller was sheltering, too, and he turned to me, and he said, 'Nice weather'.

Well, of course, it wasn't nice weather at all. In-fact it was terrible weather ...and then I got it! This was the famous British irony. I loved it!'

And I've been using irony ever since. Like the other day, I was having this barbecue for the family and a bunch of neighbours, and I burned the burgers.

And Joe, from next door, was standing there. And I turned to him, and I looked at the burgers, and I said, 'Nice weather'.

(Pause for...bewilderment, I suppose... and back to business)

Can we acknowledge, then, that the hundreds of thousands of words printed in this newspaper aren't put there just to make your fingers dirty?

Irony aside, people buy newspapers so that they can read them.

And since this is obvious to anyone with the intellect of a soap-dish, why is the newspaper not chock-full of ads for big, sexy, brands?

The short, honest answer is, stupidity.

And the combined stupidity of agencies, researchers, (yes, there's a surprise), and one hates to say it, but clients, is a terrible thing to behold.

Basically, remember, you can prove just about anything. And if you want to prove that people don't read long copy in ads, you start by proving that 'people read only a small proportion of all the editorial articles in a newspaper.'

(Television viewers, however, watch every show, every night, without ever switching channels. Note: In future, all irony will be in italics. But not all of the subsequent italicised words are ironic. Everybody clear on this?)

The fuzzy logic then goes like this: People don't read all the words in a newspaper. Therefore, people don't like to read.

Therefore, we must avoid all ads that depend on words.

Newspapers are full of words, so we must not advertise in them.

In the end, ya know, you really cannot fight determined stupidity.

I once produced a campaign for a client who published newspapers, that proved beyond doubt that you could launch a beer brand, using newspapers only, more successfully than you could on T.V. and at a fraction of the cost.

The big-brand brewers were unmoved. Having been panicked-for weeks by a press campaign that widdled all over their T.V. commercials, they ignored the evidence once the campaign was over.

So I somehow doubt that the opinions of the copywriters engaged in this 'little exercise are going to sway the prejudices of the sort of client who always knows best.

Still, we can but try.

Rule One of advertising is 'Decide who you're talking to'. It's also Rule Two.

There is no rule three or four.

So, why talk to them in a newspaper? Because, simply put, a newspaper is not a mass medium. It's personal.

You can watch TV. in a group. Posters are public. Radio is wallpaper.

But hold up a newspaper, and you have an effective barrier against the rest of the world. It is private.

Newspapers are portable. No-one tells you when or where to read them. TV. is, on the face of it, free. Radio is free. Posters are free. The internet is free. And advertising on all of them is regarded as an irritation, and rudest of all, an interruption.

People buy newspapers. You think they don't value them? Think again.

If you can't get people to read your ad in a newspaper, it's nobody's fault but your own.

(You recall that the original brief was to write an ad about how I write an ad? Well, I do it like this).

They wanted to put a big, newspaper logo down here, so you'd know who paid for the space, but I thought that'd be obvious. I didn't get paid for writing it. I truly believe in newspapers.

This message is brought to you by the Newspaper Association of America and the publishing newspapers. Neil French is the Worldwide Creative Director of Ogilvy & Mather.

MERIT AWARD
**Newspaper Over 600 Lines
Single**

ART DIRECTOR
Denis Dubrulle

WRITER
Jan Teulingkx

PHOTOGRAPHER
Christophe Gilbert

CREATIVE DIRECTOR
Marcel Ceuppens

CLIENT
Opel Berckmans

AGENCY
McCann Erickson/Hoeilaart

03113A

MERIT AWARD
**Newspaper Over 600 Lines
Single**

ART DIRECTORS
Victoria Lamppa
Laurence Thomson

WRITERS
Leon Wilson
Malin Wikerberg

CREATIVE DIRECTORS
Robert Saville
Mark Waites
Jim Thornton

CLIENT
Observer Sport Monthly

AGENCY
Mother/London

03114A

NO SEX BEFORE SPORT.
HOW DOES IT AFFECT
THE ATHLETES?

THIS SUNDAY

MERIT AWARD
Newspaper Over 600 Lines
Campaign

ART DIRECTOR
Paul Crawford

WRITER
Deb Maltzman

PHOTOGRAPHER
Greg Slater

AGENCY PRODUCERS
Linda Donlon
Sarah Murphy

CREATIVE DIRECTORS
Mary Webb
Wendy Beckett

CLIENT
The Hartford

AGENCY
Arnold Worldwide/Boston

03117A

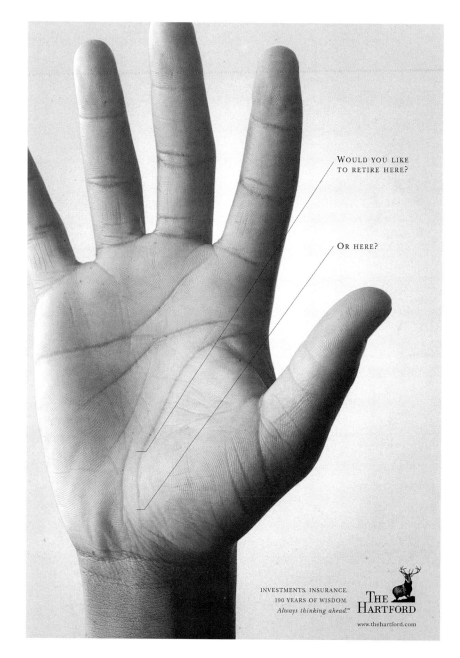

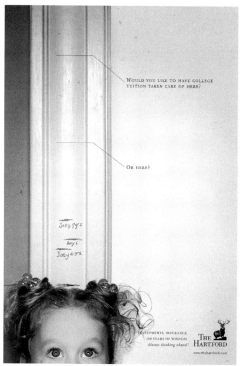

MERIT AWARD
Newspaper Over 600 Lines
Campaign

ART DIRECTORS
Molly Sheahan
Jan Jacobs

WRITER
Amber Logan

PHOTOGRAPHER
Simon Harsent

AGENCY PRODUCER
Maggie Meade

CREATIVE DIRECTORS
Tony Granger
Jan Jacobs

CLIENT
The New York Times

AGENCY
Bozell/New York

03118A

195

PRINT
MERIT

MERIT AWARD
**Newspaper Over 600 Lines
Campaign**

ART DIRECTORS
Mark Taylor
Alex Burnard

WRITERS
Ari Merkin
Steve O'Connell
Brian Tierney

PHOTOGRAPHER
Daniel Hartz

CREATIVE DIRECTORS
Alex Bogusky
Andrew Keller

CLIENT
MINI

AGENCY
Crispin Porter + Bogusky/Miami

03119A

I know we get used to it. But we shouldn't.

We get used to living in back door apartments and not having another view but the windows around. And because there is no view, sooner or later we get used to not looking outside. And because we don't look outside, sooner or later we get used to not opening the curtains. And because we don't open the curtains sooner or later we get used to turning on the light earlier. And by getting used to, we forget the sun, forget the air, and forget the magnitude.

We get used to waking up in the morning exasperated because its time. To rush into breakfast because we are late. To read the newspaper while on the bus because we can't spare any time. To eat a sandwich because we can't stop for lunch. To go home because its already night. To fall asleep in the bus because we are tired. To go to bed early and sleep heavily without having lived the day.

We get used to waiting the whole day only to hear over the phone: today I can't make it.

To smile to people without being smiled back. To be ignored when all you needed was to be seen. We get used to paying for all we want and need. And to fight to earn the money in which to pay. And to pay more than what things are worth. And to know that every time you will pay even more. And to look for more work, to make more money, to cash in the lines that charge.

We get used to pollution, to closed air-conditioned rooms and to the smell of cigarettes. To the artificial quivering light. To the impact of the natural light to the eyes. To the bacteria in drinkable water. We get used to too many things in order not to suffer. Trying not to notice, in small doses we push away here and there the pain, the resentment and the anger. If the beach is polluted we dip our toes while the rest of our body sweats. If the movie theatre is full, we sit on the first row and twist our neck a little. If there is a lot of hard work, we get relief from thinking about the weekend. And if during the weekend there isn't a lot to do, we go to bed early, satisfied as we can always catch up on our sleep.

We get used to it, so that we don't get scratched by harshness, to preserve ourselves. We get used to it to avoid wounds, bleedings, to spare the heart.

We get used to it to spear life. Them little by little we wear out and wear out so much by getting used to it, that we loose ourselves.

If one page makes you think, imagine a book.

LIBRAIRIE
FERIN

103

What else does a man need but a piece of the sea – and a boat with the name of a girl friend, and a line and a hook to fish? And while fishing, while waiting, what else does a man need but his hands, one for the cane and the other to hold his chin, so that he can loose himself in the infinite, and a bottle of rum to draw sadness, and a little thought to think until he looses himself in the infinite…

And what else does a man need but a piece of land – a very fertile piece of land – and a house, not too big, white, with a vegetable-garden and a modest orchard; and a garden – a garden is important – full of flowers to smell?

And while living, while waiting, what else does a man need but his hands to handle the soil and to scrape guitar chords when night is falling, and a bottle of whisky to draw mystery, as a house without mystery is not worth living in…

What else does a man need but a friend he likes, a friend? A man of few words, simple, someone with a look that says it all, one of those friends who doesn't deserve all of the friendship, a friend for peace and trouble, a peaceful friend, a friend for bars?

And while passing by, while waiting, what else does a man need but his hands to shake his friend's after his absence, and to pat his friend's back, and to reason with his friend and to serve his friend willingly?

And what else does a man need but a woman for him to love, a woman with breasts and a womb and a certain peculiar expression? And while thinking, while waiting, what else does a man need but the kindness of a woman when sadness brings him down, or fate carries him on its wave without direction?

Yes, and what else does a man need but his hands and a woman – the only free things left for him to fight for the sea, for the earth and for the friend…

If one page makes you think, imagine a book.

LIBRAIRIE
FERIN

37

Die slowly who doesn't travel, who doesn't read, who doesn't listen to music, who doesn't find oneself funny. Die slowly who becomes a slave of habit, going over the same tracks everyday, who doesn't change ones brand or risks wearing a new color or wont even speak to someone unknown.

Die slowly who avoids passion, who prefers black instead of white and everything in its place instead of a whirl of emotions, specially those that bring back the spark to the eye, the smiles to the yawning, hearts that tumble and feelings.

Die slowly who doesn't turn things around when is not happy with one's work, who doesn't take a chance to go after a dream, who doesn't allow oneself at least once in life to run from the conventional advices.

Die slowly who spend days complaining about one's bad luck or the heavily rain. Die slowly who drops a project before even having started it, who doesn't ask about an unknown subject or who doesn't answer when asked on something known.

Let's avoid death in small doses always reminding that being alive requires an effort greater than the simple fact of breathing.

If one page makes you think, imagine a book.

LIBRAIRIE
FERIN

46

MERIT AWARD
Newspaper Over 600 Lines Campaign

ART DIRECTOR
Carsus Dias

WRITER
Icaro Doria

CREATIVE DIRECTOR
Alexandre Okada

CLIENT
Ferin Bookstore

AGENCY
Leo Burnett/Lisbon

03120A

MERIT AWARD
**Newspaper Over 600 Lines
Campaign**

ART DIRECTOR
Michael Ancevic

WRITER
Tim Roper

PHOTOGRAPHERS
Michael Eastman
Harry DeZitter

CREATIVE DIRECTORS
Edward Boches
Michael Ancevic
Tim Roper

CLIENT
Eddie Bauer

AGENCY
Mullen/Wenham

03121A

It works best in places your cell phone never will.

The Weatheredge™ Down Parka.

In 1935, Eddie Bauer got caught in freezing rain and nearly succumbed to hypothermia because of a soggy wool overcoat. The next year, he introduced hand-stitched premium goose down to North America as a toasty, ultra-light alternative that's breathable and does a superior job of retaining body warmth. In doing so, Eddie created not just a jacket, but a revolution.

Every wrinkle, an anecdote.

Every crease, an autobiography.

The Eddie Bauer Leather Car Coat.

This Leather Car Coat is made from premium grade cowhide and was tanned by Italian leather artisans using an age-old process that results in a naturally marked finish of infinite durability. Treat it right and it'll be with you for life. In fact, one day its very texture could serve as a road map of your life's adventures.

Somewhere in a suburban strip mall, wrapped in plastic on the rack of a neighborhood dry cleaners, is another suede jacket living vicariously through yours.

Introducing Seattle Suede. Washable.

After 80 years of pioneering products that enable people to get out and go, we've dedicated the last four to perfecting a suede leather that's surprisingly low maintenance and durable enough to withstand elements even more challenging than Seattle's weather. Namely, your washing machine. So go ahead and get outdoors. Just know you'll be visiting your neighborhood dry cleaners a little less often.

MERIT AWARD
Newspaper Over 600 Lines Campaign

ART DIRECTOR
Daryl Gardiner

WRITER
Joseph Bonnici

PHOTOGRAPHER
Tom Feiler

ILLUSTRATOR
Graphex

CREATIVE DIRECTOR
Alan Russell

CLIENT
SuperPages

AGENCY
Palmer Jarvis DDB/Vancouver

03122A

199

MERIT AWARD
**Newspaper Over 600 Lines
Campaign**

ART DIRECTOR
Dan Fang

WRITER
Roger Wong

PHOTOGRAPHER
Liu Li

CREATIVE DIRECTOR
Roger Wong

CLIENT
Natural Touch Food

AGENCY
Saatchi & Saatchi/Guang Zhou

03123A

THE _____ IS THE FINEST LUXURY SEDAN IN AMERICA.

ONLY ONE LUXURY SEDAN can legitimately stake its claim on the gap in the headline above. However, the question remains: Which one?

That's exactly what the specialist researchers at Automotive Marketing Consultants Incorporated (AMCI) endeavored to determine conclusively.

AMCI is the nation's preeminent independent automotive testing company. They design objective, third-party studies to substantiate the claims that can truthfully be attributed to a particular automobile.

AMCI drives and evaluates more cars than the federal government, car-enthusiast magazines or any American organization. So consequently, most claims in broadcast car advertising have been substantiated by AMCI. But perhaps more importantly, claims that they certify are seldom challenged and none has ever been retracted.

Just how did AMCI go about identifying which luxury sedan is the finest in America?

Remain open.

In order to certify this claim, AMCI created their most sophisticated study to date, by far.

Their unprejudiced, three-phase evaluation took more than a year and 4,000 man-hours to complete. But more significantly, this study was performed "by the book." And AMCI should know—after all, they wrote the book.

When the federal guidelines were originally established for comparative vehicle advertising, AMCI was asked to assist. (Apparently, for all the driving they do, the only road they have a reputation for driving on is the high road.)

Leave nothing out.

Phase one was a thorough paper review of the most luxurious sedans available in America. The study imposed a number of basic criteria to identify only the finest automobiles and those most germane to the U.S. buyer. Ten vehicles were then promoted to the second phase, initial Comparative Vehicle Assessment (CVA®) Testing. (And, of course, far more were eliminated.)

All were carefully examined in an effort to define the most competitive set possible. An example of each was procured and carefully evaluated. From this a very clear picture emerged of exactly which luxury sedans could be considered contenders.

In all, five remarkable automobiles proceeded to the final, exacting phase, Certification Testing.

To ensure a nonpartisan evaluation of the facts, AMCI then acquired the most luxurious versions available of each of the finalist vehicles from official franchised dealers, and began the arduous process of subjecting them all to an exhaustive barrage of one

hundred and ninety-three dynamic, static and luxury feature evaluations in seven categories. Which is to say, a more comprehensive and complete evaluation would have been almost impossible to achieve.

No space for interpretation.

Needless to say, a luxury sedan is more than just the sum of its parts. But obviously, for the purpose of an objective, unbiased evaluation, AMCI needed to compare these automobiles in a measurable way.

The Rolls-Royce Silver Seraph

The BMW 750iL

The Jaguar Vanden Plas Supercharged

The Lexus LS 430

The Mercedes-Benz S600

Here's just some of what their testing discovered. Certain brands have a reputation for refinement and, in the world of luxury cars, few exemplify this more than Rolls-Royce. However, upon closer examination you may begin to question this reputation.

By way of example, if you were to sit in a Silver Seraph and count every single exposed fastener and screw head, you would find a total of sixty. Were you to attempt the same in "The Finest Luxury Sedan in America," you would not be able to find even a single one. (Astonished? So were the researchers at AMCI.)

For tests that required driving, AMCI used their most experienced test drivers. So that driving styles didn't affect results, each test was repeated until the drivers had eighteen "perfect" runs in every car.

Arguably the most significant of these trials was the 50–0 mph braking on wet pavement. In this test the BMW 750iL, a sedan that boasts a performance heritage, took 95.3 feet to reach a stop from 50 mph. "The Finest Luxury Sedan in America" stopped more than three feet sooner. And it didn't stop there.

Not only did the 750iL fail to win a single test in the performance category, it ranked third overall.

Traditionally a concours d'élégance is for cars that have been restored to their former glory. But what if you convened one for brand-new cars? Well, that is exactly what AMCI did. To judge their concours they invited nine well-respected and independent experts in their fields: three for paint, three for wood and three for leather.

Again, "The Finest Luxury Sedan in America" came out on top in this category. Just in case that makes you think it was the Jaguar Vanden Plas Supercharged, it wasn't. (Sorry, old chaps.)

In fact, no Jaguar even made it far enough into the evaluation to participate in AMCI's concours. (Oops, we've let the cat out of the bag.)

"The Finest Luxury Sedan in America" could quite possibly be the quietest. At idle, measured in the front seat, the decibel reading was 31.1. Making this automobile the most tranquil AMCI has ever tested. (Just in case you're wondering, a typical library is a deafening 40 decibels.)

All told, twelve ride-quality, interior-sound and refinement tests were completed. "The Finest Luxury Sedan in America" won the majority, and quietly drove off with victory in this category.

Ergonomics is the science of designing things that people use so that people and things interact most efficiently, effectively and safely.

Sounds somewhat Germanic, doesn't it? But apparently that stereotype is only partly true. You see, while the independent experts who evaluated this category all chose the Mercedes-Benz S600 as one of the finest German-made sedans, it still only ranked second overall to a more superior vehicle known as "The Finest Luxury Sedan in America."

Fill in the blank.

Finally, the results were carefully scrutinized, and AMCI certified that the only luxury sedan with all the credentials required to complete the headline above is the Lexus LS 430. And that's not merely their opinion. They can also prove it, unequivocally.

FOR MORE DETAILS VISIT US AT FINESTSEDAN.COM

ANY EVALUATION OF LUXURY SEDANS THAT ELIMINATES A ROLLS-ROYCE AND A BENTLEY IN THE FIRST ROUND MUST HAVE AN IMPRESSIVE WINNER.

THIS IS AN ADVERTISEMENT FOR THE FINEST LUXURY SEDAN IN AMERICA. SO WHICH LOGO BELONGS IN THE BOTTOM RIGHT-HAND CORNER?

MERIT AWARD
**Newspaper 600 Lines or Less
Single**

ART DIRECTOR
Kate Wassum

WRITERS
Al Jackson
Bryan Karr

CREATIVE DIRECTORS
Al Jackson
Duncan Stone

CLIENT
Capitol Distributing

AGENCY
Austin Kelley/Atlanta

03125A

MERIT AWARD
**Newspaper 600 Lines or Less
Single**

ART DIRECTOR
Kate Wassum

WRITERS
Al Jackson
Bryan Karr
Duncan Stone

CREATIVE DIRECTORS
Al Jackson
Duncan Stone

CLIENT
Capitol Distributing

AGENCY
Austin Kelley/Atlanta

03126A

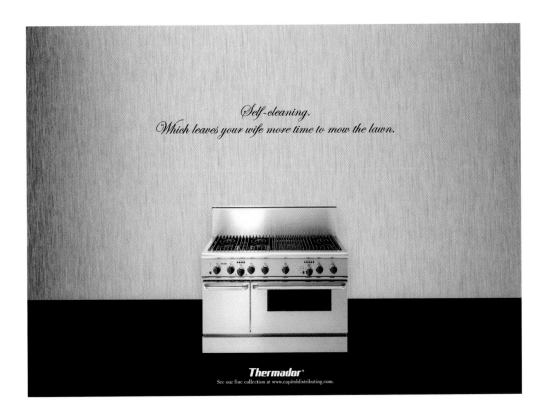

Self-cleaning.
Which leaves your wife more time to mow the lawn.

Thermador®
See our fine collection at www.capitoldistributing.com.

If other banks
are all about trust,

why are their pens
attached to chains?

For banking built on relationships,
952-431-4700.

MIDWAY BANK

Member FDIC

MERIT AWARD
**Newspaper 600 Lines or Less
Single**

ART DIRECTOR
Kevin Daley

WRITER
Chuck Pagano

PHOTOGRAPHER
Geoff Stein

AGENCY PRODUCER
Lee Hathaway

PRODUCTION COMPANY
Unigraphic

CREATIVE DIRECTORS
Marty Donohue
Tim Foley

CLIENT
Dunkin' Donuts

AGENCY
Hill Holliday/Boston

03129A

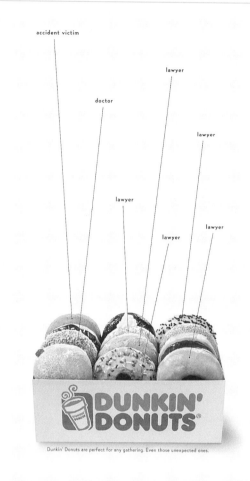

MERIT AWARD
**Newspaper 600 Lines or Less
Single**

ART DIRECTOR
Brucce Amado

WRITER
Brucce Amado

PHOTOGRAPHER
Ramiro Eduardo

CREATIVE DIRECTORS
Ramiro Eduardo
Rossana López

CLIENT
Prensa Libre

AGENCY
Ogilvy/Guatemala

03130A

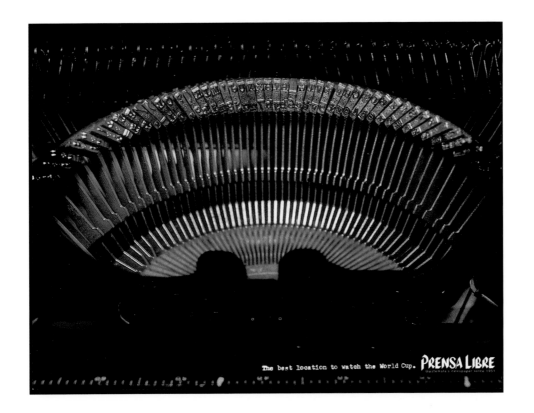

The best location to watch the World Cup. **PRENSA LIBRE**
Guatemala's newspaper since 1951

MERIT AWARD
**Newspaper 600 Lines or Less
Single**

ART DIRECTOR
Brucce Amado

WRITER
Brucce Amado

PHOTOGRAPHER
Ramiro Eduardo

CREATIVE DIRECTORS
Ramiro Eduardo
Rossana López

CLIENT
Prensa Libre

AGENCY
Ogilvy/Guatemala

03131A

MERIT AWARD
**Newspaper 600 Lines or Less
Single**

ART DIRECTORS
Jan Chalermwong
Ketchai Parponsilp

WRITER
Prasert Vijipawan

PHOTOGRAPHER
Rory Carter

CREATIVE DIRECTOR
Jureeporn Thaidumrong

CLIENT
Lea + Perrins

AGENCY
Saatchi & Saatchi/Johannesburg

03133A

Also won:
MERIT AWARD
**Collateral: Posters
Single**

205

MERIT AWARD
**Newspaper 600 Lines or Less
Campaign**

ART DIRECTOR
Thom Volarath

WRITER
Nick Gebhardt

CREATIVE DIRECTORS
Mike Lewis
Ted Nelson

CLIENT
Commune Restaurant

AGENCY
MATCH/Atlanta

03135A

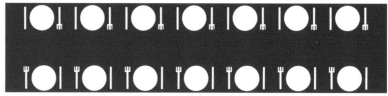

capitalist   stylist   wallflower   artist   debutante   activist   diva

foodie   matron   hippie   anarchist   poser   republican   athlete

pull up a chair.

commune
restaurant • bar • lounge

1198 howell mill rd.
westside, midtown
404 • 609 • 5000

www.communeatlanta.com

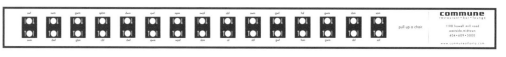

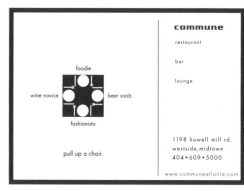

MERIT

MERIT AWARD
Newspaper 600 Lines or Less Campaign

ART DIRECTOR
William Hammond

WRITER
Steve Straw

PHOTOGRAPHER
Michael Lewis

ILLUSTRATOR
Grant Linton

CREATIVE DIRECTOR
Brett Wild

CLIENT
Guinness

AGENCY
Saatchi & Saatchi/Johannesburg

03136A

Also won:
MERIT AWARD
Collateral: Posters Single

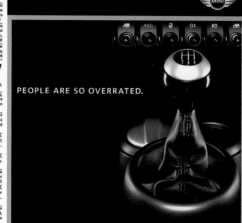

PEOPLE ARE SO OVERRATED.

The new 260 horsepower G35.

The new 260 horsepower G35.

The new 260 horsepower G35.

MERIT AWARD
Newspaper 600 Lines or Less Campaign

ART DIRECTOR
Ben Vendramin

WRITER
Pat Pirisi

CREATIVE DIRECTORS
Ben Vendramin
Pat Pirisi

CLIENT
Infiniti

AGENCY
TBWA/Chiat/Day/Toronto

03138A

MERIT AWARD
Newspaper 600 Lines or Less Campaign

ART DIRECTOR
Jayanta Jenkins

WRITER
Dylan Lee

PHOTOGRAPHERS
Sipa USA
Jean Catuffe

CREATIVE DIRECTORS
Hal Curtis
Carlos Bayala

CLIENT
Nike

AGENCY
Wieden + Kennedy/Portland

03139A

ASK MAC

Dear Mac,

I'm 16 and I've reached the point where my dad can no longer help me with my math homework. Can you help me solve this? If x2-14x+57=8, then 2x-x=?

— Stuck

Dear Stuck,

I've always loved math, so I'm glad you asked. I don't think I can show you the specific steps to solving this, because there's no better way for you to learn than to do it yourself. It would be like me playing your tournaments for you. But the answer is 7. Which is also the number of Grand Slams I've won. Very clever, Stuck. I appreciate the compliment.

— Mac

Got a problem?
askmac@nike.com

ASK MAC

Dear Mac,

My question is, I'm ambidextrous and I've played right-handed for 22 years. But you're left-handed and you dominated the tour for years. So I'm thinking I should switch to my left too. Is this wise?

— Southpaw

Dear Southpaw,

The only reason I'm answering your question is because I wanted to see if I could type imbecile with my right hand.

imbecile

— Mac

Got a problem?
askmac@nike.com

ASK MAC

Dear Mac,

Whenever I have a changeover against my regular playing partner, she does the same thing. Right when we pass each other at the net, she whispers under her breath, "Die." How should I approach her about this?

— Hearing Things

Dear Hearing Things,

If your opponent can't tell you to die out loud and in your face, then she's pretty much a coward and you can simply ignore her. Or you can just fake a heart attack. When she freaks out and runs away, that counts as a default. You win!

— Mac

Got a problem?
askmac@nike.com

Cut grass

The New Beetle Convertible.
Coming soon.

Drivers wanted.

211

MERIT AWARD
Magazine Color
Full Page or Spread: Single

ART DIRECTOR
Xavier Beauregard

WRITER
Vincent Pedrocchi

PHOTOGRAPHER
Stuart Hamilton

AGENCY PRODUCER
Sylvie Etchemaïté

CREATIVE DIRECTOR
Olivier Altmann

CLIENT
BMW

AGENCY
BDDP et Fils/Boulogne

03146A

MERIT AWARD
Magazine Color
Full Page or Spread: Single

ART DIRECTORS
Feargal Ballance
Dylan Harrison

WRITERS
Feargal Ballance
Dylan Harrison

PHOTOGRAPHER
Nick Meek

CREATIVE DIRECTORS
Ewan Paterson
Jeremy Craigen

CLIENT
Volkswagen

AGENCY
BMP DDB/London

03148A

The tough new Polo

The tough new Polo

MERIT AWARD
Magazine Color
Full Page or Spread: Single

ART DIRECTORS
Feargal Ballance
Dylan Harrison
Jeremy Craigen

WRITERS
Feargal Ballance
Dylan Harrison
Jeremy Craigen

PHOTOGRAPHER
Nick Meek

CREATIVE DIRECTORS
Ewan Paterson
Jeremy Craigen

CLIENT
Volkswagen

AGENCY
BMP DDB/London

03149A

FIVE BILLION STARS DON'T FIT
IN A TWO-SQUARE-FOOT MOON ROOF.

MERIT AWARD
Magazine Color
Full Page or Spread: Single

ART DIRECTOR
Jason Smith

WRITERS
Jim Nelson
Sheldon Clay

PHOTOGRAPHER
Chris Wimpey

CREATIVE DIRECTOR
Jim Nelson

CLIENT
Harley-Davidson

AGENCY
Carmichael Lynch/Minneapolis

03154A

MERIT AWARD
Magazine Color
Full Page or Spread: Single

ART DIRECTORS
Hans Hansen
Jeff Terwilliger

WRITERS
Eric Sorensen
Sheldon Clay

PHOTOGRAPHER
Georg Fischer

CREATIVE DIRECTOR
Jud Smith

CLIENT
Porsche Cars North America

AGENCY
Carmichael Lynch/Minneapolis

03156A

Top down. The open air on your face. A 258-hp mid-mounted engine taking you to your favorite place on the tachometer. Whenever the need for a little spontaneous wandering arises, nothing says you mean it quite like the new Boxster S. Contact us at 1-800-PORSCHE or porsche.com.

If you're going to waste an entire day, waste it with conviction.

MERIT AWARD
Magazine Color
Full Page or Spread: Single

ART DIRECTORS
Hans Hansen
Jeff Terwilliger

WRITERS
Eric Sorensen
Sheldon Clay

PHOTOGRAPHER
Georg Fischer

CREATIVE DIRECTOR
Jud Smith

CLIENT
Porsche Cars North America

AGENCY
Carmichael Lynch/Minneapolis

03157A

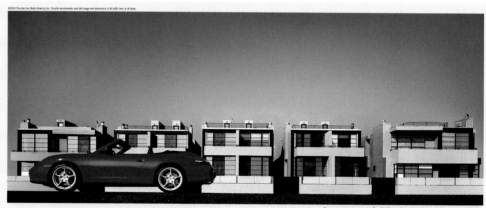

The pressure to compromise. The 911 Carrera Cabriolet is what results from never once yielding to it. The pure shape. The way the sounds and sensations of the drive resonate in the open cockpit. It wasn't, isn't, and never will be for everyone. Contact us at 1-800-PORSCHE or porsche.com.

The demands of the mass market have been noted and ignored.

©2003 Porsche Cars North America, Inc. Porsche recommends seat belt usage and observance of all traffic laws at all times.

Maybe it's the way the flawless shape works on a pair of eyes. Or the time it takes the blood in your veins to cool after a drive. This much is certain. Once experienced, the 911 Carrera will never let you go. Contact us at 1-800-PORSCHE or porsche.com.

**Is it humanly possible to walk away
without looking back?**

MERIT AWARD
**Magazine Color
Full Page or Spread: Single**

ART DIRECTORS
Hans Hansen
Jeff Terwilliger

WRITERS
Sheldon Clay
Eric Sorensen

PHOTOGRAPHER
Georg Fischer

CREATIVE DIRECTOR
Jud Smith

CLIENT
Porsche Cars North America

AGENCY
Carmichael Lynch/Minneapolis

03158A

215

MERIT AWARD
Magazine Color
Full Page or Spread: Single

ART DIRECTOR
Valerie Ang-Powell

WRITERS
Sally Hogshead
Robin Fitzgerald

CREATIVE DIRECTORS
Alex Bogusky
Andrew Keller
Sally Hogshead

CLIENT
MINI

AGENCY
Crispin Porter + Bogusky/Miami

03161A

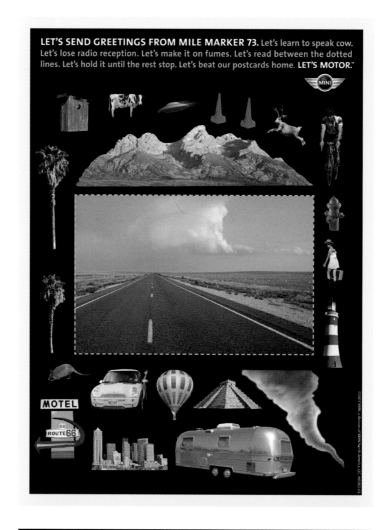

Rio. The most affordable car in America. KIA

MERIT AWARD
Magazine Color
Full Page or Spread: Single

ART DIRECTOR
Will Chau

WRITER
Chuck Meehan

PHOTOGRAPHER
Toby Pederson

CREATIVE DIRECTOR
David Angelo

CLIENT
Kia Motors America

AGENCY
davidandgoliath/Los Angeles

03162A

KILLS BUGS IN PLACES
YOU CAN'T REACH

MERIT AWARD
Magazine Color
Full Page or Spread: Single

ART DIRECTOR
Ko Min Jung

WRITER
Andrew McKechnie

PHOTOGRAPHER
Dali Meskam

CREATIVE DIRECTOR
Robert Gaxiola

CLIENT
Chin Hin

AGENCY
FCB/Singapore

03166A

MERIT AWARD
Magazine Color
Full Page or Spread: Single

ART DIRECTOR
Brett Stiles

WRITER
Chad Berry

PHOTOGRAPHER
Air Force

ILLUSTRATOR
Brett Stiles

CREATIVE DIRECTORS
Daniel Russ
Brian Born

CLIENT
Air Force

AGENCY
GSD&M/Austin

03167A

Also won:
MERIT AWARD
Collateral: Posters
Single

MERIT AWARD
Magazine Color
Full Page or Spread: Single

ART DIRECTOR
Lou Flores

WRITER
Cameron Day

CREATIVE DIRECTORS
Jeremy Postaer
David Crawford

CLIENT
Land Rover of North America

AGENCY
GSD&M/Austin

03168A

MERIT AWARD
Magazine Color
Full Page or Spread: Single

ART DIRECTOR
Nick Lim

WRITER
Yvonne Ho

PHOTOGRAPHERS
Joe Chan
Nick Lim
Eric Tong

ILLUSTRATOR
Joe Chan

CREATIVE DIRECTORS
Nick Lim
Yvonne Ho

CLIENT
Nike Hong Kong

AGENCY
J. Walter Thompson/Hong Kong

03169A

MERIT AWARD
Magazine Color
Full Page or Spread: Single

ART DIRECTORS
Luis Ghidotti
Federico Callegari

WRITERS
Ricky Vior
Matias Ballada

PHOTOGRAPHER
Vladimir Naskoff

CREATIVE DIRECTORS
Joaquín Molla
Jose Molla

CLIENT
Aiwa

AGENCY
la comunidad/Miami Beach

03171A

219

MERIT AWARD
Magazine Color
Full Page or Spread: Single

ART DIRECTOR
Jim Henderson

WRITER
Linda Birkenstock

PHOTOGRAPHERS
Terry Brennan
Tom Connors

CREATIVE DIRECTORS
Tom Kelly
Jim Henderson

CLIENT
L.L. Bean

AGENCY
Martin|Williams/Minneapolis

03178A

MERIT AWARD
Magazine Color
Full Page or Spread: Single

ART DIRECTOR
Michael Ancevic

WRITER
Tim Roper

CREATIVE DIRECTORS
Edward Boches
Michael Ancevic
Tim Roper

CLIENT
Eddie Bauer

AGENCY
Mullen/Wenham

03181A

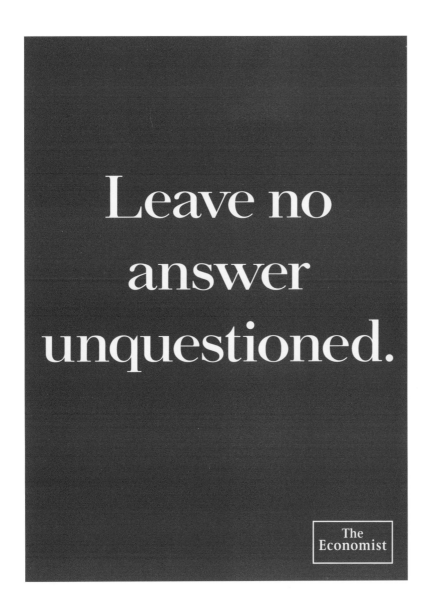

221

PRINT
MERIT

MERIT AWARD
Magazine Color
Full Page or Spread: Single

ART DIRECTOR
Simon William Johnson

WRITER
Jatinder Sandhu

PHOTOGRAPHER
Brendan Fitzpatrick

CREATIVE DIRECTOR
Sion Scott-Wilson

CLIENT
Toyota Motor Asia Pacific

AGENCY
Saatchi & Saatchi/Singapore

03187A

LEXUS
THE RELENTLESS PURSUIT OF PERFECTION

MERIT AWARD
Magazine Color
Full Page or Spread: Single

ART DIRECTOR
Stefan Leick

WRITER
Oliver Handlos

CREATIVE DIRECTORS
Stephan Ganser
Eric Urmetzer

CLIENT
Messerfabrik Victorinox

AGENCY
Scholz & Friends/Berlin

03188A

"Volkswagen Eurovan Camper – the Swiss Army Knife of family vans." • "Mitsubishi 3000 GT – the Swiss Army Knife of sports cars." • "Linux – the Swiss Army Knife of servers." • "Backseat Book. The Swiss Army Knife of books!" • "Bandana hat. The Swiss Army Knife of headwear." • "Samsung YP-700H – the Swiss Army Knife of MP3 Players." • "Mind Maps – the Swiss Army Knife of the brain." • "Fuck: The Swiss Army Knife of American English." • "MAN. The Swiss Army Knife of Advertising Agencies." • "bi.org – the Swiss Army Knife of bisexuality sites." • "BYOT – the Swiss Army Knife of self help books." • "TD GREEN Visa Card is the Swiss Army Knife of credit cards." • "VUL is the Swiss Army Knife of life insurance." • "Motivaider – the Swiss Army Knife of self improvement!" • "Perfect-Tee, the Swiss Army Knife of tees." • "Perl is the Swiss Army Knife of computer languages." • "RedBox – the Swiss Army Knife of all personal organizers." • "Heat Shock Proteins, the Swiss Army Knife of the immune system." • "ARGOS, the Swiss Army Knife of spacecraft." • "The Hummingbird generator is the Swiss Army Knife of generators." • "Scout – the Swiss Army Knife of projectors!" • "Millennium Batteries, the Swiss Army Knife of batteries." • "Cyber Tool, the Swiss Army Knife of PC repairs." • "ProMedia is the Swiss Army Knife of multimedia tools." • "Universal-Lift – the Swiss Army Knife of lifting technology." • "WinPlanet – the Swiss Army Knife of programms." • "Unschooler College, the Swiss Army Knife of education." • "The Nimda Virus is the Swiss Army Knife of malicious worms." • "The Escort is the Swiss Army Knife of transistor radios." • "The Art of War – the Swiss Army Knife of military theory." • "Internet is the Swiss Army Knife of political organizations." • "Mathematics – the Swiss Army Knife of science." • "Lavender is the Swiss Army Knife of herbs." • "Computers – the Swiss Army Knife of the classroom." • "Winner Online – the Swiss Army Knife of online gambling!" • "iPod, the Swiss Army Knife of digital devices." • "Harley-Davidson Softail Tool Kit is the Swiss Army Knife of tool bags." • "The frill of Triceratops is the Swiss Army Knife of dinosaur haberdashery." • "Ubiquitin is the Swiss Army Knife of proteins." • "The Great Facade. The Swiss Army Knife of Roman Catholic Traditionalism." • "BeAbacus – the Swiss Army Knife of Abacuses." • "Special Ministries – the Swiss Army Knife of the Notheast BSU." • "Nokia 7160 is the Swiss Army Knife of cellular phones." • "Benefon Q – the Swiss Army Knife of wireless communication." • "The 22nd Alaska State Legislature Budget Guide, the Swiss Army Knife of Budget Handbooks." • "Envisat – the Swiss Army Knife of space science." • "Enviview – the Swiss Army Knife of Envisat Data." • "Marvel G400 is the Swiss Army Knife of video cards." • "Adobe Acrobat 5, the Swiss Army Knife of knowledge base publishing." • "Radio Userland – the Swiss Army Knife of the Mac." • "EuroVan, the Swiss Army Knife of minivans." • "Cyberboy – the Swiss Army Knife of PDAs." • "The Banjo – the Swiss Army Knife of the darkside." • "The Event Control System (ECS) by Omnipotence Inc., the Swiss Army Knife of home control software." • "The OD 4000 Punch – the Swiss Army Knife of binding." • "Alumidor, the Swiss Army Knife of Cigars." • "X chart – the Swiss Army Knife of control charts." • "Panasonic TU-HDS20 – the Swiss Army Knife of TV tuners." • "netForensics – the Swiss Army Knife of enterprises." • "PowerTools, the Swiss Army Knife of HTML tools!" • "Nepheline Syenite, Table Mountain, Oregon – the Swiss Army Knife of industrial metals." • "3dJam is the Swiss Army Knife of VR animation." • "QuickTime Pro is the Swiss Army Knife of multimedia editing." • "Sony CLIE PEG-NR70V – the Swiss Army Knife of palmtops." • "The SDI – the Swiss Army Knife of training." • "The Float Cat, the Swiss Army Knife of boating." • "Jotter, the Swiss Army Knife of all the different pay-to-surf bars." • "The KLR – the Swiss Army Knife of motorcycles." • "AR-15 – the Swiss Army Knife of rifles." • "Excel – the Swiss Army Knife of the software world." • "Tcl/Tk: The Swiss Army Knife of Web Applications." • "BusyBox – The Swiss Army Knife of Embedded Linux." • "NoteTab Pro. The Swiss Army Knife of Text Editors." • "COMMUNICATE! PRO. The Swiss Army Knife of Programs!" • "Anti-matter – the Swiss Army Knife of evil science." • "KaZaA: the Swiss Army Knife of peer-to-peer agents." • "GoldBox – the Swiss Army Knife of GoldMine Tools!" • "ECM is the Swiss Army Knife of Windows management tools." • "Vypress Messenger is the Swiss Army Knife of instant messaging solutions." • "IPNetMonitorX: The Swiss Army Knife of Mac OS X Diagnostic Tools." • "The Swiss Army Knife of Video Conversion – Canopus ProCoder." • "StarTap is the Swiss Army Knife of Windows CE applications." • "Songs-DB – the Swiss Army Knife of music management software." • "Montana Jack's ATV Accessory Receiver System, the "Swiss Army Knife" of ATV Accessories!" • "The Swiss Army Knife of File Transfer." • "Troutco is the Swiss Army Knife of consulting firms." • "Marware: The Swiss Army Knife of iPod cases." • "QikFix is the Swiss Army Knife of utilities." • "Epson C80 Printer, the "Swiss Army Knife" of printers." • "The Swiss Army Knife of Sprays – the SRS." • "Space-Time Portal is the Swiss Army Knife of the STCCG world!" • "GlomaP-Z "The Swiss Army Knife of Field and Desktop Mapping Systems." • "PurgeIE is the Swiss Army Knife of Cache and Cookie Utilities." • "TW Pro is the Swiss Army Knife of Windows Desktop Management Utilities." • "C-PAS: The Swiss Army Knife of Recruiting." • "Oracle 9i: The Swiss Army Knife of databases." • "XML the Swiss Army Knife of the next generation Web." • "The CD-RW is the Swiss Army Knife of computer drives." • "Molto is the Swiss Army Knife of binary analyzers." • "CX Online the Swiss Army Knife of career education resources." • "The DX Notebook – the Swiss Army Knife of DX Sites." • "Microsoft's Excel. The Swiss Army Knife of business." • "PDF is the Swiss Army Knife of file formats." • "Crystal Reports 5.0 the Swiss Army Knife of client/server reporting tools." • "K7T Turbo is the Swiss Army Knife of mainboards." • "Snard is the Swiss Army Knife of launcher programs." • "The cohort study is the Swiss army Knife of epidemiologic designs." • "Lieberman's book is the "Swiss Army Knife" of Lie Detection Techniques." • "Altiris Vision is the Swiss Army Knife of teaching tools." • "WebInterlock is the Swiss Army Knife of Web design creation!" • "Photoshop, the Swiss Army Knife of graphics editing tools." • "Anthem AVM-20, the Swiss Army Knife of processors." • "Sage is the Swiss Army Knife of Blunt" • "Chris Harris is the Swiss Army Knife of our facilitation team." • "Groove 2.0, the Swiss Army Knife of online multimedia software." • "SCANDLES 200, the Swiss Army Knife of Fluorescent Instruments." • "GMC Snow Gloves – The Swiss Army Knife of gloves." • "Powerflash, the Swiss Army Knife of your X-10 based home automation system." • "The Swiss Army Knife of classroom learning – the TI-83 Plus Silver Edition!" • "Norton's SystemWorks is the Swiss Army Knife of utility packages." • "The new AH7B – the Swiss Army Knife of airborne weapon systems." • "SmartDraw 6: The Swiss Army Knife of Business Diagramming Software." • "EMACS – the Swiss Army Knife of editors." • "KT133A – the Swiss Army Knife of AMD chipsets." • "RPM is the Swiss Army Knife of the package manager world." • "Media Cleaner, the Swiss Army Knife of multimedia production." • "Shake, the Swiss Army Knife of HD compositing." • "The Nokia 9000 is the Swiss Army Knife of intelligent Communicators." • "Protopipe Deluxe – the Swiss Army Knife of pipes." • "Enterprise Suite 5.0 is the Swiss Army Knife of eBusiness Management solutions." • "iView, the Swiss Army Knife of image organizers." • "Anbarasan is the Swiss Army Knife of the team." • "ToolVox, the Swiss Army Knife of mic processors." • "tprof: The Swiss Army Knife of AIX performance monitoring." • "The Swiss Army Knife of aromatic oils – Lavender Mailette!" • "dsniff is the Swiss Army Knife of privacy invasion." • "lsof – the Swiss Army Knife of intrusion detection." • "Sample Search, the Swiss Army Knife of file conversions." • "Milk crates – the Swiss Army Knife of furnishing." • "DeBabelizer – the Swiss Army Knife of graphics." • "iMovie: The Swiss Army Knife of Digital Video Software." • "The LCC – the Swiss Army Knife of camera remote controllers." • "Leapfrog simulations are the Swiss Army Knife of team building experiences!" • "The Nokia 9290 Communicator is the Swiss Army Knife of gadgets." • "PHP is the Swiss Army Knife of Web tools." • "The MS1202-VLZ, the Swiss Army Knife of compact mixers." • "XML – the Swiss Army Knife of object models." • "Saw-Aid – the Swiss Army Knife of woodworking." • "The LHC is the Swiss Army Knife of particle accelerators." • "Access Virus. The Swiss Army Knife of synthesizers." • "BGBlitz is the Swiss Army Knife of backgammon programs." • "The Qbox is the Swiss Army Knife of test gear." • "Paint Shop Pro 6 is the Swiss Army Knife of digital imaging." • "PentaZip is the Swiss Army Knife of compression software." • "Ulead PhotoImpact 7 is the Swiss Army Knife of image editing packages." • "Quick Assistant is the Swiss Army Knife of marketing tools." • "Forkchops, the Swiss Army Knife of flatware!" • "Cisco 3600 series – the Swiss Army Knife of remote access solutions." • "SiSoft Sandra is the Swiss Army Knife of benchmark programs." • "Explorer Pro 6, the Swiss Army Knife of primary lights." • "Desert Twister – The Swiss Army Knife of green cards." • "CAR is the Swiss Army Knife of traffic shaping." • "Veracity is the Swiss Army Knife of data integrity!" • "Laplink is the Swiss Army Knife of file transfer." • "Genius is clearly the Swiss Army Knife of computer software." • "The X-iser Machine is the Swiss Army Knife of exercise equipment." • "The Problem Buster's Guide – The Swiss Army Knife of problem solving." • "Network ServaNT is the Swiss Army Knife of the NT/2000 administrator!" • "IEHMAP is the Swiss Army Knife of DASD mapping utilities." • "Pontiac Aztek: The Swiss Army Knife of SRVs." • "DTS is the Swiss Army Knife of ETL tools." • "QuickTime is the Swiss Army Knife of the Internet." • "Spike, the Swiss Army Knife of Fuzzers!!" • "Calculait – the Swiss Army Knife of calculators." • "Microsoft BizTalk is the Swiss Army Knife of the business world when it comes to data." • "InCharge is the Swiss Army Knife of accounting programs." • "Schiratti Control Centre is the Swiss Army Knife of flight simulator add-on's!" • "Mathcad – The Swiss Army Knife of math software." • "Library of Congress – the Swiss Army Knife of magic cards." • "Stuffit is the Swiss Army Knife of decompressors." • "DiskJockey is the Swiss Army Knife of file managers." • "Chronos Personal Organizer is the Swiss Army Knife of productivity software." • "ToolVox the Swiss Army Knife of mic processors." • "VideoFlex video camera – The Swiss Army Knife of video presentation technology!" • "SURWEB – the Swiss Army Knife of Internet-based educational applications." • "Group Organizer is the Swiss Army Knife of workgroup productivity software." • "Unrealed is the Swiss Army Knife of UT development." • "Cleaner 5 is truly the Swiss Army Knife of video compression utilities." • "DISPLAY, alias DISP, the Swiss Army Knife of DOS viewers!" • "Java is the Swiss Army Knife of languages and environments." • "The Jeep TV Lantern is the Swiss Army Knife of gadgets." • "SysCmd method is the Swiss Army Knife of access methods." • "Corel Draw is the Swiss Army Knife of graphics programs." • "Power Drawers is the Swiss Army Knife of shell extensions." • "Olympus IS-3 DLX – the Swiss Army Knife of cameras." • "Bicycling is the Swiss Army Knife of biking publications." • "Mackie MS1202-VLZ, the Swiss Army Knife of compact mixers." • "Guitar Studio – The Swiss Army Knife of guitar loops and performances." • "The Quiet Time: The Swiss Army Knife of Spiritual Disciplines." • "Barware – the Swiss Army Knife of bartending." • "Talk Switch – The Swiss Army Knife of Phone Systems." • "Dilantin, the Swiss Army Knife of drugs." • "The S-3B Viking is the Swiss Army Knife of Naval Aviation." • "The handaxe is the Swiss Army Knife of the Paleolithic Period." • "BC Adventure Harvest Moose Cap – the Swiss Army Knife of Outdoor Caps." • "Kodak's MC3 – the Swiss Army Knife of electronic gadgets." • "Jack Black Face Buff Energizing Scrub – the Swiss Army Knife of pre-shave lotions." • "Coleman's new RoadTrip Grill – the Swiss Army Knife of portable grills." • "Henry Garfath, the Swiss Army Knife of Traditional and Western Dance." • "Bess is the Swiss Army Knife of the team!" • "The Bible – the Swiss Army Knife of life."*
Always useful.
VICTORINOX
*Einige Beispiele aus mehr als 12.000 gefundenen Werbezitaten.

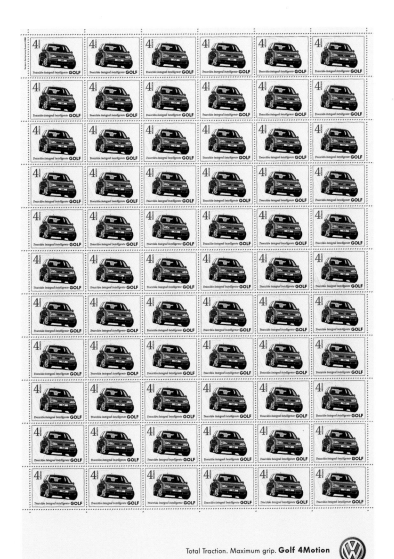

MERIT AWARD
Magazine Color
Full Page or Spread: Single

ART DIRECTOR
Hayden Pasco

WRITER
John Robertson

PHOTOGRAPHER
Robert Whitman

CREATIVE DIRECTORS
John Vitro
John Robertson

CLIENT
Taylor Guitars

AGENCY
vitrorobertson/San Diego

03191A

NOMINATED IN THE CATEGORY OF "BEST NEW ARTIST
WHO'LL NEVER PLAY FOR ANYBODY EXCEPT HER DOG".

WWW.TAYLORGUITARS.COM

MERIT AWARD
Magazine Color
Full Page or Spread: Single

ART DIRECTOR
Hayden Pasco

WRITER
John Robertson

PHOTOGRAPHER
Robert Whitman

CREATIVE DIRECTORS
John Vitro
John Robertson

CLIENT
Taylor Guitars

AGENCY
vitrorobertson/San Diego

03192A

YOU'RE RIGHT, YOU'RE PROBABLY TOO LATE TO GET INTO THE ROCK
AND ROLL HALL OF FAME. BUT YOU'RE NEVER TOO LATE TO GIVE THE
WORLD ANOTHER COVER VERSION OF "SMOKE ON THE WATER".

WWW.TAYLORGUITARS.COM

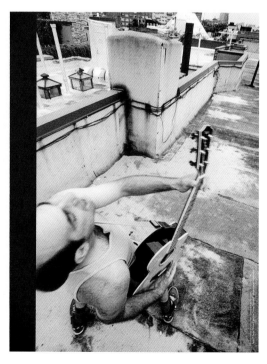

I COULD COME HOME AND DRINK AFTER A STRESSFUL DAY, INSTEAD
OF PLAYING GUITAR. BUT THEN MY WIFE WOULD NEVER COMPLIMENT
ME ON HOW MUCH MY DRINKING HAS IMPROVED.

WWW.TAYLORGUITARS.COM

MERIT AWARD
Magazine Color
Full Page or Spread: Single

ART DIRECTOR
Hayden Pasco

WRITER
John Robertson

PHOTOGRAPHER
Robert Whitman

CREATIVE DIRECTORS
John Vitro
John Robertson

CLIENT
Taylor Guitars

AGENCY
vitrorobertson/San Diego

03193A

WITHOUT SPORTS, THERE'D ONLY BE GUM

LEROY "Satchell" PAIGE

ESPN

MERIT AWARD
Magazine Color
Full Page or Spread: Single

ART DIRECTOR
Kim Schoen

WRITER
Kevin Proudfoot

CREATIVE DIRECTORS
Ty Montague
Todd Waterbury

CLIENT
ESPN

AGENCY
Wieden + Kennedy/New York

03194A

225

MERIT AWARD
Magazine Color
Full Page or Spread: Single

ART DIRECTOR
Jon Wyville

WRITER
Dave Loew

PHOTOGRAPHER
Dave Emmite

CREATIVE DIRECTORS
Jon Wyville
Dave Loew

CLIENT
NASCAR

AGENCY
Young & Rubicam/Chicago

03197A

Suddenly, a souvenir ball seems kind of lame.

MERIT AWARD
Magazine Color
Full Page or Spread: Single

ART DIRECTOR
Jon Wyville

WRITER
Dave Loew

PHOTOGRAPHER
Dave Emmite

CREATIVE DIRECTORS
Jon Wyville
Dave Loew

CLIENT
Susan Fitch

AGENCY
Young & Rubicam/Chicago

03198A

If found please return to...
oh, who am I kidding?

susan fitch

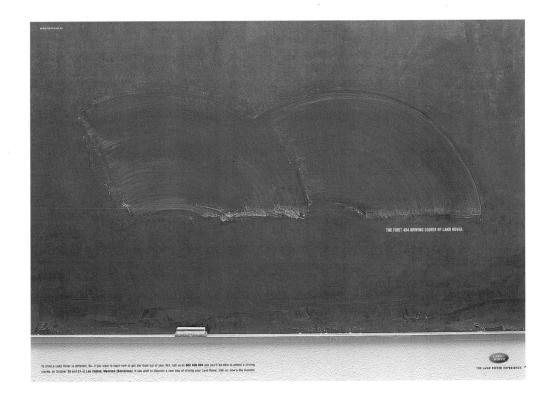

MERIT AWARD
Magazine Color
Full Page or Spread: Campaign

ART DIRECTOR
Paul Crawford

WRITER
Deb Maltzman

PHOTOGRAPHERS
Michael Schnabel
Stock

AGENCY PRODUCERS
Pam Noon
Amy Firth

CREATIVE DIRECTORS
Wendy Beckett
Bob Fitzgerald

CLIENT
Royal Caribbean

AGENCY
Arnold Worldwide/Boston

03199A

Also won:
MERIT AWARDS
Magazine Color
Full Page or Spread: Single

Collateral: Posters
Single

MERIT

MERIT AWARD
Magazine Color
Full Page or Spread: Campaign

ART DIRECTOR
Kevin Dailor

WRITER
Rob Thompson

PHOTOGRAPHER
Shawn Michienzi

AGENCY PRODUCERS
Stephanie Kailer
Karen Bronnenkant

CREATIVE DIRECTOR
Alan Pafenbach

CLIENT
Volkswagen of America

AGENCY
Arnold Worldwide/Boston

03200A

MERIT AWARD
Magazine Color
Full Page or Spread: Campaign

ART DIRECTORS
Alex Lim Thye Aun
Marthinus Strydom

WRITERS
Marthinus Strydom
Alex Lim Thye Aun

PHOTOGRAPHER
Nadav Kander

CREATIVE DIRECTOR
Steve Elrick

CLIENT
Levi Strauss Asia Pacific

AGENCY
Bartle Bogle Hegarty Asia Pacific/
Singapore

03201A

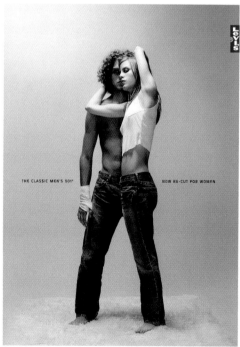

MERIT AWARD
Magazine Color
Full Page or Spread: Campaign

ART DIRECTOR
Dave Stanton

WRITER
Carlos Ricque

PHOTOGRAPHER
Richard Hamilton Smith

CREATIVE DIRECTOR
Jim Noble

CLIENT
Panama Tourism

AGENCY
BBDO/Atlanta

03202A

231

MERIT AWARD
Magazine Color
Full Page or Spread: Campaign

ART DIRECTOR
Rémy Tricot

WRITER
Olivier Couradjut

PHOTOGRAPHER
Oliver Rheindorf

AGENCY PRODUCER
Sylvie Etchemaïté

CREATIVE DIRECTOR
Olivier Altmann

CLIENT
BMW

AGENCY
BDDP et Fils/Boulogne

03203A

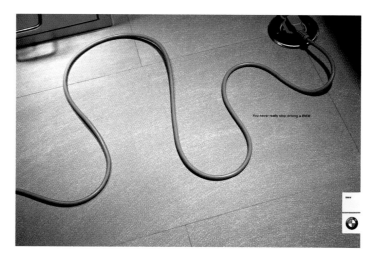

MERIT AWARD
Magazine Color
Full Page or Spread: Campaign

ART DIRECTOR
Justin Tindall

WRITER
Adam Tucker

PHOTOGRAPHER
David Gill

CREATIVE DIRECTORS
Ewan Paterson
Rob Jack

CLIENT
Lurpak

AGENCY
BMP DDB/London

03204A

233

MERIT AWARD
Magazine Color
Full Page or Spread: Campaign

ART DIRECTOR
Jason Smith

WRITERS
Sheldon Clay
Jim Nelson
Dan Roettger

PHOTOGRAPHER
Chris Wimpey

CREATIVE DIRECTOR
Jim Nelson

CLIENT
Harley-Davidson

AGENCY
Carmichael Lynch/Minneapolis

03205A

Also won:
MERIT AWARDS
Magazine Color
Full Page or Spread: Single

IF LEWIS HAD NOT MET CLARK.
IF CHURCHILL HAD NOT MET ROOSEVELT.
IF HARLEY HAD NOT MET DAVIDSON.

MERIT

THE ROAD IS ETERNAL. THE WIND IS CONSTANT.
WHAT ELSE COMES WITH A GUARANTEE LIKE THAT?

MERIT

BREATHING IS AUTOMATIC.
LIVING TAKES SOME EFFORT.

MERIT

MERIT

MERIT AWARD
Magazine Color
Full Page or Spread: Campaign

ART DIRECTORS
Martín Cacios
Marcela Augustowsky
Toto Marelli
Mercedes Tiagonce
Javier Lourenco

WRITERS
Hernán Curubeto
Martín Juárez
Roberto Leston

PHOTOGRAPHERS
Jorge Revsin
Charly Mainardi

CREATIVE DIRECTORS
Juan Cravero
Darío Lanis
Hernán Curubeto

CLIENT
Peugeot

AGENCY
CraveroLanis Euro RSCG/
Buenos Aires

03206A

Also won:
MERIT AWARDS
Magazine Color
Full Page or Spread: Single

MERIT AWARD
Magazine Color
Full Page or Spread: Campaign

ART DIRECTOR
Dave Swartz

WRITERS
Roger Hoard
Bob Cianfrone

PHOTOGRAPHERS
David Harriman
Rick Whittey

CREATIVE DIRECTORS
Alex Bogusky
Paul Keister

CLIENT
IKEA

AGENCY
Crispin Porter + Bogusky/Miami

03207A

The $99 KLITTEN chair, helping uproot the notion that wobbly, uncomfortable furniture is your lot in life. Visit unboring.com. **IKEA** unböring

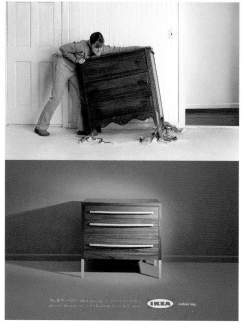

MERIT AWARD
Magazine Color
Full Page or Spread: Campaign

ART DIRECTOR
Will Chau

WRITER
Chuck Meehan

PHOTOGRAPHER
Toby Pederson

CREATIVE DIRECTOR
David Angelo

CLIENT
Kia Motors America

AGENCY
davidandgoliath/Los Angeles

03208A

WHEN YOU ALREADY HAVE LOW PRICES, YOU DON'T HAVE TO SCREAM. KIA'S SIMPLY A GOOD DEAL SALES EVENT. NOW THROUGH JANUARY 31ST.

WHEN YOU ALREADY HAVE LOW PRICES, YOU DON'T HAVE TO SCREAM. KIA'S SIMPLY A GOOD DEAL SALES EVENT. NOW THROUGH JANUARY 31ST.

WHEN YOU ALREADY HAVE LOW PRICES, YOU DON'T HAVE TO SCREAM. KIA'S SIMPLY A GOOD DEAL SALES EVENT. NOW THROUGH JANUARY 31ST.

MERIT AWARD
Magazine Color
Full Page or Spread: Campaign

ART DIRECTOR
David O'Sullivan

WRITER
Michael Lee

PHOTOGRAPHER
Julian Wolkenstein

PRODUCTION COMPANY
Look Australia

CREATIVE DIRECTOR
Garry Horner

CLIENT
Wrigleys

AGENCY
DDB/Sydney

03209A

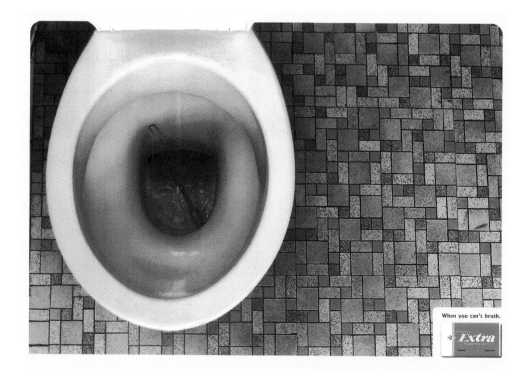

MERIT

MERIT

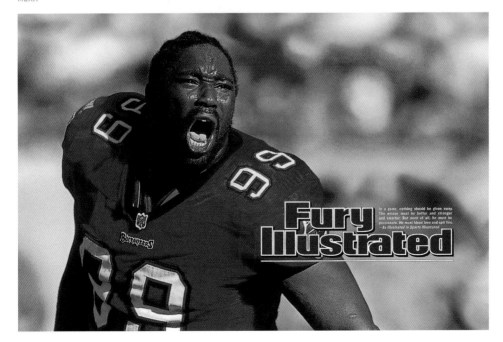

MERIT AWARD
Magazine Color
Full Page or Spread: Campaign

ART DIRECTOR
Ellen Steinberg

WRITER
Kevin Roddy

PHOTOGRAPHERS
Bill Frakes
Jacqueline Dovoisin
John W. McDonough

AGENCY PRODUCER
Louise Raicht

CREATIVE DIRECTORS
David Lubars
Kevin Roddy

CLIENT
Sports Illustrated

AGENCY
Fallon/New York

03210A

Also won:
MERIT AWARDS
Magazine Color
Full Page or Spread: Single

MERIT AWARD
**Magazine Color
Full Page or Spread: Campaign**

ART DIRECTOR
Corinna Falusi

WRITER
Thorsten Meier

PHOTOGRAPHER
Jan Willem Scholten

CREATIVE DIRECTORS
Alexander Bartel
Martin Kiessling

CLIENT
ELLE Verlag

AGENCY
Heye & Partner/Munich

03212A

MERIT AWARD
Magazine Color
Full Page or Spread: Campaign

ART DIRECTORS
Julia Meyran
Oliver Oelkers

WRITERS
Alexandra Weczerek
Tobias Holland

PHOTOGRAPHERS
Daniel M. Hartz
Oliver Rheindorf
Michaela Rehn

CREATIVE DIRECTORS
Oliver Voss
Deneke von Weltzien
Goetz Ulmer
Thomas Wildberger

CLIENT
BMW AG/MINI

AGENCY
Jung von Matt/Hamburg

03213A

241

MERIT AWARD
Magazine Color
Full Page or Spread: Campaign

ART DIRECTOR
Mo Whiteman

WRITER
Jana Liebig

PHOTOGRAPHER
Olaf Blecker

CREATIVE DIRECTORS
Hermann Waterkamp
Stefan Zschaler

CLIENT
Gruner + Jahr AG & Co./stern

AGENCY
Leagas Delaney/Hamburg

03214A

Also won:
MERIT AWARD
Newspaper Over 600 Lines
Single

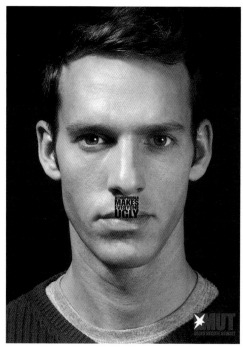

MERIT

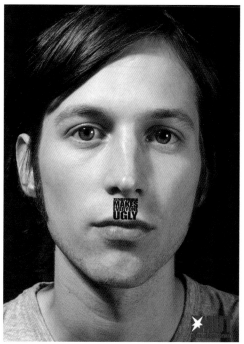

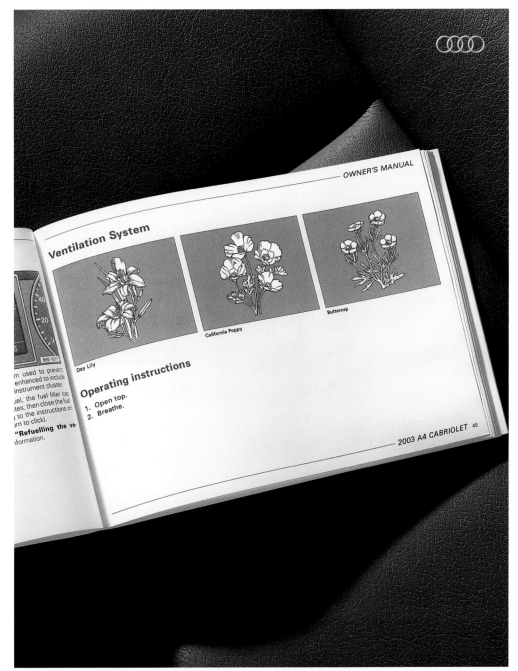

MERIT

MERIT AWARD
Magazine Color
Full Page or Spread: Campaign

ART DIRECTORS
Bob Ranew
Tony Simmons

WRITER
Lara Bridger

PHOTOGRAPHER
Michael Lewis

ILLUSTRATOR
Jim Brown

AGENCY PRODUCER
Joann Brown

CREATIVE DIRECTOR
David Baldwin

CLIENT
Audi of America

AGENCY
McKinney & Silver/Raleigh

03216A

Also won:
MERIT AWARDS
Magazine Color
Full Page or Spread: Single

MERIT

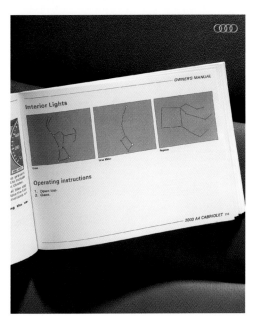

243

MERIT AWARD
Magazine Color
Full Page or Spread: Campaign

ART DIRECTOR
Will Uronis

WRITER
Shane Hutton

PHOTOGRAPHER
Tim Simmons

CREATIVE DIRECTORS
Lance Jensen
Gary Koepke

CLIENT
Hummer H2

AGENCY
Modernista!/Boston

03217A

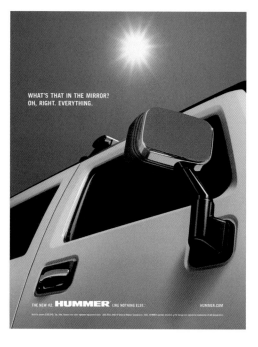

MERIT AWARD
Magazine Color
Full Page or Spread: Campaign

ART DIRECTORS
Keith Manning
Ariel Broggi

WRITERS
Ariel Broggi
Keith Manning

PHOTOGRAPHER
William Huber

CREATIVE DIRECTORS
Brian Gross
Alec Beckett

CLIENT
Atomic Ski USA

AGENCY
nail/Providence

03218A

245

MERIT AWARD
**Magazine Color
Full Page or Spread: Campaign**

ART DIRECTOR
Marcio Ribas

WRITER
Marcio Ribas

PHOTOGRAPHER
Stock

CREATIVE DIRECTOR
Alexandre Gama

CLIENT
Mitsubishi

AGENCY
NEOGAMA/BBH/São Paulo

03219A

MERIT AWARD
Magazine Color
Full Page or Spread: Campaign

ART DIRECTORS
Minh Khai Doan
Helmut Himmler

WRITER
Lars Huvart

PHOTOGRAPHER
Thomas Balzer

CREATIVE DIRECTORS
Helmut Himmler
Lars Huvart

CLIENT
American Express Germany

AGENCY
Ogilvy & Mather/Frankfurt

03221A

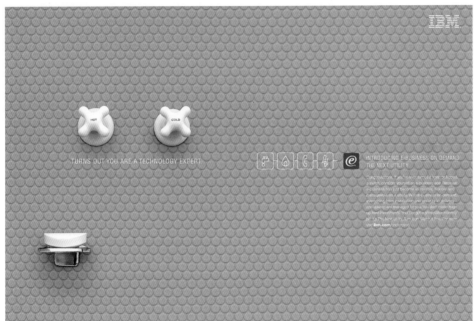

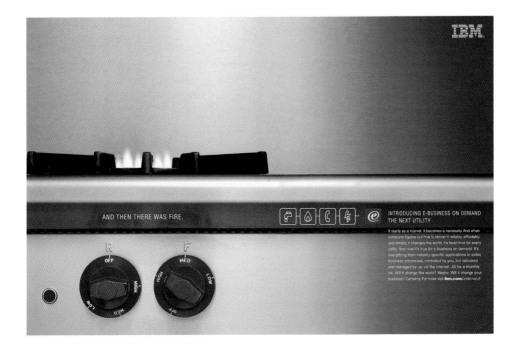

MERIT AWARD
Magazine Color
Full Page or Spread: Campaign

ART DIRECTORS
Mark Graham
Mitchell Ratchik

WRITERS
Richard Ryan
Lisa Topol

PHOTOGRAPHER
Todd Eberle

CREATIVE DIRECTORS
Chris Wall
Andy Berndt
John McNeil

CLIENT
IBM

AGENCY
Ogilvy & Mather/New York

03222A

249

MERIT AWARD
Magazine Color
Full Page or Spread: Campaign

ART DIRECTORS
Richard Johnson
Steve Hough

WRITERS
Steve Hough
Richard Johnson

PHOTOGRAPHER
Jimmy Fok

ILLUSTRATOR
Procolor

CREATIVE DIRECTOR
Craig Smith

CLIENT
Spade Magazine

AGENCY
Ogilvy & Mather/Singapore

03223A

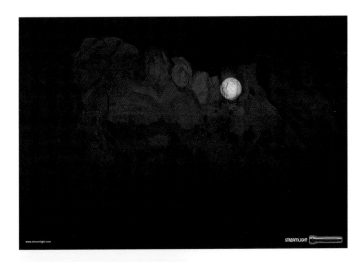

MERIT AWARD
Magazine Color
Full Page or Spread: Campaign

ART DIRECTOR
Kumphol Witpiboolrut

WRITERS
Panusard Tanashindawong
Jureeporn Thaidumrong

PHOTOGRAPHER
Fahdol na Nagara

PRODUCTION COMPANY
Studio de Nagara

CREATIVE DIRECTOR
Jureeporn Thaidumrong

CLIENT
Indosport

AGENCY
Saatchi & Saatchi/Bangkok

03224A

251

MERIT AWARD
Magazine Color
Full Page or Spread: Campaign

ART DIRECTOR
Heiko Schmidt

WRITER
Helen Kötter

PHOTOGRAPHER
Jan Steinhilber

CREATIVE DIRECTORS
Arno Lindemann
Stefan Meske

CLIENT
Dirk Rossmann GmbH

AGENCY
Springer & Jacoby/Hamburg

03225A

MERIT AWARD
Magazine Color
Full Page or Spread: Campaign

ART DIRECTOR
Justus von Engelhardt

WRITER
Florian Kähler

PHOTOGRAPHER
Iver Hansen

AGENCY PRODUCER
Mini Kotzan

CREATIVE DIRECTORS
Alexander Schill
Axel Thomsen

CLIENT
Mercedes-Benz

AGENCY
Springer & Jacoby/Hamburg

03226A

PRINT
MERIT

MERIT AWARD
Magazine Color
Full Page or Spread: Campaign

ART DIRECTOR
Louise Salas

WRITER
Jay Cranford

PHOTOGRAPHER
Wesley Hitt

CREATIVE DIRECTORS
Jay Cranford
Larry Stone

CLIENT
Arkansas Nature Conservancy

AGENCY
Stone Ward/Little Rock

03227A

Coming Soon

Nothing. That way, the bald eagle, the river otter, the bluehead shiner fish, and hundreds of other rare plant and animal species will always live here. Today. And tomorrow. And forever. Together, we're saving the last great places.

The Nature Conservancy. ARKANSAS FIELD OFFICE

Future Home

Of nesting grasshopper sparrows. And sunflowers. And Indian paintbrush. In fact, hundreds of rare plant and animal species live here. And with our help, it will always be that way. Together, we're saving the last great places.

The Nature Conservancy. ARKANSAS FIELD OFFICE

Pine Ridge Mall

Will never be built here. So this can remain the home of hundreds of rare plant and animal species. Like the red-shouldered hawk and the royal fern. Today. And a hundred years from today. Together, we're saving the last great places.

The Nature Conservancy. ARKANSAS FIELD OFFICE

MERIT AWARD
Magazine Color
Full Page or Spread: Campaign

ART DIRECTOR
Kim Schoen

WRITER
Kevin Proudfoot

PHOTOGRAPHERS
Collier Schorr
Dana Lixenburg

ILLUSTRATOR
Deanna Cheuk

CREATIVE DIRECTORS
Ty Montague
Todd Waterbury

CLIENT
ESPN

AGENCY
Wieden + Kennedy/New York

03228A

255

MERIT AWARD
Magazine Color
Full Page or Spread: Campaign

ART DIRECTOR
Andy Fackrell

WRITER
Jonathan Cude

PHOTOGRAPHER
Jake Chessum

CREATIVE DIRECTORS
Hal Curtis
Carlos Bayala

CLIENT
Nike

AGENCY
Wieden + Kennedy/Portland

03229A

MERIT AWARD
Outdoor: Single

ART DIRECTOR
Ralph Watson

WRITER
Ken Marcus

ILLUSTRATOR
Evan Hecox

CREATIVE DIRECTORS
Rick Condos
Ralph Watson
Marty Weiss

CLIENT
The Economist

AGENCY
Brand Architecture International/
New York

03232A

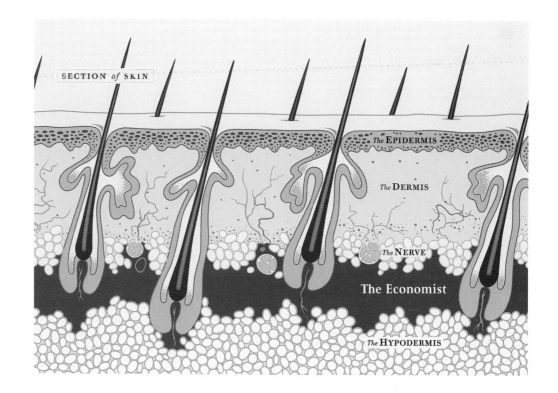

MERIT AWARD
Outdoor: Single

ART DIRECTORS
Martan
Marcela Maezono

WRITERS
Zuza Tupinambá
Luiz Musa

PHOTOGRAPHER
Hilton Ribeiro

AGENCY PRODUCERS
Claudio Dirani
Glória Afonso

CREATIVE DIRECTOR
Zuza Tupinambá

CLIENT
Citroën

AGENCY
Duezt Euro RSCG/São Paulo

03236A

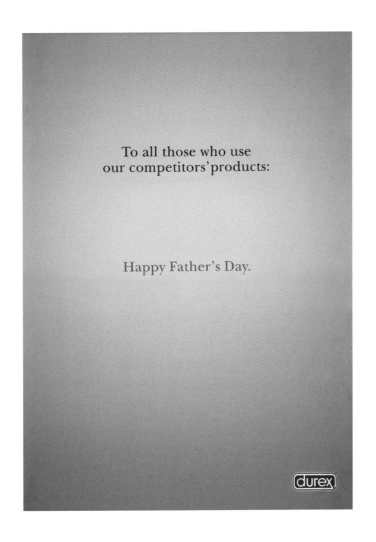

To all those who use
our competitors' products:

Happy Father's Day.

durex

MERIT AWARD
Outdoor: Single

ART DIRECTORS
Craig Smith
Michael Shackle

WRITERS
Craig Smith
Michael Shackle

PHOTOGRAPHER
Jonathan Tay

ILLUSTRATOR
Procolor

CREATIVE DIRECTORS
Andy Greenaway
Craig Smith

CLIENT
KFC

AGENCY
Ogilvy & Mather/Singapore

03239A

MERIT AWARD
Outdoor: Single

ART DIRECTOR
Sören Porst

WRITER
Türker Süer

PHOTOGRAPHERS
Andreas Burz
Stefan Reeh

CREATIVE DIRECTORS
Florian Grimm
Antje Hedde

CLIENT
DaimlerChrysler VD

AGENCY
Springer & Jacoby/Hamburg

03241A

This ad was placed on rotating advertising columns to show the effect of the smallest turning circle.

The Economist

Think outside the dodecahedron.

The Economist

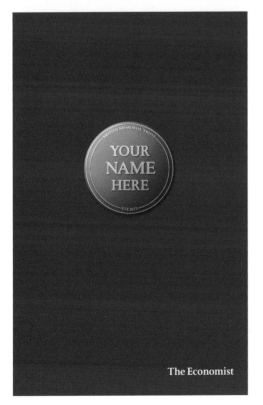

YOUR
NAME
HERE

The Economist

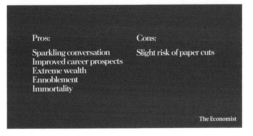

Pros:

Sparkling conversation
Improved career prospects
Extreme wealth
Ennoblement
Immortality

Cons:

Slight risk of paper cuts

The Economist

MERIT AWARD
Outdoor: Campaign

ART DIRECTORS
Mark Elwood
David May
Cameron Blackley
Paul Young
Andy McKay
Paul Brazier

WRITERS
Jeremy Carr
Chris Bardsley
Ben Kay
Tim Riley
Peter Souter

ILLUSTRATORS
Solid
Paul Barlow
A3 Studios Ltd.

CREATIVE DIRECTOR
Peter Souter

CLIENT
The Economist

AGENCY
Abbott Mead Vickers.BBDO/
London

03243A

MERIT AWARD
Outdoor: Campaign

ART DIRECTORS
Mark Taylor
Alex Burnard

WRITERS
Ari Merkin
Steve O'Connell
Brian Tierney

PHOTOGRAPHER
Daniel Hartz

CREATIVE DIRECTORS
Alex Bogusky
Andrew Keller

CLIENT
MINI

AGENCY
Crispin Porter + Bogusky/Miami

03244A

LET'S GO PARK.
Let's find a drive-in movie theater. Let's make out in the back seat. Let's make out in the front seat. Let's sit in the driveway. Let's take the keys out of the ignition. Let's rest heads on headrests.
LET'S MOTOR.™

LET'S MESS WITH PERFECTION.
Let's window-sticker. Let's bumper-sticker. Let's stripe. Let's chrome. Let's fuzzy-dice. Let's graduation-tassel. Let's dashboard-hula-girl. Let's do nothing. Let's do whatever.
LET'S MOTOR.™

LET'S MASTER THE ASPHALT ARTS.
Let's hug the corner. Let's kiss the corner. Heck, let's marry the corner. Let's clip an apex. Let's make graceful lane changes. Let's create our own techniques. Let's teach them unto others. **LET'S MOTOR.™**

LET'S JUMP IN THROUGH THE WINDOW.
Let's slide across the hood. Let's Bo and Luke-it. Let's Daisy Duke-it. Let's install the loudest Dixie horn in all of Hazzard County. But seriously folks, let's keep them wheels on the ground. **LET'S MOTOR.™**

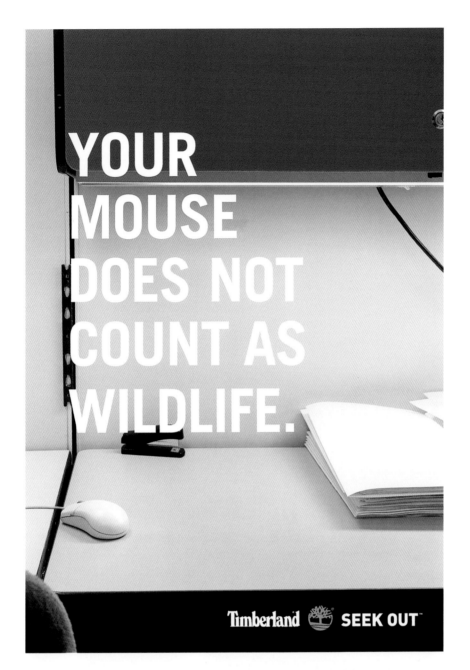

YOUR MOUSE DOES NOT COUNT AS WILDLIFE.

Timberland 🌲 SEEK OUT™

MERIT AWARD
Outdoor: Campaign

ART DIRECTOR
David Damman

WRITER
Greg Hahn

PHOTOGRAPHER
David Harriman

AGENCY PRODUCER
Louise Raicht

CREATIVE DIRECTORS
David Lubars
Kevin Roddy

CLIENT
Timberland

AGENCY
Fallon/New York

03246A

EXIT

THIS IS NOT A SIGN. IT IS A CALLING.

Timberland 🌲 SEEK OUT

BEWARE OF INTERIOR DECORATORS.

Timberland SEEK OUT

MERIT AWARD
Guerilla Advertising: Single

ART DIRECTOR
Philip Ireland

WRITER
John Davenport

PHOTOGRAPHER
Lambro

AGENCY PRODUCER
Clinton Mitri

CREATIVE DIRECTOR
Mike Schalit

CLIENT
Virgin Atlantic

AGENCY
Net#work BBDO/Johannesburg

03248A

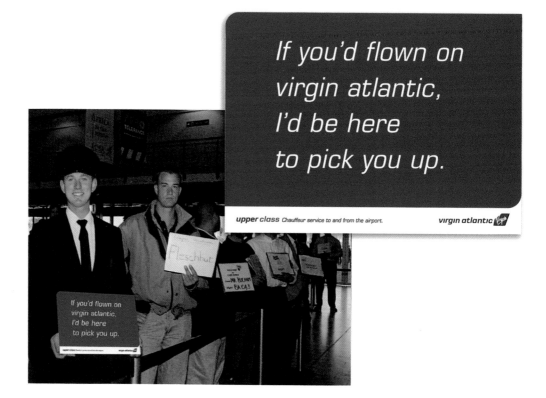

MERIT AWARD
Guerilla Advertising: Single

ART DIRECTOR
Alexander Heil

WRITER
Cora Walker

CLIENT
Ford Germany

AGENCY
Ogilvy & Mather/Frankfurt

03249A

In night club car parks, an additional door lock was stuck next to the existing one to make it difficult for people who have had too much to drink to get into their car, reminding them that their judgement is impaired after consuming alcohol.

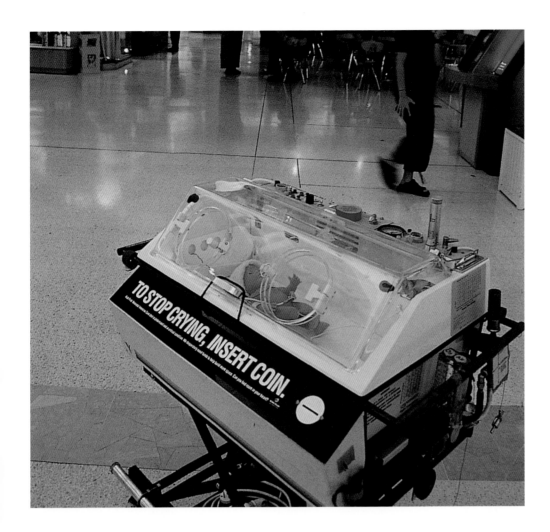

MERIT AWARD
Guerilla Advertising: Single

ART DIRECTORS
Basil Christensen
Damon O'Leary
Andrew Tinning
Andy Blood
Andy Lish
Young Rok Kim
Maxine Pattinson

WRITERS
Basil Christensen
Damon O'Leary
Andrew Tinning
Andy Blood
Andy Lish
Young Rok Kim
Maxine Pattinson

PHOTOGRAPHER
Peter Vahry

CREATIVE DIRECTOR
Andrew Tinning

CLIENT
South Auckland Health
Foundation

AGENCY
Saatchi & Saatchi/Auckland

03250A

At snack vending machines, cards can be purchased as donations to St Mungo's, the largest charity in London for the homeless.

MERIT AWARD
Guerilla Advertising: Single

ART DIRECTORS
Guy Bradbury
Eoghain Clarke

WRITERS
Eoghain Clarke
Guy Bradbury

CREATIVE DIRECTOR
Trefor Thomas

CLIENT
St Mungo's

AGENCY
Saatchi & Saatchi/London

03251A

Also won:
MERIT AWARD
Innovative Marketing

MERIT AWARD
Guerilla Advertising: Single

ART DIRECTOR
Shaun Bond

WRITER
George Low

PHOTOGRAPHER
Clive Stewart

PRODUCTION COMPANY
Beith Digital

CREATIVE DIRECTORS
Paul Warner
Cathy Thomson

CLIENT
Gary Player Country Club

AGENCY
TBWA Hunt Lascaris/
Johannesburg

03252A

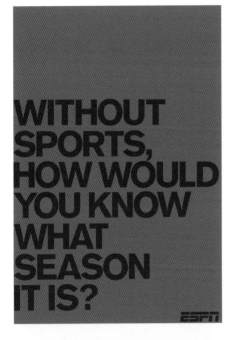

WITHOUT SPORTS, HOW WOULD YOU KNOW WHAT SEASON IT IS?

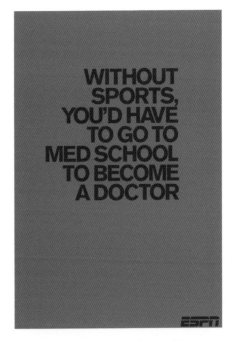

WITHOUT SPORTS, YOU'D HAVE TO GO TO MED SCHOOL TO BECOME A DOCTOR

WITHOUT SPORTS, YOU'D HAVE TO TALK ABOUT POLITICS

WITHOUT SPORTS, D.C. WOULDN'T BE UNITED

WITHOUT SPORTS, YOGI BERRA WOULDN'T MAKE ANY SENSE

MERIT AWARD
Guerilla Advertising: Campaign

ART DIRECTOR
Kim Schoen

WRITER
Kevin Proudfoot

CREATIVE DIRECTORS
Ty Montague
Todd Waterbury

CLIENT
ESPN

AGENCY
Wieden + Kennedy/New York

03253A

MERIT AWARD
Trade B/W
Full Page or Spread: Single

ART DIRECTOR
John Hobbs

WRITER
Peter Rosch

CREATIVE DIRECTOR
Kevin McKeon

CLIENT
Rolling Stone

AGENCY
Bartle Bogle Hegarty/New York

03254A

Squeaking by on a
4000 % mark-up

Somewhere in Malibu, a music exec lies on his $7000 Mies Van Der Rohe daybed, whimpering because album sales are down. A CD costs roughly 40¢ to produce and package, and despite charging twenty bucks for it, he's losing his Commes Des Garcons shirt. Premature releases featuring one good song plus forty minutes to forget won't garner much sympathy. Won't fill that six car garage either. Maybe you should charge more. No wait, you already tried that.

Rolling Stone

MERIT AWARD
Trade B/W
Full Page or Spread: Single

ART DIRECTOR
Matt Campbell

WRITER
Matt Ian

CREATIVE DIRECTOR
Kevin McKeon

CLIENT
Rolling Stone

AGENCY
Bartle Bogle Hegarty/New York

03256A

Only morons can save us now.

What can we possibly learn from MTV? How to staple our butt cheeks together? How putting eight attractive twenty-somethings in a loft guarantees a hot tub hook-up? Or that voting can change the world and it's never too late to help stamp out racism?
Maybe it's just programming for idiots. Or maybe MTV informs and inspires us while the "intellectuals" we've elected to do so are busy flirting with lobbyists. But if MTV is for morons, then remember this: it may be morons that save your planet.

Rolling Stone

Jay Chiat
(1932-1984-2002)

You'll be missed.

TBWA\CHIAT\DAY

This is how easily you could be spreading the germs that cause food poisoning.

Every year in the UK, up to 4.5 million people suffer from food poisoning. You can help prevent this with simple measures such as always washing your hands before handling food and after contact with raw meat; making sure that raw meat is kept well away from other food; and ensuring that food is always cooked properly. The Food Standards Agency is here to help keep your kitchen, and your business safe. Call us on 0845 608 6089 or visit our website at www.food.gov.uk/cleanup

FOOD SAFETY.
IT'S IN YOUR HANDS.

FOOD STANDARDS AGENCY

MERIT AWARD
Trade Color
Full Page or Spread: Single

ART DIRECTOR
Kevin Thoem

WRITER
Al Jackson

PHOTOGRAPHER
Tibor Nemeth

CREATIVE DIRECTORS
Kevin Thoem
Al Jackson

CLIENT
tibornemeth.com

AGENCY
Bubba's Deli/Atlanta

03262A

How much wood could a woodchuck chuck if a woodchuck could chuck wood?

Great photography can make you read anything. Tibor Nemeth Photography · tibornemeth.com

MERIT AWARD
Trade Color
Full Page or Spread: Single

ART DIRECTOR
Kevin Thoem

WRITER
Al Jackson

PHOTOGRAPHER
Tibor Nemeth

CREATIVE DIRECTORS
Kevin Thoem
Al Jackson

CLIENT
tibornemeth.com

AGENCY
Bubba's Deli/Atlanta

03263A

One potato, two potato, three potato, four.

Great photography can make you read anything
Tibor Nemeth Photography · tibornemeth.com

MERIT AWARD
Trade Color
Full Page or Spread: Single

ART DIRECTORS
Toby Talbot
Leo Premutico

WRITERS
Toby Talbot
Leo Premutico

PHOTOGRAPHER
Julian Wolkenstein

TYPOGRAPHER
Jacko van Deventer

CREATIVE DIRECTOR
Mike O'Sullivan

CLIENT
Julian Wolkenstein Photography

AGENCY
Colenso BBDO/Auckland

03264A

MERIT AWARD
Trade Color
Full Page or Spread: Single

ART DIRECTOR
David Damman

WRITER
Greg Hahn

PHOTOGRAPHER
David Harriman

AGENCY PRODUCER
Louise Raicht

CREATIVE DIRECTORS
David Lubars
Kevin Roddy

CLIENT
Timberland

AGENCY
Fallon/New York

03266A

MERIT AWARD
Trade Color
Full Page or Spread: Single

ART DIRECTOR
Michael Winterhagen

WRITER
Beate Steiner

PHOTOGRAPHER
Matthias Koslik

CREATIVE DIRECTORS
Martin Pross
Matthias Schmidt

CLIENT
DaimlerChrysler AG, DCVD

AGENCY
Scholz & Friends/Berlin

03270A

MERIT AWARD
Trade Color
Full Page or Spread: Single

ART DIRECTORS
Stephen Cafiero
Jorge Carreño

WRITER
Vincent Lobelle

PHOTOGRAPHER
Marc Gouby

CREATIVE DIRECTOR
Erik Vervroegen

CLIENT
Nissan

AGENCY
TBWA\Paris

03271A

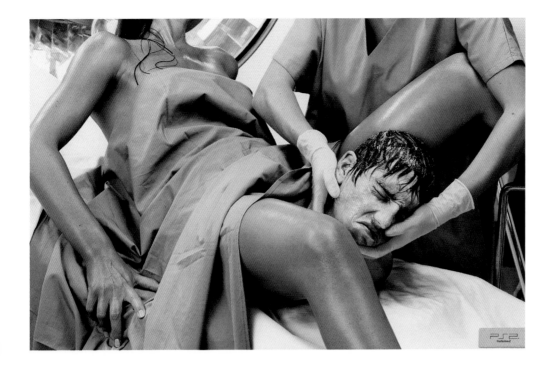

MERIT AWARD
Trade Color
Full Page or Spread: Single

ART DIRECTOR
Jorge Carreño

WRITER
Eric Helias

PHOTOGRAPHER
Dimitri Daniloff

CREATIVE DIRECTOR
Erik Vervroegen

CLIENT
Sony Playstation

AGENCY
TBWA\Paris

03272A

MERIT AWARD
Trade Color
Full Page or Spread: Single

ART DIRECTOR
Jorge Carreño

WRITER
Eric Helias

PHOTOGRAPHER
Dimitri Daniloff

CREATIVE DIRECTOR
Erik Vervroegen

CLIENT
Sony Playstation

AGENCY
TBWA\Paris

03273A

MERIT AWARD
Trade Color
Full Page or Spread: Single

ART DIRECTOR
Jorge Carreño

WRITER
Eric Helias

PHOTOGRAPHER
Marc Gouby

CREATIVE DIRECTOR
Erik Vervroegen

CLIENT
Sony Playstation

AGENCY
TBWA\Paris

03274A

Also won:
MERIT AWARD
Collateral: Point of Purchase
and In-Store

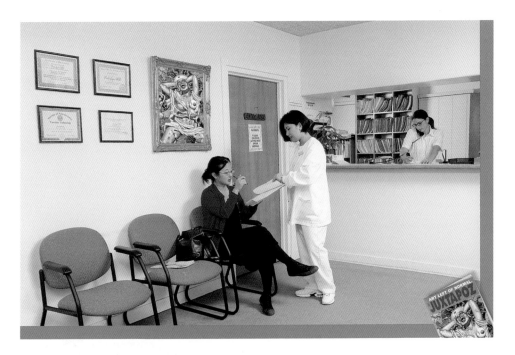

MERIT AWARD
Trade B/W or Color
Any Size: Campaign

ART DIRECTOR
Sakol Mongkolkasetarin

WRITER
Scott Wild

PHOTOGRAPHERS
Peter Samuels
Judy Wildermuth

ILLUSTRATORS
Robert Williams
Mark Ryden

CREATIVE DIRECTORS
Sakol Mongkolkasetarin
Scott Wild

CLIENT
High Speed Productions

AGENCY
Acme Advertising/San Francisco

03276A

MERIT AWARD
Trade B/W or Color
Any Size: Campaign

ART DIRECTOR
John Hobbs

WRITER
Peter Rosch

CREATIVE DIRECTOR
Kevin McKeon

CLIENT
Rolling Stone

AGENCY
Bartle Bogle Hegarty/New York

03277A

Also won:
MERIT AWARDS
Trade B/W
Full Page or Spread: Single

Where are the ugly rockstars?

They were once a shining beacon of hope to oddballs everywhere who figured, "man if I'm ever going to get laid I'd better grab a guitar." All you see on music television these days are models, socialites, and "the beautiful people." If this trend continues millions of uglies everywhere will be left in the dark, never aware that they too can "get some" with dizzying regularity. If you're remotely ugly, please get back in the game.

RollingStone

Live fast, die a
senior citizen

Burn out or fade away? How about burn brightly for dozens and dozens of years. Drugs, debauchery, trashed hotels, women half your age; today's flash-in-the-pan rock star needs a role model to keep the dream alive! We give you, Keith Richards. The gnarly 508 is an incredible guitarist, and he's written dozens of songs that knock you on your ass. Never so desperate for a hit that he and his cohorts bring in some bubble gum pop producer to craft something radio friendly. Is he a geriatric? Technically. But what's he supposed to do - dig a six-foot hole and throw himself in? Hell, at some point he probably did. You don't like him, you think he can't rock because he's pushing 60 - guess what? He doesn't give a shit.

RollingStone

666
PENTALICIOUS!

Where are the songs about Satan? What happened to the dark hidden messages that command suburban teens to submit and perform his evil biddings? You can't offend with songs about summer flings, "bling bling," or nookie. Rock, rap, pop - there really isn't anything the dark lord doesn't improve. The number of the beast has that special something that touches us all. A dark room, candles, and nineteen pentagrams scrawled onto a high school binder. Get friendly with the magic of the occult today before being nominated most likely to succeed.

RollingStone

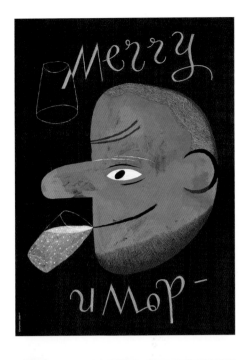

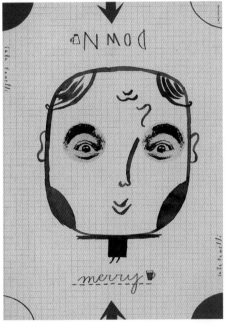
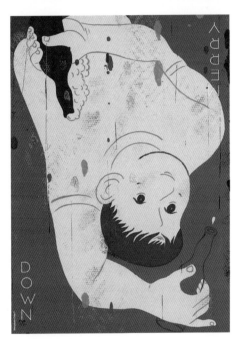
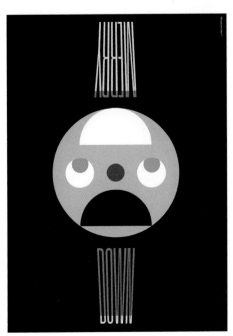

MERIT AWARD
Trade B/W or Color
Any Size: Campaign

ART DIRECTOR
Dave Dye

WRITER
Sean Doyle

ILLUSTRATORS
Gary Baseman
Clayton Bros.
Sara Fanelli
Giles Revell
Martin Haake
Michael Johnson
Jeff Fisher
Mick Marston
Olaf Hajek
Brian Cronin
Andrew Kulman
Helen Wakefield

CREATIVE DIRECTORS
Walter Campbell
Sean Doyle
Dave Dye

CLIENT
Merrydown

AGENCY
Campbell Doyle Dye/London

03278A

MERIT AWARD
Trade B/W or Color
Any Size: Campaign

ART DIRECTOR
Randy Hughes

WRITER
Glen Wachowiak

PHOTOGRAPHERS
Joe Paczkowski
RipSaw

ILLUSTRATOR
Todd apJones

CREATIVE DIRECTOR
Brian Kroening

CLIENT
American Advertising Federation

AGENCY
Carmichael Lynch/Minneapolis

03279A

At what point do national security

and common sense collide?

Join the conversation.

Have the networks finally bitten the head off

family values?

Join the conversation.

Remember when only environmentalists

would have been alarmed by this photo?

Join the conversation.

MERIT AWARD
Trade B/W or Color
Any Size: Campaign

ART DIRECTOR
Bob Barrie

WRITER
Dean Buckhorn

PHOTOGRAPHERS
Steve Liss
Michael Yarish
Daniel D. Creightoa

AGENCY PRODUCER
Paul Morita

CREATIVE DIRECTORS
David Lubars
Kevin Roddy

CLIENT
Time

AGENCY
Fallon/New York

03280A

Also won:
MERIT AWARD
Trade Color
Full Page or Spread: Single

MERIT AWARD
Trade B/W or Color
Any Size: Campaign

ART DIRECTOR
Bob Barrie

WRITER
Dean Buckhorn

PHOTOGRAPHERS
Yannis Behrakis
James Nachtwey

AGENCY PRODUCER
Paul Morita

CREATIVE DIRECTORS
David Lubars
Kevin Roddy

CLIENT
Time

AGENCY
Fallon/New York

03281A

Also won:
MERIT AWARDS
Trade Color
Full Page or Spread: Single

Our sources are not always

the obvious ones.

For more information about TIME Magazine, call your nearest representative. Hong Kong (852) 3128 5111 • London (44) (020) 7322 1032 • New York (1) (212) 522 1420
Asia · Canada · Europe · Latin America · South Pacific · United States

MERIT

And everything in between.

Music. Politics. Global economics.

(Not to mention any convergence of all three.)

For more information about TIME Magazine, call your nearest representative. Hong Kong (852) 3128 5111 • London (44) (020) 7322 1032 • New York (1) (212) 522 1420
Asia · Canada · Europe · Latin America · South Pacific · United States

For more information about TIME Magazine, call your nearest representative. Hong Kong (852) 3128 5111 • London (44) (020) 7322 1032 • New York (1) (212) 522 1420
Asia · Canada · Europe · Latin America · South Pacific · United States

MERIT

Are we over-prescribing mood drugs?

Or under-prescribing personal responsibility?

Your Body, Your Mind Issue, closing December 16th. Join the conversation.

Coolest Inventions · Person of the Year · Best Pictures of the Year · Your Body, Your Mind · 80 Days that Changed the World

Days we seized. And vice versa.

80 Days That Changed The World Issue, closing February 24th. Join the conversation.

Coolest Inventions · Person of the Year · Best Pictures of the Year · Your Body, Your Mind · 80 Days That Changed The World

Fashion's impact on design,
architecture and, occasionally,
waterfowl.

TIME Style & Design Issue, closing January 13th. Join the conversation.

Coolest Inventions · Person of the Year · Best Pictures of the Year · Your Body, Your Mind · 80 Days that Changed the World

A window into the world's most influential soul.

Person of the Year Issue, closing November 25th. Join the conversation.

Coolest Inventions · Person of the Year · Best Pictures of the Year · Your Body, Your Mind · 80 Days that Changed the World

MERIT AWARD
Trade B/W or Color
Any Size: Campaign

ART DIRECTOR
Bob Barrie

WRITER
Dean Buckhorn

PHOTOGRAPHERS
Phillipe Wojazer
Stock
Steve Dunwell
NASA/Timepix

AGENCY PRODUCER
Paul Morita

CREATIVE DIRECTORS
David Lubars
Kevin Roddy

CLIENT
Time

AGENCY
Fallon/New York

03211A

MERIT AWARD
**Trade B/W or Color
Any Size: Campaign**

ART DIRECTOR
Tom Gianfagna

WRITER
Jeremy Pippenger

CREATIVE DIRECTOR
Tom Gianfagna

CLIENT
Green Bull

AGENCY
Gianfagna Jones/New York

03282A

Also won:
MERIT AWARD
**Collateral: Posters
Single**

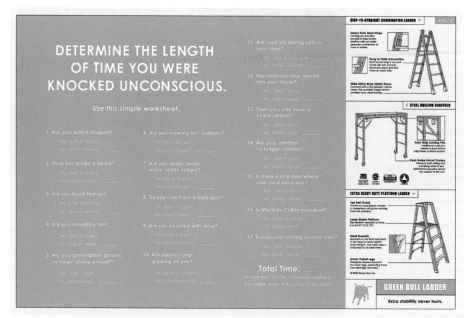

MERIT

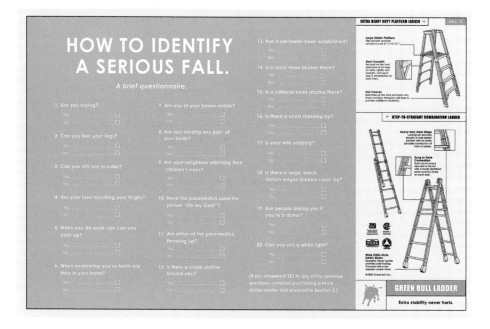

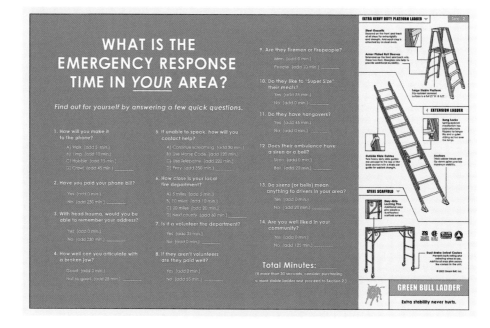

ATTENTION, CIOs, CEOs & COOs: The new *UNIVERSAL BUSINESS ADAPTER* allows you to connect all your business processes — seamlessly!

Make the incompatible compatible!
Based on carbon-coupling technology, it's the...

UNIVERSAL BUSINESS ADAPTER

Introducing the Universal Business Adapter.

It's the breakthrough you've been waiting for in integration technology. A simple device that lets you build an entirely combined infrastructure from pieces that were once thought to be entirely incompatible. With the Universal Business Adapter, your software from the Singapore office will work with your procurement system in Toledo. The calendaring features of your supply chain will work with the spreadsheets in accounting. Your benefits department timelines will work with your employee databases — even if they didn't work in the past.

With an outlet for every type of business function, from ethernet to e-mail to e-business applications, there's nothing the Universal Business Adapter can't connect. Just plug them in and let the patented conversion process do the rest.

Lose the Complexity.

Once, companies spent millions of dollars over several years to integrate their infrastructures. But with the Universal Business Adapter, it takes only fifteen minutes. It's as simple as plug and play.

The Universal Business Adapter is mainframe compatible and works with Bluetooth™ technology, XML™ Linux™ UNIX™ Java™ and even outmoded systems such as Fortran and DOS.

Exclusive Conversion Technology.

Working on the same basic principles as a universal travel adapter, the Universal Business Adapter converts all code, applications, programs and currents into one user-friendly formula. And because it's made with off-the-shelf technology, it's affordable even to the smallest of start-ups.

Yes, It Actually Works.

Who says apples and oranges don't go together? Just ask Mitchell Ratchik, CIO of Bundit, Inc. "I spent $40 million on new servers that were totally incompatible with my existing software. I thought I was finished. But with the Universal Business Adapter, I made them work together in minutes."

About Bagotronics
Bagotronics is a leading manufacturer of business devices for the serious business person. Mark Graham (B.F.A., Ph.D.), Chief Technical Officer and inventor of the UBA, has published several papers on advances in multipronged devices. He is also a recipient of the prestigious Topol Award in high-density electrical conductivity.

CONNECTS
Supply chains
Customer service
HR departments
e-mail
Call centers
Fax machines
Printers
Servers
Storage
Software
Hardware
Middleware
Pagers
Mainframes
PCs
Handhelds
Wireless devices
Executives
Workers
Help desks
Procurement

Made for Mergers

Over the next 24 months, four out of five organizations will be required to merge a department, office or entire new company into an existing system. The Universal Business Adapter eliminates the guesswork and compatibility issues that have plagued mergers in the past.

Take Jeff Compton, CIO of BlueCape, Inc. "Last year I had two of everything after a merger. Two sets of servers; two networks; two storage systems; a pair of call centers.

"The Universal Business Adapter allowed us to hit milestone consolidation dates and complete the integration ahead of schedule. It just works." Imagine what it can do for you.

Secure. Safe. Reliable.

The Universal Business Adapter was developed and manufactured with technology and expertise previously found only in university and scientific research circles.

The Universal Business Adapter is molded with pretested, virus-proof firewalling for instant intruder prevention and global viral protection. Hacker-resistant, password-protected, lithium phospho-olivine materials render the Universal Business Adapter virtually indestructible. It's weather resistant. Shock resistant. Surge resistant.

NOT SOLD AT AIRPORTS.

The Universal Business Adapter is not sold at airports. It is not a travel adapter. You can order it only from Bagotronics. For more information, or to shop securely, be sure to visit us online at: **www.bagotronics.com**

"The Universal Business Adapter has done for information systems what generations of matchmaking TV shows have done for the lovelorn – made a connection!"
— *Business Integration* magazine

BAGOTRONICS.COM

EVERYONE MUST READ
THE WALL STREET JOURNAL,
THURSDAY, Oct. 31

ATTENTION, SENIOR BUSINESS EXECUTIVES: Now, with the NEW BUSINESS TIME MACHINE, you can avoid any business crisis!

Reverse Bad Business Decisions.
Take business in a whole NEW direction: BACKWARDS.

BAGOTRONICS.COM

EVERYONE MUST READ
THE WALL STREET JOURNAL,
THURSDAY, Oct. 31

ATTENTION, SENIOR BUSINESS EXECUTIVES: Now with the NEW MAGIC BUSINESS BINOCULARS, you can avoid any business crisis!

LOOK AHEAD IN TIME.
See business outcomes BEFORE they happen!

BAGOTRONICS.COM

EVERYONE MUST READ
THE WALL STREET JOURNAL,
THURSDAY, Oct. 31

PRINT MERIT

MERIT AWARD
Trade B/W or Color
Any Size: Campaign

ART DIRECTOR
Mike Fetrow

WRITER
Mike Lescarbeau

PHOTOGRAPHER
Craig Perman

CREATIVE DIRECTOR
Mike Lescarbeau

CLIENT
Craig Perman Photography

AGENCY
One And All/Minneapolis

03284A

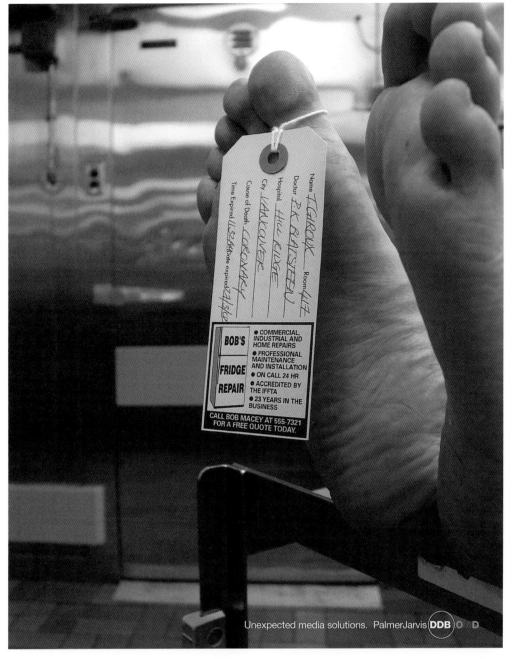

MERIT AWARD
**Collateral: Point of Purchase
and In-Store**

ART DIRECTOR
Tim Vaccarino

WRITER
Dave Weist

PHOTOGRAPHER
Melodie McDaniel

AGENCY PRODUCERS
John Gray
Andrea Ricker

CREATIVE DIRECTOR
Alan Pafenbach

CLIENT
Volkswagen of America

AGENCY
Arnold Worldwide/Boston

03286A

MERIT AWARD
**Collateral: Point of Purchase
and In-Store**

ART DIRECTORS
Erik Vervroegen
Soo Mean Chang

WRITER
Kerry Keenan

PHOTOGRAPHER
Andy Spreitzer

AGENCY PRODUCER
Deb Stotzky

CREATIVE DIRECTORS
Tony Granger
Erik Vervroegen
Kerry Keenan

CLIENT
Video World

AGENCY
Bozell/New York

03287A

MERIT AWARD
**Collateral: Point of Purchase
and In-Store**

ART DIRECTOR
Steve Mitsch

WRITER
Richard Wallace

PHOTOGRAPHER
Shannon Fagan

AGENCY PRODUCER
Hillary Frileck

CREATIVE DIRECTORS
Tony Granger
David Nobay

CLIENT
Woodwind & Brasswind

AGENCY
Bozell/New York

03288A

MERIT AWARD
**Collateral: Point of Purchase
and In-Store**

ART DIRECTORS
Dan Kiefer
Jen Fisch
Randall Erkelens
Sean Coleman

WRITERS
Chris Maley
Wil McKeand

ILLUSTRATOR
Ian McKee

CREATIVE DIRECTORS
Steve Stith
Randall Erkelens

CLIENT
Molson

AGENCY
The Integer Group/Lakewood

03290A

MERIT AWARD
**Collateral: Point of Purchase
and In-Store**

ART DIRECTOR
Jon Loke

WRITER
Victor Ng

ILLUSTRATOR
Jon Loke

CREATIVE DIRECTORS
Tay Guan Hin
Ng Tian It

CLIENT
McDonald's

AGENCY
Leo Burnett/Singapore

03291A

MERIT AWARD
**Collateral: Point of Purchase
and In-Store**

ART DIRECTOR
Goh Wee Kim

WRITER
Yu Sheng Sin

PHOTOGRAPHER
Sze Ling

TYPOGRAPHER
Goh Wee Kim

CREATIVE DIRECTORS
Linda Locke
Tay Guan Hin

CLIENT
Pacific Beauty Care

AGENCY
Leo Burnett/Singapore

03292A

MERIT AWARD
**Collateral: Point of Purchase
and In-Store**

ART DIRECTOR
Andrew Whitehouse

WRITER
Justin Gomes

PHOTOGRAPHER
Clive Stewart

CREATIVE DIRECTOR
Rob McLennan

CLIENT
Dulux

AGENCY
Lowe Bull Calvert Pace/
Johannesburg

03294A

MERIT AWARD
**Collateral: Point of Purchase
and In-Store**

ART DIRECTOR
Andrew Whitehouse

WRITER
Justin Gomes

PHOTOGRAPHER
Clive Stewart

CREATIVE DIRECTOR
Rob McLennan

CLIENT
Dulux

AGENC
Lowe Bull Calvert Pace/
Johannesburg

03293A

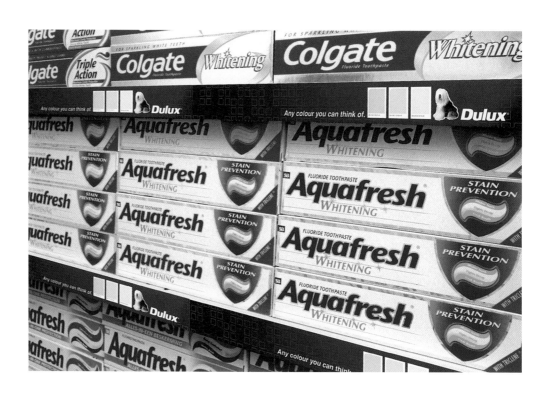

MERIT AWARD
Collateral: Point of Purchase and In-Store

ART DIRECTOR
Klaus Trapp

WRITER
Mathias Henkel

CREATIVE DIRECTORS
Andreas Heinzel
Peter Steger

CLIENT
Kellogg Company

AGENCY
Michael Conrad & Leo Burnett/
Frankfurt

03295A

MERIT AWARD
Collateral: Point of Purchase and In-Store

ART DIRECTOR
Alexandra Brunner

WRITER
Silja Spranger

PHOTOGRAPHER
Wolfgang Usbeck

CREATIVE DIRECTORS
Bernd Lange
Gregor Seitz

CLIENT
Mattel Germany

AGENCY
Ogilvy & Mather/Frankfurt

03296A

MERIT AWARD
Collateral: Self-Promotion

ART DIRECTOR
Bernie Hogya

WRITER
Brian Ahern

PHOTOGRAPHER
Clive Stewart

AGENCY PRODUCER
Maggie Meade

CREATIVE DIRECTORS
Tony Granger
Kerry Keenan

CLIENT
Art Directors Club

AGENCY
Bozell/New York

03298A

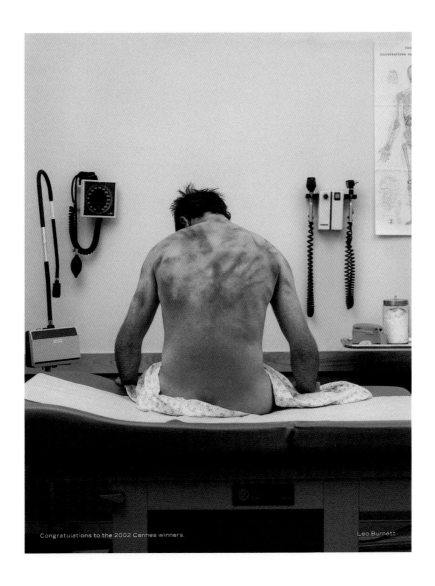

Congratulations to the 2002 Cannes winners.   Leo Burnett

MERIT AWARD
Collateral: Self-Promotion

ART DIRECTOR
Brian Shembeda

WRITER
Avery Gross

PHOTOGRAPHER
Huy Lam

CREATIVE DIRECTORS
Kash Sree
Jeff Labbé
Mark Tutssel

CLIENT
Leo Burnett/Cannes 2002

AGENCY
Leo Burnett/Chicago

03299A

MERIT AWARD
Collateral: Self-Promotion

ART DIRECTOR
Dana Neibert

WRITER
John Risser

CLIENT
San Diego Ad Club

AGENCY
Matthews|Evans|Albertazzi/
San Diego

03301A

MERIT AWARD
Collateral: Self-Promotion

ART DIRECTOR
Prasad Raghavan

WRITER
Upputuru Emmanuel

ILLUSTRATOR
Ibrahim Shaikh

CREATIVE DIRECTOR
Sunil Vysyaprath

CLIENT
Losers

AGENCY
Ogilvy & Mather/New Delhi

03300A

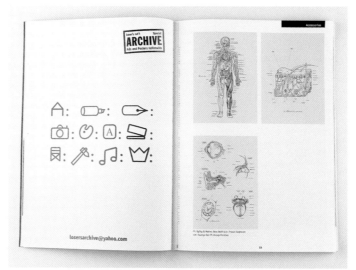

Palmer Jarvis DDB ■
Ideas ■

MERIT AWARD
Collateral: Self-Promotion

ART DIRECTOR
Dean Lee

WRITER
James Lee

PHOTOGRAPHER
CWS

ILLUSTRATOR
Artefact

CREATIVE DIRECTOR
Alan Russell

CLIENT
Palmer Jarvis DDB

AGENCY
Palmer Jarvis DDB/Vancouver

03302A

MERIT AWARD
Collateral: Self-Promotion

ART DIRECTOR
David Emmitt

WRITER
Tony Hirsch

PHOTOGRAPHER
Lance Clayton

CREATIVE DIRECTOR
David Emmitt

CLIENT
Utah Advertising Federation

AGENCY
The RobertsEmmitt Agency/
Salt Lake City

03303A

295

MERIT AWARD
Collateral: Self-Promotion

ART DIRECTOR
Marcus Rebeschini

WRITER
Robert Kleman

CLIENT
Dave and John

AGENCY
TBWA/Singapore

03304A

EMPLOY
DAVID DROGA &
JOHN HEGARTY
FOR A FRACTION
OF THE COST.

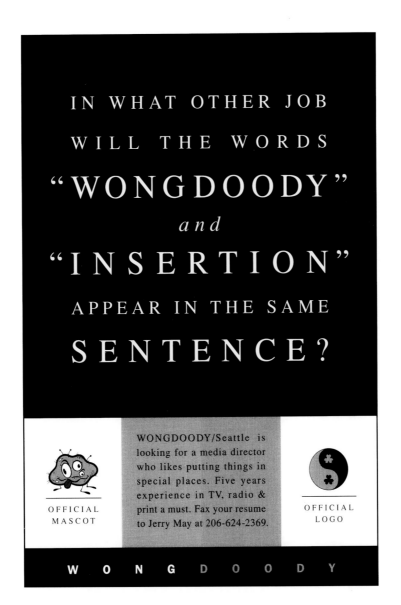

MERIT AWARD
**Collateral: Posters
Single**

ART DIRECTOR
Andrew Grant

WRITER
Andrew Hicks

ILLUSTRATOR
Andrew Grant

CREATIVE DIRECTORS
Peter Badenhorst
Mark Fisher

CLIENT
Audi SA

AGENCY
Ogilvy & Mather/Johannesburg

03316A

MERIT AWARD
**Collateral: Posters
Single**

ART DIRECTORS
Richard Johnson
Tham Khai Meng
Kelly Dickinson

WRITER
Andy Greenaway

PHOTOGRAPHERS
Kelly Dickinson
Julian Watt

ILLUSTRATOR
Richard Johnson

CREATIVE DIRECTORS
Andy Greenaway
Craig Smith

CLIENT
Gaelic Inns

AGENCY
Ogilvy & Mather/Singapore

03317A

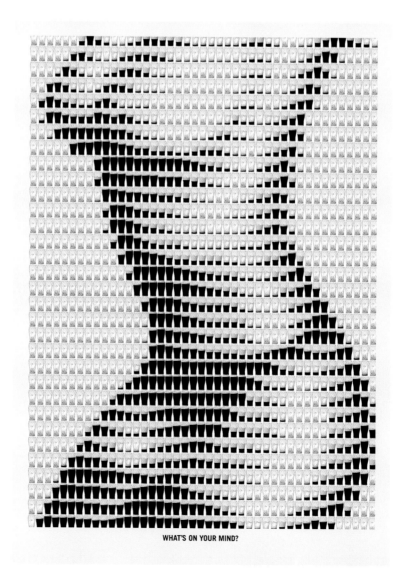

MERIT AWARD
Collateral: Posters
Single

ART DIRECTOR
Surapat Chaiyongyos

WRITERS
Kittinan Sawasdee
Jureeporn Thaidumrong

PHOTOGRAPHER
Anuchai Sricharunputong

PRODUCTION COMPANY
Remix Studio Bangkok

CREATIVE DIRECTOR
Jureeporn Thaidumrong

CLIENT
Suvimol

AGENCY
Saatchi & Saatchi/Bangkok

03318A

MERIT AWARD
**Collateral: Posters
Single**

ART DIRECTOR
David Nien-Li Yang

WRITERS
Bob Volkman
Michael Herlehy

PHOTOGRAPHERS
Crain's Staff Photographers

CREATIVE DIRECTOR
Robin Yount

CLIENT
Crain's Chicago Business

AGENCY
Tom Dick & Harry/Chicago

03321A

MERIT AWARD
**Collateral: Posters
Campaign**

ART DIRECTOR
Bernie Hogya

WRITER
Brian Ahern

PHOTOGRAPHER
Bernie Hogya

CREATIVE DIRECTORS
Tony Granger
Kerry Keenan

CLIENT
Art Directors Club

AGENCY
Bozell/New York

03322A

301

MERIT AWARD
**Collateral: Posters
Campaign**

ART DIRECTOR
Karen Lilje

WRITERS
Trevor Olive
Justin Dodd

ILLUSTRATOR
Karen Lilje

CREATIVE DIRECTOR
Graham Warsop

CLIENT
AFGEM

AGENCY
The Jupiter Drawing Room
(South Africa)/Johannesburg

03324A

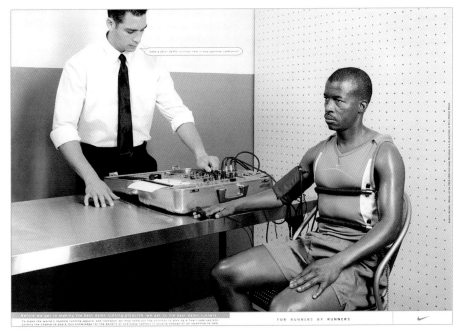

MERIT

MERIT AWARD
**Collateral: Posters
Campaign**

ART DIRECTORS
Graeme Erens
Michael Bond

WRITERS
Graeme Erens
Bernard Hunter

PHOTOGRAPHER
Michael Lewis

CREATIVE DIRECTOR
Graham Warsop

CLIENT
Nike

AGENCY
The Jupiter Drawing Room
(South Africa)/Johannesburg

03323A

Also won:
MERIT AWARD
**Magazine Color
Full Page or Spread: Single**

MERIT AWARD
**Collateral: Posters
Campaign**

ART DIRECTOR
Doug Pedersen

WRITER
Doug Pedersen

CREATIVE DIRECTOR
Jim Mountjoy

CLIENT
Richard McCoy Financial
Services

AGENCY
Loeffler Ketchum Mountjoy/
Charlotte

03325A

Also won:
MERIT AWARDS
**Collateral: Posters
Single**

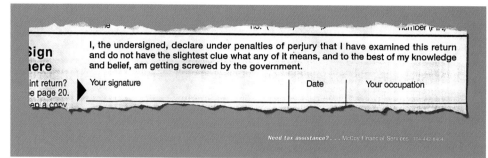

MERIT

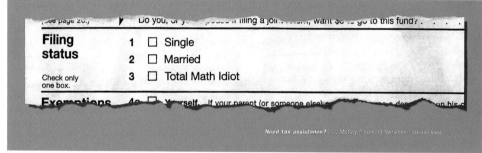

MERIT

MERIT AWARD
**Collateral: Posters
Campaign**

ART DIRECTORS
Pann Lim
Andrew Lok

WRITERS
Andrew Lok
Pann Lim

ILLUSTRATORS
Pann Lim
Andrew Lok

CLIENT
The Dubliner Irish Pub

AGENCY
onemanbrand.com/Singapore

03326A

I heard this story about a couple that had a huge wedding with hundreds of guests. Some of them had flown or driven great distances to be there. The ceremony went off smoothly and then everybody settled in for a lavish dinner.

When it was time for the groom to make a toast and give his speech, he thanked everyone for the wonderful gifts and for taking the trouble to travel so far to share the happy occasion. He said he was so grateful that he had arranged a present for every person at the reception. All they had to do was look under their chairs and each would find an envelope stuck to the bottom with a gift in it. Of course, the guests quickly reached down and retrieved their envelopes.

They were shocked and horrified at the contents! Each package contained 8x10 colour glossy photos of the bride and the best man having sex in every position imaginable on a pool table.

The groom spoke. "I suspected they were having an affair, so I hired an investigator who took these shots." He turned to the father of the bride. "Thanks for the $30,000 dinner and party, but I'm out of here." Then he walked out of the hall with his pint of Guinness.

AT LEAST THERE'S ONE LEGEND YOU CAN ALWAYS **BELIEVE**

I wish to warn you about a new criminal ring targeting business travellers. This gang is organized, well funded, highly skilled, and very active in Asia.

The crime begins when a business traveller goes to a lounge for a drink at the end of the day. Someone in the bar walks up and offers to buy him one.

The last thing the traveller remembers, until he wakes up in a hotel room bathtub with his body submerged to the neck in ice, is sipping that drink. There is a note taped to the wall instructing him not to move and to call for an ambulance. A phone is on a table next to the tub.

He calls emergency services, which have now become quite familiar with this felony. The business traveller is instructed by the operator to carefully reach behind and feel for a tube protruding from his lower back.

He finds it and the operator tells him to remain still, having already sent the paramedics to help. The operator knows that both the man's kidneys have been harvested for sale in the black market.

And that this new victim of a heinous organ-smuggling ring is condemned to a life of dialysis, as well as abstinence from alcoholic beverages like Guinness.

AT LEAST THERE'S ONE LEGEND YOU CAN ALWAYS **BELIEVE**

I was doing research for a science project when I stumbled upon this charming anecdote. "One small step for man, one giant leap for mankind." wasn't the only memorable remark made by Neil Armstrong during Apollo Mission 11. In the landing craft, when they were drinking a celebratory toast to America's victory in the space race, he quipped enigmatically "Here's to you, Mr. Gorsky."

Many people at NASA thought it was a casual comment concerning some rival Soviet Cosmonaut. However, upon checking, there was no Gorsky in either the Russian or American space programs. Over the years, many people questioned Armstrong as to what "Here's to you, Mr. Gorsky." meant, but he always just smiled.

On July 5, 1995 (in Tampa Bay, Florida), while answering questions following a speech, a reporter brought up the 26-year old query to Armstrong. This time he finally responded as Mr. Gorsky had already passed away.

When he was a kid, his neighbours were Mr. and Mrs. Gorsky. He was playing baseball with his buddy in the backyard when his friend hit a fly ball, which landed in the front lawn below the Gorskys' bedroom windows.

As he ran over to pick up the ball, young Armstrong heard Mrs. Gorsky shouting at her husband, "Oral sex! You want oral sex?! You'll get oral sex when the kid next door walks on the moon with a Guinness!"

AT LEAST THERE'S ONE LEGEND YOU CAN ALWAYS **BELIEVE**

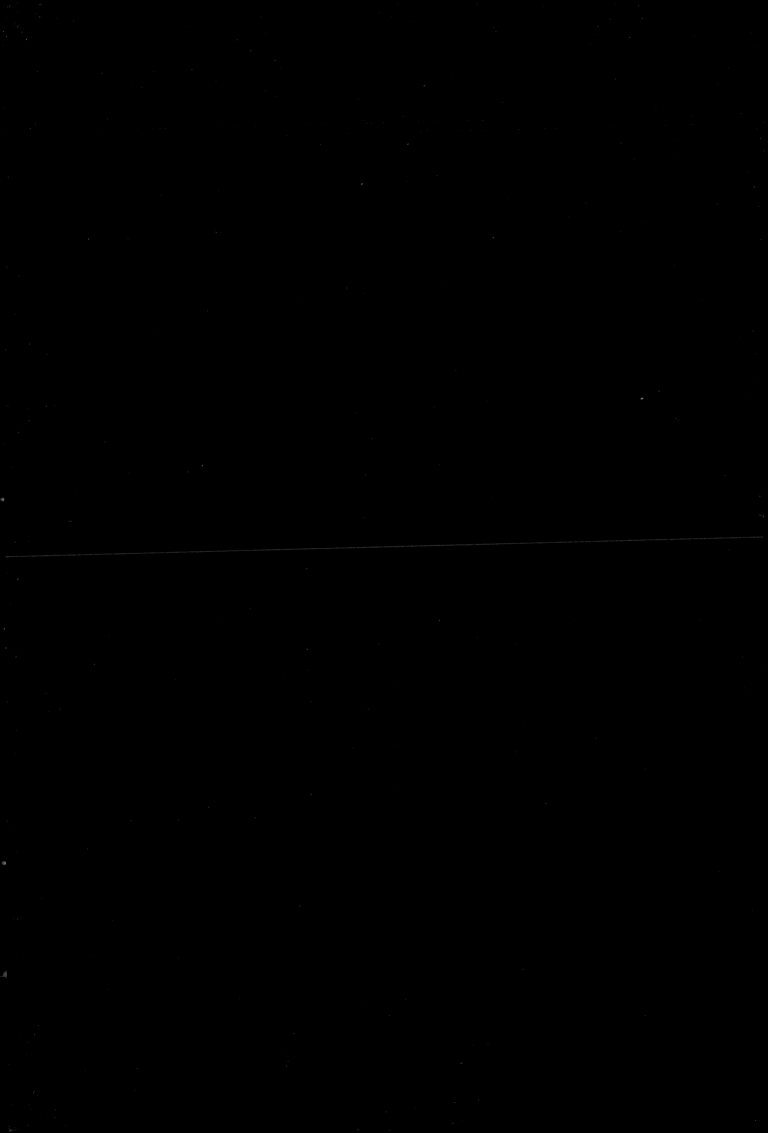

MERIT AWARD
Annual Report

DESIGNER
Jason Jones

ART DIRECTOR
Dave Ritter

WRITER
Reid Armbruster

PHOTOGRAPHER
Charlie Simokaitis

CREATIVE DIRECTOR
Dana Arnett

CLIENT
Harley-Davidson

AGENCY
VSA Partners/Chicago

03055D

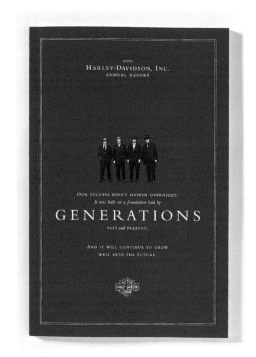

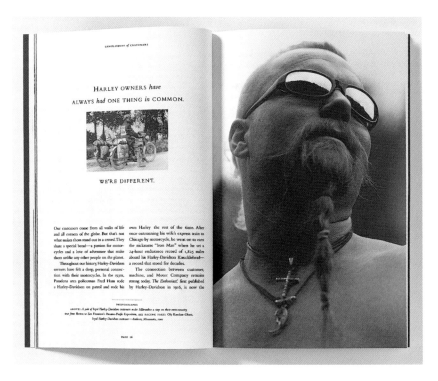

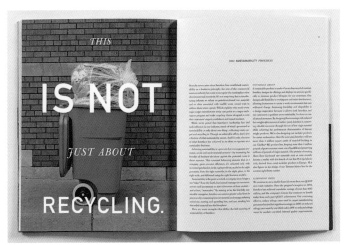

MERIT AWARD
Annual Report

DESIGNER
Dan Knuckey

ART DIRECTOR
Dan Knuckey

WRITER
Andy Blankenburg

PHOTOGRAPHER
Tom Maday

CREATIVE DIRECTOR
Jamie Koval

CLIENT
Interface

AGENCY
VSA Partners/Chicago

03056D

MERIT AWARD
Booklet/Brochure

ART DIRECTOR
Tomas Lorente

WRITER
Carlos Domingos

PHOTOGRAPHERS
Several

CREATIVE DIRECTORS
Tomas Lorente
Carlos Domingos

CLIENT
Age. Comunicações

AGENCY
Age. Comunicações/São Paulo

03058D

MERIT AWARD
Booklet/Brochure

DESIGNER
Brian Dixon

ART DIRECTOR
Brian Dixon

WRITER
Justin Dobbs

CREATIVE DIRECTOR
Gary Backaus

CLIENT
Clark Tower

AGENCY
archer malmo/Memphis

03059D

MERIT AWARD
Booklet/Brochure

DESIGNERS
Vanessa Eckstein
Frances Chen

ART DIRECTOR
Vanessa Eckstein

PHOTOGRAPHER
Antoine Bootz

CREATIVE DIRECTOR
Vanessa Eckstein

CLIENT
The Nienkamper Store

AGENCY
Blok Design/Mexico City

03060D

MERIT AWARD
Booklet/Brochure

DESIGNERS
Heidi Chisholm
Peet Pienaar

PHOTOGRAPHER
Gareth Chisholm

CREATIVE DIRECTORS
Heidi Chisholm
Peet Pienaar

CLIENT
RSA Litho

AGENCY
Daddy buy me a Pony/Cape Town

03057D

PERFEKTION ENTSTEHT NICHT IRGENDWO.
DIE GLÄSERNE MANUFAKTUR IN DRESDEN.

MERIT AWARD
Booklet/Brochure

ART DIRECTORS
Maik Kähler
Thore Jung

WRITERS
Christoph Nann
Ralf Heuel

PHOTOGRAPHERS
Christoph Morlinghaus
Kai-Uwe Gundlach
Carsten Heidmann
Peter Bialobrzeski

ILLUSTRATOR
Katharina Wlodasch

CREATIVE DIRECTORS
Ralf Heuel
Ralf Nolting

CLIENT
Volkswagen

AGENCY
Grabarz & Partner Werbeagentur/
Hamburg

03062D

MERIT AWARD
Booklet/Brochure

DESIGNER
Andrew Plymin

ART DIRECTOR
Andrew Plymin

WRITER
Nigel Dawson

PHOTOGRAPHER
Stuart Crossett

CREATIVE DIRECTOR
Nigel Dawson

CLIENT
MND

AGENCY
Grey Worldwide/Melbourne

03063D

Also won:
MERIT AWARD
Direct Mail
Single

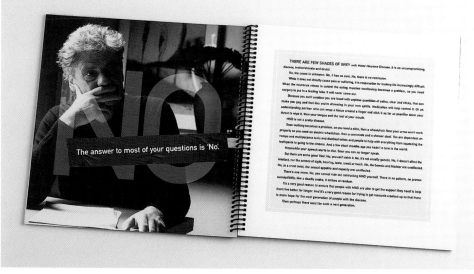

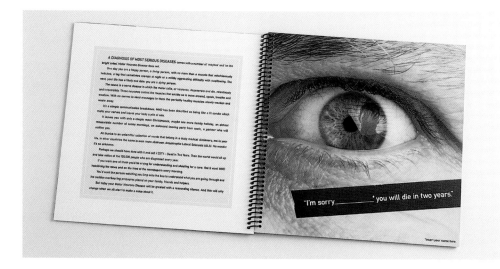

MERIT AWARD
Booklet/Brochure

ART DIRECTOR
Anthony Yumul

CREATIVE DIRECTOR
Douglas Lloyd

CLIENT
CFDA

AGENCY
Lloyd (+ co)/New York

03066D

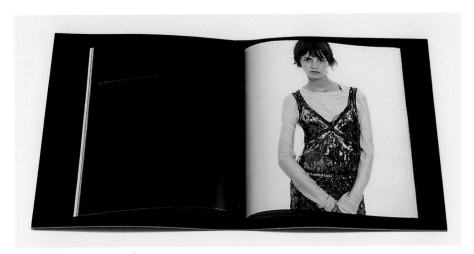

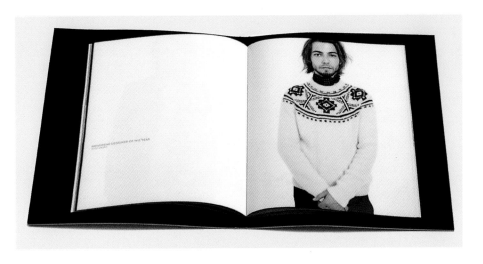

MERIT AWARD
Booklet/Brochure

DESIGNERS
Giovanni Carrieri Russo
Pace Kaminsky

ART DIRECTOR
Pace Kaminsky

WRITER
Windsor Press

PHOTOGRAPHER
Francois Halard

CREATIVE DIRECTOR
Giovanni Carrieri Russo

CLIENT
Windsor

AGENCY
No. 11 Incorporated/New York

03068D

"CULTURE IS AN IMPORTANT PART OF THE SPIRIT OF A COMMUNITY, SO IT IS ONLY NATURAL THAT ART AND ARTISTS SHOULD BECOME PART OF THE FABRIC OF THIS PLACE."

MERIT AWARD
Booklet/Brochure

DESIGNER
Prasad Raghavan

ART DIRECTOR
Prasad Raghavan

WRITER
Upputuru Emmanuel

ILLUSTRATOR
Ibrahim Shaikh

CREATIVE DIRECTOR
Sunil Vysyaprath

CLIENT
Losers

AGENCY
Ogilvy & Mather/New Delhi

03067D

DESIGN
MERIT

MERIT AWARD
Booklet/Brochure

DESIGNERS
David Israel
Carolina Trigo
Maja Blazejewska

WRITER
Vel Richey-Rankin

CREATIVE DIRECTORS
Brian Collins
David Israel

CLIENT
Dove

AGENCY
Ogilvy & Mather/Brand
Integration Group/New York

03069D

She can discern hype from quality, and will happily pay a premium for the latter. She is in that group of women who could be called "beauty pragmatists." To her, the cost of a beauty product isn't the main issue. What she is interested in is whether it is going to work.

"I'd rather have fewer quality items than a whole wardrobe full of cheap T-shirts."

JULIA

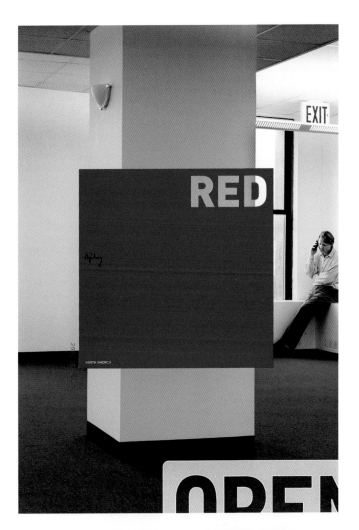

MERIT AWARD
Booklet/Brochure

DESIGNERS
David Israel
Maja Blazejewska

WRITER
Tonice Sgrignoli

CREATIVE DIRECTORS
Rick Boyko
Brian Collins

CLIENT
Ogilvy & Mather

AGENCY
Ogilvy & Mather/Brand
Integration Group/New York

03071D

MERIT AWARD
Booklet/Brochure

DESIGNERS
David Israel
Maja Blazejewska
Leigh Okies

WRITER
Tonice Sgrignoli

CREATIVE DIRECTORS
Rick Boyko
Brian Collins

CLIENT
Ogilvy & Mather

AGENCY
Ogilvy & Mather/Brand
Integration Group/New York

03072D

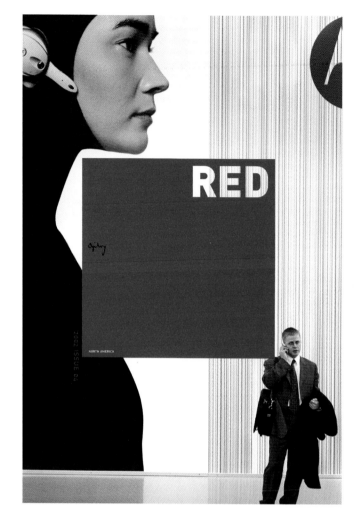

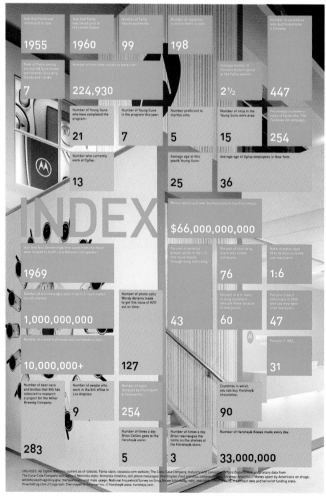

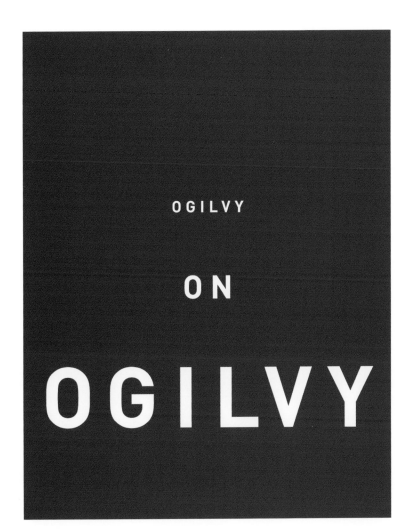

MERIT AWARD
Booklet/Brochure

DESIGNERS
Brian Collins
Tuan Ching

CREATIVE DIRECTOR
Brian Collins

CLIENT
Ogilvy & Mather

AGENCY
Ogilvy & Mather/Brand
Integration Group/New York

03070D

MERIT AWARD
Booklet/Brochure

DESIGNERS
Kevin Finn
Julian Melhuish

ART DIRECTORS
Kevin Finn
Julian Melhuish

WRITERS
Kevin Finn
Julian Melhuish
Noah Regan
Justin Drape

PHOTOGRAPHER
Ingvar Kenne

CREATIVE DIRECTOR
Malcolm Poynton

CLIENT
Spicers Paper, Australia

AGENCY
Saatchi Design/Sydney

03073D

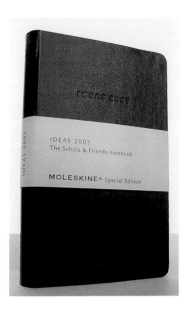

MERIT AWARD
Booklet/Brochure

DESIGNERS
Petra Reichenbach
Sven Sochaczewsky

ART DIRECTORS
Bettina Fortak
Petra Reichenbach
Sven Sochaczewsky
Sandra Weinmann
Niko Willborn

WRITERS
Matthias Schmidt
Karin von Huelsen

PHOTOGRAPHER
Matthias Koslik

CREATIVE DIRECTOR
Sebastian Turner

CLIENT
Scholz & Friends Group

AGENCY
Scholz & Friends/Berlin

03074D

323

DESIGN
MERIT

MERIT AWARD
Booklet/Brochure

DESIGNER
Niki Fleming

ART DIRECTOR
Jane Hope

WRITER
Gary McGuire

PHOTOGRAPHER
Chris Gordaneer

CREATIVE DIRECTOR
Jane Hope

CLIENT
Taxi

AGENCY
Taxi/Toronto

03075D

MERIT AWARD
Booklet/Brochure

DESIGNER
Nichole Dillon

ART DIRECTOR
Jamie Koval

WRITER
Andy Blankenburg

PHOTOGRAPHERS
Tom Maday
Maria Rebledo

CREATIVE DIRECTOR
Jamie Koval

CLIENT
MeadWestvaco Papers Group

AGENCY
VSA Partners/Chicago

03077D

DESIGN
MERIT

MERIT AWARD
Booklet/Brochure

DESIGNER
Nichole Dillon

ART DIRECTOR
Nichole Dillon

WRITER
Andy Blankenburg

PHOTOGRAPHER
Geof Kern

CLIENT
Telwares Communications

AGENCY
VSA Partners/Chicago

03078D

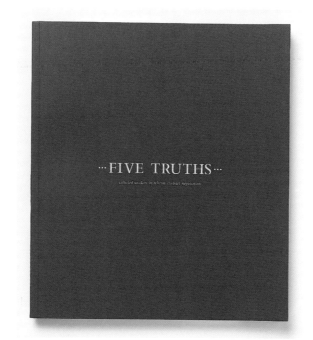

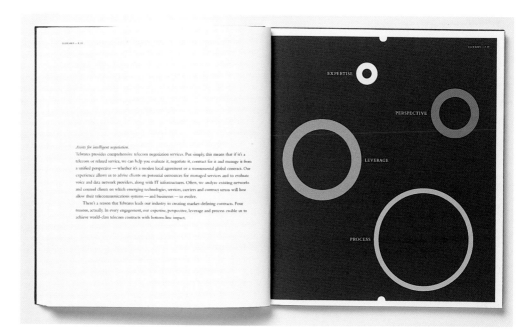

MERIT AWARD
Booklet/Brochure

DESIGNERS
Ken Matsubara
Jonathan Barnbrook

ART DIRECTOR
Ken Matsubara

WRITERS
Sumiko Sato
Barton Corley

CREATIVE DIRECTORS
John C. Jay
Sumiko Sato

CLIENT
Mori Building

AGENCY
Wieden + Kennedy/Tokyo

03079D

MERIT AWARD
Booklet/Brochure

DESIGNER
Shintaro Tanabe

ART DIRECTOR
Philip Lord

WRITERS
Koji Iida
Bobbito Garcia

ILLUSTRATORS
Shuhei Urano
Yosuke Hasegawa
Toshio Sasagawa

CREATIVE DIRECTORS
John C. Jay
Sumiko Sato

CLIENT
Nike Japan

AGENCY
Wieden + Kennedy/Tokyo

03080D

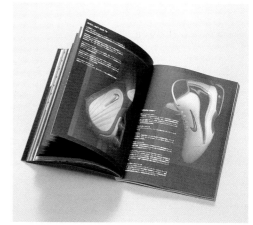

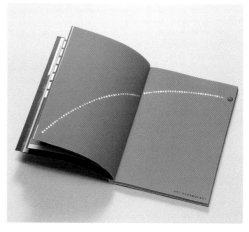

MERIT AWARD
Booklet/Brochure

DESIGNER
Paul Marince

ART DIRECTOR
Paul Marince

WRITERS
Karen Barnes
Ricky Perkins
Roseann Rush
Maureen Hall
Peter Mitchell
Keith Borshak
Mark Pingitore
Judith Yates

CREATIVE DIRECTOR
Ricky Perkins

CLIENT
The Woodbine Agency

AGENCY
The Woodbine Agency/
Winston-Salem

03076D

MERIT AWARD
Corporate Identity

DESIGNER
Glenda Venn

WRITER
Desirée Brown

ILLUSTRATOR
Glenda Venn

CLIENT
Fibs Restaurant

AGENCY
Bingo Communications/
Johannesburg

03082D

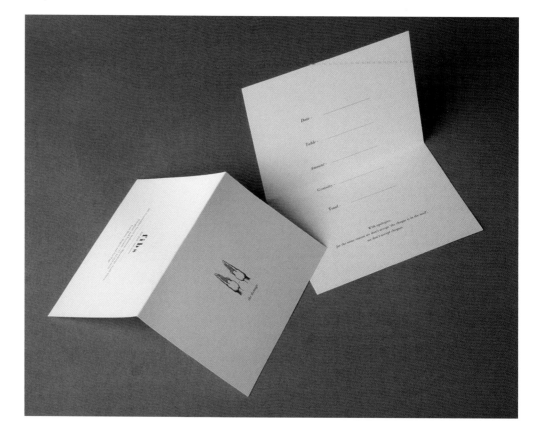

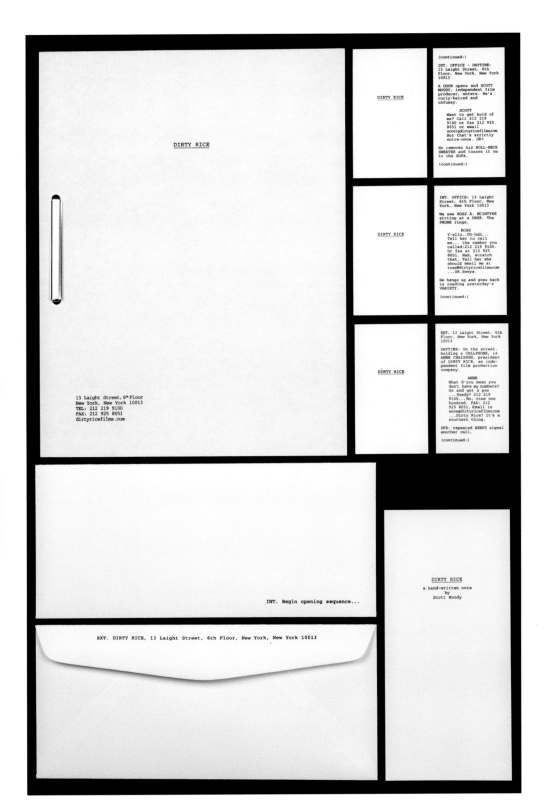

MERIT AWARD
Corporate Identity

DESIGNER
Graham Clifford

ART DIRECTOR
Callum MacGregor

WRITER
Guy Barnett

CREATIVE DIRECTORS
Guy Barnett
Callum MacGregor

CLIENT
Dirty Rice

AGENCY
The Brooklyn Brothers/New York

03094D

MERIT AWARD
Corporate Identity

DESIGNERS
Graham Clifford
Young Seo
Vidhu Kapur

ART DIRECTOR
Callum MacGregor

WRITER
Guy Barnett

CREATIVE DIRECTORS
Guy Barnett
Callum MacGregor

CLIENT
Sabrina Huffman

AGENCY
The Brooklyn Brothers/New York

03095D

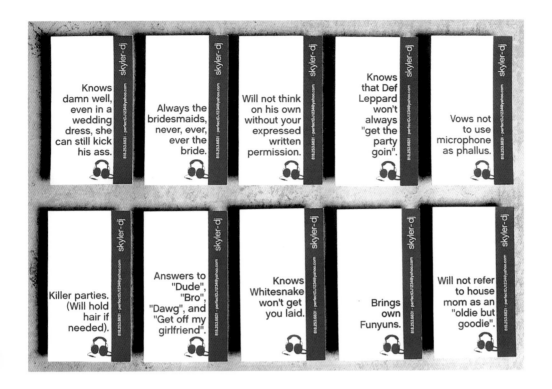

MERIT AWARD
Corporate Identity

DESIGNER
Brady Waggoner

ART DIRECTOR
Brady Waggoner

WRITER
John Ferin

CREATIVE DIRECTOR
Joe Clipner

CLIENT
Skyler, DJ

AGENCY
CANNON/Grand Rapids

03083D

MERIT AWARD
Corporate Identity

DESIGNER
Peet Pienaar

CREATIVE DIRECTOR
Peet Pienaar

CLIENT
Vulindlela

AGENCY
Daddy buy me a Pony/Cape Town

03081D

MERIT AWARD
Corporate Identity

DESIGNER
Toshihiro Onimaru

ART DIRECTOR
Toshihiro Onimaru

CREATIVE DIRECTOR
Takanori Aiba

CLIENT
Will Planning Inc.

AGENCY
Graphics and Designing Inc./
Tokyo

03084D

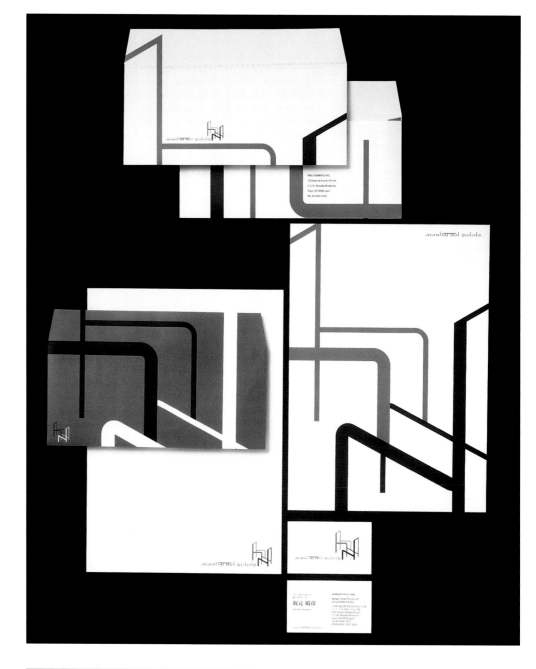

MERIT AWARD
Corporate Identity

DESIGNER
Brandt Bates

CREATIVE DIRECTOR
Joanne Thomas

CLIENT
Cape Town Major Events
Company

AGENCY
The Jupiter Drawing Room
(South Africa)/Cape Town

03096D

DESIGN
MERIT

MERIT AWARD
Corporate Identity

DESIGNERS
Rita Thinnes
Patrick Bittner

ART DIRECTORS
Rita Thinnes
Patrick Bittner

WRITER
Germaine Paulus

PHOTOGRAPHER
André Mailänder

CREATIVE DIRECTOR
Ivica Maksimovic

CLIENT
Dittgen Bauunternehmen

AGENCY
Maksimovic & Partners/
Saarbrücken

03086D

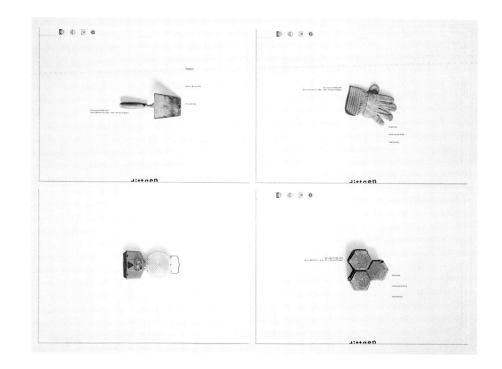

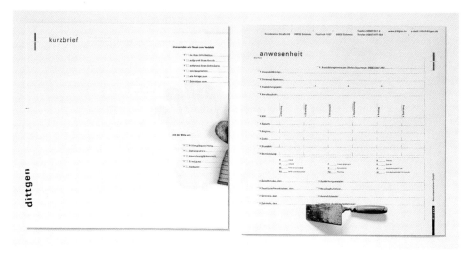

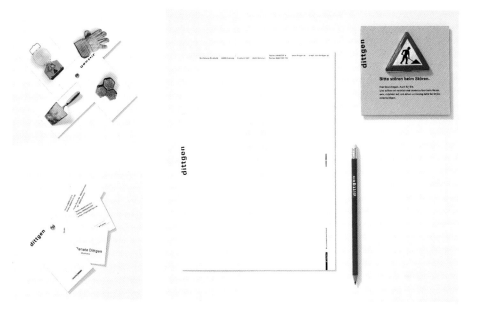

MERIT AWARD
Corporate Identity

DESIGNERS
Steve Sandstrom
James Parker

ART DIRECTOR
Steve Sandstrom

WRITER
Neil Webster

ILLUSTRATOR
James Parker

CREATIVE DIRECTOR
Steve Sandstrom

CLIENT
Portland Trail Blazers

AGENCY
Sandstrom Design/Portland

03087D

337

MERIT AWARD
Corporate Identity

DESIGNERS
Kobe Suvongse
Alan Leusink
Jeff Johnson
Jason Walzer

WRITER
Billy Jurewicz

CREATIVE DIRECTOR
Billy Jurewicz

CLIENT
space150

AGENCY
space150/Minneapolis

03088D

MERIT AWARD
Corporate Identity

DESIGNERS
Alan Leusink
Todd Bartz

WRITER
Billy Jurewicz

CREATIVE DIRECTOR
Billy Jurewicz

CLIENT
space150

AGENCY
space150/Minneapolis

03089D

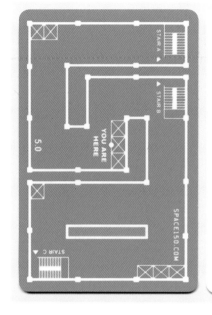

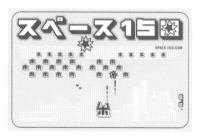

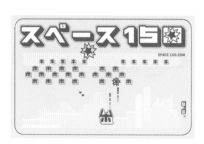

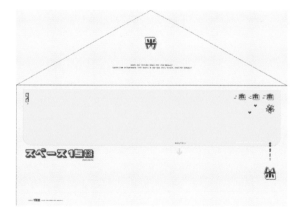

MERIT AWARD
Corporate Identity

DESIGNERS
Todd Bartz
Jeff Johnson
Jason Walzer

WRITER
Billy Jurewicz

CREATIVE DIRECTOR
Billy Jurewicz

CLIENT
space150

AGENCY
space150/Minneapolis

03090D

MERIT AWARD
Corporate Identity

DESIGNER
Dave Watson

CREATIVE DIRECTOR
Steve Mykolyn

CLIENT
Butterfield & Robinson

AGENCY
Taxi/Toronto

03091D

MERIT AWARD
Corporate Identity

DESIGNER
Spencer Buck

ART DIRECTOR
Ryan Wills

WRITERS
Spencer Buck
Ryan Wills
Alex Bane

CREATIVE DIRECTORS
Spencer Buck
Ryan Wills
Alex Bane

CLIENT
Taxi Studio Ltd.

AGENCY
Taxi Studio Ltd./Bristol

03092D

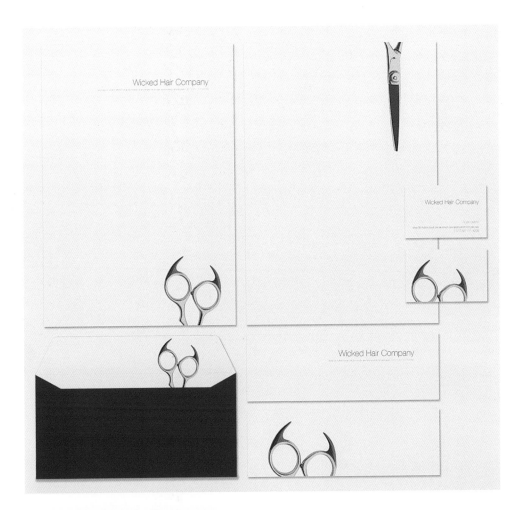

MERIT AWARD
Corporate Identity

DESIGNER
Terri Santos

CREATIVE DIRECTOR
Nathan Reddy

CLIENT
Wicked Hair Company

AGENCY
TBWA/Gavin/Reddy/Johannesburg

03093D

MERIT AWARD
Corporate Identity

DESIGNERS
Ai Osada
Travis Kramer
Craig Neuman
Darren Abbott
Kathy Johnson

ART DIRECTOR
Craig Neuman

WRITER
Brian Brooker

PHOTOGRAPHER
Tim Pott

ILLUSTRATOR
Travis Kramer

CREATIVE DIRECTOR
Craig Neuman

CLIENT
40 Sardines Restaurant

AGENCY
Three Wide Marketing/Kansas City

03097D

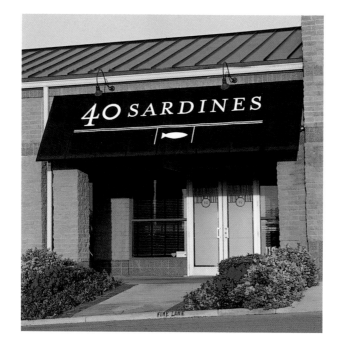

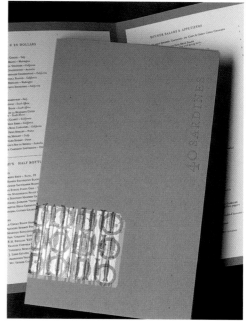

MERIT AWARD
Corporate Identity

DESIGNERS
Janice Davison
Anthony Biles

TYPOGRAPHERS
Janice Davison
Mike Pratley

CREATIVE DIRECTORS
Bruce Duckworth
David Turner

CLIENT
Boa Housewares

AGENCY
Turner Duckworth/London

03098D

MERIT AWARD
Corporate Identity

DESIGNER
Gabriel Hueso

ART DIRECTORS
Gabriel Hueso
Uschi Henkes

CREATIVE DIRECTORS
Uschi Henkes
Urs Frick

CLIENT
Jesus Galindo

AGENCY
Zapping/Madrid

03085D

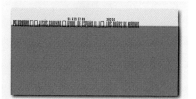

MERIT AWARD
Logo/Trademark

DESIGNER
Travis Olson

CREATIVE DIRECTOR
Bill Thorburn

CLIENT
Harley-Davidson

AGENCY
Carmichael Lynch Thorburn/
Minneapolis

03099D

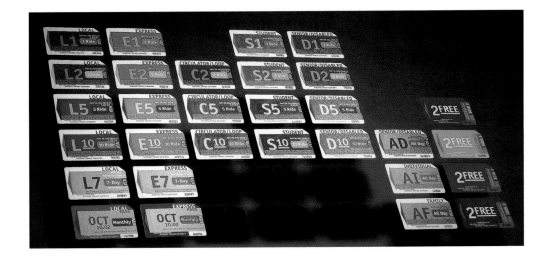

MERIT AWARD
Commercial Product Packaging

ART DIRECTORS
Ana Laura Gomes
Alberto Kim
Jacqueline Lemos

WRITER
Mariana D'Horta

ILLUSTRATOR
José Carlos Lollo

CREATIVE DIRECTOR
Carlos Silvério

CLIENT
Souza Cruz

AGENCY
DPZ/São Paulo

03102D

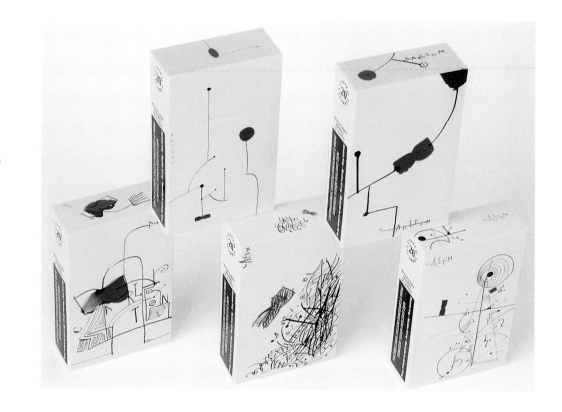

MERIT AWARD
Commercial Product Packaging

DESIGNER
Rikus Ferreira

WRITER
Anton Visser

ILLUSTRATOR
Rikus Ferreira

CREATIVE DIRECTOR
Joanne Thomas

CLIENT
Gabriel Shock Absorbers

AGENCY
The Jupiter Drawing Room
(South Africa)/Cape Town

03109D

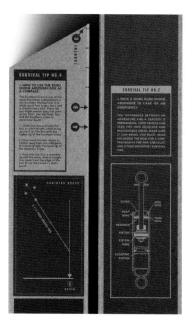

MERIT AWARD
Commercial Product Packaging

DESIGNERS
Matthew Clark
the karacters design team

ART DIRECTOR
Matthew Clark

ILLUSTRATOR
Matthew Clark

CREATIVE DIRECTOR
Maria Kennedy

CLIENT
Clearly Canadian Beverage
Corporation

AGENCY
karacters design group/Vancouver

03103D

MERIT AWARD
Commercial Product Packaging

ART DIRECTOR
Aunnop Boonthong

CREATIVE DIRECTOR
Douglas Lloyd

CLIENT
Energy Brands

AGENCY
Lloyd (+ co)/New York

03104D

347

MERIT AWARD
Commercial Product Packaging

ART DIRECTOR
Alfredo Castro

CREATIVE DIRECTOR
Douglas Lloyd

CLIENT
Gucci Parfum

AGENCY
Lloyd (+ co)/New York

03105D

MERIT AWARD
Commercial Product Packaging

DESIGNER
Neil Powell

ART DIRECTOR
Neil Powell

WRITER
Josh Rogers

CREATIVE DIRECTOR
Neil Powell

CLIENT
Rheingold Brewing Company

AGENCY
Powell/New York

03106D

MERIT AWARD
Commercial Product Packaging

DESIGNER
Luke Manning

ART DIRECTORS
Ryan Wills
Alex Bane

ILLUSTRATORS
Dave Clark
Peter Bane

CREATIVE DIRECTOR
Spencer Buck

CLIENT
Somerfield

AGENCY
Taxi Studio Ltd./Bristol

03107D

MERIT AWARD
Commercial Product Packaging

DESIGNERS
Spencer Buck
Ryan Wills
Alex Bane

ART DIRECTORS
Ryan Wills
Alex Bane

WRITER
Spencer Buck

ILLUSTRATOR
Bill Ledger

CREATIVE DIRECTORS
Spencer Buck
Ryan Wills
Alex Bane

CLIENT
Somerfield

AGENCY
Taxi Studio Ltd./Bristol

03108D

MERIT AWARD
Commercial Product Packaging

DESIGNER
Anthony Biles

TYPOGRAPHERS
Jeremy Tankard
Anthony Biles

CREATIVE DIRECTORS
Bruce Duckworth
David Turner

CLIENT
Boa Housewares

AGENCY
Turner Duckworth/London

03110D

MERIT AWARD
Commercial Product Packaging

DESIGNER
Anthony Biles

PHOTOGRAPHER
David Gill

ILLUSTRATOR
Peter Ruane

CREATIVE DIRECTORS
Bruce Duckworth
David Turner

CLIENT
Marks & Spencer

AGENCY
Turner Duckworth/London

03111D

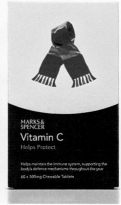

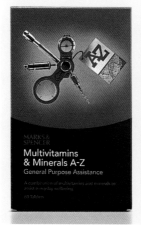

MERIT AWARD
Commercial Product Packaging

DESIGNER
Bruce Duckworth

CREATIVE DIRECTORS
Bruce Duckworth
David Turner

CLIENT
Superdrug

AGENCY
Turner Duckworth/London

03112D

MERIT AWARD
**Promotional and Point of
Purchase Posters: Single**

DESIGNER
Andy Lee Chow Wei

ART DIRECTOR
Andy Lee Chow Wei

PHOTOGRAPHER
Joyce Choo

CREATIVE DIRECTOR
Tan Sin Kuan

CLIENT
Asia Pacific Breweries

AGENCY
Associates In Design/Singapore

03113D

MERIT AWARD
**Promotional and Point of
Purchase Posters: Single**

DESIGNER
Eric Yeo

ART DIRECTOR
Eric Yeo

WRITER
Jay Phua

PHOTOGRAPHER
Teo Studio

CREATIVE DIRECTORS
Rob Sherlock
Robert Gaxiola

CLIENT
KHL Marketing

AGENCY
FCB/Singapore

03115D

MERIT AWARD
**Promotional and Point of
Purchase Posters: Single**

DESIGNER
Eric Yeo

ART DIRECTORS
Eric Yeo
Ko Min Jung

WRITER
Andrew McKechnie

PHOTOGRAPHER
Teo Studio

CREATIVE DIRECTORS
Rob Sherlock
Robert Gaxiola

CLIENT
KHL Marketing

AGENCY
FCB/Singapore

03116D

MERIT AWARD
**Promotional and Point of
Purchase Posters: Single**

DESIGNER
Eric Yeo

ART DIRECTOR
Eric Yeo

WRITER
Raymond Quah

PHOTOGRAPHER
Teo Studio

CREATIVE DIRECTORS
Rob Sherlock
Robert Gaxiola

CLIENT
KHL Marketing

AGENCY
FCB/Singapore

03117D

MERIT AWARD
**Promotional and Point of
Purchase Posters: Single**

DESIGNER
Eric Yeo

ART DIRECTOR
Eric Yeo

WRITER
Robert Gaxiola

PHOTOGRAPHER
Stock

CREATIVE DIRECTORS
Rob Sherlock
Robert Gaxiola

CLIENT
Terminal One

AGENCY
FCB/Singapore

03118D

MERIT AWARD
Promotional and Point of
Purchase Posters: Single

DESIGNER
Jonathan Nah

ART DIRECTOR
Jonathan Nah

WRITER
Noel Yeo

PHOTOGRAPHERS
Jimmy Fok
Calibre Pictures

ILLUSTRATOR
Rhapsodi Digital Art

CREATIVE DIRECTOR
Lim Soon Huat

CLIENT
Swissotel The Stamford,
Singapore

AGENCY
Gosh Advertising/Singapore

03119D

MERIT AWARD
Promotional and Point of
Purchase Posters: Single

ART DIRECTORS
Grant Jacobsen
Martin Schlumpf

WRITER
Sammy Jane Every

ILLUSTRATOR
Andre Schwartz

CREATIVE DIRECTOR
Alan Irvin

CLIENT
Johannesburg Zoo

AGENCY
Grey Worldwide/Johannesburg

03120D

ペットのための健康保険があります。　anicom

MERIT AWARD
**Promotional and Point of
Purchase Posters: Single**

DESIGNERS
Kozue Asano
Shin Nagashima

ART DIRECTOR
Shin Nagashima

WRITER
Tomoki Harada

PHOTOGRAPHER
Tetsuya Tsuji

CLIENT
Anicom

AGENCY
Hakuhodo/Tokyo

03125D

MERIT AWARD
**Promotional and Point of
Purchase Posters: Single**

ART DIRECTOR
Masahiko Gonda

CLIENT
Sakai, Sake Brewing

AGENCY
Hakuhodo/Tokyo

03121D

355

MERIT AWARD
**Promotional and Point of
Purchase Posters: Single**

DESIGNER
Mikael Blom

ART DIRECTOR
Mikael Blom

CREATIVE DIRECTOR
Anders Kornestedt

CLIENT
Röhsska Design Museum

AGENCY
Happy Forsman & Bodenfors/
Göteborg

03123D

MERIT AWARD
**Promotional and Point of
Purchase Posters: Single**

DESIGNER
Andreas Kittel

ART DIRECTOR
Andreas Kittel

WRITER
Andreas Kittel

ILLUSTRATOR
Nicodemus Tessin

CREATIVE DIRECTOR
Anders Kornestedt

CLIENT
Swedish Museum of Architecture

AGENCY
Happy Forsman & Bodenfors/
Göteborg

03124D

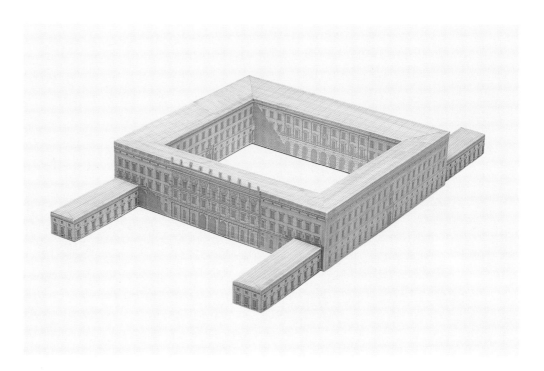

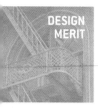

MERIT AWARD
**Promotional and Point of
Purchase Posters: Single**

ART DIRECTOR
Till Schaffarczyk

WRITER
Till Schaffarczyk

PHOTOGRAPHER
Joachim Bacherl

CLIENT
Buchladen Lesecafe

AGENCY
Ogilvy & Mather/Frankfurt

03128D

MERIT AWARD
**Promotional and Point of
Purchase Posters: Single**

ART DIRECTOR
Ute Sonntag

WRITERS
Paul von Mühlendahl
Pit Kho

ILLUSTRATOR
Peter Langpeter

CREATIVE DIRECTOR
Pit Kho

CLIENT
IBM Germany

AGENCY
Ogilvy & Mather/Frankfurt

03129D

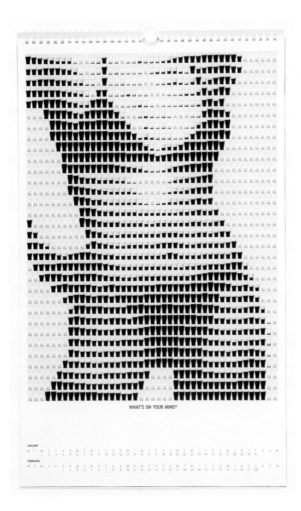

WHAT'S ON YOUR MIND?

MERIT AWARD
**Promotional and Point of
Purchase Posters: Single**

ART DIRECTORS
Tham Khai Meng
Richard Johnson
Kelly Dickinson

WRITER
Andy Greenaway

PHOTOGRAPHERS
Julian Watt
Kelly Dickinson

ILLUSTRATOR
Richard Johnson

CREATIVE DIRECTORS
Andy Greenaway
Craig Smith

CLIENT
Gaelic Inns

AGENCY
Ogilvy & Mather/Singapore

03130D

The
Time
of
Your
Life

STEPPENWOLF
MAINSTAGE THEATRE
Dates SEPT 12 - NOV 3, 2002
(312)335-1650
WWW.STEPPENWOLF.ORG

MERIT AWARD
**Promotional and Point of
Purchase Posters: Single**

DESIGNER
Steve Sandstrom

ART DIRECTOR
Steve Sandstrom

ILLUSTRATOR
Steve Sandstrom

CREATIVE DIRECTOR
Joe Sciarrotta

CLIENT
Ogilvy & Mather

AGENCY
Sandstrom Design/Portland

03131D

359

MERIT AWARD
**Promotional and Point of
Purchase Posters: Single**

DESIGNER
Jim McDonough

ART DIRECTOR
Jim McDonough

WRITER
Jeff Heath

PHOTOGRAPHER
Giles Hancock

CREATIVE DIRECTORS
Jim McDonough
Jeff Heath

CLIENT
Shaws Hand-Made Chocolate

AGENCY
THEORY/San Francisco

03132D

MERIT AWARD
**Promotional and Point of
Purchase Posters: Single**

DESIGNERS
Dana Arnett
Hans Seeger

ART DIRECTOR
Dana Arnett

WRITER
Dana Arnett

CREATIVE DIRECTOR
Dana Arnett

CLIENT
Dallas/Ft. Worth AIGA

AGENCY
VSA Partners/Chicago

03133D

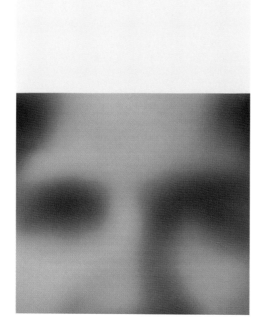

MERIT

MERIT AWARD
**Promotional and Point of
Purchase Posters: Campaign**

DESIGNERS
Luis Peña
Hanni El-Khatib

ART DIRECTOR
Luis Peña

ILLUSTRATORS
Hanni El-Khatib
Luis Peña

CREATIVE DIRECTOR
Luis Peña

CLIENT
J-Boogie

AGENCY
Butler, Shine & Stern/PeñaBrand/
Sausalito

03134D

Also won:
MERIT AWARD
**Promotional and Point of
Purchase Posters: Single**

MERIT AWARD
**Promotional and Point of
Purchase Posters: Campaign**

DESIGNERS
Haruhiko Sugiyama
Shinichi Ohnuma

ART DIRECTOR
Taka Naito

WRITER
Taka Naito

PHOTOGRAPHER
Shoji Uchida

ILLUSTRATOR
Hideki Minami

CREATIVE DIRECTOR
Taka Naito

CLIENT
Elecom

AGENCY
Hakuhodo/Osaka

03135D

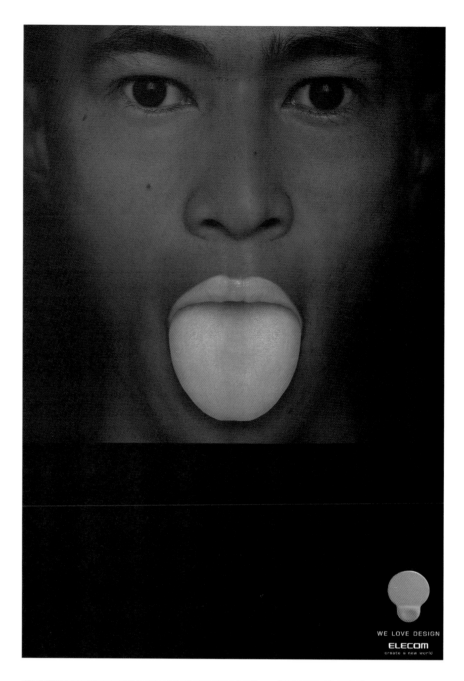

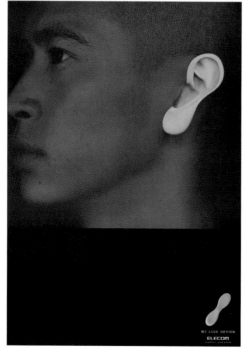

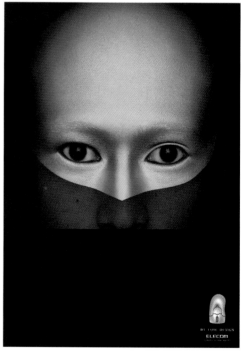

MERIT AWARD
**Promotional and Point of
Purchase Posters: Campaign**

DESIGNER
Lisa Careborg

ART DIRECTOR
Lisa Careborg

PHOTOGRAPHER
Henrik Lindvall

CREATIVE DIRECTOR
Anders Kornestedt

CLIENT
Swedish Museum of Architecture

AGENCY
Happy Forsman & Bodenfors/
Göteborg

03136D

Also won:
**MERIT AWARD
Public Service/Political
Posters: Campaign**

363

DESIGN MERIT

MERIT AWARD
**Promotional and Point of
Purchase Posters: Campaign**

ART DIRECTOR
Christan Boshoff

WRITER
Paula Lang

PHOTOGRAPHER
Graham Kietzmann

CREATIVE DIRECTOR
Graham Warsop

CLIENT
Nedbank

AGENCY
The Jupiter Drawing Room
(South Africa)/Johannesburg

03137D

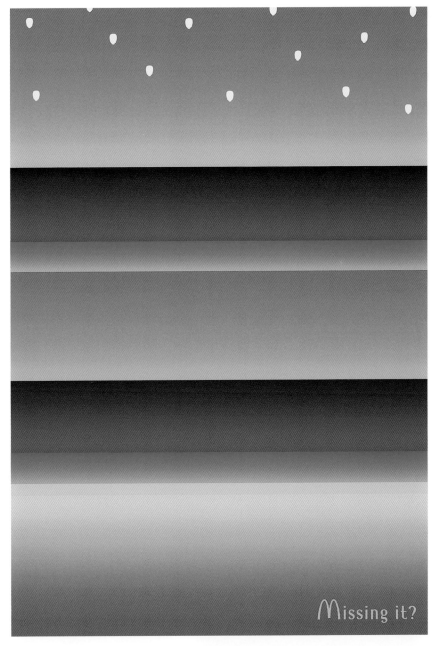

MERIT AWARD
**Promotional and Point of
Purchase Posters: Campaign**

ART DIRECTORS
Jon Loke
Victor Ng

WRITERS
Victor Ng
Jon Loke

ILLUSTRATORS
Jon Loke
Lay Leng

CREATIVE DIRECTORS
Tay Guan Hin
Ng Tian It

CLIENT
McDonald's

AGENCY
Leo Burnett/Singapore

03138D

365

MERIT AWARD
Promotional and Point of
Purchase Posters: Campaign

DESIGNER
Prasad Raghavan

ART DIRECTOR
Prasad Raghavan

WRITER
Upputuru Emmanuel

PHOTOGRAPHER
Manoj K. Jain

ILLUSTRATOR
Ramesh Arora

CREATIVE DIRECTOR
Sunil Vysyaprath

CLIENT
Dr. Morepen

AGENCY
Ogilvy & Mather/New Delhi

03139D

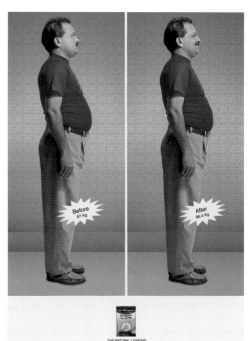

MERIT AWARD
Promotional and Point of Purchase Posters: Campaign

DESIGNER
Jiten Thukral

ART DIRECTOR
Sunil Vysyaprath

WRITER
Nirmal Pulickal

PHOTOGRAPHER
Bharat Sikka

CREATIVE DIRECTORS
Josy Paul
Sunil Vysyaprath

CLIENT
www.Indiatimes.com

AGENCY
RMG David/New Delhi

03140D

367

MERIT AWARD
**Promotional and Point of
Purchase Posters: Campaign**

DESIGNER
Daisuke Kokubo

ART DIRECTOR
Shintaro Tanabe

WRITER
Barton Corley

CREATIVE DIRECTORS
John C. Jay
Sumiko Sato

CLIENT
Nike Japan

AGENCY
Wieden + Kennedy/Tokyo

03141D

MERIT AWARD
**Environmental Design
Retail, Office, Restaurant,
Outdoor**

DESIGNERS
Brian Collins
Edward Chiquitucto
Weston Bingham
Roman Luba
Alan Orr

CREATIVE DIRECTOR
Brian Collins

CLIENT
Hershey

AGENCY
Ogilvy & Mather/Brand
Integration Group/New York

03143D

MERIT AWARD
**Environmental Design
Retail, Office, Restaurant,
Outdoor**

DESIGNERS
Sandra Schilling
Tim Stuebane

ART DIRECTORS
Sandra Schilling
Tim Stuebane

WRITERS
Peter Quester
Brigit van den Valentyn

CREATIVE DIRECTORS
Martin Pross
Matthias Schmidt
Robert Krause

CLIENT
DaimlerChrysler AG, DCVD

AGENCY
Scholz & Friends/Berlin

03144D

MERIT AWARD
**Environmental Design
Retail, Office, Restaurant,
Outdoor**

DESIGNER
Sandra Schilling

ART DIRECTOR
Sandra Schilling

WRITER
Peter Quester

PHOTOGRAPHER
Ralph Baiker

CREATIVE DIRECTORS
Martin Pross
Matthias Schmidt

CLIENT
DaimlerChrysler AG, DCVD

AGENCY
Scholz & Friends/Berlin

03145D

MERIT AWARD
Book Jacket Design

DESIGNER
Jason Jones

ART DIRECTORS
Ken Fox
Mike Petersen

WRITER
Herbert Wagner

PHOTOGRAPHERS
Harley-Davidson Archives
Various

CREATIVE DIRECTOR
Dana Arnett

CLIENT
Harley-Davidson

AGENCY
VSA Partners/Chicago

03146D

MERIT AWARD
Book Jacket Design

DESIGNER
Nichole Dillon

ART DIRECTOR
Jamie Koval

WRITER
Andy Blankenburg

PHOTOGRAPHER
Jim Krantz

CLIENT
Quantum Printing

AGENCY
VSA Partners/Chicago

03147D

MERIT AWARD
Book Jacket Design

DESIGNERS
Miki Araki
Lyle Owerko

ART DIRECTOR
Lyle Owerko

WRITER
Lyle Owerko

PHOTOGRAPHER
Lyle Owerko

CREATIVE DIRECTOR
Lyle Owerko

CLIENT
Wonderlust

AGENCY
Wonderlust Industries Inc./
New York

03148D

DESIGN
MERIT

MERIT AWARD
Consumer Magazine Full Issue

DESIGNER
Mark Diaper

ART DIRECTOR
Mark Diaper

CLIENT
Phaidon

AGENCY
Eggers + Diaper/Berlin

03149D

MERIT AWARD
Consumer Magazine Full Issue

DESIGNER
Mark Diaper

ART DIRECTOR
Mark Diaper

CLIENT
The Public Art Fund/Artangel

AGENCY
Eggers + Diaper/Berlin

03150D

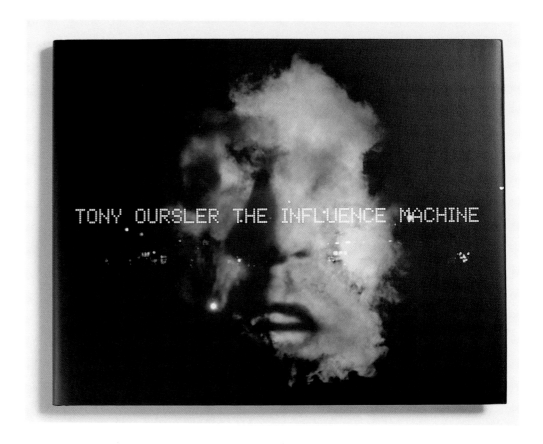

MERIT AWARD
Trade Magazine Full Issue

DESIGNERS
David Lerch
Haesun Lerch
Lee Nichols
Wes Jones

ART DIRECTOR
David Lerch

WRITERS
Phil Hollenbeck
Diana Hickerson
Aaron Barker
Brandi Knox Beck

PHOTOGRAPHER
Phil Hollenbeck

ILLUSTRATORS
Brad Holland
Sandra Dionisi
Marc Burkhardt
Timothy Cook
Brian Cronin

CREATIVE DIRECTOR
Tom Hair

CLIENT
Dallas Society for Visual Arts

AGENCY
Axiom Design Group/Houston

03151D

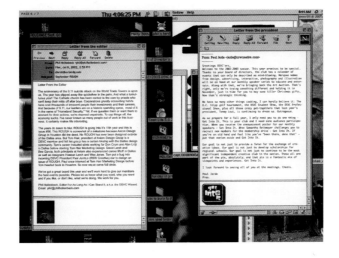

MERIT AWARD
**Direct Mail
Single**

ART DIRECTOR
Ian Mitchell

WRITER
Richard Johnson

PHOTOGRAPHER
Nick Veasey

CREATIVE DIRECTORS
Graham Mills
Jac Nolan

CLIENT
Philips

AGENCY
Arc Marketing/London

03152D

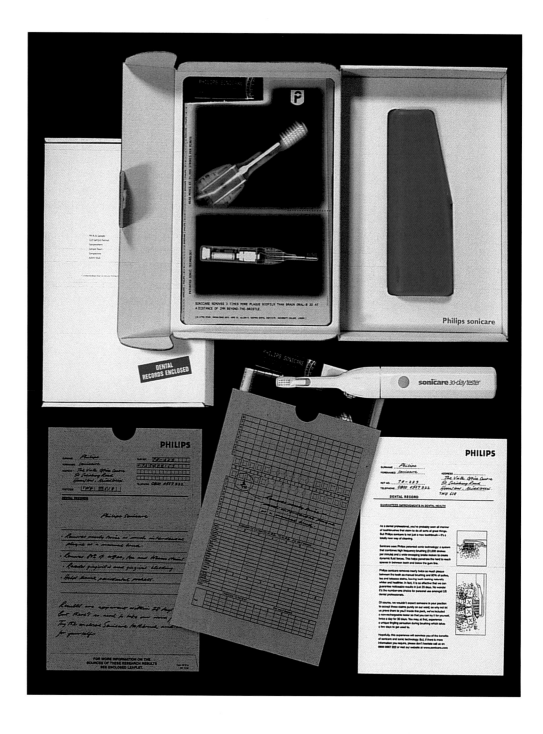

Your door handle requested these.
(It gets lonely when you're not around.)

arnoldworldwide

Out sick.
My everything hurts.

arnoldworldwide

Out busting my ass
for a client. (No, really.)

arnoldworldwide

Winter Wellness Day.
(Na-na-na-na
nah-nah.)

arnoldworldwide

On vacation.
Thinking about coming back.

arnoldworldwide

Personal Day.
My life needs me.

arnoldworldwide

Summer Friday.
(Let me kiss the hand of
whoever dreamt this up.)

arnoldworldwide

MERIT AWARD
**Direct Mail
Single**

DESIGNERS
Lara Gislason
Dan Vlahos

WRITER
Eitan Chitayat

CREATIVE DIRECTORS
Rene Payne
Clif Wong

CLIENT
Arnold Worldwide

AGENCY
Arnold Worldwide/Boston

03153D

MERIT AWARD
**Direct Mail
Single**

DESIGNERS
Katsue Kikita
Chie Arakawa

ART DIRECTOR
Marcus Woolcott

WRITER
Emi Kanda

ILLUSTRATOR
Katsue Kikita

CREATIVE DIRECTORS
Marcus Woolcott

CLIENT
B-She

AGENCY
Beacon Communications/Tokyo

03154D

MERIT AWARD
Direct Mail
Single

DESIGNER
Ray Fesenmaier

ART DIRECTOR
Ray Fesenmaier

WRITER
Brad Gilmore

PHOTOGRAPHERS
Walt Denson
Chris Sheehan

CREATIVE DIRECTOR
Jim Nelson

CLIENT
Harley-Davidson

AGENCY
Carmichael Lynch/Minneapolis

03156D

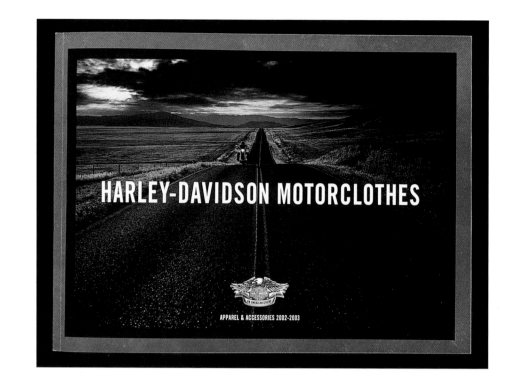

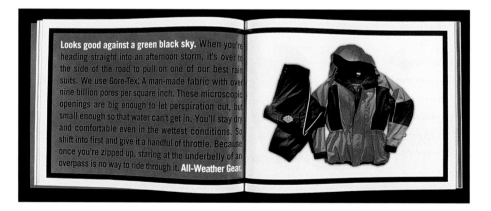

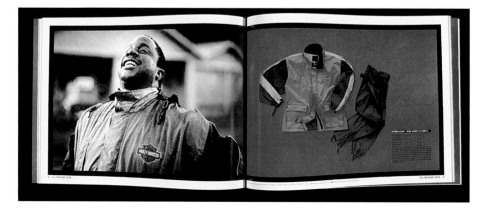

MERIT AWARD
Direct Mail
Single

DESIGNER
Jacob Escobedo

ART DIRECTOR
Kevin Fitzgerald

WRITERS
Jennifer Titus
Heather Johnson

ILLUSTRATORS
Bryan Mon
Kevin Mackenzie

CREATIVE DIRECTOR
Gary Albright

CLIENT
Cartoon Network Marketing

AGENCY
Cartoon Network/Creative Services/
Atlanta

03157D

MERIT AWARD
Direct Mail
Single

DESIGNERS
Paulina Reyes
Nathan Hinz

ART DIRECTOR
Alan Leusink

WRITER
Mark Wirt

PHOTOGRAPHER
Maria Erikson

CREATIVE DIRECTORS
Alan Colvin
Joe Duffy

CLIENT
Archipelago

AGENCY
Duffy/Minneapolis

03158D

MERIT AWARD
**Direct Mail
Single**

ART DIRECTOR
Maik Kähler

WRITER
Christoph Nann

ILLUSTRATOR
Björn Erbslöh

CREATIVE DIRECTOR
Ralf Nolting

CLIENT
Farbraum Digital Art & Litho

AGENCY
Grabarz & Partner Werbeagentur/
Hamburg

03159D

MERIT AWARD
Direct Mail
Single

ART DIRECTOR
Cris Lucke

WRITER
Débora Tenca

PHOTOGRAPHER
Maurício Nahas

CREATIVE DIRECTORS
Cibar Ruiz
José Luiz Mendieta

CLIENT
Litokromia

AGENCY
Grottera/São Paulo

03161D

MERIT AWARD
Direct Mail
Single

DESIGNER
Andreas Kittel

ART DIRECTORS
Andreas Kittel
Anders Kornestedt

WRITER
Björn Engström

CREATIVE DIRECTOR
Anders Kornestedt

CLIENT
Munkedals

AGENCY
Happy Forsman & Bodenfors/
Göteborg

03163D

MERIT AWARD
Direct Mail
Single

DESIGNER
Andreas Kittel

ART DIRECTORS
Andreas Kittel
Anders Kornestedt

WRITER
Björn Engström

CREATIVE DIRECTOR
Anders Kornestedt

CLIENT
Munkedals

AGENCY
Happy Forsman & Bodenfors/
Göteborg

03162D

MUNKEN LYNX 100 g/m²

29 May 2002

Hi!

If you're wonder-

ing why I'm

writing in such

a large font with

such wide line

MUNKEN PURE 13 100 g/m²

spacing, it's

because I'd like

to take this

opportunity to show

off some of our

different Munken

papers, seeing as

MUNKEN PURE 13 100 g/m²

books, please feel

free to contact

me on tel

+46 (0) 524 172 46,

owe.lundberg@munke-

dals.se or visit

www.munkenpapers.com

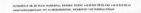

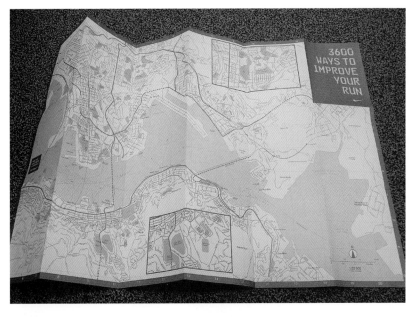

MERIT AWARD
Direct Mail
Single

ART DIRECTOR
Eric Tong

WRITERS
Thomas Tsang
Jinnie Kim

ILLUSTRATOR
Eric Tong

CREATIVE DIRECTORS
Nick Lim
Yvonne Ho

CLIENT
Nike Hong Kong

AGENCY
J. Walter Thompson/Hong Kong

03164D

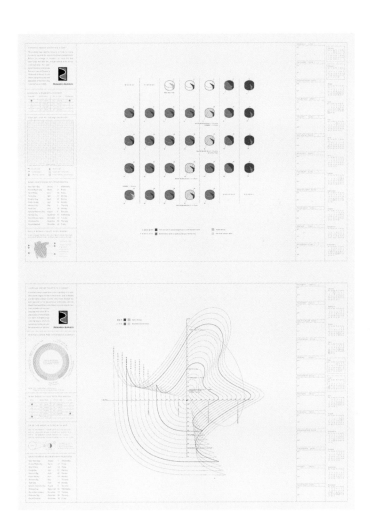

MERIT AWARD
Direct Mail
Single

DESIGNER
Mark Stead

ART DIRECTOR
Mark Stead

WRITER
Livio Tronchin

CREATIVE DIRECTOR
Jenny Ehlers

CLIENT
Research Surveys

AGENCY
King James RSVP/Cape Town

03165D

MERIT AWARD
Direct Mail
Single

ART DIRECTOR
Roy Yung

WRITERS
Bernard Chan
Irene Fung

CREATIVE DIRECTOR
Bernard Chan

CLIENT
Prudential

AGENCY
Leo Burnett/Hong Kong

03167D

MERIT AWARD
Direct Mail
Single

DESIGNER
Anuar Abu

ART DIRECTOR
Tay Guan Hin

WRITERS
Gerard Lim
Yu Sheng Sin

ILLUSTRATOR
Anuar Abu

CREATIVE DIRECTORS
Linda Locke
Tay Guan Hin

CLIENT
Discovery Channel

AGENCY
Leo Burnett/Singapore

03166D

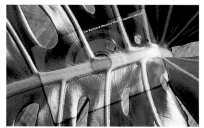

MERIT AWARD
**Direct Mail
Single**

DESIGNER
Ness Higson

ART DIRECTOR
Ness Higson

WRITER
Sarah Coker

PHOTOGRAPHER
Spider Martin

CREATIVE DIRECTOR
Spencer Till

CLIENT
Alabama Bureau of Tourism
& Travel

AGENCY
Lewis Communications/
Birmingham

03168D

MERIT AWARD
Direct Mail
Single

DESIGNER
LOBO

PHOTOGRAPHER
Sandra Bordin

CREATIVE DIRECTOR
Mateus de Paula Santos

CLIENT
Jum Nakao

AGENCY
LOBO/São Paulo

03169D

MERIT AWARD
**Direct Mail
Single**

DESIGNER
Vineet Mahajan

ART DIRECTOR
Vineet Mahajan

WRITER
Rahul Johri

CREATIVE DIRECTOR
Sunil Vysyaprath

CLIENT
Business World

AGENCY
Ogilvy & Mather/New Delhi

03172D

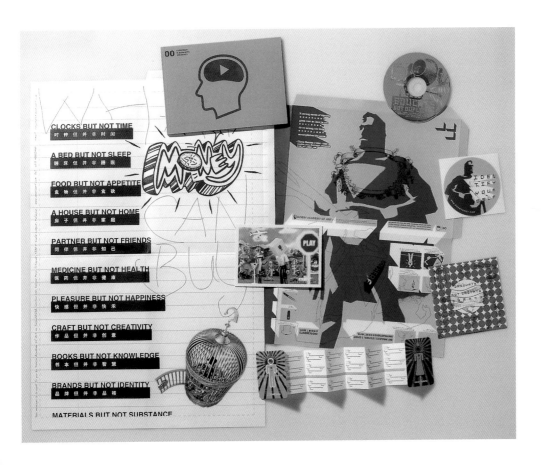

MERIT AWARD
Direct Mail
Single

DESIGNERS
Chong Khong Lum
Lee Kim Yee
Herbie Phoon

ART DIRECTORS
Jesmond Ng
Chung Wei Fung

WRITERS
Herbie Phoon
Soo Man Heng

PHOTOGRAPHER
Lee Kong How

ILLUSTRATOR
Chong Chin Yen

CREATIVE DIRECTOR
Herbie Phoon

CLIENT
Dasein Academy of Art

AGENCY
Option 5/Dasein Art/Kuala Lumpur

03173D

MERIT AWARD
Direct Mail
Single

DESIGNERS
Myrna Newcomb
Kit Hinrichs

ART DIRECTOR
Kit Hinrichs

WRITER
Delphine Hirasuna

CREATIVE DIRECTOR
Kit Hinrichs

CLIENT
Pentagram Design

AGENCY
Pentagram Design/San Francisco

03174D

DESIGN MERIT

DESIGNERS
Takayo Muroga
Kit Hinrichs

ART DIRECTOR
Kit Hinrichs

WRITER
Delphine Hirasuna

PHOTOGRAPHER
Terry Heffernan

CREATIVE DIRECTOR
Kit Hinrichs

CLIENT
Pentagram Design

AGENCY
Pentagram Design/San Francisco

03175D

MERIT AWARD
Direct Mail
Single

DESIGNER
Sheila Smith

WRITER
Victoria List

PHOTOGRAPHERS
Various

CREATIVE DIRECTOR
Kay Ritta

CLIENT
BMW of North America

AGENCY
Ritta & Associates/Englewood

03176D

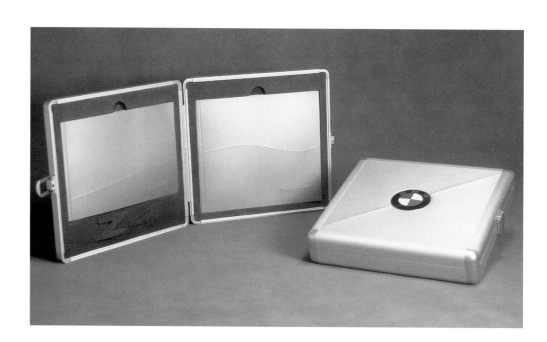

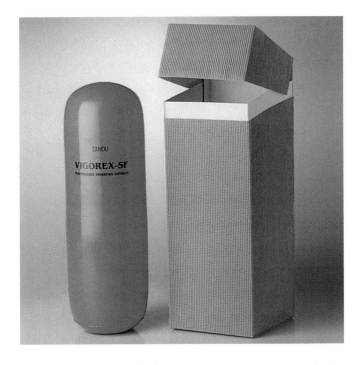

MERIT AWARD
Direct Mail
Single

DESIGNER
Ashok Laxmitukaram Lad

ART DIRECTOR
Ashok Laxmitukaram Lad

WRITER
Ashok Laxmitukaram Lad

PHOTOGRAPHER
Sajan Chandrapaian

ILLUSTRATOR
Vinay Patil

CREATIVE DIRECTOR
Sen Colaco

CLIENT
Zandu Works

AGENCY
Saatchi & Saatchi/Bangalore

03177D

An enlarged capsule of Vigorex-SF (a sexual performance enhancer) was mailed to doctors. When struck, the capsule collapses, but promptly bounces back, leaving no doubt as to what the product's promise is.

MERIT AWARD
Direct Mail
Single

ART DIRECTOR
Michelle Tranter

WRITERS
Michelle Tranter
Rafiq Lehmann

CREATIVE DIRECTORS
Sion Scott-Wilson
Michelle Tranter

CLIENT
Republic of Singapore Navy

AGENCY
Saatchi & Saatchi/Singapore

03178D

MERIT AWARD
Direct Mail
Single

DESIGNER
Steve Sandstrom

ART DIRECTOR
Steve Sandstrom

CREATIVE DIRECTOR
Steve Sandstrom

CLIENT
Sandstrom Design

AGENCY
Sandstrom Design/Portland

03179D

MERIT AWARD
Direct Mail
Single

DESIGNERS
Christine Taylor
Jana Folmert

ART DIRECTOR
Boris Schwiedrzik

WRITER
Helge Bloeck

ILLUSTRATOR
Susann Greuel

CREATIVE DIRECTORS
Kurt-Georg Dieckert
Stefan Schmidt

CLIENT
Sony Computer Entertainment
Germany/PlayStation2

AGENCY
TBWA/Berlin

03180D

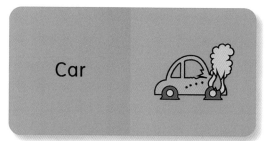

MERIT AWARD
Direct Mail
Single

ART DIRECTORS
Blind
Jessica Edelstein

WRITERS
Neal Hughlett
Suzanne Kisbye

PHOTOGRAPHERS
Photonica
Index
Corbis Images
Don Wong
Getty Images
NASA
Timepix
Magnum Photos
Digital Domain
Broadcast

CREATIVE DIRECTORS
Rob Schwartz
Chris Graves

CLIENT
Nissan

AGENCY
TBWA/Chiat/Day/Los Angeles

03181D

MERIT AWARD
Direct Mail
Single

DESIGNER
Mark Waters

CREATIVE DIRECTORS
Bruce Duckworth
David Turner

CLIENT
Turner Duckworth

AGENCY
Turner Duckworth/London

03182D

DESIGN MERIT

MERIT AWARD
Direct Mail
Single

DESIGNERS
Dan Knuckey
Penny Richards

ART DIRECTOR
Jamie Koval

WRITER
Andy Blankenburg

PHOTOGRAPHERS
Michael Mundy
Jim Koch

CREATIVE DIRECTOR
Jamie Koval

CLIENT
Baker

AGENCY
VSA Partners/Chicago

03183D

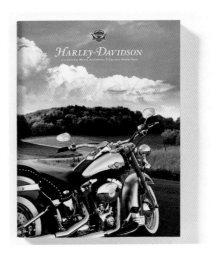

MERIT AWARD
Direct Mail
Single

DESIGNERS
Jason Jones
Andrew Reeves
Ron Berkheimer

ART DIRECTORS
Jason Jones
Dave Carnegie

WRITER
Reid Armbruster

PHOTOGRAPHER
Mid Coast Studio

CREATIVE DIRECTOR
Dana Arnett

CLIENT
Harley-Davidson

AGENCY
VSA Partners/Chicago

03184D

MERIT AWARD
Direct Mail
Single

ART DIRECTOR
Barbara Schirmer

WRITER
Kay Eichner

PHOTOGRAPHER
Hans Starck

CREATIVE DIRECTORS
Michael Reissinger
Kay Eichner

CLIENT
Endless Pain Studio

AGENCY
Weigertpirouzwolf/Hamburg

03185D

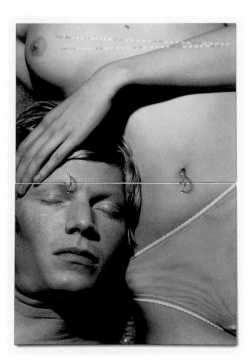

MERIT AWARD
**Direct Mail
Campaign**

DESIGNERS
Lori Butler
Ben Belsky

ART DIRECTOR
Lori Butler

WRITERS
Ariel Lustig
Mary Michael Stewart

CREATIVE DIRECTOR
Nick Cohen

CLIENT
Maximum PC

AGENCY
Mad Dogs and Englishmen/
San Francisco

03187D

397

MERIT AWARD
**Public Service/Political
Posters: Single**

ART DIRECTOR
Scott Lambert

WRITER
Mark Ringer

PHOTOGRAPHER
Alex Aslangul

CREATIVE DIRECTORS
Mark Ringer
Scott Lambert

CLIENT
Victorian Darts Association

AGENCY
FCB/Melbourne

03188D

MERIT AWARD
**Public Service/Political
Posters: Single**

DESIGNER
Andreas Kittel

ART DIRECTOR
Andreas Kittel

PHOTOGRAPHER
Mikael Olsson

CREATIVE DIRECTOR
Anders Kornestedt

CLIENT
Röhsska Design Museum

AGENCY
Happy Forsman & Bodenfors/
Göteborg

03189D

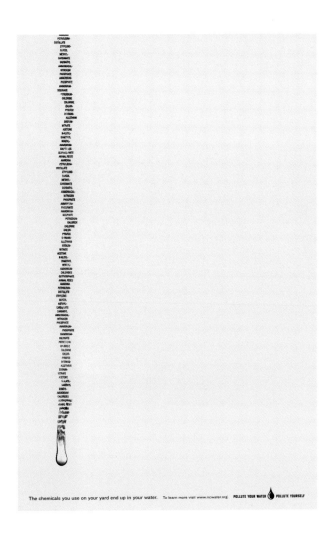

The chemicals you use on your yard end up in your water.   To learn more visit www.ncwater.org.   POLLUTE YOUR WATER ⬤ POLLUTE YOURSELF

MERIT AWARD
Public Service/Political
Posters: Single

ART DIRECTOR
Doug Pedersen

WRITER
Doug Pedersen

PHOTOGRAPHER
Pat Staub

CREATIVE DIRECTOR
Jim Mountjoy

CLIENT
North Carolina Department
of Energy

AGENCY
Loeffler Ketchum Mountjoy/
Charlotte

03190D

WATER
IS COMPRISED OF TWO HYDROGEN ATOMS
AND ONE OXYGEN ATOM.

AT LEAST IT USED TO BE.

Once the source of all life, our water is fast becoming the opposite. Pollution from seemingly harmless actions such as overwatering lawns and not recycling used motor oil ends up poisoning not just our water but also ourselves. To learn more about what you can do to help stop water pollution, visit www.ncwater.org or call 1-919-733-4064.

POLLUTE YOUR WATER ⬤ POLLUTE YOURSELF

MERIT AWARD
Public Service/Political
Posters: Single

ART DIRECTOR
Doug Pedersen

WRITER
Doug Pedersen

CREATIVE DIRECTOR
Jim Mountjoy

CLIENT
North Carolina Department
of Energy

AGENCY
Loeffler Ketchum Mountjoy/
Charlotte

03191D

MERIT AWARD
**Public Service/Political
Posters: Single**

ART DIRECTOR
Rick Bryson

WRITER
Brett Compton

PHOTOGRAPHER
Imagination Brewery

CREATIVE DIRECTOR
Bart Cleveland

CLIENT
Georgia Tech

AGENCY
Sawyer Riley Compton/Atlanta

03192D

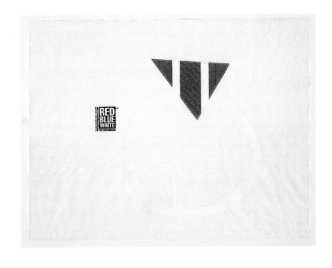

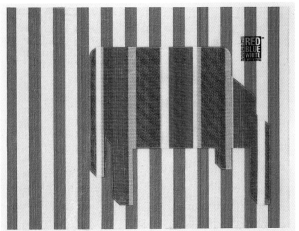

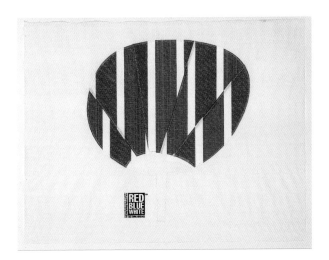

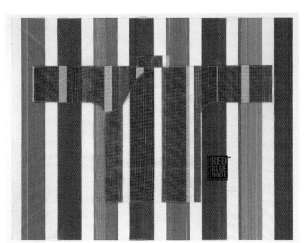

MERIT AWARD
Public Service/Political
Posters: Campaign

DESIGNER
Wai-Ki Kwok

ART DIRECTOR
Stanley Wong

ILLUSTRATOR
Stanley Wong

CREATIVE DIRECTOR
Stanley Wong

CLIENT
Hong Kong Heritage Museum

AGENCY
Anothermountainman/Hong Kong

03197D

DESIGN
MERIT

MERIT AWARD
**Public Service/Political
Booklet/Brochure & Other
Collateral**

DESIGNER
Lisa Careborg

ART DIRECTOR
Lisa Careborg

PHOTOGRAPHER
Jesper Sundelin

CREATIVE DIRECTOR
Anders Kornestedt

CLIENT
Swedish Museum of Architecture

AGENCY
Happy Forsman & Bodenfors/
Göteborg

03194D

MERIT AWARD
Public Service/Political
Booklet/Brochure & Other
Collateral

DESIGNERS
Deepak Dogra
Hemant Anant Jain

ART DIRECTOR
Deepak Dogra

WRITER
Hemant Anant Jain

ILLUSTRATOR
Deepak Dogra

CREATIVE DIRECTOR
Sunil Vysyaprath

CLIENT
Mid Land Bookshop

AGENCY
Ogilvy & Mather/New Delhi

03195D

403

MERIT AWARD
Public Service/Political Booklet/Brochure & Other Collateral

DESIGNER
Brock Haldeman

WRITERS
Brock Haldeman
Jeremy Bokor

CREATIVE DIRECTOR
Brock Haldeman

CLIENT
Pivot Design

AGENCY
Pivot Design/Chicago

03196D

The fallout continues; corporate energy giant, once rated as among the world's top ten conglomerates, dissolves amidst scandal. Democrats and Republicans say no deal possible on 2003 budget, but no **love** lost. Another victim today; sniper still on the loose. Bishops revamping policy on abusive priests; draft expected next week. Iraq vents fury at U.N. resolution **giving** rise to speculation about sanctions compliance. Tornado death toll climbs to 38. House gives Bush authority for war. Lack of corporate management **kindness** cited as major cause of employee stress. British royals hold rape case counseling talks. Unemployment rises; **prosperity** for many doubtful until second quarter of next year. New study finds lymphatic-related cancers increasing. Al Qaeda tied to Bali blast that killed 180. Infamous New York crime **family** at it again says Feds. Where is Bin Laden, are we any closer to knowing? Cloning reaches new roadblock; stem cell research halted. The **joy** is gone; divorce rates on the rise. Threat of dock workers' strike looms at all major ports. ILWU is persistent, but major ports' execs say 'proposal stinks'. Medicare, **health** care costs to skyrocket in 2002. Most major airlines hit hard in wake of towers' tragedy. New accusations in murder-for-hire case. Corporations' lack of **generosity** seen as driving force in class action suit. 130 indicted in cocaine arrests; biggest bust in state's history. More trouble in the Middle East as **peace** talks between Arabs and Jews dissolve; violence escalates. Retirement plans evaporate as stocks tumble again today.

love

giving

kindness

prosperity

family

joy

health

generosity

peace

uℓısǝpivot

On behalf of our clients,
a donation will be made this year
to America's Second Harvest.
Seeing things to be thankful for
often means looking beyond the headlines.
From all of us at Pivot Design,
best wishes for a warm and wonderful
holiday season,
and a peaceful new year.

America's Second Harvest is the nation's largest domestic
hunger relief organization. Through a network of over
200 food banks and food-rescue programs, they distribute
food to 26 million hungry Americans each year, 8 million of
whom are children. Last year, America's Second Harvest
distributed 1.4 billion pounds of food to needy Americans
across all 50 states and Puerto Rico.

uℓısǝpivot

On behalf of our clients,
a donation will be made this year
to America's Second Harvest.

From all of us at Pivot Design,
best wishes for a warm and wonderful
holiday season,
and a peaceful new year.

America's Second Harvest is the nation's largest domestic
hunger relief organization. Through a network of over
200 food banks and food-rescue programs, they distribute
food to 26 million hungry Americans each year, 8 million of
whom are children. Last year, America's Second Harvest
distributed 1.4 billion pounds of food to needy Americans
across all 50 states and Puerto Rico.

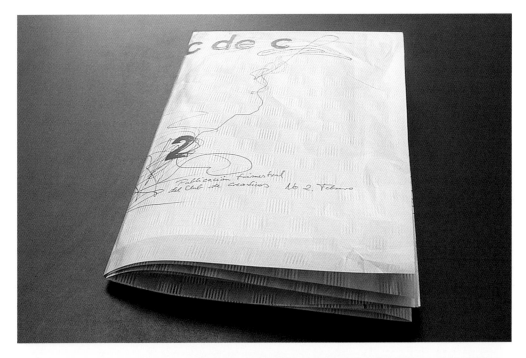

MERIT AWARD
**Public Service/Political
Booklet/Brochure & Other
Collateral**

DESIGNERS
Ed Irujo
Uschi Henkes

ART DIRECTOR
Uschi Henkes

WRITERS
Jose Luis Moro
David Palacios
Concha Wert

CREATIVE DIRECTORS
Uschi Henkes
Urs Frick

CLIENT
C de C

AGENCY
Zapping/Madrid

03193D

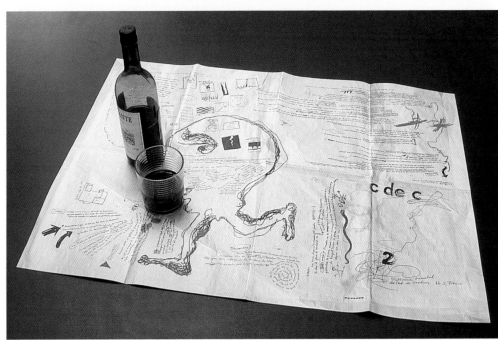

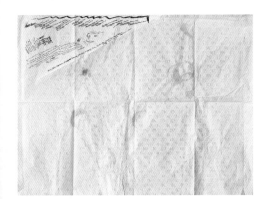

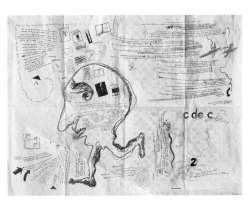

405

PUBLIC

SERVICE

MERIT

MERIT AWARD
Public Service/Political Newspaper or Magazine Single

ART DIRECTOR
Paul Brazier

WRITER
Nick Worthington

PHOTOGRAPHER
Rik Pinkcombe

CREATIVE DIRECTORS
Paul Brazier
Nick Worthington

CLIENT
DFT

AGENCY
Abbott Mead Vickers.BBDO/ London

03327A

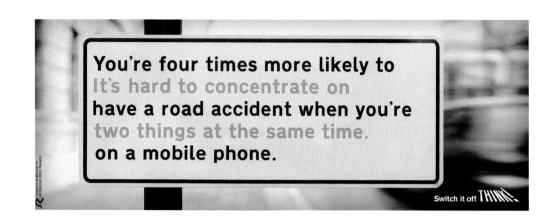

MERIT AWARD
Public Service/Political Newspaper or Magazine Single

ART DIRECTORS
Rob Baird
Alex Burnard
Mike Del Marmol

WRITER
Roger Baldacci

PHOTOGRAPHERS
Rob Baird
Alex Burnard
Greg Carter
Mike Del Marmol

ILLUSTRATOR
Jasper Goodall

AGENCY PRODUCERS
Aidan Finnan
Sally Hunter
Andrea Ricker

CREATIVE DIRECTORS
Ron Lawner
Alex Bogusky
Pete Favat
Ari Merkin
Roger Baldacci

CLIENT
American Legacy Foundation

AGENCY
Arnold Worldwide/Boston and Crispin Porter + Bogusky/Miami

03330A

MERIT AWARD
**Public Service/Political
Newspaper or Magazine
Single**

ART DIRECTORS
Rob Baird
Alex Burnard
Mike Del Marmol

WRITER
Roger Baldacci

PHOTOGRAPHERS
Rob Baird
Alex Burnard
Greg Carter
Mike Del Marmol

ILLUSTRATOR
Jasper Goodall

AGENCY PRODUCERS
Aidan Finnan
Sally Hunter
Andrea Ricker

CREATIVE DIRECTORS
Ron Lawner
Alex Bogusky
Pete Favat
Ari Merkin
Roger Baldacci

CLIENT
American Legacy Foundation

AGENCY
Arnold Worldwide/Boston and
Crispin Porter + Bogusky/Miami

03331A

409

MERIT AWARD
Public Service/Political
Newspaper or Magazine
Single

ART DIRECTOR
James Clunie

WRITER
Tim Cawley

ILLUSTRATOR
James Clunie

AGENCY PRODUCERS
Audrey Cullen
Christine Moe

CLIENT
Cub Scouts

AGENCY
Carmichael Lynch/Minneapolis

03332A

AS LONG AS THERE ARE OLD LADIES WHO
STINK AT CROSSING STREETS, WE'LL BE HERE.

CUB SCOUT ENROLLMENT IS HERE. CALL 763-545-4550 OR VISIT JOINCUBS.COM

MERIT AWARD
**Public Service/Political
Newspaper or Magazine
Single**

ART DIRECTOR
Wayne Antill

WRITER
Ulric Charteris

PHOTOGRAPHER
Michael Lewis

CREATIVE DIRECTOR
Wayne Antill

CLIENT
SA Scouts Association

AGENCY
FCB/Johannesburg

03335A

MERIT AWARD
**Public Service/Political
Newspaper or Magazine
Single**

ART DIRECTOR
Mandy Kennedy

WRITER
Charlie Cook

ILLUSTRATOR
Jeremy Andrew

CREATIVE DIRECTOR
Tom McFarlane

CLIENT
Qantas

AGENCY
M&C Saatchi/Sydney

03336A

MERIT AWARD
**Public Service/Political
Newspaper or Magazine
Single**

ART DIRECTOR
Tom Gibson

WRITER
Joe Alexander

PHOTOGRAPHER
Jacques Lowe

CREATIVE DIRECTOR
Joe Alexander

CLIENT
John F. Kennedy Library
Foundation

AGENCY
The Martin Agency/Richmond

03337A

MERIT AWARD
**Public Service/Political
Newspaper or Magazine
Single**

ART DIRECTORS
Gregory Yeo
Steve Hough

WRITERS
Steve Hough
Gregory Yeo

PHOTOGRAPHER
Museum Archive

ILLUSTRATORS
Dreamimaging
Procolor
Hybrid Studio

CREATIVE DIRECTOR
Craig Smith

CLIENT
Changi Museum

AGENCY
Ogilvy & Mather/Singapore

03338A

Also won:
MERIT AWARD
**Public Service/Political
Outdoor and Posters
Single**

MERIT AWARD
Public Service/Political Newspaper or Magazine Single

ART DIRECTOR
William Hammond

WRITER
George Low

ILLUSTRATOR
Grant Linton

CREATIVE DIRECTOR
Brett Wild

CLIENT
Adopt-a-Minefield

AGENCY
Saatchi & Saatchi/Johannesburg

03339A

MERIT AWARD
Public Service/Political Newspaper or Magazine Single

ART DIRECTOR
John Foster

WRITER
David Thackray

PHOTOGRAPHER
Teo Chai Guan

CREATIVE DIRECTOR
Sion Scott-Wilson

CLIENT
International Aid for Korean Animals & Korea Animal Protection Society

AGENCY
Saatchi & Saatchi/Singapore

03186A

413

MERIT AWARD
**Public Service/Political
Newspaper or Magazine
Campaign**

ART DIRECTOR
Rob Baird

WRITER
Roger Baldacci

PHOTOGRAPHER
Richard Avedon

AGENCY PRODUCERS
Aidan Finnan
Katherine Hennesy
Greg Carter

CREATIVE DIRECTORS
Ron Lawner
Pete Favat
Roger Baldacci

CLIENT
American Legacy Foundation

AGENCY
Arnold Worldwide/Boston

03342A

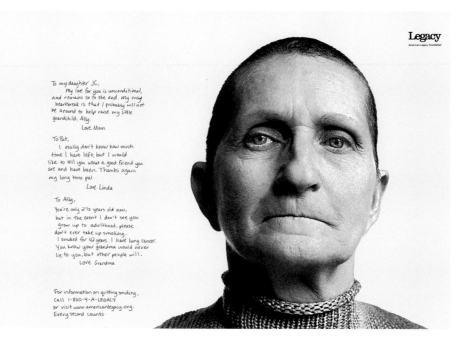

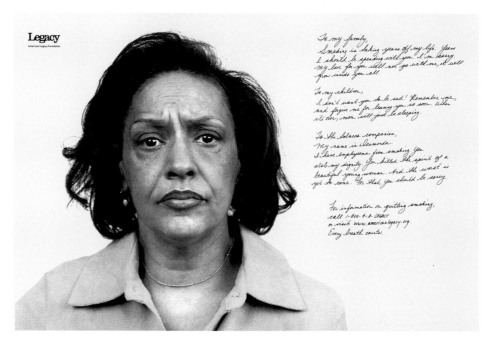

MERIT

MERIT

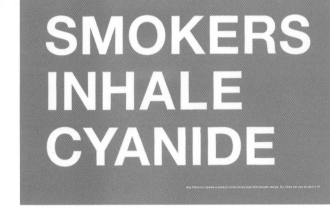

CIGARETTE SMOKE HAS ARSENIC

A little hint the tobacco industry forgot to mention. So, what can you do about it?

SMOKERS INHALE CYANIDE

Big Tobacco creates a product more poisonous than people realize. So, what can you do about it?

AMMONIA IS ADDED TO CIGARETTES

One of the 599 ingredients the tobacco industry puts in cigarettes. So, what can you do about it?

MERIT AWARD
Public Service/Political Newspaper or Magazine Campaign

ART DIRECTOR
Paul Stechschulte

WRITER
Ari Merkin

PHOTOGRAPHER
Sebastian Gray

AGENCY PRODUCERS
Julieana Wilson
Jessica Hoffman

CREATIVE DIRECTORS
Ron Lawner
Alex Bogusky
Pete Favat
Ari Merkin
Roger Baldacci

CLIENT
American Legacy Foundation

AGENCY
Arnold Worldwide/Boston and
Crispin Porter + Bogusky/Miami

03341A

Also won:
MERIT AWARDS
Public Service/Political Newspaper or Magazine Single

415

MERIT AWARD
**Public Service/Political
Newspaper or Magazine
Campaign**

ART DIRECTOR
Drew Lees

WRITER
Farrokh Madon

PHOTOGRAPHERS
Teo Chai Guan
Teo Studio

ILLUSTRATOR
Procolor

CREATIVE DIRECTOR
Chris Mitchell

CLIENT
Singapore Red Cross Society

AGENCY
Batey/Singapore

03343A

THIS MUCH CAN SAVE A BABY'S LIFE.

Every little helps. Give blood. Give life.

THIS MUCH CAN SAVE A CHILD'S LIFE.

Every little helps. Give blood. Give life.

THIS MUCH CAN SAVE AN ADULT'S LIFE.

Every little helps. Give blood. Give life.

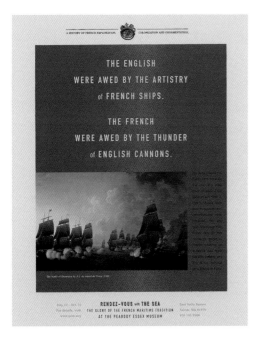

THE ENGLISH
WERE AWED BY THE ARTISTRY
of FRENCH SHIPS.

THE FRENCH
WERE AWED BY THE THUNDER
of ENGLISH CANNONS.

RENDEZ-VOUS with THE SEA
THE GLORY OF THE FRENCH MARITIME TRADITION
AT THE PEABODY ESSEX MUSEUM

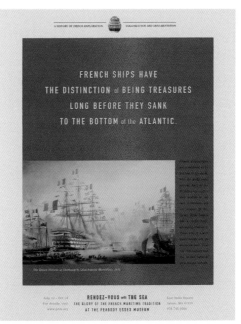

FRENCH SHIPS HAVE
THE DISTINCTION of BEING TREASURES
LONG BEFORE THEY SANK
TO THE BOTTOM of the ATLANTIC.

RENDEZ-VOUS with THE SEA
THE GLORY OF THE FRENCH MARITIME TRADITION
AT THE PEABODY ESSEX MUSEUM

ONLY THE FRENCH COULD
USE 2/3 of THE
EARTH'S SURFACE AS
AN EXCUSE TO DECORATE.

RENDEZ-VOUS with THE SEA
THE GLORY OF THE FRENCH MARITIME TRADITION
AT THE PEABODY ESSEX MUSEUM

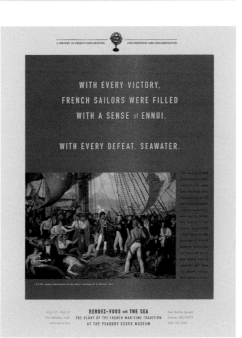

WITH EVERY VICTORY,
FRENCH SAILORS WERE FILLED
WITH A SENSE of ENNUI.

WITH EVERY DEFEAT, SEAWATER.

RENDEZ-VOUS with THE SEA
THE GLORY OF THE FRENCH MARITIME TRADITION
AT THE PEABODY ESSEX MUSEUM

MERIT AWARD
**Public Service/Political
Newspaper or Magazine
Campaign**

ART DIRECTOR
Michael Ancevic

WRITER
Tim Roper

CREATIVE DIRECTOR
Edward Boches

CLIENT
Peabody Essex Museum

AGENCY
Mullen/Wenham

03344A

417

MERIT AWARD
**Public Service/Political
Newspaper or Magazine
Campaign**

ART DIRECTOR
Sergio Lacueva

WRITER
Giovanni Maletti

PHOTOGRAPHER
Graham Kietzmann

ILLUSTRATOR
Sergio Lacueva

CREATIVE DIRECTORS
Sergio Lacueva
Peter Badenhorst

CLIENT
READ

AGENCY
Ogilvy & Mather/Johannesburg

03345A

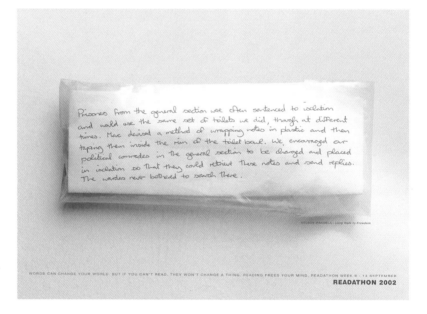

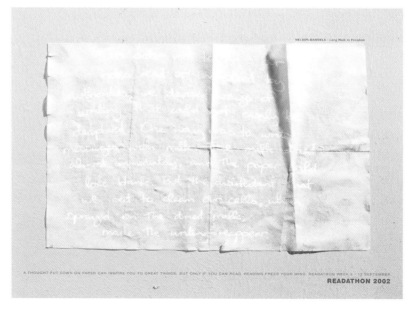

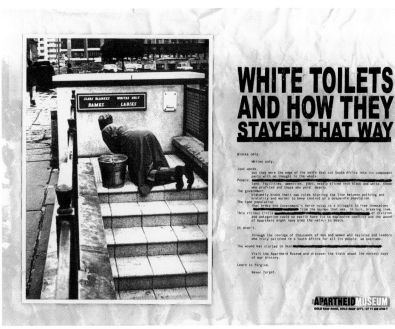

MERIT AWARD
Public Service/Political Newspaper or Magazine Campaign

ART DIRECTOR
Marike Stapleton

WRITER
Felix Kessel

PHOTOGRAPHERS
Ernst Cole
Stock

ILLUSTRATOR
Marike Stapleton

CREATIVE DIRECTOR
Louis Gavin

CLIENT
Apartheid Museum

AGENCY
TBWA/Gavin/Reddy/Johannesburg

03346A

MERIT AWARD
**Public Service/Political
Outdoor and Posters
Single**

ART DIRECTORS
Jessica Foster
Rich Wakefield

WRITER
Jean Weisman

PHOTOGRAPHER
Jim Fiscus

CREATIVE DIRECTORS
Bill Pauls
Rich Wakefield

CLIENT
Save the Children

AGENCY
BBDO/Atlanta

03347A

MERIT AWARD
**Public Service/Political
Outdoor and Posters
Single**

ART DIRECTOR
Mariana Sa

WRITER
Manir Fadel

PHOTOGRAPHER
Marcel Valvassori

CREATIVE DIRECTORS
Jader Rossetto
Pedro Cappeletti
Erh Ray

CLIENT
MASP Museum of Art of São Paulo

AGENCY
DM9 DDB/São Paulo

03350A

MERIT AWARD
**Public Service/Political
Outdoor and Posters
Single**

ART DIRECTOR
Nuno Vasco

WRITER
Tiago Fonseca

PHOTOGRAPHER
David Prior

ILLUSTRATOR
Nuno Vasco

CREATIVE DIRECTOR
Tiago Fonseca

CLIENT
Red Cross Mozambique

AGENCY
Golo Publicidade/Maputo

03351A

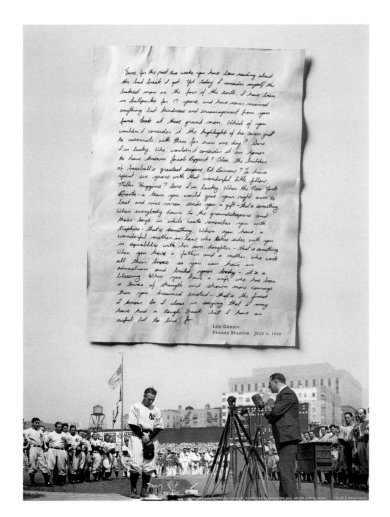

MERIT AWARD
**Public Service/Political
Outdoor and Posters
Single**

ART DIRECTOR
David Estoye

WRITER
Julie Rath

PHOTOGRAPHERS
Mario Parnell
Stock

AGENCY PRODUCER
Hillary DuMoulin

CREATIVE DIRECTORS
Jeffrey Goodby
Rich Silverstein

CLIENT
The ALS Association

AGENCY
Goodby, Silverstein & Partners/
San Francisco

03352A

MERIT AWARD
**Public Service/Political
Outdoor and Posters
Single**

ART DIRECTORS
Jens Frank
Thomas Hofbeck

WRITERS
Jörg Schrod
Dr. Stephan Vogel

PHOTOGRAPHER
Gernot Stracke

CREATIVE DIRECTORS
Thomas Hofbeck
Dr. Stephan Vogel

CLIENT
Doctors Against Animal Testing

AGENCY
Ogilvy & Mather/Frankfurt

03353A

MERIT AWARD
**Public Service/Political
Outdoor and Posters
Single**

ART DIRECTORS
Jens Frank
Thomas Hofbeck

WRITERS
Jörg Schrod
Dr. Stephan Vogel

PHOTOGRAPHER
Stock

CREATIVE DIRECTORS
Thomas Hofbeck
Dr. Stephan Vogel

CLIENT
Doctors Against Animal Testing

AGENCY
Ogilvy & Mather/Frankfurt

03354A

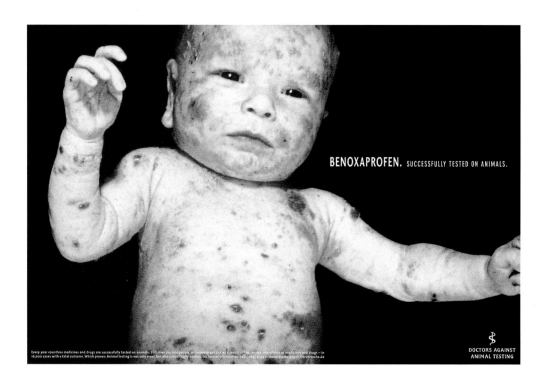

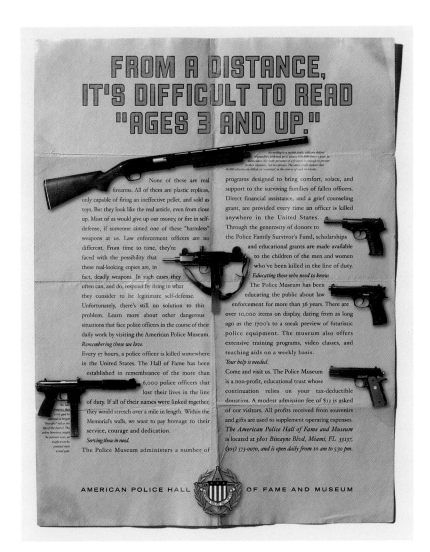

MERIT AWARD
**Public Service/Political
Outdoor and Posters
Campaign**

ART DIRECTOR
Sarah Congdon

WRITER
Aaron DaSilva

PHOTOGRAPHERS
Bradley Smith
Brian Wilder

AGENCY PRODUCERS
Tom Black
Lisa Elliot
Gysele Maas

CREATIVE DIRECTORS
Mick O'Brien
Doug Chapman

CLIENT
Jazz Musicians' Emergency Fund

AGENCY
Allen & Gerritsen/Watertown

03358A

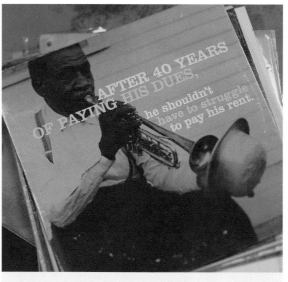

MERIT AWARD
**Public Service/Political
Outdoor and Posters
Campaign**

ART DIRECTOR
Hansong Lin

WRITERS
Daming Zheng
Zhibin Mai

CREATIVE DIRECTOR
Daming Zheng

CLIENT
Polytrade Paper Corporation

AGENCY
Blueflame/Guang Zhou.

03359A

TRANSLATION: Hi, I'm Milky-Mulberry, one of the last two Milky-Mulberry trees in the tropical rainforest on the lower reaches of Amazon (before being made into this piece of paper).

425

MERIT AWARD
**Public Service/Political
Outdoor and Posters
Campaign**

ART DIRECTOR
Phil Mimaki

WRITER
David Oakley

PHOTOGRAPHER
Pat Staub

ILLUSTRATOR
Terence Reynolds

CREATIVE DIRECTORS
David Oakley
John Boone

CLIENT
Spectrum Speakers

AGENCY
BooneOakley/Charlotte

03360A

279	MARCH/APRIL 1998	COMMUNICATION ARTS
271	MARCH/APRIL 1997	COMMUNICATION ARTS
283	SEPTEMBER/OCTOBER 1998	COMMUNICATION ARTS
293	DECEMBER 1999 • ADVERTISING ANNUAL	COMMUNICATION ARTS
299	SEPTEMBER/OCTOBER 2000	COMMUNICATION ARTS
310	JANUARY/FEBRUARY 2002	COMMUNICATION ARTS
306	AUGUST 2001 • PHOTOGRAPHY ANNUAL	COMMUNICATION ARTS
295	MARCH/APRIL 2000	COMMUNICATION ARTS
287	MARCH/APRIL 1999	COMMUNICATION ARTS
301	DECEMBER 2000 • ADVERTISING ANNUAL	COMMUNICATION ARTS
302	JANUARY/FEBRUARY 2001	COMMUNICATION ARTS
303	MARCH/APRIL 2001	COMMUNICATION ARTS
299	SEPTEMBER/OCTOBER 2000	COMMUNICATION ARTS
309	DECEMBER 2001 • ADVERTISING ANNUAL	COMMUNICATION ARTS
307	SEPTEMBER/OCTOBER 2001	COMMUNICATION ARTS
296	MAY/JUNE 2000	COMMUNICATION ARTS
297	JULY 2000 • ILLUSTRATION ANNUAL	COMMUNICATION ARTS
290	AUGUST 1999 • PHOTOGRAPHY ANNUAL	COMMUNICATION ARTS
286	JANUARY/FEBRUARY 1999	COMMUNICATION ARTS
291	SEPTEMBER/OCTOBER 1999	COMMUNICATION ARTS
292	NOVEMBER 1999 • DESIGN ANNUAL	COMMUNICATION ARTS
001	ADVERTISING IS 1% BLACK	COMMUNICATION ARTS
298	AUGUST 2000 • PHOTOGRAPHY ANNUAL	COMMUNICATION ARTS
304	MAY/JUNE 2001	COMMUNICATION ARTS
300	NOVEMBER 2000 • DESIGN ANNUAL	COMMUNICATION ARTS

TO FIND OUT HOW TO MAKE YOUR AGENCY MORE DIVERSE, CALL 318-449-1720. **SPECTRUM SPEAKERS PROGRAM**

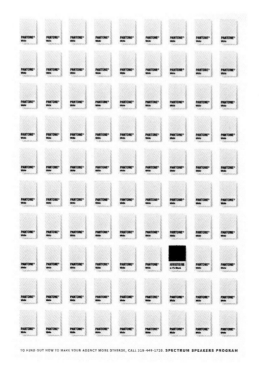

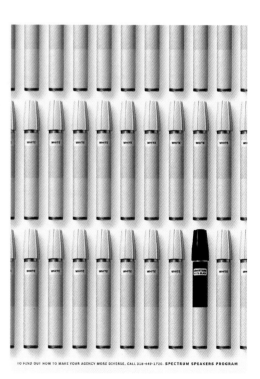

VERY FEW CRIME REPORTS START WITH "THE SUSPECT, A FORMER CUB SCOUT, WAS LAST SEEN..."
CUB SCOUT ENROLLMENT IS HERE. WWW.JOINCUBS.COM

MERIT

IDLE HANDS ARE TROUBLE. HANDS STUCK IN MELTED MARSHMALLOW, LESS SO.
CUB SCOUT ENROLLMENT IS HERE. WWW.JOINCUBS.COM

FUNNY HOW ALL THE COLLEGE SCHOLARSHIPS SEEM TO GO TO KIDS WITH "INTERESTS."
CUB SCOUT ENROLLMENT IS HERE. WWW.JOINCUBS.COM

HE'S BETTER OFF WITH SCRAPES ON HIS ELBOWS THAN COUCH MARKS ON HIS BUTT.
CUB SCOUT ENROLLMENT IS HERE. WWW.JOINCUBS.COM

MERIT AWARD
**Public Service/Political
Outdoor and Posters
Campaign**

ART DIRECTOR
James Clunie

WRITER
Tim Cawley

ILLUSTRATOR
James Clunie

AGENCY PRODUCERS
Audrey Cullen
Christine Moe

CLIENT
Cub Scouts

AGENCY
Carmichael Lynch/Minneapolis

03361A

Also won:
MERIT AWARD
**Public Service/Political
Outdoor and Posters
Single**

427

MERIT AWARD
**Public Service/Political
Outdoor and Posters
Campaign**

ART DIRECTOR
Mark Sorensen

WRITER
Troy Longie

AGENCY PRODUCER
Terri Herber

CREATIVE DIRECTOR
Jac Coverdale

CLIENT
MCASA

AGENCY
Clarity Coverdale Fury/
Minneapolis

03362A

Also won:
MERIT AWARD
**Public Service/Political
Outdoor and Posters
Single**

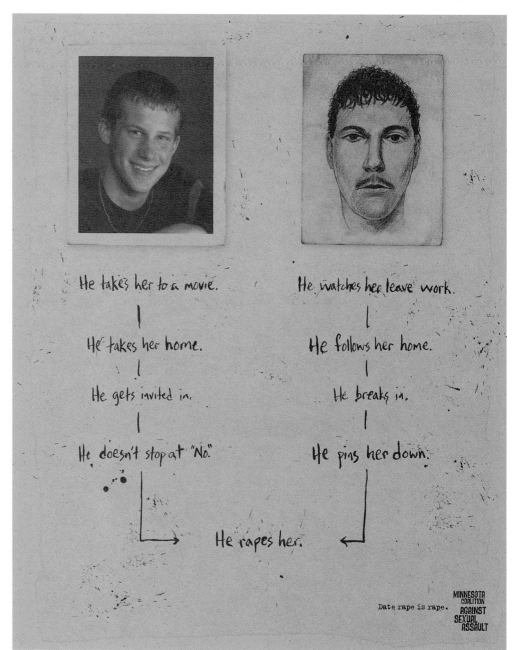

MERIT

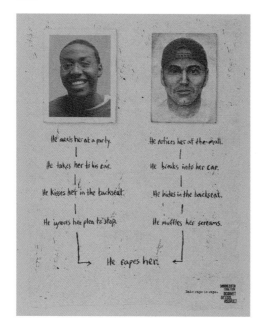

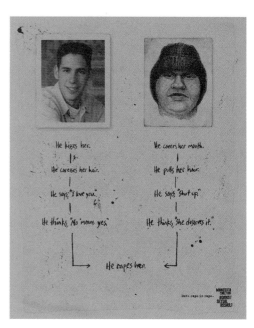

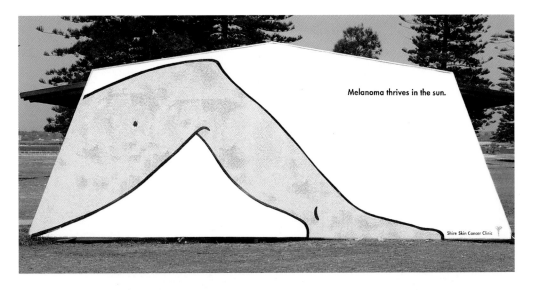

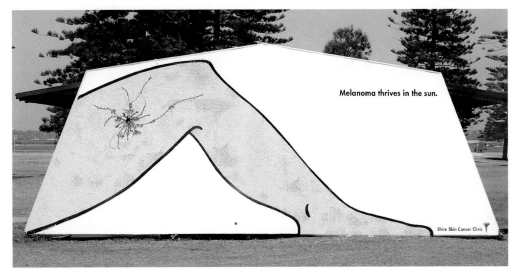

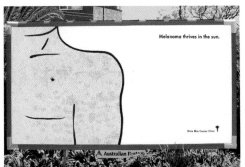

MERIT AWARD
**Public Service/Political
Outdoor and Posters
Campaign**

ART DIRECTORS
Toby Talbot
Leo Premutico

WRITERS
Toby Talbot
Leo Premutico

ILLUSTRATORS
Scott Wilson
Ben Lockwood

CREATIVE DIRECTOR
Mike O'Sullivan

CLIENT
Shire Skin Cancer Clinic

AGENCY
Colenso BBDO/Auckland

03363A

429

MERIT AWARD
**Public Service/Political
Outdoor and Posters
Campaign**

ART DIRECTOR
Steve Drifka

WRITER
Mike Holicek

PHOTOGRAPHER
Tim Waite

ILLUSTRATORS
Bill Kaminski
Jim McDonald

AGENCY PRODUCER
Jules Miller

CREATIVE DIRECTORS
Rich Kohnke
David Hanneken

CLIENT
William F. Eisner Museum of
Advertising & Design

AGENCY
Kohnke Hanneken/Milwaukee

03364A

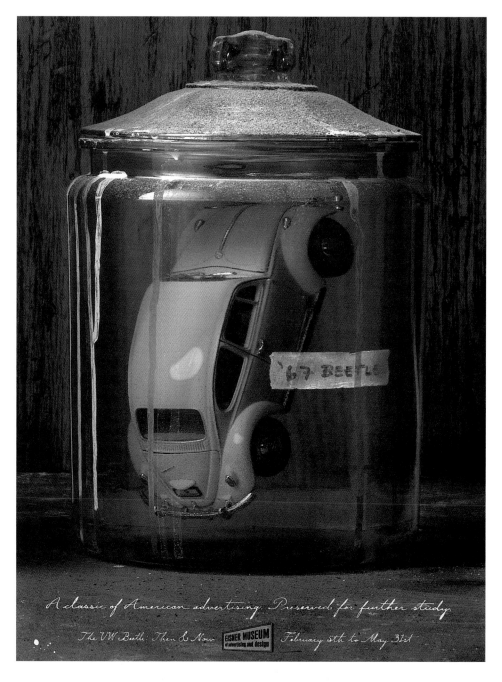

MERIT AWARD
**Public Service/Political
Outdoor and Posters
Campaign**

ART DIRECTORS
David Cucinello
Paolo Grippa

WRITER
Steve Porcaro

CREATIVE DIRECTOR
Basil Mina

CLIENT
Torture Museum of Prague

AGENCY
Leo Burnett/Prague

03365A

MERIT AWARD
**Public Service/Political
Outdoor and Posters
Campaign**

ART DIRECTOR
Sunil Vysyaprath

WRITER
Satbir Singh

PHOTOGRAPHER
Manoj Adhikari

CREATIVE DIRECTOR
Sunil Vysyaprath

CLIENT
HOPE

AGENCY
Ogilvy & Mather/New Delhi

03366A

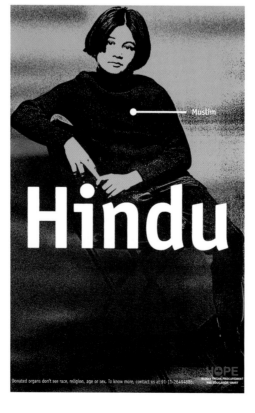

UNIVERSAL DECLARATION OF HUMAN RIGHTS

COUNTRIES THAT SIGNED IT	COUNTRIES THAT INFRINGED IT
Canada	Canada
Colombia	Colombia
Cuba	Cuba
Costa Rica	Costa Rica
Chile	Chile
China	China
Denmark	Denmark
Greece	Greece
Republic Dominicana	Republic Dominicana
Haiti	Haiti
Egypt	Egypt
El Salvador	El Salvador
Ethiopia	Ethiopia
France	France
Guatemala	Guatemala
Island	Island
India	India
Iran	Iran
Irak	Irak
Lybane	Lybane
Liberia	Liberia
Brasil	Brasil
Mexico	Mexico
Netherland	Netherland
Belgique	Belgique
New Zeland	New Zeland
Nicaragua	Nicaragua
Norway	Norway
Pakistan	Pakistan
Panama	Panama
Paraguay	Paraguay
Peru	Peru
The Philippines	The Philippines
Siam	Siam
Bolivia	Bolivia
Syria	Syria
Turkey	Turkey
United Kingdom	United Kingdom
U.S.A.	U.S.A.
Uruguay	Uruguay
Venezuela	Venezuela
Afghanistan	Afghanistan
Argentina	Argentina

Amnistía Internacional
Sección Española Tel.: 902 119 133
www.a-i.es

UNIVERSAL DECLARATION OF HUMAN RIGHTS

PROCLAIMED RIGHTS	RESPECTED RIGHTS
- Right to life.	
- Right to liberty.	
- Right to security of person.	
- Right to recognition every-where as a person before the law.	
- Right to an effective remedy by the competent national tribunals.	
- Right to an independent and impartial tribunal.	
- Right to be presumed inno-cent.	
- Right of equal before the law.	
- Right to freedom of movement and residence.	
- Right to leave any country.	
- Right to seek and to enjoy in other countries asylum from persecution.	
- Right to nationality.	
- Right to marry.	
- Right to found a family.	
- Right to own property alone as well as in association with others.	
- Right to freedom of thought, conscience and religion.	
- Right to freedom of opinion and expression.	
- Right to freedom of peaceful assembly and association.	
- Right to take part in the government of your country.	
- Right of equal access to pu-blic service in your country.	
- Right to free and secret vote.	
- Right to social security.	
- Right to work.	
- Right to equal pay for equal work.	
- Right to form and to join trade unions for the protec-tion of your interests.	
- Right to rest and leisure.	
- Right to a standard of living	
- Right to motherhood and child hood.	
- Right to education.	
- Right to protection of the moral and material interest.	

Amnistía Internacional

UNIVERSAL DECLARATION OF HUMAN RIGHTS

SIGNED	INFRINGED
1948	1948, 1949,
	1950, 1951,
	1952, 1953,
	1954, 1955,
	1956, 1957,
	1958, 1959,
	1960, 1961,
	1962, 1963,
	1964, 1965,
	1966, 1967,
	1968, 1969,
	1970, 1971,
	1972, 1973,
	1974, 1975,
	1976, 1977,
	1978, 1979,
	1980, 1981,
	1982, 1983,
	1984, 1985,
	1986, 1987,
	1988, 1989,
	1990, 1991,
	1992, 1993,
	1994, 1995,
	1996, 1997,
	1998, 1999,
	2000, 2001;
	2002;

Amnistía Internacional

MERIT AWARD
Public Service/Political Outdoor and Posters Campaign

ART DIRECTOR
Vicente Navarro

WRITER
Paco Conde

ILLUSTRATOR
Mayte De Nicolas

CREATIVE DIRECTOR
Cesar Garcia

CLIENT
Amnesty International

AGENCY
Saatchi & Saatchi/Madrid

03367A

433

MERIT AWARD
**Public Service/Political
Outdoor and Posters
Campaign**

ART DIRECTOR
Philip Bonnery

WRITER
Anselmo Ramos

PHOTOGRAPHER
Public Domain

CREATIVE DIRECTOR
Armando Hernandez

CLIENT
Abolitionist Action Committee

AGENCY
Young & Rubicam/Miami

03369A

Name: William Hamilton Little

DOB: 10 / 25 / 60   Race: white

Height: 6-1   Weight: 191

Eyes: Brown   Hair: Brown

Date of Execution: 6 / 1 / 99

Ex 6-1-99

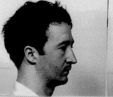

D.R.# 788

Last Meal Request:

Fifteen slices of cheese, three fried eggs, three buttered toasts, two
hamburger patties with cheese, 2 tomato sliced, one sliced onion, french
fries with salad dressing, 2 lb. of crispy fried bacon, one quart
chocolate milk and one pint of fresh strawberries.

-Lost your appetite?

**9th Annual FAST & VIGIL
to Abolish the Death Penalty**

U.S. Supreme Court in Washington, D.C., June 29 to July 2, 2002
Everyone is encouraged to participate. Fasting is optional.
For registration forms, including details on lodging, travel
and other logistics, to help with funding or to volunteer,
please contact the Abolitionist Action Committee c/o CUADP
(800)973-6548, aac@abolition.org, www.abolition.org

Name: Jeffrey Dillingham

DOB: 3 / 6 / 73   Race: white

Height: 6-1   Weight: 205

Eyes: hazel   Hair: Brown

Date of Execution: 11 / 1 / 00

Executed
#74

D.R.# 999071

Last Meal Request:

1 Cheeseburger with American, Cheddar and Mozzarella Cheese, without
mayonnaise, mustard or onions; Large French Fries; Bowl of Macaroni and
Cheese; Lasagna with 2 slices of Garlic Bread; 4 oz. of Nacho Cheese; 3
Large Cinnamon Rolls; 5 Scrambled Eggs; 8 pints of Chocolate Milk.

-Lost your appetite?

**9th Annual FAST & VIGIL
to Abolish the Death Penalty**

U.S. Supreme Court in Washington, D.C., June 29 to July 2, 2002
Everyone is encouraged to participate. Fasting is optional.
For registration forms, including details on lodging, travel
and other logistics, to help with funding or to volunteer,
please contact the Abolitionist Action Committee c/o CUADP
(800)973-6548, aac@abolition.org, www.abolition.org

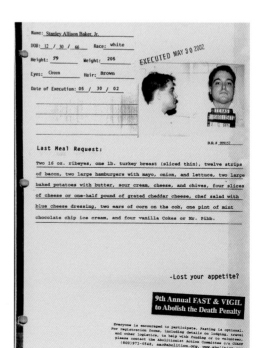

Name: Stanley Allison Baker, Jr.

DOB: 12 / 30 / 66   Race: white

Height: 59   Weight: 205

Eyes: Green   Hair: Brown

Date of Execution: 05 / 30 / 02

EXECUTED MAY 30 2002

D.R.# 999157

Last Meal Request:

Two 16 oz. ribeyes, one lb. turkey breast (sliced thin), twelve strips
of bacon, two large hamburgers with mayo, onion, and lettuce, two large
baked potatoes with butter, sour cream, cheese, and chives, four slices
of cheese or one-half pound of grated cheddar cheese, chef salad with
blue cheese dressing, two ears of corn on the cob, one pint of mint
chocolate chip ice cream, and four vanilla Cokes or Mr. Pibb.

-Lost your appetite?

**9th Annual FAST & VIGIL
to Abolish the Death Penalty**

Everyone is encouraged to participate. Fasting is optional.
For registration forms, including details on lodging, travel
and other logistics, to help with funding or to volunteer,
please contact the Abolitionist Action Committee c/o CUADP
(800)973-6548, aac@abolition.org, www.abolition.org

Media & creative. Isn't it time they started talking to each other?

Of course it is. And it starts on the 26th November with the first of a two-part evening conference arranged by the IPA so some of the most senior agency names and media owners will be there to demonstrate how reuniting with each other can help us to create the campaigns we all long to produce. The beer

will be free and afterwards there'll be a preview screening of a major and exclusive new film release. Part One will be at 6.00pm on the 26th November at Planet Hollywood and Part Two will be on the 3rd December at MPC. **Tickets are £50 for both parts, available from the** IPA on 0207 201 8232.

MERIT AWARD

Public Service/Political Collateral: Brochures and Direct Mail

ART DIRECTOR
Rob Fletcher

WRITER
David Alexander

CREATIVE DIRECTORS
Rob Fletcher
David Alexander

CLIENT
Institute of Practitioners in Advertising

AGENCY
Banks Hoggins O'Shea FCB/ London

03370A

TOMMY LING
ST. PAUL, MN

PACK 174

The kids in Tommy Ling's neighborhood were never doing anything cool. They'd just hang out and slouch in front of the TV, like a bunch of sponge cakes. Tommy had waaaay too much energy and imagination for that, so he joined the Cub Scouts. Suddenly, Tommy was having adventures the kids in the neighborhood couldn't imagine, becoming a "man of the world." Tommy was psyched. He told his buddies. They joined Cub Scouts. They got psyched. Soon, everyone was totally psyched.

GRADE: 4th **RANK:** Webelos **HEIGHT:** 4'5" **WEIGHT:** 59
INTERESTS: eating cereal, dinosaurs, football

If you're in grades 1-5, you could be a Cub Scout, too. Just ask your parents, then visit joincubs.com

©2002 Indianhead and Viking Councils, BSA

TOMMY LING — PACK 174 — ST. PAUL, MN

GARY PORTER — PACK 362 — RAMSEY, MN

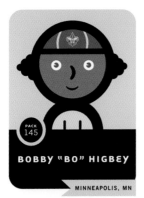

BOBBY "BO" HIGBEY
MINNEAPOLIS, MN

PACK 145

Bobby's goal in life is to be an astronaut. Joining the Cub Scouts seemed a logical first step. In the Cub Scouts, Bobby is learning all about computers, and stars, and the history of flight. So when the day comes, and the President asks him to put on his space suit, fly to Mars, and make peace with the aliens on behalf of all mankind, Bobby will be ready.

GRADE: 3rd **RANK:** Bear **HEIGHT:** 4'7" **WEIGHT:** 57
INTERESTS: toy robots, planetariums, kickball

If you're in grades 1-5, you could be a Cub Scout, too. Just ask your parents, then visit joincubs.com

©2002 Indianhead and Viking Councils, BSA

BOBBY "BO" HIGBEY — PACK 145 — MINNEAPOLIS, MN

LEO WHITIN — PACK 54 — RIVER FALLS, WI

MERIT AWARD

Public Service/Political Collateral: Brochures and Direct Mail

ART DIRECTOR
James Clunie

WRITER
Tim Cawley

ILLUSTRATOR
James Clunie

AGENCY PRODUCERS
Audrey Cullen
Christine Moe

CLIENT
Cub Scouts

AGENCY
Carmichael Lynch/Minneapolis

03371A

SRINI KUMARAKOM
SAVAGE, MN

PACK 239

Srini moved to Minnesota from a big city on the East Coast, so he didn't know a lot about outdoorsy stuff like streams, birds and frogs. Being a Cub Scout changed all that in a hurry. Now, Srini and his new friends go camping and hiking and bug collecting. They venture bravely into the woods…free-spirited…and under adult supervision. From a shy city kid has emerged: Srini Crockett, King of the Wild Frontier.

GRADE: 4th **RANK:** Webelos **HEIGHT:** 4'7" **WEIGHT:** 61
INTERESTS: building forts, nature walks, hide & seek

If you're in grades 1-5, you could be a Cub Scout, too. Just ask your parents, then visit joincubs.com

©2002 Indianhead and Viking Councils, BSA

SRINI KUMARAKOM — PACK 239 — SAVAGE, MN

STEVE CRONOPOLOUS — PACK 237 — NEW LONDON, MN

MERIT AWARD
**Public Service/Political
Collateral: Brochures and
Direct Mail**

ART DIRECTOR
Hans-Juergen Kaemmerer

WRITER
Robert Junker

PHOTOGRAPHERS
Bilderberg
Dorothea Schmidt

CREATIVE DIRECTOR
Hans-Juergen Kaemmerer

CLIENT
Amnesty International

AGENCY
Michael Conrad & Leo Burnett/
Frankfurt

03373A

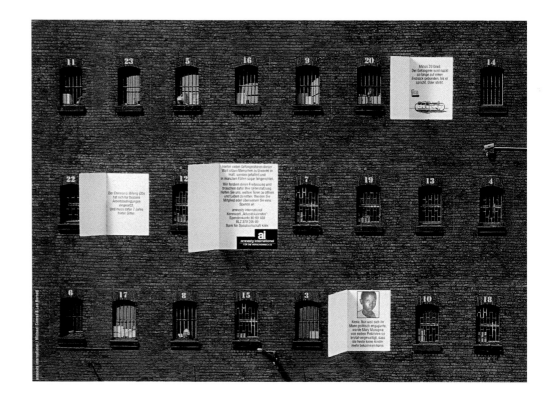

WOMEN'S REFUGE
"BRUISED AMBASSADORS"

MERIT AWARD
**Public Service/Political
Collateral: Brochures and
Direct Mail**

ART DIRECTORS
Steve Cooper
Gavin Bradley

WRITER
Ken Double

CREATIVE DIRECTOR
Gavin Bradley

CLIENT
Women's Refuge

AGENCY
Saatchi & Saatchi New Zealand/
Wellington

03374A

From: Bridie Wilkinson
Sent: Monday, 22 July 2002 12:52 p.m.
Subject: BRUISED FACE

You might have noticed my impressive bruising this morning. Thanks to those of you
who were so concerned and sympathetic. You were all really kind. I'm not sure what
you thought of my excuse as to how it happened, but it wasn't actually the truth.

The bruising was the work of a make-up artist. Around the country this morning,
people like me arrived noticeably "bruised" at work to help Women's Refuge publicise
its annual appeal. Embarrassing and duplicitous as it was, I agreed to do it because
any day in the real world any of us might meet a woman who carries the scars of an
abusive relationship. Like me, they'll make up an excuse for those scars.

Women's Refuge gives these women and their children a chance to put their lives
back on track. Education programmes, abuse counselling, legal assistance, a 24
hour crisis service and safe houses are all available depending on need.

If you're able to, you can help by giving whatever you can to the street collectors for
the Women's Refuge Annual Appeal this week – or you can call 0900 REFUGE from
your home phone and a $20 donation will be automatically added to your Telecom
account.

With thanks
Bridie

WOMEN'S REFUGE "BRUISED AMBASSADORS"

First thing Monday, on the week of the Women's
Refuge Annual Appeal, 27 women in Auckland,
Wellington and Christchurch started their day with bruises,
false but quite convincing, applied to their faces. Each
was briefed to tell friends and colleagues that
the injuries were the result of a trivial accident.

Later in the day, the women sent a prepared email
to the people in their workplace revealing the truth,
highlighting the purpose of the exercise and pointing
out the presence of a donation box in reception.

Press and television coverage continued the story. In
interviews the women talked about their unsettling
morning and the reaction their "injuries" provoked. They
reported a marked tendency to ignore the bruises.

Only one or two people had expressed concern to
the women, though several professed to be greatly
relieved when the deception was uncovered. Among
those who said nothing there was an almost universal
assumption that the bruises were the result of violence.

Emails like this one were sent by
the Bruised Ambassadors to work-
mates later in the day.

437

MERIT AWARD
**Public Service/Political
Radio: Single**

WRITER
Annie Finnegan

AGENCY PRODUCER
Chris Jennings

PRODUCTION COMPANY
Blast Audio

CREATIVE DIRECTORS
Ron Lawner
Alex Bogusky
Pete Favat
Ari Merkin
Roger Baldacci

CLIENT
American Legacy Foundation

AGENCY
Arnold Worldwide/Boston and
Crispin Porter + Bogusky/Miami

03012R

MAN: Hello?

JEFF: My name is Jeff and I am taking a 60-second survey about a well-known product.

MAN: Okay.

JEFF: I'd like to get your opinion on some flavors currently added to this product. Please rate them on a scale of one to 10, with 10 as most delicious. Cocoa.

MAN: Five.

JEFF: Licorice.

MAN: Ah, seven.

JEFF: Peppermint.

MAN: Ah, four.

JEFF: Ammonia.

MAN: Zero.

JEFF: Methylbutyric Acid.

MAN: Zero.

JEFF: 6-10, Di-menthyl-5-9 undecadien-2-one.

MAN: What kind of stupid questions are these?

JEFF: Well, these are just ingredients some tobacco companies say they add to cigarettes for flavor, sir.

MAN: Oh, is that right?

JEFF: Yes, sir. Well, thank you for your time today.

MAN: Okay.

JEFF: Your opinion matters.

ANNOUNCER: Knowledge is contagious. Infect truth.

WOMAN: Hello?

TRUTH: Hi. I'm taking a quick survey about a well-known product. Would you mind participating?

WOMAN: Ah ha.

TRUTH: Okay. Please rate the following statements as positive, negative, or neutral.

WOMAN: This product comes in different flavors.

WOMAN: Positive.

TRUTH: This product fits in your pocket.

WOMAN: Positive.

TRUTH: This product typically costs under five dollars.

WOMAN: Negative.

TRUTH: This product gives off cyanide.

WOMAN: Ew. Oh, terrible. No. Negative.

TRUTH: This product kills people who use it.

WOMAN: Negative.

TRUTH: How about, this product kills people who don't even use it. They just have to stand nearby.

WOMAN: Oh, negative.

TRUTH: What if the price were lower, like four dollars. Still negative?

WOMAN: Oh, no, no, no. Definitely.

TRUTH: Do you know what the product is?

WOMAN: I have no idea.

TRUTH: Cigarettes. Thank you for sharing your opinions today.

WOMAN: Ah, okay.

ANNOUNCER: Knowledge is contagious. Infect truth.

MERIT AWARD
**Public Service/Political
Radio: Single**

WRITER
Annie Finnegan

AGENCY PRODUCER
Chris Jennings

PRODUCTION COMPANY
Blast Audio

CREATIVE DIRECTORS
Ron Lawner
Alex Bogusky
Pete Favat
Ari Merkin
Roger Baldacci

CLIENT
American Legacy Foundation

AGENCY
Arnold Worldwide/Boston and
Crispin Porter + Bogusky/Miami

03013R

SFX: Phone ringing.

JENNY: I'll get it.

MOTHER: Sit down.

JENNY: Hello? Uh, hold on.

MOTHER: Hey, get back in here, finish your dinner. *(Silence.)* I mean it, Jenny. Now. *(Silence.)* What is it, honey?

JENNY: It's for...dad.

MOTHER: Give me it. Hello? No, no he's not. He's not here. No, thank you. Listen. He hasn't been with us for over a year, okay? It's hard enough without you people calling around here trying to stir him up. That was my daughter who you asked about her dead daddy. And all for a sale? I wish he was here. He'd pull you through the phone by your—

ANNOUNCER: On November 25, Vladimir Meckel was killed by a drunk driver, leaving behind a wife and two children because someone got behind the wheel drunk. Vladimir died. But for those left behind, the pain will last forever. Friends don't let friends drive drunk. A message from the US Department of Transportation and the Ad Council.

MERIT AWARD
**Public Service/Political
Radio: Single**

WRITER
James Bray

AGENCY PRODUCER
Mike Doran

PRODUCTION COMPANY
Howard Schwartz Recording

CREATIVE DIRECTOR
John Staffen

CLIENT
Ad Council

AGENCY
DDB/New York

03014R

MERIT AWARD
**Public Service/Political
Television: Single**

ART DIRECTOR
Brett Channer

WRITER
Brett Channer

AGENCY PRODUCER
Karen Peterman

PRODUCTION COMPANY
Untitled

DIRECTOR
David Tennant

CREATIVE DIRECTORS
Brett Channer
Patrick Allossery

CLIENT
Canadian Landmine Foundation

AGENCY
A Good Cause/Toronto

03375A

[Military personnel are shown working in a field with landmine detectors. A man kneels near a dug-up landmine.]

SUPER: This is how you find a landmine when you have the money to do it right.

[The landmine slowly dissolves into a puddle. A group of laughing children run by. One steps in the puddle, where the landmine is hidden.]

SUPER: This is how you find one when you don't. Help us do it right. Adopt-a-Minefield logo. www.canadianlandmine.com.

[Two teens with hidden cameras walk into a mail service company, carrying a big brown box.]

TEEN 1: Good morning. I'd like to ship this arsenic and cyanide-spreading mechanism.

CLERK: Arsenic and cyanide?

TEEN 1: Right.

CLERK: You're going to ship that?

TEEN 1: Right, but, you know, it's packed up pretty good, it's not like it's leaking out.

CLERK: It's hazardous materials.

CUSTOMER IN LINE: That's illegal, isn't it?

CLERK: Yeah, I mean, that's just ridiculous.

TEEN 1: I'm not trying to do anything illegal.

CLERK: Sending arsenic and cyanide is not illegal?

TEEN 1: I just want to ship these cigarettes.

[The teen opens the box, revealing cigarettes. A sticker on the box reads: "There are over 4,000 chemicals in cigarette smoke."]

CLERK: I don't think we're going to let you ship it.

SUPER: *Knowledge is contagious. Infect truth.

MERIT AWARD
Public Service/Political Television: Single

ART DIRECTOR
Amee Shah

WRITER
Scott Linnen

AGENCY PRODUCER
Spring Clinton-Smith

PRODUCTION COMPANY
Harvest Films

DIRECTOR
Baker Smith

CREATIVE DIRECTORS
Ron Lawner
Alex Bogusky
Pete Favat
Ari Merkin
Roger Baldacci

CLIENT
American Legacy Foundation

AGENCY
Arnold Worldwide/Boston and Crispin Porter + Bogusky/Miami

03379A

[A woman undergoing cancer treatment speaks to a home video camera.]

WOMAN: Okay, there we go. Hi, Emma. It's mommy. And this is you. Emma, mommy's really sick, so I wanted to do this so you'll always know how much I love you. *[Singing, she struggles not to cry.]* You are my sunshine, my only sunshine. You make me happy when skies are gray. You'll never know, dear, how much I love you. Please don't take my sunshine away.

SUPER: Be there tomorrow. Stop smoking today.

ANNOUNCER: If you're ready to stop smoking, we can help you learn to quit. Call us today.

SUPER: 1-877-270-STOP. Minnesota's Tobacco Helpline. Minnesota Partnership for Action Against Tobacco.

MERIT AWARD
Public Service/Political Television: Single

ART DIRECTOR
Mark Sorensen

WRITER
Troy Longie

AGENCY PRODUCER
Jenee Schmidt

PRODUCTION COMPANIES
Film Graphics
Steam Films

DIRECTOR
Mat Humphrey

CREATIVE DIRECTORS
Jac Coverdale
Jerry Fury

CLIENT
MAPPT

AGENCY
Clarity Coverdale Fury/ Minneapolis

03376A

PUBLIC
SERVICE
MERIT

MERIT AWARD
**Public Service/Political
Television: Single**

ART DIRECTORS
Toby Talbot
Leo Premutico
Mike O'Sullivan

WRITERS
Toby Talbot
Leo Premutico
Mike O'Sullivan

AGENCY PRODUCER
Alesa Tong

PRODUCTION COMPANY
Curious Films

DIRECTOR
Brendon Dixon

CREATIVE DIRECTOR
Mike O'Sullivan

CLIENT
Auckland Regional Council

AGENCY
Colenso BBDO/Auckland

03377A

ANNOUNCER: This ad is an experiment.

(Two men, on top of Mt. Eden, put an electronic tracking device inside a piece of litter. Then they throw it in a stormwater drain and follow its path down to the harbor. Eventually they recover it, washed up on the beach, 11.4 kilometers away. It takes just three hours and 49 minutes to get there.)

SUPER: Street litter doesn't stay on the street. The Big Clean Up. 0800 JOIN IN. arc.govt.co.nz. ARC logo.

MERIT AWARD
**Public Service/Political
Television: Single**

ART DIRECTOR
Mark Taylor

WRITER
Tom Adams

AGENCY PRODUCER
Michelle Lazzarino

PRODUCTION COMPANY
Stink

DIRECTOR
Ivan Zacharias

CREATIVE DIRECTOR
Alex Bogusky

CLIENT
Florida Department of Health

AGENCY
Crispin Porter + Bogusky/Miami

03380A

(Two workers take down a Marlboro billboard by the side of a road in Senegal, Africa.)

ANNOUNCER: In 1998, Marlboro cigarettes voluntarily took down all their advertising in Senegal, Africa. And kept it down...

(They finish the job, resting in the back of their truck. A convoy of limos, with American flags on the hoods, drives by. As soon as the convoy passes, the workers start to put the billboard back up.)

ANNOUNCER: ...Until the President of the United States left. What the tobacco industry says they don't do, they just don't do in the US.

SUPER: Truth.

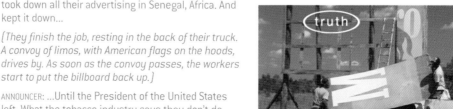

ANNOUNCER: On September 26, Jeff Adams will climb the 1,766 stairs of the CN Tower in his wheelchair.

(Jeff, training for the climb, starts rolling his chair up a down escalator, staying in the same spot as if he were on a treadmill.)

ANNOUNCER: Naturally, he'll have some training to do.

SUPER: Canadian Foundation For Physically Disabled Persons.

ANNOUNCER: Help Jeff build a barrier-free society. Buy a step.

SUPER: www.stepuptochange.com.

MERIT AWARD
Public Service/Political Television: Single

ART DIRECTOR
Paul Wallace

WRITER
David Ross

AGENCY PRODUCER
Christine Pacheco

PRODUCTION COMPANY
Avion Films

DIRECTOR
Jana Peck

CREATIVE DIRECTOR
Neil McOstrich

CLIENT
Jeff Adams Step Up To Change

AGENCY
Palmer Jarvis DDB/Toronto

03381A

(This spot is played in segments, interrupted by other commercials. A digital display counter indicates three minutes in real time.)

ANNOUNCER: In the next few minutes, you could make a cup of tea, go to the loo, or see to the kids.

(A woman leaves her living room. A carelessly placed cigarette sets fire to the chair, then the rest of the room. As the fire rages, other commercials break into the scene. The counter continues marking the time.)

SUPER: A smoke alarm would have sounded about now.

MOTHER: Ryan!

CHILD: Mommy!

(The room reaches flash point. The windows blow out.)

ANNOUNCER: What you've just witnessed took under three minutes. Never, ever underestimate the speed of fire. Get out, call the fire service, and for God's sake, stay out.

SUPER: New Zealand Fire Service logo.

MERIT AWARD
Public Service/Political Television: Single

ART DIRECTOR
Andrew Tinning

WRITER
Andrew Tinning

AGENCY PRODUCER
Esther Watkins

PRODUCTION COMPANY
The Sweet Shop

DIRECTOR
Jessica Bluck

CREATIVE DIRECTOR
Andrew Tinning

CLIENT
NZ Fire Service

AGENCY
Saatchi & Saatchi/Auckland

03382A

RADIO

THE WORLD'S GREATEST

MERIT

MERIT AWARD
Consumer Radio: Single

WRITER
John Immesoete

AGENCY PRODUCER
Sally Naylor

PRODUCTION COMPANY
Chicago Recording Company

CREATIVE DIRECTOR
John Immesoete

CLIENT
Anheuser-Busch

AGENCY
DDB/Chicago

03015R

ANNOUNCER: Bud Light presents, "Real Men of Genius."

CHOIR: *(Singing.)* Real Men of Genius.

ANNOUNCER: Today we salute you, Mr. Fancy Coffee Shop Coffee Pourer.

CHOIR: *(Singing.)* Mr. Fancy Coffee Shop Coffee Pourer.

ANNOUNCER: What do you do with a master's degree in art history? You get a nose ring and pour coffee for a living.

CHOIR: *(Singing.)* Pour it on now!

ANNOUNCER: Why is it called a latte? Maybe because it costs a latte and it takes a latte time to make.

CHOIR: *(Singing.)* Whole lot o' latte!

ANNOUNCER: Someone ordered a cappuccino? Step aside. Let the man who works the milk foamer take over.

CHOIR: *(Singing.)* Step aside!

ANNOUNCER: Sure, you charge five bucks for a cup of coffee. It's putting that tip jar out that takes real guts.

CHOIR: Yeah!

ANNOUNCER: So crack open an ice cold Bud Light, Guru of the Ground Roast. It's not the caffeine that gives us the buzz, it's you.

CHOIR: *(Singing.)* Mr. Fancy Coffee Shop Coffee Pourer.

ANNOUNCER: Bud Light Beer. Anheuser-Busch. St. Louis, Mo.

MERIT AWARD
Consumer Radio: Single

WRITERS
Bill Cimino
Mark Gross

AGENCY PRODUCER
Sally Naylor

PRODUCTION COMPANY
Chicago Recording Company

CREATIVE DIRECTORS
John Immesoete
Mark Gross
Bill Cimino

CLIENT
Anheuser-Busch

AGENCY
DDB/Chicago

03016R

ANNOUNCER: Bud Light presents, "Real Men of Genius."

CHOIR: *(Singing.)* Real Men of Genius.

ANNOUNCER: Today we salute you, Mr. Giant Inflatable Pink Gorilla Maker.

CHOIR: *(Singing.)* Mr. Giant Inflatable Pink Gorilla Maker.

ANNOUNCER: The automotive industry's most convincing marketing tool: the giant gas-filled pink gorilla.

CHOIR: *(Singing.)* Such a big monkey.

ANNOUNCER: Factory rebates. Zero percent financing. Poppycock! Nothing sells cars like a helium-happy primate.

CHOIR: *(Singing.)* You said it, brother!

ANNOUNCER: Why a gorilla? Because who'd buy a car from a dealer with a giant inflatable hamster?

CHOIR: *(Singing.)* Not gonna buy it.

ANNOUNCER: So crack open an ice cold Bud Light, oh King of The Automotive Jungle. When we say you're the greatest, we're not just blowing hot air.

CHOIR: *(Singing.)* Mr. Giant Inflatable Pink Gorilla Maker.

ANNOUNCER: Bud Light Beer. Anheuser-Busch. St. Louis, Mo.

ANNOUNCER: *[In the style of a racetrack announcer.]* And they're off. Out of the gate is "Dinner Date." "Dinner Date" starts strong. But here comes "No Reservation," followed by "Hours of Waiting." Now "Idle Chit-Chat" is making a move. But "Idle Chit-Chat" is no match for "Awkward Silence." It's "Idle Chit-Chat." It's "Awkward Silence." And here comes "Table By The Kitchen" and "Snooty Waiter," followed by "Undercooked Chicken." I don't believe it, out of nowhere comes "Declined Credit Card" and "Utter Humiliation." As they come down the stretch, "First Base" is nowhere in sight. And finally, it's "Peck On The Cheek" and "Let's Just Be Friends."

ANNOUNCER: For a better time, go to the track. National Thoroughbred Racing. We bet you love it.

MERIT AWARD
Consumer Radio: Single

WRITERS
Brad Emmett
Lee Seidenberg
Erik Fahrenkopf
Anthony DeCarolis

AGENCY PRODUCER
Barbara Michelson

PRODUCTION COMPANY
McHale/Barone

DIRECTOR
Joe Barone

CREATIVE DIRECTOR
Sal DeVito

CLIENT
National Thoroughbred Racing
Association

AGENCY
DeVito/Verdi/New York

03018R

ANNOUNCER: *[In the style of a racetrack announcer.]* And they're off. Out of the gate, it's "Go To The Mall" and "Do Some Shopping." Looking good early is "Your Girlfriend," "Trying On Jeans," and "Tight Squeeze." And here comes the favorite, "Does My Butt Look Big?" Followed by, "Not Really." Immediately followed by, "What's That Supposed To Mean?" And now it's "Sweetie Pie," "Snookums," and "Baby Cakes." But they're no match for "Cold Shoulder" and "Silent Treatment." And in a last ditch effort, it's "Begging." It's "Pleading." It's "Groveling." It's "Begging." But in the end, it's gonna be "Mother Was Right" and "I Should've Stayed With Bob."

ANNOUNCER: For a better time, go to the track. National Thoroughbred Racing. We bet you love it.

MERIT AWARD
Consumer Radio: Single

WRITERS
Erik Fahrenkopf
Anthony DeCarolis
Brad Emmett
Lee Seidenberg

AGENCY PRODUCER
Barbara Michelson

PRODUCTION COMPANY
McHale/Barone

DIRECTOR
Joe Barone

CREATIVE DIRECTOR
Sal DeVito

CLIENT
National Thoroughbred Racing
Association

AGENCY
DeVito/Verdi/New York

03019R

MERIT AWARD
Consumer Radio: Single

WRITER
Clay Hudson

AGENCY PRODUCER
Dan Brown

CREATIVE DIRECTORS
Mark Ray
Brent Ladd
Clay Hudson

CLIENT
7-Eleven

AGENCY
GSD&M/Austin

03020R

MAN 1: Hey, uh, you gonna be much longer?

MAN 2: Almost through.

MAN 1: 'Cause you know, money's been coming out of that Vcom check-cashing machine for about five minutes now.

MAN 2: Just cashing the old paycheck.

MAN 1: Yeah. Me, too.

MAN 1: So, what do you do?

MAN 2: I'm CEO of a global telecommunications company.

MAN 1: Wow.

MAN 2: Well, it pays the rent.

MAN 1: I wouldn't expect a guy like you to, you know, be at 7-Eleven, cashing a check at the Vcom machine at three in the morning.

MAN 2: Well, nobody else has self-service check cashing. Which means I don't have to wait on somebody to help me and it puts me in control. Plus I got a five-dollar coupon check for signing up! Five whole bucks!

MAN 1: You dropped a hundred there.

MAN 2: Oh, thanks.

ANNOUNCER: Introducing Vcom 24-hour check cashing at any participating 7-Eleven store. Plus money orders, wire transfers and more. Sign up now and get your first and tenth checks cashed for free. Vcom, only at 7-Eleven. Cash paychecks for a low one percent fee.

SFX: Slurp.

ANNOUNCER: Oh, thank heaven.

SFX: Ahh.

MERIT AWARD
Consumer Radio: Single

WRITER
Mark Ray

AGENCY PRODUCER
Susan Lazarus

PRODUCTION COMPANY
Oink Ink Radio

CREATIVE DIRECTORS
Mark Ray
Brent Ladd
Steve Miller

CLIENT
Southwest Airlines

AGENCY
GSD&M/Austin

03021R

MAN: January 8th?

WOMAN: Nope.

MAN: January 11th?

WOMAN: Nope.

MAN: January 21st?

WOMAN: Nope.

MAN: February 12th?

WOMAN: Nope.

MAN: February 17th?

WOMAN: Nope.

(The man continues to name dates; the woman continues to answer in the negative.)

MAN: November 19th?

WOMAN: Nope.

MAN: December 2nd?

WOMAN: Nope.

MAN: December 25th?

WOMAN: Are you kidding?

MAN: January...

ANNOUNCER: What good are frequent flyer miles if you can't use them? With Rapid Rewards from Southwest Airlines, you can fly where you want, when you want. No seat restrictions. Very few blackout dates.

MAN: June 22nd?

WOMAN: Nope.

MAN: This doesn't bother you at all, does it?

WOMAN: Nope.

ANNOUNCER: So don't miss out. Visit southwest.com to learn how to become a Rapid Rewards Member. Southwest Airlines.

SFX: Ding.

PILOT: You are now free to move about the country.

SFX: Roller coaster at the beginning of ride.

MAN: Whoa, this is gonna be great.

WOMAN: Yeah. This thing goes really high, doesn't it?

MAN: If you're scared, just hang onto me.

WOMAN: Oh.

MAN: Here we go!

SFX: Roller coaster rushing down first slope. High-pitched, blood-curdling, girlie screaming.

WOMAN: Honey! Snap out of it! It's embarrassing.

MAN: Oh, sorry.

ANNOUNCER: Playland. Now open weekends.

MERIT AWARD
Consumer Radio: Single

ART DIRECTOR
Joe Piccolo

WRITER
Andy Linardatos

AGENCY PRODUCER
Ailsa Brown

PRODUCTION COMPANY
Wave Productions

CREATIVE DIRECTORS
Ian Grais
Chris Staples

CLIENT
Playland

AGENCY
Rethink/Vancouver

03023R

TOM: Hi, Tom Bodett here. I've always wondered what exactly dogs are dreaming about when they're moving their paws and yipping in their sleep. Some say that the dream state lets the soul slip free of its earthbound shell to resume a past life. That just maybe Buster harbors the reincarnated spirit of Constantine the Eleventh, last of the Byzantine emperors, who each night gallops once again through the rubble, tears of rage falling from one eye, tears of sorrow from the other, as the ancient walls are breached. Personally, I'm betting dogs are just dreaming about table scraps or chasing the neighbor's cat. Just something to contemplate as you watch your dog's paws twitch in your room at Motel 6, where they have the lowest price of any national chain, and where pets are welcome. I'm Tom Bodett for Motel 6, and we'll leave the light on for you and your best friend Buster... the Eleventh.

ANNOUNCER: Motel 6 is an Accor hotel and a proud sponsor of The Humane Society of the United States.

MERIT AWARD
Consumer Radio: Single

WRITER
David Canright

AGENCY PRODUCER
Sheri Cartwright

PRODUCTION COMPANY
Bad Animals

CREATIVE DIRECTOR
Mike Malone

CLIENT
Motel 6

AGENCY
The Richards Group/Dallas

03025R

MERIT AWARD
Consumer Radio: Single

WRITERS
Sue Anderson
Theo Ferreira

AGENCY PRODUCER
Melanie Gray

PRODUCTION COMPANY
Sterling Sound

CREATIVE DIRECTOR
Sue Anderson

CLIENT
BMW VALVETRONIC

AGENCY
TBWA Hunt Lascaris/
Johannesburg

03024R

ANNOUNCER: *[Nose blocked. Struggling to pronounce words.]* Try to take a breath whilst blocking your nose. A little difficult to get air into those lungs, isn't it? This is how conventional spark-ignition engines work. By using a throttle, they restrict the air into the engine, restricting performance, restricting efficiency. So what would happen if there were no throttle? *[Voice is now normal.]* Your engine would breathe more easily for greater performance. Greater efficiency. Valvetronic by BMW.

MERIT AWARD
Consumer Radio: Campaign

WRITERS
Bill Cimino
Mark Gross

AGENCY PRODUCER
Sally Naylor

PRODUCTION COMPANY
Chicago Recording Company

CREATIVE DIRECTORS
John Immesoete
Bill Cimino
Mark Gross

CLIENT
Anheuser-Busch

AGENCY
DDB/Chicago

03027R

ANNOUNCER: Bud Light presents, "Real Men of Genius."

CHOIR: *[Singing.]* Real Men of Genius.

ANNOUNCER: Today we salute you, Mr. Beach Metal Detector Guy.

CHOIR: *[Singing.]* Mr. Beach Metal Detector Guy.

ANNOUNCER: Some seek their fortune on the stock market, others in real estate. But you, you look for loose change in the sand.

CHOIR: *[Singing.]* Hitting the jackpot.

ANNOUNCER: Armed with a five-foot Geiger counter and the world's largest set of earphones, you live your life with a simple code of honor: "Finders keepers, losers weepers."

CHOIR: *[Singing.]* Finders keepers.

ANNOUNCER: Sure, people mock you, but he who holds 92 cents, a gold-plated earring, and a steel-toed boot gets the last laugh.

CHOIR: *[Singing.]* Who's laughing now?

ANNOUNCER: So crack open an ice cold Bud Light, oh Sultan of The Sand. We'd give you a medal, but you probably already found one.

CHOIR: *[Singing.]* Mr. Beach Metal Detector Guy.

ANNOUNCER: Bud Light Beer. Anheuser-Busch. St. Louis, Mo.

ANNOUNCER: *(In the style of a racetrack announcer.)* And they're off. Out of the gate it's "Let's Get Together" and "Go Camping." But here comes "Raining" and "Pouring," And now it's "Five Guys In A Two-Man Tent." I don't believe it, it's "Nature Calling." And now it looks like it's gonna be "Number Two In The Woods." And "Toilet Paper" is nowhere in sight. But here comes "Handful Of Leaves." And what's this, it's "Itching," followed by "Scratching." It's "Itching." It's "Scratching." "Scratching" and "Itching." And now it's "Spreading," coming up from the rear. And in the end it's "The Worst Three Days Of Your Life."

ANNOUNCER: For a better time, go to the track. National Thoroughbred Racing. We bet you love it.

BUD LIGHT ANNOUNCER: Bud Light has arrived in Calgary and we at the Bud Light Institute are going to make a commercial for each and every beer-drinking guy in town. In order to do this, we purchased a database of Calgary males from a credit card company.

BEER GUY ANNOUNCER: Brad Rosen, you're the reason we brew Bud Light. Because you're the kind of 27-year-old systems analyst who has worked at McCrory Industries on Third Avenue for two years and pulls in 58 big ones a year. And you never back down from a challenge. Not you. Not unless your boss really disagrees. So why is Bud Light your beer, Brad Rosen? Because you always have time for your buddies. Because you don't let your webbed feet interfere with your golf game. And because you always remember that your girlfriend of five years, Helen, likes black lingerie while your assistant, Teresa, prefers red. Yeah, that's why we brew Bud Light for you, Brad.

BUD LIGHT ANNOUNCER: Calgary, Bud Light's here for you. This calls for a Bud Light.

MERIT AWARD
Consumer Radio: Campaign

WRITERS
Jonathan Commerford
Alistair King

AGENCY PRODUCER
Alexis Roberts

PRODUCTION COMPANY
Spaced Out Sound

CREATIVE DIRECTOR
Alistair King

CLIENT
Cape Argus Newspaper

AGENCY
King James Advertising/
Cape Town

03030R

ANNOUNCER: Recently, we spoke to the father of a Cape Town schoolboy and informed him that a pack of condiments was found in his son's pocket. This was his response.

MAN 1: Condiments? What?

MAN 2: I'm afraid it's true, sir.

MAN 1: But, no, no, no. He's only 11! His voice hasn't even broken yet, man!

MAN 2: They start young these days.

MAN 1: Where did he get it?

MAN 2: He claims they hand them out at the school tuck shop.

MAN 1: Hand them out? At the tuck shop? That's insane. What kind of school is that?

MAN 2: And apparently they were flavored.

MAN 1: Flavored, nog al! Hell's teeth! I'm telling you, it's all the bloomin' TV they watch.

MAN 2: Have you ever made use of condiments, sir?

MAN 1: Ja, ja, ja. Long time ago. But I wasn't 11.

MAN 2: Reading the newspaper not only improves your general knowledge. It can increase your vocabulary, too. So keep your head fed. Pick up a "Cape Argus" today. It's news you can use.

MERIT AWARD
Consumer Radio: Campaign

WRITERS
Oliver Devaris
Graham Johnson

AGENCY PRODUCER
Julia Ferguson

PRODUCTION COMPANY
Beamo Music

CREATIVE DIRECTOR
Tom McFarlane

CLIENT
ABC Radio

AGENCY
M&C Saatchi/Sydney

03031R

Also won:
MERIT AWARD
Consumer Radio: Single

FEMALE TRIO: *(Singing in the style of a sickeningly sweet 1950's soap powder jingle.)* Anthrax, anthrax, la, la, la. Anthrax, anthrax, la, la, la. Anthrax, anthrax, la, la, la. Anthrax, anthrax, la, la, la. Anthrax, anthrax…

ANNOUNCER: We can make light of even the most serious subjects. Backberner on ABC. A different look at the week's news. Tonight on ABC TV.

SFX: Sneeze.

MAN: *(As if coming over a police two-way radio.)* Do you hear that?

SFX: Radio chatter.

MAN: You hear it? Those are police sirens off in the distance…If you're the guy who just stole the pick-up truck from BC Place, you just stole what's called a Bait Car…We've been tracking you for blocks…We're about to cut the power to your car…Then we're going to arrest you.

SFX: Radio chatter.

MAN: Do you hear those sirens yet?

ANNOUNCER: The Bait Car Program from the Vancouver Police.

MERIT AWARD
Consumer Radio: Campaign

WRITER
Paul Little

AGENCY PRODUCER
Sue Bell

PRODUCTION COMPANY
GGRP

CREATIVE DIRECTOR
Alan Russell

CLIENT
Insurance Corporation of
British Columbia

AGENCY
Palmer Jarvis DDB/Vancouver

03032R

BRADY BUNCH FAMILY CHOIR: *(To the tune of The Brady Bunch theme song.)* Sunday, Monday, Happy Days. Tuesday, Wednesday, Thursday, Friday, Happy Days. These Happy Days are yours and mine. These Happy Days are yours and mine, Happy Days!

ANNOUNCER: From Happy Days to The Brady Bunch, the classics come together in TV Land. Call your cable company to subscribe.

MERIT AWARD
Consumer Radio: Campaign

ART DIRECTOR
Joe Piccolo

WRITERS
Grant Fraggalosch
Rob Tarry

PRODUCTION COMPANY
Wave Productions

CREATIVE DIRECTORS
Ian Grais
Chris Staples

CLIENT
TV Land

AGENCY
Rethink/Vancouver

03033R

MERIT AWARD
Consumer Television
Over :30 Single

ART DIRECTORS
Gerry Graf
Harold Einstein

WRITERS
Gerry Graf
Harold Einstein

PHOTOGRAPHER
John Lindley

AGENCY PRODUCER
Elise Greiche

PRODUCTION COMPANY
hungry man

DIRECTOR
Bryan Buckley

CREATIVE DIRECTORS
Gerry Graf
Ted Sann

CLIENT
FedEx

AGENCY
BBDO/New York

03394A

■

(A well-dressed man with a long beard and long hair rings the doorbell of a suburban home.)

MAN: Hi.

LADY: Hi.

MAN: I was marooned on an island for five years, with this package, and I swore that I would deliver it to you, because I work for FedEx. *(We flash back to the man on the island, wearing almost nothing. He yells at the top of his lungs, then he tries in vain to open up a coconut, with the dirty FedEx package sitting beside him.)*

LADY: That's very admirable, thank you.

MAN: By the way, what's in the package?

LADY: Nothing, really. Just a satellite phone, GPS locator, fishing rod, water purifier, and some seeds...just silly stuff. Thank you again. You keep up the good work.

COP 1: *(To Wile E. Coyote.)* Just take your time. Don't worry. They can't see you. Think back to that sunny day in the desert. You were wearing springs on your feet. You're chasing someone.

(Wile E., looking at the line up, holds up a "#4" sign.)

BEAKY BUZZARD: Uh, nope, nope, nope.

COP 1: Have 'em read the card.

COP 2: Number one, read the card, please.

TWEETY BIRD: Beep-beep.

COP 2: Number two.

FOGHORN LEGHORN: I say, I say...

COP 2: Number two. Read the card.

LAWYER: Detective.

COP 2: Number two.

FOGHORN LEGHORN: Beep-beep, son.

COP 2: Number three.

(Cop 1 and Cop 2 look at each other confidently.)

ROAD RUNNER: Beep-beep.

(Wile E. Coyote slowly raises up the "#4" sign again. Cop 1 can't believe it.)

LAWYER: We're done here.

COP 1: Let 'em go.

ROAD RUNNER: Beep-beep.

COP 1: *(To Wile E.)* You know he's just gonna go back out there and do this to you again. *(To Cop 2.)* Sometimes I hate this job.

COP 2: It was three, right?

COP 1: It's always three.

(Sad piano music plays. A woman carries a lamp to the trash, and goes back into the house. It begins to rain on the lamp. The woman in her living room enjoys the light of a new IKEA lamp. She lovingly touches it. We see the cold, lonely, wet lamp on the curb with the trash.)

SWEDISH MAN: Many of you feel bad for this lamp. This is because you are crazy. It has no feelings. And the new one is much better.

SUPER: IKEA logo. Unböring. unboring.com.

MERIT AWARD
Consumer Television
Over :30 Single

WRITER
Chris Bieger

AGENCY PRODUCER
Ashley Nixon

PRODUCTION COMPANY
Space Program

ANIMATION PRODUCTION
Renegade Animation

DIRECTOR
Rocky Lane

DIRECTOR OF ANIMATION
Darrell Van Citters

CREATIVE DIRECTOR
Pete Johnson

CLIENT
Cartoon Network

AGENCY
Cartoon Network On-Air/Atlanta

03384A

MERIT AWARD
Consumer Television
Over :30 Single

ART DIRECTORS
Mark Taylor
Steve Mapp

WRITER
Ari Merkin

AGENCY PRODUCER
Rupert Samuel

PRODUCTION COMPANY
MJZ

DIRECTOR
Spike Jonze

CREATIVE DIRECTORS
Alex Bogusky
Paul Keister

CLIENT
IKEA

AGENCY
Crispin Porter + Bogusky/Miami

03385A

[The driver of a MINI Cooper pulls over. A policeman approaches. But this is not your typical highway patrolman; it's a British bobby.]

BOBBY: [With a thick, British accent.] You do realize you were driving on the wrong side of the road.

MOTORER: This is America, man.

BOBBY: Right then. Good show. Carry on.

SUPER: MINI. Now in America. MINI logo.

MERIT AWARD
Consumer Television
Over :30 Single

ART DIRECTOR
Amee Shah

WRITER
Scott Linnen

AGENCY PRODUCERS
David Rolfe
Rupert Samuel

PRODUCTION COMPANY
Harvest Films

DIRECTOR
Baker Smith

CREATIVE DIRECTORS
Alex Bogusky
Andrew Keller

CLIENT
MINI

AGENCY
Crispin Porter + Bogusky/Miami

03393A

Also won: MERIT AWARD **Consumer Television :30/:25 Single**

MERIT AWARD
Consumer Television
Over :30 Single

ART DIRECTOR
Carlos Anuncibay

WRITER
Keith Bickel

AGENCY PRODUCER
Colin Hickson

PRODUCTION COMPANY
Academy Films

DIRECTOR
Frederic Planchon

CREATIVE DIRECTORS
Malcolm Green
Gary Betts

CLIENT
Vauxhall Motors

AGENCY
Delaney Lund Knox Warren/
London

03386A

[A group of Vauxhall Corsas engages in a game of hide-and-seek.]

SUPER: Put the fun back into driving. Corsa. Vauxhall logo. www.Vauxhall.co.uk/corsafun.

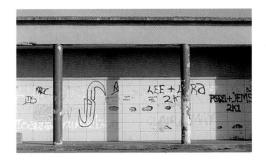

MUSIC: Minnie Riperton's "Loving You."

(In this commercial, we see structures in the shape of soccer goalposts, including a hill with two fence posts in center frame; the entrance to a block of flats with two pillars; a boarded-up shop front; a rectangular, corrugated iron shed by the side of the road; a brick wall with two bollards; a park with a lamppost and a tree beside a path; a wire fence with a hole in it; and so on. The last shot shows two park benches center frame, with an old man seated on each.)

SUPER: Umbro logo.

MERIT AWARD
**Consumer Television
Over :30 Single**

ART DIRECTOR
Richard Flintham

WRITER
Andy McLeod

AGENCY PRODUCER
Kate Sturgess

PRODUCTION COMPANY
HLA

DIRECTOR
John Hardwick

CREATIVE DIRECTORS
Andy McLeod
Richard Flintham

CLIENT
Umbro

AGENCY
Fallon/London

03388A

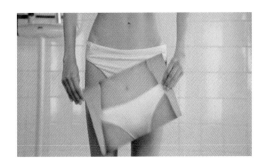

(A naked young woman looks in the mirror. When a photo in front of her chest is removed, we see that she is actually a boy. A boy in Kosovo is holding a water gun. The water gun is actually a photo. As the picture of the water gun is removed, we see a real gun in his hand. A woman sits miserably in front of the door. When she removes a photo covering her face, we see her black eye. Next, we see a woman's abdomen. A photo, positioned in front of her, is dropped to reveal that she is anorexic. We see a forest, then a Brazilian girl in front of a pile of cut-down trees; she is holding the photo of the lush forest that once was. An old woman sits on a couch, holding a young woman's hand. As the old woman removes a photo, we see that there is no young woman. An African boy sits on a soccer field. When he removes a photo of his leg, we see he has only one leg.)

SUPER: Fotoprix. Perfect pictures for an imperfect world. Fotoprix logo.

MERIT AWARD
**Consumer Television
Over :30 Single**

ART DIRECTORS
Javier Furones
Judith Francisco

WRITERS
Natalia Martin
Jose Maria Pujol

PRODUCTION COMPANY
Errecerre

DIRECTOR
Xavier Rosello

CREATIVE DIRECTORS
Jose Maria Pujol
Javier Furones

CLIENT
Fotoprix

AGENCY
The Farm/Madrid

03389A

459

MERIT AWARD
Consumer Television
Over :30 Single

ART DIRECTOR
Mark Wenneker

WRITER
Jamie Barrett

AGENCY PRODUCER
James Horner

PRODUCTION COMPANY
Biscuit Filmworks

DIRECTOR
Noam Murro

CREATIVE DIRECTOR
Jamie Barrett

CLIENT
Saturn

AGENCY
Goodby, Silverstein & Partners/
San Francisco

03392A

[People are shown moving up and down streets usually reserved for cars. A man jogs backwards out of his driveway. A group of people shuffles toward a traffic light. A crowd of people moves down a street at night. They hold flashlights as though they were headlights. A cluster of young students, led by an adult, shuffles down the street; the group is in an invisible school bus. Hundreds of people hurry down a highway. And so on.]

ANNOUNCER: When we design our cars, we don't see sheet metal. We see the people who may one day drive them. Introducing the redesigned L, the VUE, and the all new ION. It's different in a Saturn.

SUPER: It's different in a Saturn.

MERIT AWARD
Consumer Television
Over :30 Single

ART DIRECTOR
Simon Hepton

WRITER
Matt Crabtree

AGENCY PRODUCER
Sarah Martin

PRODUCTION COMPANY
Streetlight Films

DIRECTOR
Paul Street

CREATIVE DIRECTOR
Luke White

CLIENT
Greene King

AGENCY
McCann-Erickson/London

03396A

[A young man on a bicycle tumbles straight off the edge of a mountain, finally stopping on the road below. He lifts his head and opens his eyes, only a little bruised. Just then, we see a truck heading straight for him.]

SFX: Smack!

[Amazingly, the man lifts his head. As he gathers his thoughts, a huge meteorite from the sky lands on him. Cut to a pub, where the grim reaper is taking a sip of his Greene King IPA. He sighs with contentment, glancing at his watch.]

SUPER: Greene King IPA logo.

ANNOUNCER: Greene King IPA. Could you say no to another?

[The young man is struck by lightning. Once again, he opens his eyes, looks himself up and down, and wonders what he's doing alive.]

[In a junkyard, a worker reluctantly puts a beat-up 60's Mercedes into the car crusher. As the car gets crushed, the life of the Mercedes flashes before us. This includes: driving down Route 66; going through a car wash; pulling up at a red carpet event; driving through a blizzard; avoiding an accident; "for sale" written in soap on the windshield; a young couple buying the car. There is a bright flash. Inside a Mercedes factory, the fresh, new C-Class pulls up to a lot where other C-Classes are parked.]

ANNOUNCER: The outside may change, but the soul remains the same. The C-Class.

SUPER: Soul like no other. Mercedes-Benz logo.

MERIT AWARD
**Consumer Television
Over :30 Single**

ART DIRECTOR
Dawn McCarthy

WRITER
Laura Fegley

AGENCY PRODUCER
Chris Ott

PRODUCTION COMPANY
Go Film

DIRECTOR
Rad-ish

CREATIVE DIRECTORS
Andy Hirsch
Randy Saitta

CLIENT
Mercedes-Benz USA

AGENCY
Merkley Newman Harty Partners/
New York

03390A

SUPER: Santo Presents. A Santo Production. Of a commercial by Santo. The greatest auto dealer commercial of all time!

[Thus begins a dazzling, over-the-top display of pyrotechnics, dancing, singing, and acrobatics, including Scott Thomason himself rising up in a white tuxedo from a ring of fire.]

SCOTT: If you don't come see me today, I can't save you any money.

[The Portland Area All Star Gospel Group breaks into song. Skateboarders circle Scott, who does a series of amazing flips. When he lands, he is surrounded by the Portland Trailblazer dance team. Next, Scott, dressed as a prince with a key on a pillow, leads a ballerina to a car.]

SUPER: You are still watching the greatest auto dealer commercial of all time.

ANNOUNCER: And then Scott came to her in a dream with the golden key and he said to her...

SCOTT: If you don't come see me today, I can't save you any money.

[Two ninjas jump-kick dollar signs in half. To the soundtrack of "2001 A Space Odyssey," Scott plants a Thomason Flag on the moon. He then releases a flutter of white doves. Cut to a montage of clips, including NASA footage; stampeding buffalo; a Viking; stallions at sunset; a puppy and kitten; and so on. With the final crescendo, the music and lights cut.]

SUPER: *[Car alarms in the background.]* Fini.

MERIT AWARD
**Consumer Television
Over :30 Single**

ART DIRECTORS
Matt Peterson
Dena Blevins

WRITER
Ian Cohen

AGENCY PRODUCER
Kevin Diller

PRODUCTION COMPANY
Moxie Pictures

DIRECTOR
Spencer Chinoy

CREATIVE DIRECTOR
Austin Howe

CLIENT
Thomason Autogroup

AGENCY
Nerve/Portland

03397A

MERIT AWARD
**Consumer Television
Over :30 Single**

ART DIRECTOR
Bil Bungay

WRITER
Trevor Beattie

AGENCY PRODUCER
Lucy Wood

PRODUCTION COMPANY
Buggg Films

DIRECTORS
Stephen Ward
Bil Bungay

CREATIVE DIRECTOR
Trevor Beattie

CLIENT
Five

AGENCY
TBWA/London

03398A

(Michael Jackson's features, over the course of this commercial, evolve seamlessly from a chubby African American infant to the pale, emotionless, death-masked adult of today.)

SUPER: If this is what's happening outside, what's going on inside?

MERIT AWARD
**Consumer Television
Over :30 Single**

ART DIRECTOR
Rachid Ahouyek

WRITERS
Carlo Cavallone
Paul Shearer

AGENCY PRODUCER
Jasmine Kimera

PRODUCTION COMPANY
Outsider

DIRECTOR
Dom&Nic

CREATIVE DIRECTOR
Paul Shearer

CLIENT
Nike Europe

AGENCY
Wieden + Kennedy/Amsterdam

03403A

(A woman, stretching as she prepares for a run, is accidentally splashed by a man as he jogs through a puddle. She sprints after him and "accidentally" splashes him. This starts a fast-paced competition to see who can soak the other, culminating in the two being deluged in the wake of a bus driving through a giant puddle.)

SUPER: Enjoy the weather. Swoosh.

(Fans, watching their respective teams, are shown talking to their TV sets.)

FAN 1: We're still in it. Let's do it.

FAN 2: Look at the game. Watch who got the ball, watch who got the ball.

FAN 3: Now that is mad dog defense. That's a good defense. If they just work it a little more like that.

FAN 4: Impossible.

FAN 5: Here we go.

FAN 6: Nice tip, nice tip. Way to crash the board.

FAN 7: Basketball 101. Basketball 101.

FAN 8: They need to hurry up. What are they taking their time for?

FAN 2: Tackle somebody. Tackle somebody now!

FAN 3: That's bush league. That's all it is. Nothing but bush league.

FAN 6: Fourth quarter they always collapse.

FAN 9: Push it, Fisher.

FAN 10: Come on!

FAN 11: Terry's open, he's open, he's open!

FAN 1: Run baby, run. Run.

FAN 10: Knock him down!

FAN 4: Don't foul.

FAN 11: Foul him!

FAN 12: Let it go!

MERIT AWARD
**Consumer Television
Over :30 Single**

ART DIRECTOR
Kim Schoen

WRITER
Kevin Proudfoot

AGENCY PRODUCER
Brian Cooper

PRODUCTION COMPANY
Epoch Films

DIRECTOR
Stacy Wall

CREATIVE DIRECTORS
Ty Montague
Todd Waterbury

CLIENT
ESPN

AGENCY
Wieden + Kennedy/New York

03399A

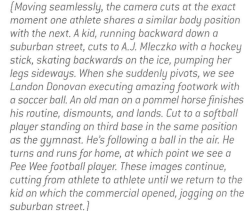

(Moving seamlessly, the camera cuts at the exact moment one athlete shares a similar body position with the next. A kid, running backward down a suburban street, cuts to A.J. Mleczko with a hockey stick, skating backwards on the ice, pumping her legs sideways. When she suddenly pivots, we see Landon Donovan executing amazing footwork with a soccer ball. An old man on a pommel horse finishes his routine, dismounts, and lands. Cut to a softball player standing on third base in the same position as the gymnast. He's following a ball in the air. He turns and runs for home, at which point we see a Pee Wee football player. These images continue, cutting from athlete to athlete until we return to the kid on which the commercial opened, jogging on the suburban street.)

MERIT AWARD
**Consumer Television
Over :30 Single**

ART DIRECTOR
Hal Curtis

WRITERS
Mike Byrne
Kash Sree

AGENCY PRODUCER
Vic Palumbo

PRODUCTION COMPANY
RSA USA

DIRECTOR
Jake Scott

CREATIVE DIRECTORS
Hal Curtis
Carlos Bayala

CLIENT
Nike

AGENCY
Wieden + Kennedy/Portland

03400A

Nike Shox

MERIT AWARD
Consumer Television
Over :30 Single

ART DIRECTOR
Matt Stein

WRITER
Jonathan Cude

AGENCY PRODUCER
Jennifer Smieja

PRODUCTION COMPANY
Gorgeous Enterprises

DIRECTOR
Frank Budgen

CREATIVE DIRECTORS
Hal Curtis
Ty Montague
Mike Byrne

CLIENT
Nike

AGENCY
Wieden + Kennedy/Portland

03402A

ANNOUNCER 1: It's absolutely atrocious, Alan. I can't believe he missed that.

ANNOUNCER 2: The reverse angle showed that was a good call for offside.

ANNOUNCER 1: Oh my word, I think we've got an...

ANNOUNCER 2: Extra man on the pitch.

ANNOUNCER 1: Can't imagine he'll get too far, though.

ANNOUNCER 2: Well, I don't know, though. So far, he's given the police nothing but a good look at his backside.

ANNOUNCER 1: I don't know if this is a cry for help, but it's certainly got my attention.

ANNOUNCER 2: Oh dear, that image is going to stay with me for a very long time.

ANNOUNCER 1: Scorched into my retina.

ANNOUNCER 2: I do hope he's not heading for the royal box.

ANNOUNCER 1: Ooh, that's going to leave a mark...Back to the game.

ANNOUNCER 2: Furlong to Denick.

ANNOUNCER 1: We have contact. Looks like he has more souvenirs for the crowd.

ANNOUNCER 2: I think he's got the shoes to thank.

ANNOUNCER 1: A minute ago they were all chanting who had all the pies. I think there's your answer.

SUPER: More go.

ANNOUNCER 2: And he's off like a bull with gas.

SUPER: Nike Shox. Swoosh logo.

MERIT AWARD
Consumer Television
Over :30 Single

ART DIRECTOR
Monica Taylor

WRITER
Mike Byrne

AGENCY PRODUCER
Andrew Loevenguth

PRODUCTION COMPANY
HSI

DIRECTOR
Gerard de Thame

CREATIVE DIRECTOR
Hal Curtis

CLIENT
Nike

AGENCY
Wieden + Kennedy/Portland

03470A

SFX: Stampeding wild horses.

[Storm clouds gather over rolling hills as the earth shakes. A herd of runners moves through the land like a pack of wild horses. Dirt flies. The group disappears down a hill.]

SFX: More intense stampeding.

[They scatter and separate. A smaller group heads into a wooded area, darting in and out of the trees. As a group they suddenly move left and meet up with the bigger group. They run to the top of a ridge, and one by one fly down the other side of the hill.]

SUPER: Swoosh logo. Nike.

(Treacherous weather lashes a beach. Hardened surfers seek shelter in their vans. A guy in a VW Polo turns up and goes surfing.)

SUPER: Careful it doesn't go to your head. The tough new Polo.

MERIT AWARD
**Consumer Television
Over :30 Campaign**

ART DIRECTORS
Rob Jack
Michael Kaplan
Feargal Ballance
Dylan Harrison

WRITERS
Ewan Paterson
Tim Charlesworth
Feargal Ballance
Dylan Harrison

AGENCY PRODUCERS
Maggie Blundell
Lucy Westmore

PRODUCTION COMPANIES
@radical.media
Harry Nash Films

DIRECTORS
Frederik Bond
Ringan Ledwidge
Lenard Dorfman

CREATIVE DIRECTORS
Ewan Paterson
Jeremy Craigen
Dave Buchanan
Mike Hannett

CLIENT
Volkswagen

AGENCY
BMP DDB/London

03404A

MERIT AWARD
**Consumer Television
Over :30 Campaign**

ART DIRECTOR
Gerard Caputo

WRITER
Mike Gibbs

AGENCY PRODUCERS
Mark Sitley
Tom Anderson

PRODUCTION COMPANY
Independent Media

DIRECTORS
Alfonso Cuaron
Francois Girard

CREATIVE DIRECTORS
David Lubars
Bruce Bildsten

CLIENT
PBS

AGENCY
Fallon/Minneapolis

03405A

(A pet fish in a fish bowl is watching a PBS show about salmon returning upriver. Inspired, the fish begins an amazing series of leaps and flips in order to make its way back home. It jumps from the bowl into a glass of water, then out the window. Splashing from puddle to puddle, he eventually lands in a jug. A man places the jug on a truck and drives off. The fish watches the passing scenery. As the truck crosses a bridge, the fish leaps from the jug into the river, swimming upstream beside the salmon.)

SUPER: Be more empowered. Be More. PBS logo.

465

MERIT AWARD
**Consumer Television
Over :30 Campaign**

ART DIRECTORS
Paul Foulkes
Joel Clement
Rich Silverstein

WRITERS
Tyler Hampton
Matt Elhardt
Jeffrey Goodby

AGENCY PRODUCERS
Diane Hill
Colleen Wellman
Debbie King

PRODUCTION COMPANIES
Academy Films
MJZ
@radical.media

DIRECTORS
Frederic Planchon
Frederik Bond
Ralf Schmerberg

CREATIVE DIRECTORS
Steve Simpson
Steve Luker

CLIENT
Hewlett-Packard

AGENCY
Goodby, Silverstein & Partners/
San Francisco

03406A

Also won:
MERIT AWARD
**Consumer Television
Over :30 Single**

[Three thieves, discussing their next heist, sit in a Parisian restaurant. Suddenly, a computer arrow grabs one of the crooks by the shirt and drags him out through the restaurant doors. The arrow continues to drag the crook down the street, around a corner and then throws him in a police van.]

ANNOUNCER: Using HP mobile technology to get information quickly and easily, the world's police forces now fight crime digitally.

SUPER: Crime fighters + hp = everything is possible.

SALESMAN: So that's $8,795.

WOMAN: Is that the—

[Her husband nudges her, as if to say, "for God's sake, shut up!" The salesman hands over the keys.]

SALESMAN: The car's just out there on the forecourt. I'll come out with you.

MAN: No, that's fine. We've seen it. We're very happy. Really happy with that. Bye now.

[The couple walks out quickly.]

MAN: *[Whispering.]* Just keep walking. Keep walking!

SUPER: No. We haven't got the price wrong. Polo E SDI. Reduced by £620. VW logo.

MERIT AWARD
**Consumer Television
:30/:25 Single**

ART DIRECTOR
Peter Heyes

WRITER
Matt Lee

AGENCY PRODUCER
Maggie Blundell

PRODUCTION COMPANY
Academy Films

DIRECTOR
Peter Cattaneo

CREATIVE DIRECTORS
Ewan Paterson
Jeremy Craigen

CLIENT
Volkswagen

AGENCY
BMP DDB/London

03407A

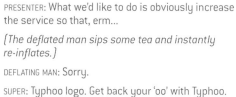

PRESENTER: So if we look at this line here...

[A man at the meeting, obviously bored, starts to deflate like a balloon.]

PRESENTER: We can see that the units have slowly increased.

[A long raspberry noise emanates from the man's body as he deflates. The others try to ignore him. Another man at the table makes himself a cup of Typhoo.]

PRESENTER: So we can meet our target of increased growth.

[Suddenly, the deflating man shoots around the room before coming to a halt on the table. The tea maker hands a cup of tea to the now totally deflated man, who is sprawled out on the table.]

PRESENTER: What we'd like to do is obviously increase the service so that, erm...

[The deflated man sips some tea and instantly re-inflates.]

DEFLATING MAN: Sorry.

SUPER: Typhoo logo. Get back your 'oo' with Typhoo.

PRESENTER: Right. Where was I? The three percent...

MERIT AWARD
**Consumer Television
:30/:25 Single**

ART DIRECTOR
Christer Andersson

WRITER
Alex Ball

AGENCY PRODUCER
Tracey Johnston

PRODUCTION COMPANY
Godman

DIRECTOR
Barney Cokeliss

CREATIVE DIRECTOR
Charles Inge

CLIENT
Typhoo

AGENCY
Clemmow Hornby Inge/London

03408A

MERIT AWARD
Consumer Television
:30/:25 Single

ART DIRECTOR
Aaron Adler

WRITER
Ari Weiss

AGENCY PRODUCER
Clair Grupp

PRODUCTION COMPANY
Harvest Films

DIRECTOR
Baker Smith

CREATIVE DIRECTOR
Eric Silver

CLIENT
Fox Sports Net

AGENCY
Cliff Freeman & Partners/
New York

03409A

MERIT AWARD
Consumer Television
:30/:25 Single

ART DIRECTOR
Aaron Adler

WRITER
Ari Weiss

AGENCY PRODUCER
Clair Grupp

PRODUCTION COMPANY
Harvest Films

DIRECTOR
Baker Smith

CREATIVE DIRECTOR
Eric Silver

CLIENT
Fox Sports Net

AGENCY
Cliff Freeman & Partners/
New York

03410A

[It starts to rain on the pedestrians at a city bus stop. A man in a Nets shirt and hat is not only getting wet, but is being pelted by hail. He takes a few steps to the side, but the hail follows him. He steps under an umbrella, but this is unsuccessful. Hailstones fall even harder. Finally, the Nets fan falls to the ground, surrendering to his fate.]

SUPER: God is a Celtics Fan. Boston Celtics logo.

[Among a group of people walking down the street, a guy is decked out in a Knicks sweatshirt and hat. A sudden gust of wind blows off his hat. But the only person affected by the wind is the Knicks fan. He retrieves his hat. A harder gust of wind blows him into a garbage can. Again, the Knicks fan is the only one affected. As he gets back on his feet, the largest gust sends him into the sky. He comes crashing down onto a parked car across the street.]

SUPER: God is a Celtics Fan. Boston Celtics logo.

GOD IS A CELTICS FAN

(Opens on a door with sign reading, "Test Room #3. Testing In Progress.")

TESTER: Hello, my friend. Which would you rather have? This oven toasted sub...? *(Uncovers Quiznos toasted sub.)*

SUBJECT: I like toasted.

TESTER: ...Or this untoasted sub with a lot of, shall we say, lettuce.

(He uncovers untoasted sub lying in a pile of cash. The subject stuffs the bills in his pockets.)

TESTER: *(Speaking into small tape recorder.)* Uh-huh. Clearly prefers the untoasted sub with the lettuce.

ANNOUNCER: The only way to beat a Quiznos toasted sub is to cheat.

SUPER: Quiznos logo. Oven Toasted Tastes Better™.

MERIT AWARD
**Consumer Television
:30/:25 Single**

ART DIRECTOR
Guy Shelmerdine

WRITER
Richard Bullock

AGENCY PRODUCER
Matt Bijarchi

PRODUCTION COMPANY
JGF

DIRECTOR
Jeff Gorman

CREATIVE DIRECTOR
Taras Wayner

CLIENT
Quiznos

AGENCY
Cliff Freeman & Partners/
New York

03425A

(A couple argues in a kitchen.)

MAN: Why do you always bring her up? It was nothing. Nothing happened.

WOMAN: That's what you say. While I'm stuck in here like some prisoner, you're out prowling the streets.

MAN: What?

WOMAN: That's exactly what you're doing, isn't it? You want to keep me here so you can have the stability of all this.

(A man wearing an IKEA shirt walks into the scene.)

IKEA MAN: So, what do you guys think?

(The camera reveals that the couple is in the kitchen section of the IKEA store.)

MAN: It feels really good.

WOMAN: Yeah, we'll take it.

SUPER: Shop Unböring. IKEA logo. unboring.com.

MERIT AWARD
**Consumer Television
:30/:25 Single**

ART DIRECTOR
Paul Stechschulte

WRITER
Tom Adams

AGENCY PRODUCER
Rupert Samuel

PRODUCTION COMPANY
Moxie Pictures

DIRECTOR
Wes Anderson

CREATIVE DIRECTORS
Alex Bogusky
Paul Keister

CLIENT
IKEA

AGENCY
Crispin Porter + Bogusky/Miami

03411A

MERIT AWARD
Consumer Television
:30/:25 Single

ART DIRECTOR
Paul Stechschulte

WRITER
Tom Adams

AGENCY PRODUCER
Rupert Samuel

PRODUCTION COMPANY
Moxie Pictures

DIRECTOR
Wes Anderson

CREATIVE DIRECTORS
Alex Bogusky
Paul Keister

CLIENT
IKEA

AGENCY
Crispin Porter + Bogusky/Miami

03412A

[In a living room, a family is having a conversation.]

MOTHER: Tell me what's wrong.

DAUGHTER: I'm pregnant.

MOTHER: Oh, my.

FATHER: I knew it! I knew it! It's that creepy boyfriend of yours, isn't it? I told you this would happen.

DAUGHTER: Dad, stop.

MOTHER: So it's my fault now.

FATHER: Where do you think she learns this kind of behavior? Not from me. You're the one that smoked pot in college.

[An IKEA employee walks into the room.]

IKEA MAN: So, what do you think?

[The camera reveals that the family is actually at an IKEA store, in a living room display.]

MOTHER: I like it. We'll take it.

SUPER: Shop Unböring. IKEA logo. unboring.com.

MERIT AWARD
Consumer Television
:30/:25 Single

WRITER
John Immesoete

AGENCY PRODUCERS
Greg Popp
Gary Gassel

PRODUCTION COMPANY
MJZ

DIRECTOR
Kuntz & Maguire

CREATIVE DIRECTORS
John Immesoete
John Hayes
Barry Burdiak

CLIENT
Anheuser-Busch

AGENCY
DDB/Chicago

03414A

MOM: Greg. This one you gotta see.

LESLIE: Oh, Mom.

MOM: That's Leslie's first bath. Look at that little tushy.

GREG: That's her little tushy, all right. That cute little tushy that belongs to such an attractive, beautiful woman. 'Cause it's grown up into something else...nice, big round...tushy. You know. Have you seen it? Have you seen it lately?

SUPER: Budweiser logo. TRUE. www.budweiser.com.

GREG: Is dinner coming soon, or is it...

WOMAN: *[Carefully reviewing greeting cards at the store.]* You truly are my true love...Our love shines like a beacon.

[Plunking down a 6-pack at a gas station, a guy sees a greeting card at the register. He grabs it.]

SUPER: Budweiser logo. TRUE. www.budweiser.com.

WOMAN: *[At the dinner table, she opens the card her boyfriend has picked out; she is moved.]* It's perfect.

MERIT AWARD
**Consumer Television
:30/:25 Single**

ART DIRECTOR
Adam Glickman

WRITER
Craig Feigen

AGENCY PRODUCERS
Greg Popp
Gary Gassel

PRODUCTION COMPANY
MJZ

DIRECTOR
Kuntz & Maguire

CREATIVE DIRECTORS
John Immesoete
John Hayes
Barry Burdiak

CLIENT
Anheuser-Busch

AGENCY
DDB/Chicago

03416A

BARTENDER: How you doing?

GUY 1: How you doing?

GUY 2: How you doing?

BARTENDER: How you doing?

OUT OF TOWNER: Well, thanks for asking. I'm doing fine. Just got in today. My brother-in-law picked me up at the airport. Mighty big airport you all got. And the people here are so nice.

BARTENDER: You want a beer?

OUT OF TOWNER: I want a Bud.

GUY 3: How you doing?

GUYS 1 & 2: *[Together.]* How you doing?

GUY 3: How you doing?

BARTENDER: How you doing?

GUY 3: How you doing?

OUT OF TOWNER: I'm doing fine. I just got here today. My brother-in-law picked me up at the airport, and the people sure are nice.

GUY 3: Nice people.

GUY 4: How you doing?

BARTENDER: How you doing?

GUY 4: How you doing?

OUT OF TOWNER: I'm doing fine. I just got here. My brother-in-law picked me up at the airport. Mighty big airport.

SUPER: Budweiser logo. TRUE. www.budweiser.com.

MERIT AWARD
**Consumer Television
:30/:25 Single**

ART DIRECTORS
Scott Smith
Vinny Warren
Pat Burke

WRITERS
Vinny Warren
Pat Burke
Scott Smith

AGENCY PRODUCER
Kent Kwiatt

PRODUCTION COMPANY
hungry man

DIRECTOR
Allen Coulter

CREATIVE DIRECTORS
John Immesoete
John Hayes
Barry Burdiak

CLIENT
Anheuser-Busch

AGENCY
DDB/Chicago

03417A

471

GREG: When I look at Steve and Jenny, I just think, wow! Don't they look great, especially Jenny. We all remember what she used to look like, you know, really plump and not fat, you know, big boned, you know, wide, you know, she had girth, you know. Diets, there were tons of them but the one that worked best for her was stoppin' eatin', you know, there's no food in here.

SUPER: Budweiser logo. TRUE. www.budweiser.com.

MERIT AWARD
Consumer Television
:30/:25 Single

WRITER
John Immesoete

AGENCY PRODUCERS
Greg Popp
Gary Gassel

PRODUCTION COMPANY
Radke Films

DIRECTORS
John Immesoete
Greg Popp

CREATIVE DIRECTORS
John Immesoete
John Hayes
Barry Burdiak

CLIENT
Anheuser-Busch

AGENCY
DDB/Chicago

03418A

MERIT AWARD
Consumer Television
:30/:25 Single

ART DIRECTOR
Dan Pawych

WRITER
Ben Weinberg

AGENCY PRODUCER
Bev Cornish

PRODUCTION COMPANY
Steam Films

DIRECTOR
David Kellogg

CREATIVE DIRECTOR
Dan Pawych

CLIENT
Anheuser-Busch

AGENCY
Downtown Partners DDB/Toronto

03419A

COUNSELOR: Let's start with you, Jennifer.

JENN: There's no communication. None.

COUNSELOR: Um-huh.

JENN: He just sits there like a lump watching the satellite TV.

COUNSELOR: How many channels?

JEFF: Dude, a lot. I mean, there's, like, two just for volleyball.

COUNSELOR: Surround?

JEFF: Oh, yeah.

COUNSELOR: Flat Screen?

JEFF: Plasma. 43 inch. Hi def.

COUNSELOR: Extended viewing angle?

JEFF: Oh, yeah, you can see it from the bathroom if you leave the door open.

COUNSELOR: Sweet. You know what you need to do?

JENN: What?

COUNSELOR: *(Signaling for Jenn to be quiet.)* You need—how big is your woofer?

JEFF: Like 18 inches.

COUNSELOR: God, that's a big woofer.

SUPER: TRUE. Budweiser. www.budweiser.com.

GIRLFRIEND: Oh, sweety, it's perfect!

SALES CLERK: That's great! It fits him really well in the shoulders. It's Italian.

GIRLFRIEND: Oh, it's Italian.

BEAUTIFUL WOMAN: Nice sweater.

GUY: Okay.

GIRLFRIEND: Okay?

GUY: Yup.

[The guy then goes to a bar to meet his friends in his new Italian sweater.]

GUY: Guys, what's going on?

[Shocked, his friends look from one to another and burst into laughter.]

SUPER: TRUE. Budweiser. www.budweiser.com.

MERIT AWARD
Consumer Television
:30/:25 Single

ART DIRECTOR
Rich Pryce-Jones

WRITER
David Chiavegato

AGENCY PRODUCER
Johnny Chambers

PRODUCTION COMPANIES
Imported Artists
@radical.media

DIRECTORS
Rick Lemoine
Steve Miller

CREATIVE DIRECTOR
Dan Pawych

CLIENT
Anheuser-Busch

AGENCY
Downtown Partners DDB/Toronto

03420A

SUPER: 1999.

EXECUTIVE 1: Just so I understand, is it a chip?

GUY 1: I hesitate to call it a chip.

EXECUTIVE 2: And it fuels the Internet?

GUY 1: Helps to fuel—It helps to fuel the Internet.

EXECUTIVE 3: Is it, like, software?

GUY 1: Software is like a really weird word.

EXECUTIVE 3: That's a weird word?

EXECUTIVE 4: Do you guys have a Web Site?

GUY 1: Yeah. We have one under construction.

EXECUTIVE 1: So you're on the Web, the World Wide Web?

EXECUTIVE 2: This is fantastic!

EXECUTIVE 4: I think we'd be idiots not to fund this.

GUY 1: Really?

SUPER/ANNOUNCER: Times have changed. So have we.

ANNOUNCER: The new E*TRADE. More of what you need to stay ahead in today's economy.

SUPER: Planning. Investing. Banking. Lending. Advice. E*TRADE Financial.

MERIT AWARD
Consumer Television
:30/:25 Single

ART DIRECTOR
Sean Farrell

WRITER
Colin Nissan

AGENCY PRODUCER
Cindy Fluitt

PRODUCTION COMPANY
Biscuit Filmworks

DIRECTOR
Noam Murro

CREATIVE DIRECTORS
Rich Silverstein
Jeffrey Goodby

CLIENT
E*TRADE

AGENCY
Goodby, Silverstein & Partners/
San Francisco

03421A

473

TELEVISION
MERIT

MERIT AWARD
**Consumer Television
:30/:25 Single**

ART DIRECTOR
Jeff Church

WRITER
Steve McElligott

AGENCY PRODUCERS
Michelle Price
Monique Veillete

PRODUCTION COMPANY
Anonymous Content

DIRECTOR
John Dolan

CREATIVE DIRECTOR
Court Crandall

CLIENT
ESPN Mohr Sports

AGENCY
Ground Zero/Los Angeles

03423A

MERIT AWARD
**Consumer Television
:30/:25 Single**

ART DIRECTOR
Jeff Church

WRITER
Steve McElligott

AGENCY PRODUCERS
Michelle Price
Monique Veillete

PRODUCTION COMPANY
Anonymous Content

DIRECTOR
John Dolan

CREATIVE DIRECTOR
Court Crandall

CLIENT
ESPN Mohr Sports

AGENCY
Ground Zero/Los Angeles

03424A

KIDS: Life on the farm is soooo sweet...and there's so much good food to eat! We love carrots! We love carrots! We love corn! We love corn! We love potatoes! We love potatoes! We love tomatoes! We love tomatoes! We love beets! We love beets!

JAY MOHR: *(Pointing off camera to a boy's mother.)* You know, your mom's hot. You know what I'd like to do to your mom? It involves a tomato and some corn and a lot of beets.

SUPER: Jay Mohr. Wrong for them. Just right for us. Mohr Sports logo.

KURT: And we're back with 4 News on your side. Let's see what's happening outside. You know, I actually saw my breath last night.

SHARON: Really? Well, that means hot cocoa weather is on the way!

KURT: Ah ah ah!

SHARON: Well, looks like we're in for a little rain. Jay?

JAY MOHR: That's right, Sharon. We are. And you know what? If you ever say "hot cocoa weather" again, I'm gonna go to the trailer park and kick over your house.

SUPER: Jay Mohr. Wrong for them. Just right for us. Mohr Sports logo.

FEMALE HOST: I actually happen to be wearing one. This is what we call a Legacy Piece because this is sure to stay in your family for many, many generations. It's Goldique, with 1.85 carats of Crystalle. And Jay, wouldn't you agree that, for all our gentlemen viewers out there, this is just the perfect gift for that special lady in your life.

JAY: All our gentlemen callers? Both of them? Yeah, that's nice. You can tip your hooker with it.

SUPER: Jay Mohr. Wrong for them. Just right for us. Mohr Sports logo.

MERIT AWARD
Consumer Television
:30/:25 Single

ART DIRECTOR
Jeff Church

WRITER
Steve McElligott

AGENCY PRODUCERS
Michelle Price
Monique Veillette

PRODUCTION COMPANY
Anonymous Content

DIRECTOR
John Dolan

CREATIVE DIRECTOR
Court Crandall

CLIENT
ESPN Mohr Sports

AGENCY
Ground Zero/Los Angeles

03422A

DAD: Hi, son. How's it going?

SON: Well, dad, I'm having real trouble with my revision.

DAD: Well, no one said becoming a doctor was going to be easy. Here, try one of these.

SON: Rowntree's Fruit Pastilles?

DAD: That's right. They're fruity, they're chewy, and they'll help you pass those exams.

(As if all is suddenly clear, the son scribbles away happily. Years later, the son is wearing what looks like a doctor's white coat.)

BOY: Hi, dad!

(The camera reveals that the son is actually working behind the counter in a chip shop.)

DAD: *(Guiltily.)* Erm, small cod and chips please, son.

ANNOUNCER: Rowntree's Fruit Pastilles. They're fruity. They're chewy. What more do you want?

SUPER: Rowntree's logo. You'll love these.

MERIT AWARD
Consumer Television
:30/:25 Single

ART DIRECTOR
Tony Barry

WRITER
Damon Collins

AGENCY PRODUCER
Russell Benson

PRODUCTION COMPANY
MJZ

DIRECTOR
Kuntz & Maguire

CREATIVE DIRECTOR
Paul Weinberger

CLIENT
Nestle Rowntrees

AGENCY
Lowe/London

03426A

MERIT AWARD
Consumer Television
:30/:25 Single

ART DIRECTOR
Neil Sullivan

WRITERS
Gordon Graham
Geoff Smith

AGENCY PRODUCER
Natashka Coleman

PRODUCTION COMPANIES
Harry Nash Films
Tool of North America

DIRECTOR
Tom Routson

CREATIVE DIRECTOR
Paul Weinberger

CLIENT
Nestlè UK

AGENCY
Lowe/London

03097A

[Throughout, young children engage in acts of violence, with adults as the victims, in order to get a packet of Milkybar Munchies. In one scene, a mother is pushing her toddler in a grocery store cart. Nearby, a young man is eating Milkybar Munchies. When the mother bends to pick something up, the baby pinches her bottom. Thinking the young man is the culprit, the mother slaps him. In the final scene, a mom in a parked car shares some Milkybar Munchies with her friend. The kids look on forlornly from the back seat.]

ANNOUNCER: New Milkybar Munchies are made for adults.

[Mom sets off down the drive, but someone has attached a rope from the car to the front porch. The rope, now taut, pulls down the porch. The children smile mischievously.]

ANNOUNCER: But try explaining that to kids.

MERIT AWARD
Consumer Television
:30/:25 Single

ART DIRECTOR
Dave Douglas

WRITER
Pete Breton

AGENCY PRODUCER
Sandy Cole

PRODUCTION COMPANY
Untitled

DIRECTOR
Tim Godsall

CREATIVE DIRECTORS
Marta Cutler
David Kelso
Chad Borlase
Gary Watson

CLIENT
Rogers AT&T Wireless

AGENCY
Maclaren McCann/Toronto

03427A

Also won:
MERIT AWARD
Consumer Television
Under $50,000 Budget

[A man with pantyhose on his head runs up to the window of a gas station.]

MAN: Fill the bag.

[Suddenly, his cell phone rings.]

SFX: "Push It," by Salt N' Peppa.

ATTENDANT: Kevin? Remember, we met at Nancy's? It's me, Andrea.

[Kevin backs slowly away, his robbery foiled.]

ATTENDANT: You look good.

SUPER: Personalize your ring tone. Rogers AT&T logo.

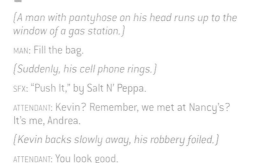

Personalize your ringtone

MUSIC: Dean Martin's "Let it Snow."

[Corporate CEOs feverishly shred paper and dump it out of top floor windows, tricking the people partying on floors below into thinking that even more Christmas spirit is upon them.]

SUPER: To all those who were not naughty this year, happy holidays. Heineken logo.

MERIT AWARD
**Consumer Television
:30/:25 Single**

ART DIRECTOR
Rob Perillo

WRITERS
Bryan Johnson
Rob Lenois

AGENCY PRODUCER
Colin Pearsall

PRODUCTION COMPANY
Minder Media

DIRECTOR
Tony Kaye

CREATIVE DIRECTORS
Lee Garfinkel
Steve Doppelt
John Liegey

CLIENT
Heineken

AGENCY
Publicis/New York

03428A

MERIT AWARD
**Consumer Television
:30/:25 Single**

ART DIRECTOR
Nick Spahr

WRITER
Kevin Frank

AGENCY PRODUCER
Stacey Higgins

PRODUCTION COMPANY
Tool of North America

DIRECTOR
Tom Routson

CREATIVE DIRECTORS
Greg Bell
Paul Venables

CLIENT
HBO Home Video-OZ

AGENCY
Venables, Bell & Partners/
San Francisco

03432A

[A guy puts a quarter in a newspaper box and takes out a paper. As he opens his paper, he notices that he took two by mistake. This is followed by a sequence of disturbing clips from "OZ." The guy then puts another quarter in the box to replace the extra newspaper.]

SUPER: Eight full hours of OZ. It'll make you think twice. The entire first season on DVD and VHS.

ANNOUNCER: Your British sailor circa 1740 knew that citrus fruit could prevent scurvy. Now that's gotta be the only conceivable reason that a man would put a lime in his beer. Then again, how bad can scurvy be? A certain amount of risk goes hand in hand...with living the high life.

SUPER: Miller High Life logo.

MERIT AWARD
Consumer Television
:30/:25 Single

ART DIRECTOR
Jeff Williams

WRITER
Jed Alger

AGENCY PRODUCER
Jeff Selis

PRODUCTION COMPANY
@radical.media

DIRECTOR
Errol Morris

CREATIVE DIRECTORS
Susan Hoffman
Roger Camp

CLIENT
Miller Brewing Company

AGENCY
Wieden + Kennedy/Portland

03436A

MERIT AWARD
Consumer Television
:30/:25 Single

ART DIRECTOR
Monica Taylor

WRITER
Mike Byrne

AGENCY PRODUCER
Andrew Loevenguth

PRODUCTION COMPANY
Omaha Pictures

DIRECTOR
Rupert Sanders

CREATIVE DIRECTOR
Hal Curtis

CLIENT
Nike

AGENCY
Wieden + Kennedy/Portland

03462A

SFX: A single drum throughout.

[Two men on the street, surrounded by a crowd, get ready to compete. We then see feet moving up and down. A crowd beneath an elevated subway track looks up, cheering. The contestants do pull ups from the rail just beneath the train tracks. They continue, looking at one another intensely, the crowd cheering. As they begin to show strain, a subway car approaches. The contestants stare at one another, holding on; finally, one contestant lets go and falls.]

SUPER: Nike logo. Swoosh. Apparel. Made to Move.

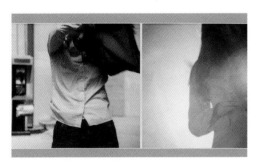

49 hwy/42 city

■

(A young woman is wearing a heavy down parka, a scarf, and gloves. She begins to shed her heavy clothes. Soon, she is down to a fleece shirt and pants. She continues, taking off the fleece shirt. Finally, she's in a tank top. We then see a TDI powered Volkswagen zipping down a highway. The environment is hot and dry like the desert.)

ANNOUNCER: You could go from Aspen to Phoenix on just one tank. The fuel-efficient Golf TDI.

MERIT AWARD
**Consumer Television
:30/:25 Campaign**

ART DIRECTOR
Paul Renner

WRITER
Dave Weist

AGENCY PRODUCER
Bill Goodell

PRODUCTION COMPANY
Bob Industries

DIRECTOR
Dayton/Faris

CREATIVE DIRECTOR
Alan Pafenbach

CLIENT
Volkswagen of America

AGENCY
Arnold Worldwide/Boston

03437A

MERIT AWARD
**Consumer Television
:30/:25 Campaign**

ART DIRECTOR
Peter Heyes

WRITER
Matt Lee

AGENCY PRODUCER
Maggie Blundell

PRODUCTION COMPANY
Academy Films

DIRECTOR
Peter Cattaneo

CREATIVE DIRECTORS
Ewan Paterson
Jeremy Craigen

CLIENT
Volkswagen

AGENCY
BMP DDB/London

03438A

■

WOMAN: Go on.

MAN: I'm really sorry for not paying the right amount for my Volkswagen Passat last week. I should have told you you undercharged me, but it seemed like a good idea at the time. Please don't tell the police. We got a baby.

SUPER: No. We haven't got the price wrong. Passat SE TDI 100 PS. Reduced by £825. VW logo.

SHAVE 3-4 STROKES
OFF YOUR SCORE.

MERIT AWARD
Consumer Television
:30/:25 Campaign

ART DIRECTORS
Dean Wagner
Steven Makransky

WRITERS
LeAnn Wilson McGuire
Andy Tyer

AGENCY PRODUCER
Lyn Stovall

PRODUCTION COMPANY
CornerBooth Productions

DIRECTOR
Frank Swoboda

CREATIVE DIRECTOR
LeAnn Wilson McGuire

CLIENT
Golf Pride (a Division of
Eaton Corporation)

AGENCY
BURRIS/Greensboro

03439A

WITHOUT BREAKING A SWEAT.

INSTRUCTOR: Good morning! And welcome to Gene Greer's Golf Academy. As promised, we're going to show you how to shave three to four strokes off your score. Today! Let's get started. Regrip your clubs...with Golf Pride. *(Waves.)* Thank you all for coming!

SUPER: Shave 3-4 strokes off your score.

(Instructor walks away, leaving students alone.)

SUPER: Without breaking a sweat. Golf Pride logo.

MERIT AWARD
Consumer Television
:30/:25 Campaign

ART DIRECTOR
Rob Carducci

WRITERS
Dan Kelleher
Richard Bullock

AGENCY PRODUCER
Ed Zazzera

PRODUCTION COMPANY
Oil Factory

DIRECTOR
Hughes Bros.

CREATIVE DIRECTOR
Eric Silver

CLIENT
Fox Sports Net

AGENCY
Cliff Freeman & Partners/
New York

03440A

(Mike Tyson is gently rocking an infant in his arms, singing a lullaby. John Kruk, host of "The Best Damn Sports Show Period," observes quietly at the doorway of his child's room. Kruk's wife appears. Together they happily observe the tender moment.)

KRUK: Okay, Mike, we'll be back around midnight.

MRS. KRUK: He's so sweet.

(Cut to Tyson on the set of "The Best Damn Sports Show Period.")

HOST: Please welcome, Mike Tyson!

SUPER: Athletes really want to be on The Best Damn Sports Show Period.

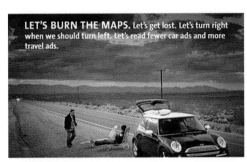

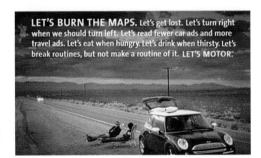

[Two guys hang out on the side of the road next to their parked MINI.]

SUPER: Let's burn the maps. Let's get lost. Let's turn right when we should turn left. Let's read fewer car ads and more travel ads. Let's eat when hungry. Let's drink when thirsty. Let's break routines, but not make a routine of it. Let's motor. MINI.

MERIT AWARD
**Consumer Television
:30/:25 Campaign**

ART DIRECTORS
Mark Taylor
Alex Burnard

WRITERS
Ari Merkin
Steve O'Connell

AGENCY PRODUCERS
David Rolfe
Rupert Samuel

DIRECTOR
Plus

CREATIVE DIRECTORS
Alex Bogusky
Andrew Keller

CLIENT
MINI

AGENCY
Crispin Porter + Bogusky/Miami

03441A

[A customer is standing extremely close to a Saturn salesperson.]

CUSTOMER: $9,995 for the Saturn Special Edition SL?

SALESPERSON: That's right.

CUSTOMER: With A/C?

SALESPERSON: Yup.

CUSTOMER: That's incredible. Is there anything else I should know?

SALESPERSON: You're like an inch away from my face, and it is really freaking me out.

CUSTOMER: *[Stepping away from the salesperson.]* How's that?

SUPER: The Saturn "Maybe A Little Too Honest" Spring Sales Event.

SALESPERSON: That is much, much better.

SUPER: 2002 Saturn SL Starting at $9,995. Saturn logo.

MERIT AWARD
**Consumer Television
:30/:25 Campaign**

ART DIRECTOR
Dave Laden

WRITERS
Matt Smukler
Jamie Barrett

AGENCY PRODUCER
David Yost

PRODUCTION COMPANY
MJZ

DIRECTOR
Kuntz & Maguire

CREATIVE DIRECTOR
Jamie Barrett

CLIENT
Saturn

AGENCY
Goodby, Silverstein & Partners/
San Francisco

03442A

MERIT AWARD
**Consumer Television
:30/:25 Campaign**

ART DIRECTORS
Demian Fore
Tom Gilmore

WRITERS
Carole Hurst
Rich Tlapek

AGENCY PRODUCERS
Karen Jacobs
Khrisana Edwards

PRODUCTION COMPANIES
hungry man
Ritts Hayden

DIRECTORS
David Shane
Daniel Kleinman

CREATIVE DIRECTORS
Rich Tlapek
Tom Gilmore

CLIENT
Dial

AGENCY
GSD&M/Austin

03443A

(During an office party, a guy photocopies his butt. Retrieving the copy, he quickly exits the copy room. A different guy enters and smushes his face down on the glass.)

SFX: Copy machine noise.

SUPER: You're not as clean as you think. Dial logo.

SFX: Shower sound.

[A man and woman are in a conference room. The woman notices one last donut. The man reaches toward the table. Seeing this, the woman lunges, grabbing the donut.]

ANNOUNCER: Dunkin' Donuts delicious donuts. Just the thing with your morning coffee.

[She composes herself and takes a bite. At this point we realize that he was reaching for a pen on the table near the box.]

SUPER: Dunkin' Donuts. Just the thing.

MERIT AWARD
**Consumer Television
:30/:25 Campaign**

ART DIRECTORS
Eric Peterson
Tim Foley

WRITERS
John Hart
Marty Donohue

AGENCY PRODUCERS
Wendy Hudson
Tom Foley

PRODUCTION COMPANIES
Biscuit Filmworks
@radical.media

DIRECTORS
Noam Murro
Frank Todaro

CREATIVE DIRECTORS
Marty Donohue
Tim Foley

CLIENT
Dunkin' Donuts

AGENCY
Hill Holliday/Boston

03444A

[A woman is at the kitchen table. Her husband walks in, opens the fridge, and takes out a carton of milk. He gives her a conspiratorial look, then drinks straight from the carton. He spits out the sour milk.]

WIFE: The fridge is broken.

SUPER/ANNOUNCER: Refrigerators on sale. Sears. Where else?

MERIT AWARD
**Consumer Television
:30/:25 Campaign**

ART DIRECTORS
Mitch Gordon
Chris Tag
Stuart Cohn

WRITERS
Chris Sadlier
Michael Stout
Josh Kemeny

AGENCY PRODUCER
Ray Lyle

PRODUCTION COMPANIES
MJZ
Tool of North America
Avenue Edit
Ashe and Spencer

DIRECTORS
Craig Gillespie
Sean Ehringer

CREATIVE DIRECTORS
Mitch Gordon
Joe Sciarrotta

CLIENT
Sears Roebuck and Co.

AGENCY
Ogilvy & Mather/Chicago

03446A

MERIT AWARD
**Consumer Television
:30/:25 Campaign**

ART DIRECTORS
John LaMacchia
Mitchell Ratchik
Jeff Curry
Jeff Compton

WRITERS
Lisa Topol
Chris Wall
Tom Bagot
Maggie Powers

AGENCY PRODUCER
Lee Weiss

PRODUCTION COMPANY
Pytka Productions

DIRECTOR
Joe Pytka

CREATIVE DIRECTORS
Tom Bagot
Chris Wall
Jeff Curry

CLIENT
IBM

AGENCY
Ogilvy and Mather/New York

03445A

SENIOR MANAGER: What is it?

INVENTOR: It's a UBA.

GUY 1: A UBA?

INVENTOR: Universal Business Adapter.

SENIOR MANAGER: What's it do?

INVENTOR: It connects anything to everything.

SENIOR MANAGER: What's this for?

INVENTOR: Your laptop. Your mainframe. Call center.
Unix servers. Linux servers. Internet. Supply chain.
Payroll system. HR. E-mail.

SENIOR MANAGER: Slick.

GAL 1: Is it affordable?

GAL 2: Fast?

GUY 2: Easy?

INVENTOR: Very.

SENIOR MANAGER: Does it work in Europe?

INVENTOR: You need an adapter.

SUPER: There is no Universal Business Adapter.
Get Websphere Integration Software. e-business
on demand. IBM.

(On a suburban school parking lot, a group of guys tests a real-life version of a weapon from the video game, "Ratchet & Clank.")

CAMERAMAN: Okay, today we're gonna try and hit that target with the Devastator, a rocket launcher in "Ratchet & Clank."

(A guy fires the enormous weapon. The rocket misses its target, creating a huge explosion. Some of the guys laugh, some run, some are in complete shock.)

CAMERAMAN: Wow.

(Cut to the Devastator in game graphics.)

ANNOUNCER: The Devastator. One of 36 weapons not fit for this world.

SUPER: Live in your world. Play in ours. Playstation2 logo.

MERIT AWARD
Consumer Television :30/:25 Campaign

ART DIRECTOR
Lew Willig

WRITER
Scott Duchon

AGENCY PRODUCERS
Elizabeth Giersbrook
Julie Rousseau

PRODUCTION COMPANY
Biscuit Filmworks

DIRECTOR
Noam Murro

CREATIVE DIRECTOR
Jerry Gentile

CLIENT
Sony Playstation

AGENCY
TBWA/Chiat/Day/Los Angeles

03447A

EIGHT FULL HOURS OF OZ. IT'LL MAKE YOU THINK TWICE.

Also won: **MERIT AWARD** Consumer Television :30/:25 Single

(A guy standing at a crosswalk is obviously in a hurry to get somewhere. The light at the opposite side of the intersection clearly reads, "don't walk." To the left and right, there is not a car in sight. The light still reads, "don't walk." The guy begins to take a step into the intersection. This is followed by a sequence of disturbing clips from "OZ." The guy takes his foot out of the intersection.)

SUPER: Eight full hours of OZ. It'll make you think twice. The entire first season on DVD and VHS.

MERIT AWARD
Consumer Television :30/:25 Campaign

ART DIRECTOR
Nick Spahr

WRITER
Kevin Frank

AGENCY PRODUCER
Stacey Higgins

PRODUCTION COMPANY
Tool of North America

DIRECTOR
Tom Routson

CREATIVE DIRECTORS
Paul Venables
Greg Bell

CLIENT
HBO Home Video-OZ

AGENCY
Venables, Bell & Partners/
San Francisco

03448A

MERIT AWARD
Consumer Television
:30/:25 Campaign

ART DIRECTOR
Ted Royer

WRITER
Jeff Bitsack

AGENCY PRODUCERS
Chris Noble
Andrew Loevenguth

PRODUCTION COMPANY
hungry man

DIRECTOR
David Shane

CREATIVE DIRECTORS
Ty Montague
Todd Waterbury

CLIENT
ESPN

AGENCY
Wieden + Kennedy/New York

03449A

MERIT AWARD
Consumer Television
:30/:25 Campaign

ART DIRECTORS
Joe Shands
Jayanta Jenkins

WRITERS
Roger Camp
Dylan Lee

AGENCY PRODUCER
Jennifer Fiske

PRODUCTION COMPANIES
Harvest Films
Stock Footage

DIRECTOR
Baker Smith

CREATIVE DIRECTORS
Roger Camp
Tim Hanrahan
Todd Waterbury

CLIENT
Powerade

AGENCY
Wieden + Kennedy/Portland

03450A

ESPN OFFICES
12:38AM

Also won: MERIT AWARD Consumer Television :30/:25 Single

SUPER: ESPN offices. 12:38 am.

[Dan Patrick types at his computer. Suddenly the lights flicker and go out. He walks down the stairs and through a low-lit basement. He reaches a door that says, "Danger. High Voltage." He opens the door to reveal Lance Armstrong resting on a stationary bike.]

DAN: Lance, hey, what's the story?

LANCE: Hey. Hey, Dan, sorry. I thought everyone left for the night.

[Lance begins peddling the bike and the lights come back on in response.]

DAN: Can I get you an energy bar? How 'bout some water?

LANCE: No, nah, I'm okay.

DAN: You good?

LANCE: Thanks.

DAN: All right.

SUPER: This is SportsCenter.

[An angry Andy Roddick, after questioning a judge's call on his first serve, serves his second one so hard it is driven into the clay surface.]

SUPER: Very Real Power. Powerade.

WOMAN CO-HOST: And Jackie is wearing this wonderfully elegant, two-piece ensemble made of cotton and rayon that's guaranteed to impress. What do you think, Jay?

JAY MOHR: That's gonna impress, all right. Does it come with a bedpan and a walker? Ugh.

SUPER: Jay Mohr. Wrong for them. Just right for us. Mohr Sports logo.

Shop on-line anywhere

(A man is trapped under a log in a forest. A delivery man arrives and has the trapped man sign for a package. He opens it. Inside is a book called: "So, you're Trapped under a Log.")

SUPER: Shop online anywhere. Rogers AT&T logo.

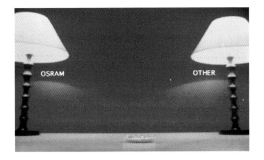

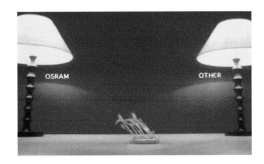

AMERIT AWARD
Consumer Television
:20 and Under: Single

ART DIRECTOR
Hylton Mann

WRITER
George Low

AGENCY PRODUCER
Natalie Johnson

PRODUCTION COMPANY
Have Bolex Will Travel

DIRECTOR
Brett Wild

CREATIVE DIRECTOR
Brett Wild

CLIENT
Osram

AGENCY
Saatchi & Saatchi/Johannesburg

03453A

[Bean sprouts have been planted beneath two lamps. The one on the left contains an Osram full-spectrum bulb, the other, on the right, a standard light bulb Time-elapsed photography tracks the growth of the beans as they rise up and sprout toward the Osram bulb.]

SUPER: Osram Natural Daylight Bulbs.

MERIT AWARD
Consumer Television
:20 and Under: Single

ART DIRECTOR
Kim Schoen

WRITER
Kevin Proudfoot

AGENCY PRODUCER
Chris Noble

PRODUCTION COMPANY
hungry man

DIRECTOR
David Shane

CREATIVE DIRECTORS
Ty Montague
Todd Waterbury

CLIENT
ESPN

AGENCY
Wieden + Kennedy/New York

03454A

[Joe Montana in cooking attire searches feverishly for something.]

VOICE 1: C'mon people, we gotta find this thing. Let's go!

VOICE 2: Anything?

VOICE 3: Check under the refrigerator!

[Meanwhile, Dan Patrick, Scott Campbell, Rich Eisen, and Stuart Scott are eating in cafeteria. Dan finds something in his soup.]

RICH: What?

[Dan spits out a Super Bowl ring.]

RICH: Oh.

SCOTT: Oh my. Wow.

STUART: *[Putting the ring on.]* Wait, wait.

RICH: Wow. Looks good. Nice. I like that, very nice. Bling bling.

■

(Victor and John are playing shelfball.)

VICTOR: I'm talkin' about rules. It doesn't hit the back.

JOHN: Those aren't the rules. You're talking about making up the rules.

VICTOR: I'm talking about—

(Emmit sees the boss walk in.)

EMMIT: *(Holding out a document.)* I'm talking about...this. *(The boss walks out of frame.)*

VICTOR: You don't even know what you're talking about!

SUPER: Without sports, a shelf would just be a shelf. ESPN logo.

VICTOR: I know how to play the game!

EMMIT: You know what I'm talkin' about.

MERIT AWARD
**Consumer Television
:20 and Under: Single**

ART DIRECTOR
Kim Schoen

WRITER
Kevin Proudfoot

AGENCY PRODUCER
Brian Cooper

PRODUCTION COMPANY
RSA USA

DIRECTOR
ACNE

CREATIVE DIRECTORS
Ty Montague
Todd Waterbury

CLIENT
ESPN

AGENCY
Wieden + Kennedy/New York

03455A

MERIT AWARD
Consumer Television
:20 and Under: Campaign

ART DIRECTORS
Karen Costello Malave
Yooly Mukai

WRITERS
Chris Ribeiro
Michael Everard

AGENCY PRODUCER
Alex Brook

PRODUCTION COMPANY
Bob Industries

DIRECTOR
Chris Hooper

CREATIVE DIRECTOR
Eric Hirshberg

CLIENT
California Milk Advisory Board

AGENCY
Deutsch/Los Angeles

03456A

MERIT AWARD
Consumer Television
:20 and Under: Campaign

ART DIRECTORS
Justine Gallacher
Rob Hibbert

WRITERS
Rob Hibbert
Justine Gallacher

AGENCY PRODUCER
Joanne Alach

PRODUCTION COMPANY
Exit Films

DIRECTOR
Boyd Hicklin

CREATIVE DIRECTOR
Scott Whybin

CLIENT
Melbourne International Comedy
Festival

AGENCY
Whybin TBWA/Melbourne

03457A

DIRECTOR: California Cheese, take six. And, action!
SFX: Cell phone ringing.
DIRECTOR: Somebody turn that off.
COW: Should I go?
DIRECTOR: Cut!
ANNOUNCER: Great cheese comes from happy cows.
SUPER: Real California Cheese. It's the cheese.

SUPER: The Prague Medieval Swimming Festival.

CZECHOSLOVAKIAN OFFICIAL: *(In Czech.)* On your marks,
get set, go.

(Four medieval knights awkwardly jump into the pool.)

SUPER: Almost as silly as The Melbourne International
Comedy Festival. Comedy festival Web Site and logo.
March 28–April 21. Book at Ticketmaster
7 1300 66 00 13.

(Feet float down a set of stairs without actually touching them. Two red Chinese restaurant doors open and close, revealing the set of stairs behind them. The feet and legs float down the steps again, then back up the steps.)

SUPER: nikelab.com.

MERIT AWARD
**Consumer Television
:20 and Under: Campaign**

ART DIRECTORS
Danielle Flagg
Jeff Williams
Susan Hoffman

WRITERS
Simon Mainwaring
Carlos Bayala

AGENCY PRODUCERS
Ben Grylewicz
Katie Shields

PRODUCTION COMPANIES
The Design Assembly
Hunter Gatherer
Wieden + Kennedy
Joint

DIRECTORS
Thomas Wagner
Hunter Gatherer
Eric David Johnson

CREATIVE DIRECTORS
Carlos Bayala
Susan Hoffman

CLIENT
Nike

AGENCY
Wieden + Kennedy/Portland

03458A

MERIT AWARD
Consumer Television
Varying Lengths Campaign

ART DIRECTORS
Paul Silburn
Chris Bovill
John Allison

WRITERS
Paul Silburn
Chris Bovill
John Allison

AGENCY PRODUCER
Diane Croll

PRODUCTION COMPANY
Spectre

DIRECTOR
Daniel Kleinman

CREATIVE DIRECTORS
Trevor Beattie
Paul Silburn

CLIENT
John Smiths

AGENCY
TBWA/London

03459A

ANNOUNCER: Three divers to go. And this is Darren Croll of Australia. Oh, that's a good dive.

[The judges hold up scores.]

ANNOUNCER: 642.2. And now, Petit of Canada. Oh, even better. This final is really hotting up. Now the favorite. John Smith of Great Britain. What can he do?

[Fat guy does a cannon ball.]

ANNOUNCER: Oh, terrific. The crowd loves it. And so do the judges. Top bombing.

SUPER: No nonsense.

MERIT AWARD
Consumer Television
Varying Lengths Campaign

ART DIRECTORS
Ted Royer
Bill Lee

WRITERS
Jeff Bitsack
Ilicia Winokur

AGENCY PRODUCERS
Chris Noble
Temma Shoaf

PRODUCTION COMPANY
hungry man

DIRECTOR
David Shane

CREATIVE DIRECTORS
Ty Montague
Todd Waterbury

CLIENT
ESPN

AGENCY
Wieden + Kennedy/New York

03460A

SUPER: ESPN Cafeteria. June 21, 12:15 pm.

SIMONE GAGNE: You can imagine how big it was for Canada to win that gold medal. We waited a long time and now after 50 years the gold medal is back.

SCOTT VAN PELT: Tell me something. What kind of cheese you got there?

SIMONE GAGNE: American.

SCOTT VAN PELT: That's right. American cheese. American cheese.

SUPER: This is SportsCenter. ESPN logo.

SCOTT VAN PELT: American cheese.

■

SUPER: Le Poulet en colere. *(Subtitles.)* The Angry Chicken.

ANNOUNCERS: *(French under, English over.)* A young man is being chased by a chicken. When a chicken in this neighborhood gets angry, it will chase you down. There goes the young man. Look, there he goes. Okay, there is the chicken. No, he cannot fool the chicken. But wait. All right, he has fooled the chicken.

SUPER: Presto. Swoosh logo. Nike-presto.com.

MERIT AWARD
Consumer Television
Varying Lengths Campaign

ART DIRECTOR
Danielle Flagg

WRITER
Mike Byrne

AGENCY PRODUCER
Jennifer Smieja

PRODUCTION COMPANY
Partizan

DIRECTOR
Traktor

CREATIVE DIRECTORS
Susan Hoffman
Carlos Bayala

CLIENT
Nike

AGENCY
Wieden + Kennedy/Portland

03461A

Also won:
MERIT AWARD
Consumer Television
Over :30 Single

MERIT AWARD
Non Broadcast
Cinema

ART DIRECTORS
James Ioveno
Rafael Soberal

WRITER
Miguel Fernández

CREATIVE DIRECTORS
John Gellos
Gregg Wasiak
Griffin Stenger
Will Morrison

CLIENT
Latino Film Festival

AGENCY
The Concept Farm/New York

03464A

Cast In Order of Appearance

Gardener — Antonio Soto

Bus Boy — Ignacio Matos

Pregnant Teen — Isabel Fernández

Carjacker — Rafael Soberal

Drunk Bum — Alejandra Umpierre

Cartel Thug — Edgardo Sol

Machete Mugger — José Vega

Are you content with the role
of Latinos in film?

Not your stereotypical week at the movies

(In the last scene of a generic movie, a man and
boy walk off into the sunset. The image fades to
black and credits start rolling.)

SUPER: (Credits rolling.) Cast in order of appearance:
Gardener, Antonio Soto; Bus Boy, Ignacio Matos;
Pregnant Teen, Isabel Fernández; Carjacker, Rafael
Soberal; Whore, Pilar Sosa; Drunk Bum, Alejandra
Umpierre; Cartel Thug, Edgardo Sol.

SUPER: Are you content with the role of Latinos in film?
The New York International Latino Film Festival. Not
your stereotypical week at the movies.

MERIT AWARD
Non Broadcast
Cinema

ART DIRECTOR
Patrizio Marini

WRITER
Emanuele Madeddu

PRODUCTION COMPANY
Mercurio Cinematografica

DIRECTOR
Gigi Piola

CLIENT
The Face

AGENCY
Fagan Reggio del Bravo/Rome

03465A

(In a parody of the award-winning Levi's commercial
of the previous year, a young man, trying to run
through a wall, crashes into it and falls down dead.)
SUPER: Need a post facility? The Face—Milan.

need a post facility?

■

(A 15-year-old kid in his room is watching MTV. When his mom knocks on the door, he grabs the remote control and changes the channel—to hard-core porn.)

MOM: Hi, son, how are you?

SON: Fine, mom.

MOM: How was school?

SON: Fine.

MOM: That's good, darling. Listen, dinner is ready. Please don't take long or it will get cold.

(The moment his mom leaves, the kid flips the channel back to MTV.)

SUPER: I watched MTV once.

MERIT AWARD
Non Broadcast Cinema

ART DIRECTORS
Ricky Vior
Luis Ghidotti
Mariano Cassisi
Federico Callegari

WRITERS
Jose Molla
Joaquín Molla
Leo Prat
Matias Ballada

AGENCY PRODUCERS
Facundo Perez
Fernando Lazzari

PRODUCTION COMPANIES
Emma sin Emma
La Banda Films

DIRECTOR
Jose Antonio Prat

CREATIVE DIRECTORS
Jose Molla
Joaquín Molla
Cristian Jofre

CLIENT
MTV

AGENCY
la comunidad/Miami Beach

03466A

MERIT AWARD
Foreign Language Television

ART DIRECTOR
Gloria Linaza

WRITER
Nacho Guilló

AGENCY PRODUCERS
Marta Delgado
Miguel Ramis

PRODUCTION COMPANY
BVS

DIRECTOR
Mónica Herrera

CREATIVE DIRECTORS
Pablo Monzón
Jorge López

CLIENT
Action Against Hunger

AGENCY
Cathedral The Creative Center/
Madrid

03467A

MARCH 22ND. WORLD WATER DAY.

(A hand places a glass of water in front of a picture
of an undernourished African child. Due to the
optical effect of the glass of water, the part of the
child's body that is behind the glass appears fat.)

5 December. International Volunteer Day.

MERIT AWARD
Foreign Language Television

ART DIRECTORS
Carlos Rubio
Jorge López

WRITERS
Noelia Terrer
Pablo Monzón

AGENCY PRODUCERS
Marta Delgado
Miguel Ramis

PRODUCTION COMPANY
Miss Wasabi

DIRECTOR
Isabel Coixet

CREATIVE DIRECTORS
Pablo Monzón
Jorge López

CLIENT
Red Cross

AGENCY
Cathedral The Creative Center/
Madrid

03468A

■

(A young man runs forward, against the direction of a crowd of people who are running away from something. We discover that he is a Red Cross Volunteer, heading to the place where his help is needed.)

MERIT AWARD
Foreign Language Television

WRITER
Kazunori Saito

AGENCY PRODUCER
Tsuguyuki Saito

PRODUCTION COMPANY
YES OPEN

DIRECTOR
Jun Kawanishi

CREATIVE DIRECTORS
Ichiro Kinoshita
Kazunori Saito

CLIENT
Nissin Food Products

AGENCY
Dentsu/Tokyo

03469A

■

SUPER: Sausage High School.

TEACHER: *(Bumping his sausage head on the door-frame.)* Ouch! *(To sausage students.)* What are you laughing at? Here are the results of your job interviews. Aoki. Hot dog. Abe. American dog. Amano. Japanese stew! Quiet! Grindy. Cup Noodles!

STUDENTS: Grindy! Grindy! Grindy!

SUPER: Ground pork. Cup Noodles Sausage makes its debut in society.

GRINDY: I'll do my best.

MERIT AWARD
Innovative Marketing
Category Sponsor:
Yahoo!

WRITER
Scott Greggory

CREATIVE DIRECTOR
Scott Greggory

CLIENT
Toledo Towing

AGENCY
BusinessVoice/Toledo

03009G

[Messages heard by callers placed on hold.]

ANNOUNCER: Season's greetings and thanks for calling Toledo Towing and Recovery. Do you belong to an auto club? Just let us know and we'll lop 10% off your repair bill. Are you a senior citizen? Then guess what?! You, too, can save 10% on your repairs. Are you a man or a woman? Prove it, and we'll take 10% off your repair total. If you live on land, if you still have your own tongue or if you cringe at least a little bit when renting bowling shoes, give yourself a 10% discount. Got milk? Then good news, friend: You get 10% off. In fact, just give us any reason to give you 10% off your repair bill, and we'll do it. We're easy that way. You might even say slutty.

ANNOUNCER: Mike Mills is a rich and famous rock star, the bass player for the band R.E.M. But few people know about the other Mike Mills; he's the Service Manager here at Toledo Towing. While Mike Mills the musician enjoys a life of privilege, including champagne baths and nightly orgies, our Mike Mills spends most of the day complaining that he isn't the other Mike Mills, the Mike Mills everyone likes and respects; the Mike Mills who gets to wear sparkly clothes on stage. Oh, sure, our Mike Mills could wear sparkly clothes, but he'd get beat up by the other guys who work here. Nope, life isn't easy for the other Mike Mills. So, whatta you say, cut him some slack the next time he acts like a jerk.

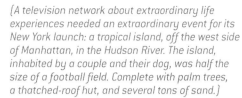

(A television network about extraordinary life experiences needed an extraordinary event for its New York launch: a tropical island, off the west side of Manhattan, in the Hudson River. The island, inhabited by a couple and their dog, was half the size of a football field. Complete with palm trees, a thatched-roof hut, and several tons of sand.)

MERIT AWARD
Innovative Marketing

ART DIRECTOR
Valerie Ang-Powell

WRITERS
Robin Fitzgerald
Sally Hogshead

CREATIVE DIRECTOR
Sally Hogshead

CLIENT
Fine Living

AGENCY
Crispin Porter + Bogusky/
Los Angeles

03010G

This ambient media execution was placed on university athletic tracks during a week-long training period. It utilized the existing starting grid of the 200 meter race, but the numeral 8 was removed from its original place and repositioned further back on the track.

MERIT AWARD
Innovative Marketing

ART DIRECTOR
Michael Bond

WRITER
Bernard Hunter

PHOTOGRAPHER
David Prior

CREATIVE DIRECTOR
Graham Warsop

CLIENT
Nike

AGENCY
The Jupiter Drawing Room
(South Africa)/Johannesburg

03011G

MERIT AWARD
Innovative Marketing

ART DIRECTORS
Dena Blevins
Matt Peterson
Tia Doar

WRITERS
Ian Cohen
Mark Radcliffe
Geoff Rogers
Joel Thomas

AGENCY PRODUCERS
Kevin Diller
Alysia Alder
Eric Lepire
Claire McNally

PRODUCTION COMPANY
Moxie Pictures

DIRECTOR
Spencer Chinoy

CREATIVE DIRECTORS
Austin Howe
Ian Cohen

CLIENT
Thomason Autogroup

AGENCY
Nerve/Portland

03012G

See 03397A

MERIT AWARD
Innovative Marketing

ART DIRECTOR
Calvin Chu

WRITERS
Michael Eilperin
Blake Callaway

PHOTOGRAPHER
Bethany Jensen

CREATIVE DIRECTOR
Michael Eilperin

CLIENT
SCI FI Channel

AGENCY
SCI FI Channel/New York

03014G

This surprise photo pack insert, placed in actual packs of developed film, blurred the line between science fiction and science fact, involving the consumer in the long history of UFO sightings that TAKEN explored.

MERIT AWARD
Innovative Marketing

ART DIRECTOR
Jon Wyville

WRITER
Dave Loew

CREATIVE DIRECTORS
Jon Wyville
Dave Loew

CLIENT
NASCAR

AGENCY
Young & Rubicam/Chicago

03015G

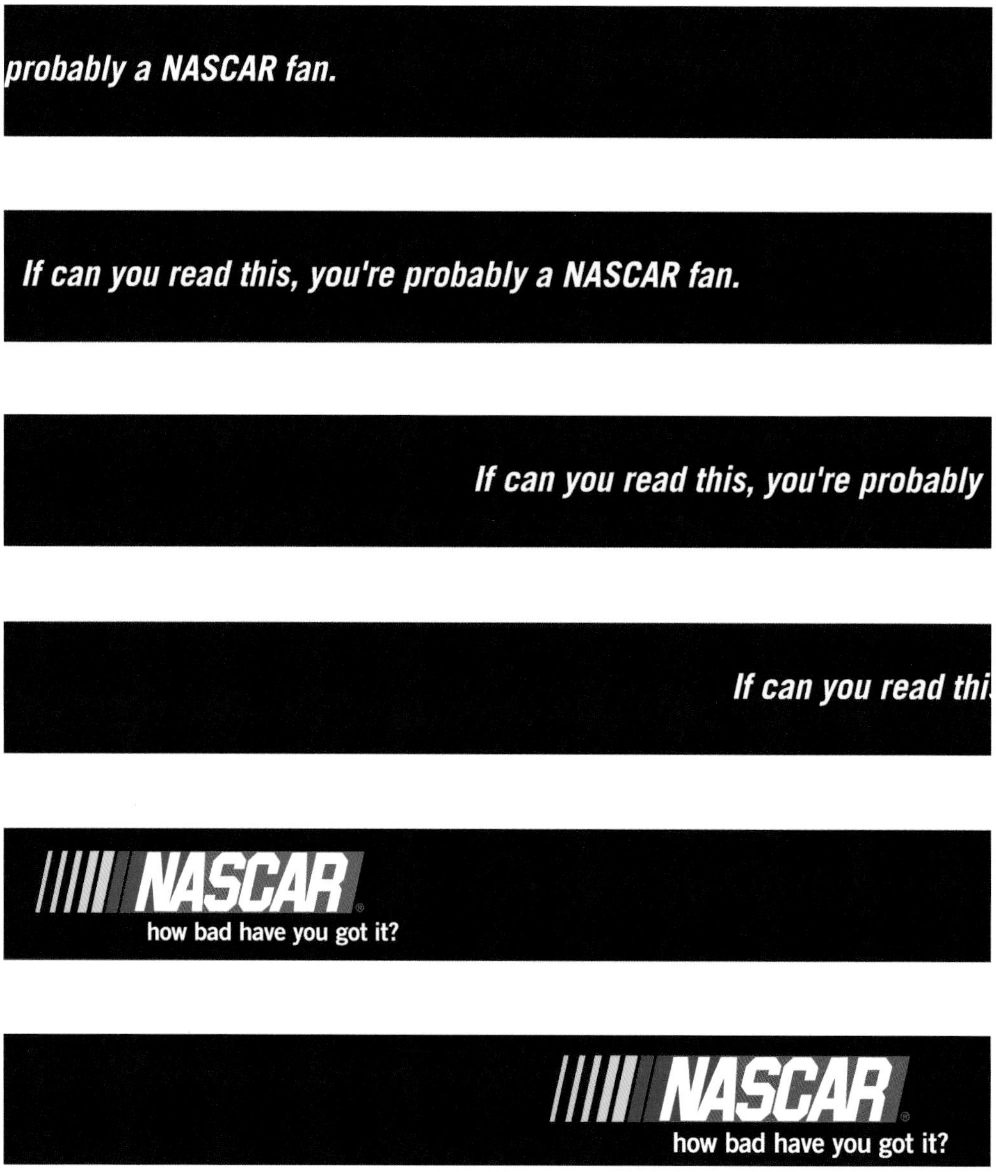

probably a NASCAR fan.

If can you read this, you're probably a NASCAR fan.

If can you read this, you're probably

If can you read thi

how bad have you got it?

how bad have you got it?

MERIT AWARD
Integrated Branding

ART DIRECTORS
Julian Newman
Adele Ellis
Mike Gatti

WRITERS
Alex Russell
Tim Brunelle

PHOTOGRAPHER
Tom Nagy

ILLUSTRATOR
Evan Hecox

AGENCY PRODUCERS
Paul Shannon
Andrea Ricker
Ken Kingdon

PRODUCTION COMPANIES
Psyop NYC
The Barbarian Group

CREATIVE DIRECTORS
Ron Lawner
Alan Pafenbach
Chris Bradley
Tim Brunelle

CLIENT
Volkswagen of America

AGENCY
Arnold Worldwide/Boston

03016G

ANNOUNCER: What kind of people finish something but are never quite done with it? I mean, aren't you done when you're finished? See, these people have an idea. But as soon as they're finished with it, they realize they're not finished. So they keep fiddlin'. Trying to make it just a little bit better. Then they have another idea. And it's good, too. But they can't leave that one alone either. Of course, more ideas pop up. And they can't keep their hands off any of 'em. You know they might spend a month trying to tweak this little part here or drive themselves crazy smoothing out that shape there just to make every Volkswagen a little better. So, no matter what they finish, they're never really—finished. Ever. Maybe these people have some kinda weird DNA, these engineers and designers. Well, they sure are smart. Smart, but kooky. I wonder what they're gonna think up next?

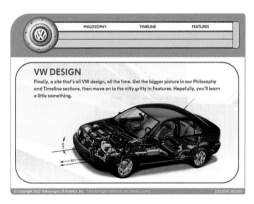

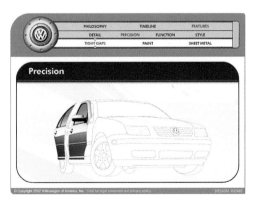

MERIT AWARD
Integrated Branding

ART DIRECTORS
Toby Talbot
Leo Premutico
Mike O'Sullivan

WRITERS
Toby Talbot
Leo Premutico
Mike O'Sullivan

CREATIVE DIRECTOR
Mike O'Sullivan

CLIENT
Auckland Regional Council

AGENCY
Colenso BBDO/Auckland

03017G

ANNOUNCER: This ad is an experiment.

[Two men, on top of Mt. Eden, put an electronic tracking device inside a piece of litter. Then they throw it in a stormwater drain and follow its path down to the harbor. Eventually they recover it, washed up on the beach, 11.4 kilometers away. It takes just three hours and 49 minutes to get there.]

SUPER: Street litter doesn't stay on the street. The Big Clean Up. 0800 JOIN IN. arc.govt.co.nz. ARC logo.

MAN: This is my Micka. She is not a very good mouse catcher, but she is very friendly. She loves our porch, but she'll get used to yours. If I can't find a bone marrow donor.

SUPER: Call 02 510 20 510.

MERIT AWARD
Integrated Branding

ART DIRECTOR
Jiri Langpaul

WRITER
Martin Charvat

PHOTOGRAPHER
Petr Skurne

AGENCY PRODUCERS
Premysl Grepl
Nikola Lapackova

PRODUCTION COMPANY
Stillking

DIRECTOR
Ivan Zacharias

CREATIVE DIRECTOR
Martin Charvat

CLIENT
The Foundation for the
Transplantation of Bone Marrow

AGENCY
Leo Burnett/Prague

03019G

WOMAN: This piano you are hearing, I got from my grandfather when I was five. So, it's been mine, well, for the last 24 years. I spent a lot of hours on it, but I never became a concert pianist. Hmm, it needs a little tuning. I don't need it anymore, so, if you are interested in it, it's yours. For free. They have not found a bone marrow donor for me yet.

ANNOUNCER: If you want to help, call 02 510 20 510.

TRANSLATION: Free. For low price, almost new Skoda. Only 25,000 km, fully loaded, passenger-side airbag, aluminum wheels. If I can't find a bone marrow donor. Please call 02 510 20 510.

TRANSLATION: Looking for anybody who would like to take up fully equipped flat. Color TV, phone, fridge, washing machine, very close to public transportation. If I can't find a bone marrow donor. Please call 02 510 20 510.

MERIT AWARD
Integrated Branding

ART DIRECTORS
Jeff Curry
Jeff Compton
John McNeil
Mitchell Ratchik
Greg Kaplan
John LaMacchia

WRITERS
Chris Wall
Tom Bagot
Maggie Powers
Lisa Topol
George Tannenbaum

AGENCY PRODUCERS
Lee Weiss
Pamela Shulman

PRODUCTION COMPANY
Pytka Productions

DIRECTOR
Joe Pytka

CREATIVE DIRECTORS
Chris Wall
Tom Bagot
Jeff Curry

CLIENT
IBM

AGENCY
Ogilvy & Mather/New York

03020G

SENIOR MANAGER: What is it?

INVENTOR: It's a UBA.

GUY 1: A UBA?

INVENTOR: Universal Business Adapter.

SENIOR MANAGER: What's it do?

INVENTOR: It connects anything to everything.

SENIOR MANAGER: What's this for?

INVENTOR: Your laptop. Your mainframe. Call center. Unix servers. Linux servers. Internet. Supply chain. Payroll system. HR. E-mail.

SENIOR MANAGER: Slick.

GAL 1: Is it affordable?

GAL 2: Fast?

GUY 2: Easy?

INVENTOR: Very.

SENIOR MANAGER: Does it work in Europe?

INVENTOR: You need an adapter.

SUPER: There is no Universal Business Adapter. Get Websphere Integration Software. e-business on demand. IBM.

Open daily starting June 15th. Admission includes unlimited access to over 25 rides. See pne.bc.ca for details.

[A high-speed boat races across a lake. The boat starts to bounce on the water. Suddenly, the boat takes flight and flips through the air.]

SFX: Screaming.

[Just before the boat hits the water, the picture freezes, then reverses. The boat flips backwards and lands safely, racing away in reverse.]

SFX: Laughter, then sound of amusement park ride.

[The whole action starts again.]

SUPER: Playland logo.

Open daily starting June 15th. Admission includes unlimited access to over 25 rides. See pne.bc.ca for details.

MERIT AWARD
Integrated Branding

ART DIRECTORS
Ian Grais
Joe Piccolo

WRITERS
Ian Grais
Andy Linardatos

PHOTOGRAPHER
Hans Sipma

AGENCY PRODUCERS
Lynn Bonham
Chris Raedcher

PRODUCTION COMPANIES
JMB Post
Wave Productions

CREATIVE DIRECTORS
Ian Grais
Chris Staples

CLIENT
Playland

AGENCY
Rethink/Vancouver

03021G

SFX: Amusement park sounds.

SON: I don't know about that ride, dad. I'm kinda scared.

DAD: Son, sometimes we do things in life because they scare us. That's how you grow as a person. It's not easy. But in the end, it's worth it. Now whatta you say?

SON: All right, dad. I'll do it.

DAD: 'Atta boy.

SFX: Safety bar being snapped shut on ride.

SON: Aren't you getting on with me?

DAD: What are you, nuts? Have you seen how fast this thing goes?

SFX: Ride starting up.

SON: Daddy?

DAD: Don't "daddy" me. You picked it.

SON: Daddy!

ANNOUNCER: Playland. Now open weekends.

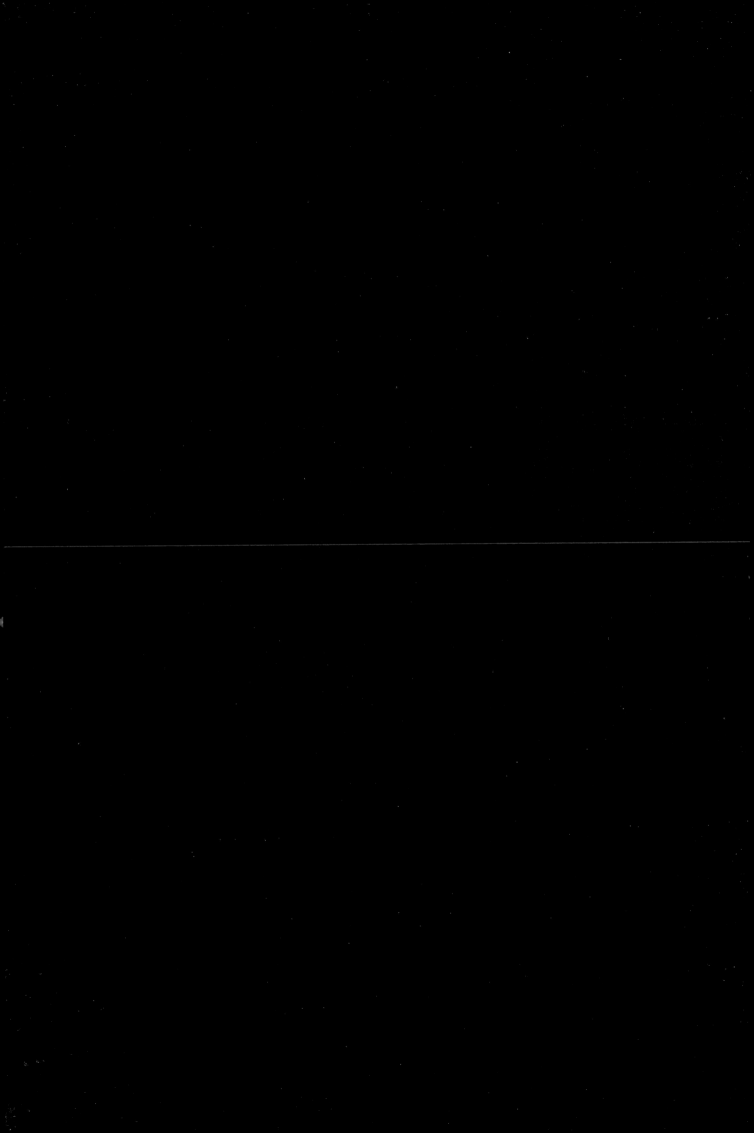

COLLEGE

MERIT

MERIT AWARD
Advertising

ART DIRECTORS
Tatum Cardillo
Mike Lee

WRITER
David Ciano

SCHOOL
Academy of Art College/
San Francisco

CC341

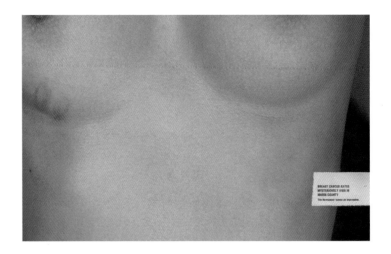

MERIT AWARD
Advertising

ART DIRECTOR
Allen Yu

WRITER
Allen Yu

DESIGNER
Allen Yu

SCHOOL
Academy of Art College/
San Francisco

CC057

Assignment:
Promote newspaper readership
among young adults. Sponsored
by The Newspaper Association
of America.

MERIT AWARD
Advertising

ART DIRECTORS
Thomas Pastrano
Kirsten Pederson

WRITERS
Thomas Pastrano
Kirsten Pederson

DESIGNERS
Thomas Pastrano
Kirsten Pederson

SCHOOL
California State University/
Long Beach

CC320

MERIT AWARD
Advertising

ART DIRECTOR
Grant Simpson

WRITER
Grant Simpson

SCHOOL
Chicago Portfolio School/Chicago

CC321

511

MERIT AWARD
Advertising

ART DIRECTOR
Steve Anderson

WRITER
Priti Damle

DESIGNER
Steve Anderson

SCHOOL
The Creative Circus/Atlanta

CC278

MERIT AWARD
Advertising

ART DIRECTOR
John Baker

WRITERS
Patrick Almaguer
Robert Calabro

SCHOOL
The Creative Circus/Atlanta

CC270

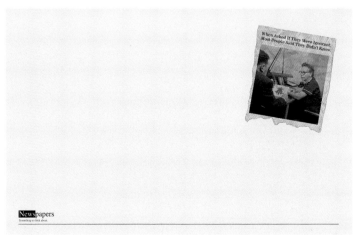

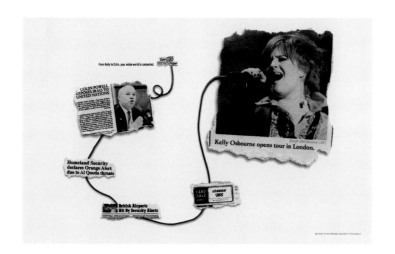

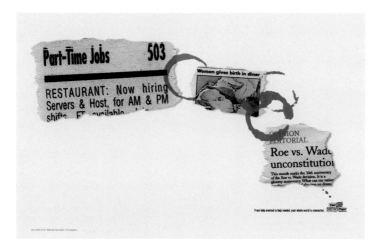

MERIT AWARD
Advertising

ART DIRECTORS
Jinho Kim
Marjorieth San Martin

WRITER
Jinho Kim

SCHOOL
Miami Ad School/Miami Beach

CC076

MERIT AWARD
Advertising

ART DIRECTOR
Gretchen Heim

WRITER
Cheryllyne Vaz

DESIGNER
Gretchen Heim

SCHOOL
Miami Ad School/Minneapolis

CC152

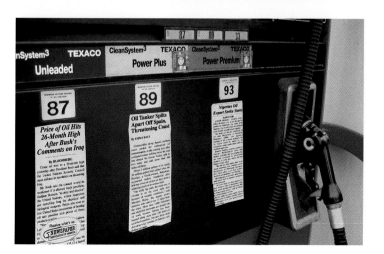

515

MERIT AWARD
Advertising

ART DIRECTORS
Emily Strand
Cindy Potter

WRITER
Amber Lashmett

SCHOOL
Miami Ad School/San Francisco

CC335

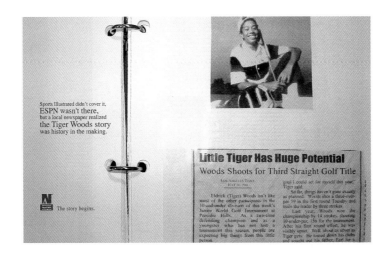

MERIT AWARD
Advertising

ART DIRECTOR
Spencer Canon

WRITER
Spencer Canon

SCHOOL
Portfolio Center/Atlanta

CC021

MERIT AWARD
Advertising

ART DIRECTORS
Terri Dann
Brian Rosenkrans

WRITERS
Nik Bristow
Kelly Quinlan

SCHOOL
Portfolio Center/Atlanta

CC037

MERIT AWARD
Advertising

ART DIRECTORS
Julia Blackburn
Mike Houston

WRITERS
Julia Blackburn
Mike Houston

SCHOOL
School of Visual Concepts/Seattle

CC002

517

MERIT AWARD
Advertising

ART DIRECTOR
Kiran Koshy

WRITER
Kiran Koshy

SCHOOL
Texas A&M University/Commerce

CC135

MERIT AWARD
Advertising

ART DIRECTORS
Jeremy S. Boland
Andy Dao

WRITER
Tyler Carner

SCHOOL
University of Colorado/Boulder

CC242

MERIT AWARD
Advertising

ART DIRECTORS
Julia Veinberg
Katrina Ford

WRITERS
Julia Veinberg
Katrina Ford

SCHOOL
University of Colorado/Boulder

CC244

MERIT AWARD
Advertising

ART DIRECTORS
Matt Miller
January Vernon

WRITER
Scott Ginsberg

SCHOOL
University of Colorado/Boulder

CC243

519

COLLEGE
MERIT

MERIT AWARD
Advertising

ART DIRECTOR
Jonathan Byrne

WRITER
Leah Dieterich

SCHOOL
University of Colorado/Boulder

CC090

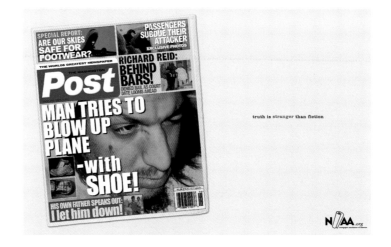

MERIT AWARD
Advertising

ART DIRECTORS
Nick Munoz
Leslie Ziegler

WRITER
Whitney Presley

SCHOOL
University of Texas/Texas Creative/
Austin

CC430

MERIT AWARD
Advertising

ART DIRECTOR
Charles Moore

WRITER
Brian Kille

SCHOOL
University of Texas/Texas Creative/
Austin

CC432

MERIT AWARD
Advertising

ART DIRECTOR
Aziz Rawat

WRITER
Michael Tuton

SCHOOL
VCU Adcenter/Richmond

CC315

MERIT AWARD
Advertising

ART DIRECTOR
Mark Bangerter

WRITER
William Burks Spencer

SCHOOL
VCU Adcenter/Richmond

CC008

MERIT AWARD
Advertising

ART DIRECTOR
Pooja Wadhawan

WRITER
Lyle P. Yetman

SCHOOL
VCU Adcenter/Richmond

CC010

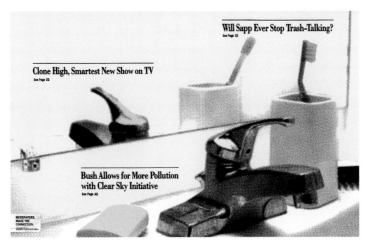

MERIT AWARD
Advertising

ART DIRECTOR
Matthew Trego

WRITER
Madhu Kalyanaraman

SCHOOL
VCU Adcenter/Richmond

CC063

MERIT AWARD
Advertising

ART DIRECTOR
Dan Ware

WRITER
Scott Johnson

SCHOOL
VCU Adcenter/Richmond

CC119

523

COLLEGE
MERIT

MERIT AWARD
Design

ART DIRECTORS
Nathan Orensten
Annie Williams
Ferry Tanumihardjo

WRITERS
Nathan Orensten
Annie Williams

DESIGNERS
Nathan Orensten
Annie Williams
Ferry Tanumihardjo

SCHOOL
Columbus College of Art & Design/
Columbus

CCD003

MERIT AWARD
Design

ART DIRECTORS
Stedson McIntyre
Nick Coakley

WRITER
Stedson McIntyre

DESIGNER
Stedson McIntyre

SCHOOL
Columbus College of Art & Design/
Columbus

CCD014

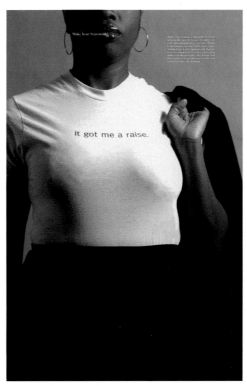

MERIT AWARD
Design

WRITERS
Ranielle Barbas
Toni Jordan
Scott Tredeau

DESIGNERS
Ranielle Barbas
Toni Jordan
Scott Tredeau

PHOTOGRAPHER
Kristin Phagan

SCHOOL
The Creative Circus/Atlanta

CCD056

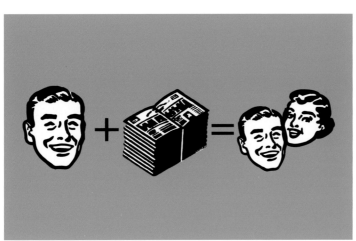

MERIT AWARD
Design

DESIGNER
Clara Sims

SCHOOL
James Madison University/
Harrisonburg

CCD076

525

MERIT AWARD
Design

DESIGNER
Nathaniel K. Arey

SCHOOL
James Madison University/
Harrisonburg

CCD077

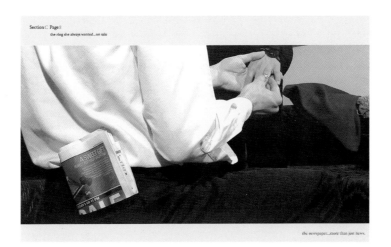

MERIT AWARD
Design

WRITER
Emersson Barillas

DESIGNER
Emersson Barillas

SCHOOL
James Madison University/
Harrisonburg

CCD029

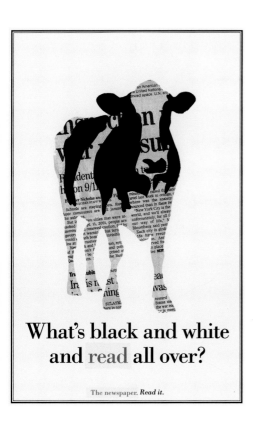

What's black and white
and read all over?

The newspaper. *Read it.*

What's black and white
and read all over?

The newspaper. *Read it.*

MERIT AWARD
Design

ART DIRECTORS
Frank Baseman
Barbara Metzger

WRITER
Barbara Metzger

DESIGNER
Barbara Metzger

SCHOOL
Philadelphia University/
Philadelphia

CCD067

MERIT AWARD
Design

DESIGNER
Ben Ginnel

SCHOOL
Portfolio Center/Atlanta

CCD008

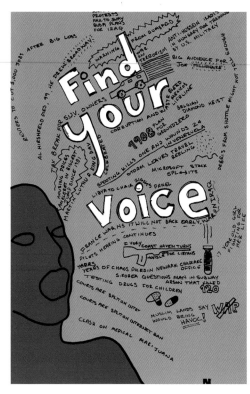

MERIT AWARD
Design

DESIGNERS
Luis Bravo
Russell Austin

SCHOOL
Portfolio Center/Atlanta

CCD009

MERIT AWARD
Design

ART DIRECTOR
Elizabeth Salkoff

WRITER
Allison Khoury

SCHOOL
VCU Adcenter/Richmond

CCD072

THE ANNUAL PATRICK KELLY SCHOLARSHIP AWARD

Established by EURO RSCG MVBMS Partners in conjunction with The One Club to honor the late Patrick Kelly, the scholarship is awarded to a student of advertising based on the merits of his or her portfolio, essays, and teacher recommendations. Below is an excerpt from Amy Hollrah's response to the topic: "Explain why you chose advertising."

I chose advertising because I cannot not choose advertising. Advertising changes the world. Every day. Normal people don't even realize it. It's unbelievable to me that something like a slogan or song can influence the masses. That's why I do it. I cannot not write advertising. It's in me. It's something I have to do or else it feels like something's missing. It's an obsessive-compulsive disorder I cannot control. I will never tire of trying to change people's minds with an ad. And I will never tire of wanting to find the exact perfect way to say something. Plus, some of the hardest working people I have ever known are in this business.

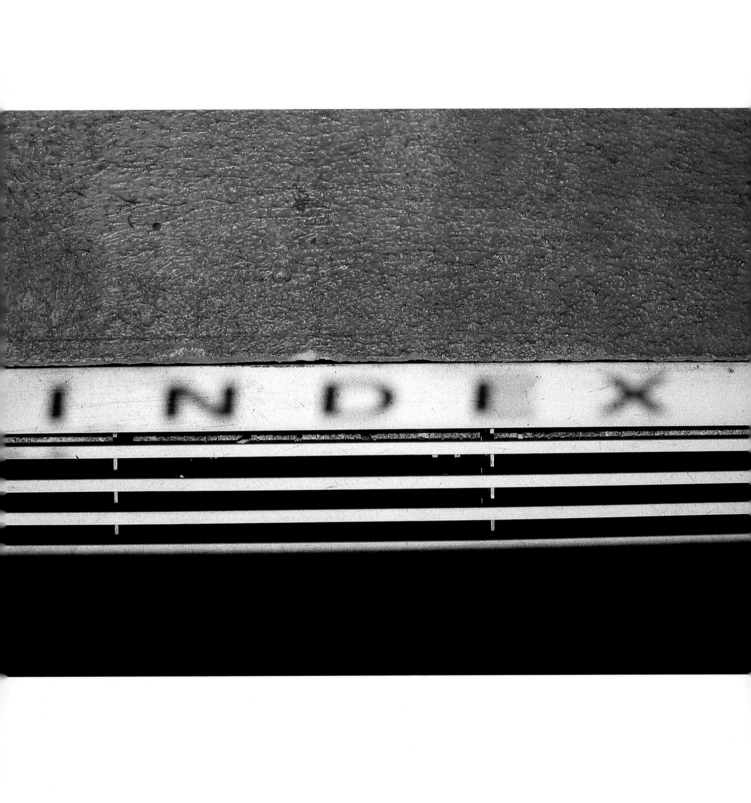

PRODUCER

PRODUCTION COMPANY

DATE DUE

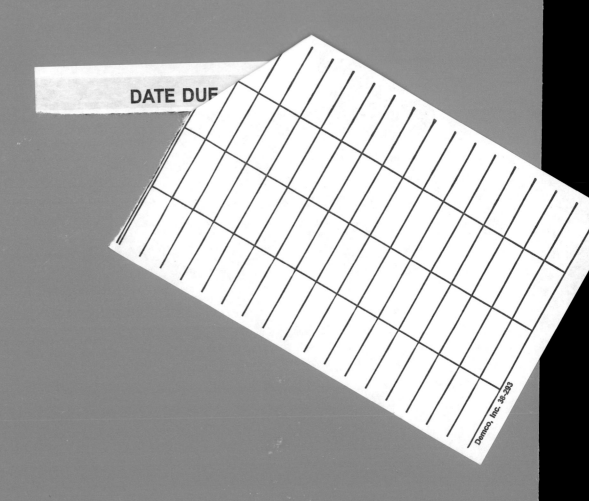

Autora: Ifeoma Onyefulu
Versión castellana: Montserrat Riera
Dirección: Santi Bolíbar

Publicado por primera vez en Gran Bretaña en 1993 por Frances Lincoln Limited;
4, Torriano News, Torriano Avenue, London, NW5 2RZ.

Coordinación de la producción: Elisa Sarsanedas

ISBN: 84-89970-67-X

Impreso en China

A de ÁFRICA

Ifeoma Onyefulu

intermón
FUNDACIÓN PARA EL TERCER MUNDO
Miembro de Oxfam Internacional

Nota del Autor

Este libro está basado en mis imágenes favoritas del África que conozco. Soy de la tribu Igbo y crecí en el sudeste de Nigeria, pero las personas y los objetos de las fotografías reflejan la rica diversidad de todo el continente. Hay ejemplos de influencias musulmanas y árabes del norte, además de trajes y ornamentos del sur, donde predominan las religiones animistas o cristianas.

Hay nueces de kola, el tinte añil y varios tipos de joyas y adornos para las mujeres, que muestran parte de la diversa riqueza africana. Y aunque otros africanos pueden usar otro tipo de nuez, un tinte de otro color y joyas aparentemente distintas, los significados y costumbres asociados con ellos son los mismos.

Sin embargo, también deseo plasmar todo aquello que la población africana tiene en común: el estilo de vida tradicional en los pueblos, los estrechos vínculos familiares y sobretodo la hospitalidad por la cual es famosa.

Este libro muestra qué representa África para mi, pero también quiere enseñar a todos los niños este vasto, amistoso y colorido continente.

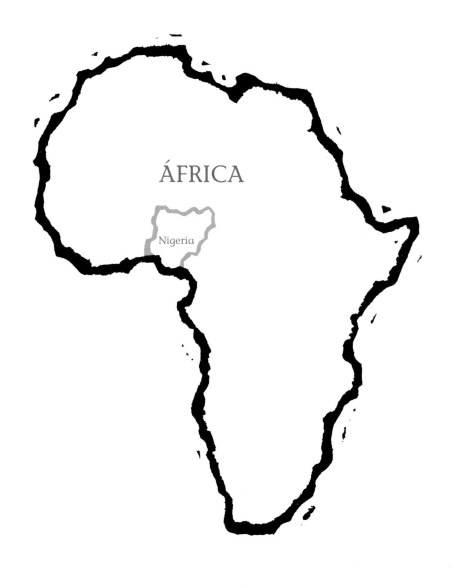

ÁFRICA

Nigeria

África

Tilahum, Oone y Zewge son tres niños africanos. Siempre están a punto para explicar cosas. Serán nuestros guías en este paseo por **África**.

-¡**África** es muy grande! –dicen–. Hay muchas cosas que ver, que explicar... ¿Por dónde empezamos?

-¡Hagamos un juego! –exclaman–. Cada uno escogerá por turno alguna cosa de **África** que le parezca importante y después elegiremos juntos alguna cosa en la que estemos de acuerdo los tres.

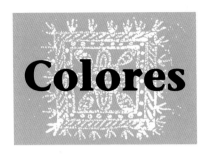

Colores

-¡Yo primero! –dice Oone–. Para empezar escogeré una cosa que tiene muchos **colores**, por ejemplo, por ejemplo… los collares hechos con semillas de **colores**.
Si juntas muchas semillas, combinando los **colores** más vivos, salen unos adornos fantásticos para ponértelos en el pelo, collares, pulseras…

Canoa

-Eso está bien –dice Tilahum–, pero otra cosa importante de verdad es una **canoa**.

Con una **canoa** puedes dar grandes paseos. Puedes ir a pescar, llevar cosas a vender, ir a la escuela. La **canoa** es un medio de transporte indispensable, en el que, además, cabe mucha gente.

Tambores

-A mí, lo que me gusta –dice Zewge– es el sonido de los **tambores**. Si queremos comunicarnos alguna cosa importante entre distintos poblados... ¡tam, tam!... y se entera todo el mundo. Y no digamos a la hora de bailar, nadie puede quedarse sentado cuando oye su ritmo. También los utilizamos para dar la bienvenida a los niños cuando nacen.

Abrazo

-Ya hemos dicho tres cosas, una cada uno. Ahora nos toca decir una a los tres a la vez.

-Tenemos que escoger los tres la misma –les recuerda Tilahum–.

-… **Abrazo**. En África demostramos que nos queremos con un gran **abrazo**, cuando estamos muy contentos.

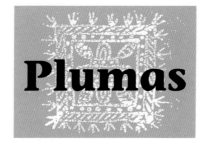

Plumas

-Vamos a jugar otra vez –dice Zewge–: **plumas**.

Las **plumas** indican quién es el jefe del poblado. Todo el mundo respeta al que las lleva. El jefe de mi poblado se llama Olusegun, yo le conozco. Es un gran jefe. Las plumas que lleva son de águila.

Las plumas pasan de padres a hijos cuando los niños se hacen mayores. Las mujeres no llevan plumas.

Abuela

-**Abuela** –dice Tilahum–, la **abuela** cuenta historias y leyendas de animales y de nuestros antepasados, y a todos nos gusta escucharlas. Todo el mundo respeta mucho a las abuelas.

Choza

-**Chozas**, casas… En casa se está bien por la noche –dice Oone–. Mi **choza** está hecha de adobe con el techo de caña, mijo o maíz. Estos materiales acumulan el calor del día y por la noche nos protegen del frío.

Tintes

-Ahora –dice Zewge– nos toca proponer una cosa a los tres.
Tilahum piensa, Oone también y Zewge finalmente dice: –el **tinte**, el color y especialmente el color azul.
-Sí, sí, el azul más intenso, el color más bonito –coinciden los tres–. Nuestros vestidos tienen distintos colores, que se consiguen con los **tintes**. Para hacer el **tinte** se mezclan los pigmentos con agua en unos grandes hoyos en el suelo.

Saltar

-Otra ronda… –empieza Tilahum–. Ya lo tengo: salto, ¡nos gusta tanto **saltar**!
Tenemos juegos en los que sólo saltamos. A veces hay que **saltar** muy alto y otras se trata de ver quien salta más lejos. Es uno de nuestros juegos preferidos.

Fruta

-**Fruta**, **fruta** de cualquier tipo, que se encuentra en árboles muy altos –mientras lo está diciendo, Oone se chupa los dedos–. Comería fruta a todas horas. Se la ofrecemos a nuestros amigos en las grandes ocasiones, pero antes los ancianos dicen las oraciones. ¿Queréis fruta?

Lámparas

-**Lámparas**. Las fabricamos con botes de hojalata, que llenamos de aceite o de parafina. Las lámparas de aceite nos iluminan por la noche hasta la hora de dormir.

Máscara

-Una los tres a la vez… ¡**máscara**!
¡Ésta sí que es buena!
Cuando aparece una **máscara** seguro que hay una fiesta. Los artistas hacen los dibujos para las máscaras y las elaboran; después bailamos todos a su alrededor.

Vecinos

-¿Dejamos de jugar? –pregunta Oone.
-No, no, sigamos con este juego, es muy divertido –protesta
Tilahum–. Yo tengo otra: **vecinos**. Es fantástico tener **vecinos**
como vosotros: les puedes explicar todo, te ayudan y les puedes
ayudar. Nunca estás solo.

Adornos

-**Adornos** –añade Zewge–. Es bonito adornarte el cuerpo con collares, dibujos o tatuajes. Fijaos en mis hermanas, les encanta engalanarse.

Arcilla

–**Arcilla**, cacharros de barro, de cualquier tamaño –dice Oone, que se ha vuelto a animar–. Se pueden llenar de lo que quieras, pero sobre todo mantienen el agua fresca cuando hace calor.

Reina

-Una **reina**. La **reina** siempre va engalanada. Antes había más **reinas**, ahora ya no hay tantas, pero las auténticas **reinas** siempre van cubiertas de adornos y son muy amables.

Río

-Una los tres juntos… una que signifique un lugar donde lo pasamos muy bien, que nos gusta mucho… **¡río!** el **río** es fantástico. Hay sitio para todo el mundo y para hacer muchas cosas distintas. Hay sitios para bañarse, otros para pescar, para lavar la ropa… ¡Qué bien se está en el **río**!

Saludo

-¡Yo, yo, ahora yo! –exclama Tilahum–: **saludo**. En África nos saludamos con la mano. Nuestro jefe Olusegun saluda con la palma de la mano porque es la persona más importante. También nos saludamos enlazando los dedos, o con un apretón de manos.

Turbante

-**Turbante** –añade Zewge–. Todo el mundo los lleva para protegerse del calor. Los que practican la religión islámica también llevan un turbante y tienen que ir a la Meca por lo menos una vez a lo largo de su vida. Las mujeres lo llevan cuando tienen que cargar alguna cosa en la cabeza.

Paraguas

Oone ya está listo para decir la próxima: – **paraguas**. Los **paraguas** son de colorines y protegen del sol y del calor. Los que van a vender al mercado los colocan encima de sus mercancías.

Poblado

-**Poblado** –dicen los tres a la vez, al recordar que ahora les tocaba elegir una palabra juntos–.
En el **poblado** se está bien, cada uno tiene su casa y cada **poblado** tiene costumbres y tradiciones diferentes que los mayores enseñan a los jóvenes.

Tejidos

-Ya hemos dicho muchas cosas, podríamos dejarlo… –comenta Tilahum–.

-¡Vale! La última vuelta –les anima Zewge–. Los **tejidos**. Las telas más bonitas, las que tienen más colores, son de algodón y las hacemos artesanalmente. Se utilizan para hacer vestidos, alfombras… Los padres enseñan a sus hijos e hijas el arte de tejer.

Xilófono

-Un instrumento de música, una música muy agradable… es el **xilófono**.

Su sonido nos invita a la fiesta, cantamos y bailamos cuando lo oímos. Cada madera produce un sonido diferente cuando el músico la toca.

Mientras lo explica, Oone mueve las manos como si estuviera tocando.

Ñames

-Empiezo a tener hambre –dice Zewge tocándose la barriga–. Los **ñames**. Se cultivan en huertos y son como las patatas pero más largos, y bien cocinados con aceite de palma… están deliciosos.

Zigzag

-Ha sido un juego divertido, pero tal vez, el paseo ha sido un poco extraño. Hemos ido de aquí para allá, dando rodeos… Ha sido parecido a los caminos que encontramos por toda África… Pero, atención, nos falta la última palabra… Aquí está: **zigzag**. Nuestro paseo ha sido como un **zigzag**, como muchos de nuestros caminos.

Oone, Zewge y Tilahum emprenden el camino de regreso a casa y nos dicen hasta pronto.